A Collection of Wisdom

Rodney Ohebsion

Immediex Publishing

Immediex Publishing

www.immediex.com

For retail or wholesale orders, visit www.immediex.com

ISBN: 1-932968-19-9

Categories:

Self Development
Eastern & Western Philosophy
Reference / Quotes / Proverbs

Contents

Introduction

Six Definitions of Wisdom
1 knowledge that is of supreme relevancy and rank **2** knowledge combined with the knowledge of how to make use of one's knowledge **3** the sum of learning throughout history **4** skill in judgment, decision making, and in determining the best way to achieve the best result **5** understanding the true nature of things **6** the book *A Collection of Wisdom*

A Collection of Wisdom is the book that the entire world has been writing for thousands and thousands of years through its thoughts, observations, insights, experiences, teachings, lessons, and writings. And it is the result of my personal quest to experience this wisdom, and to *unleash* it in one book—and give you the best of the best of the best of the best. This book captures the essence of an amazing abundance and variety of the universe's accumulated wisdom—and even more importantly—puts it in an incredibly clear, efficient, and dynamic format.

It is my aim to give you treasured teachings from all corners—from the teachings of Confucius to the proverbs of Africa; from Cyrus the Great's *Human Rights Charter* to Sun Tzu's *The Art of War*; from the Mulla Nasrudin Tales to the Lakota Native American cultural teachings; from *The Prince* by Niccolo Machiavelli to lessons based on the life of Oprah Winfrey; from the business methods of Andrew Carnegie to the coaching methods of Phil Jackson; and from the best of Hillary Clinton to the best of Zen Buddhism—there is almost no stone this book leaves unturned.

And instead of just throwing page after page of uninteresting and obscure texts at you, this book has done just the opposite. Material has been organized, books have been summarized, simple explanations have been made, passages from foreign translations have been clarified to reflect modern English, the obscure has been made clear, irrelevant and redundant information has been taken out, and everything has been made to ensure that it will be totally vibrant and captivating.

The result is a book that is more useful than a stack of typical self-help books, more interesting than a collection of conventional philosophy books, and more captivating and informative than a pile of quote and proverb books.

(Note: In a section of chapters towards the end of this book, I have also included wisdom-related material from various religions. It is not my goal to promote or dispromote any types of religions or beliefs in this book. See the preface to the religion section for more information on this.)

Lakota Native Americans

The Lakota are a group of Native Americans that are characterized by their emphasis on ideals such as **community, affinity, generosity, cooperation,** and **strength**. The term Lakota roughly translates to "an alliance of people."

The Lakota are part of a larger tribe of Native Americans known as the Sioux, and are sometimes referred to as the Teton Sioux. (For a background of the Native Americans, see the Native American Proverbs, Quotes, and Chants chapter of this book).

Note: Modern day Lakota (most of whom currently occupy parts of South Dakota and surrounding states) are for the most part much different than those of several generations ago. This chapter generally describes the earlier Lakota, and therefore refers to them mostly in the past tense.

Family and the Tiyospaye

Throughout most of Lakota history, family and community were the foundations of life. And for the Lakota, family did not just end at one's immediate relatives (i.e., siblings, parents, and children). Instead, different families that were bound by blood or marriage ties united together to form a social unit called a *tiyospaye,* which translates to "member extended family."

For the Lakota, each person's acts were often measured in terms of its impact on the entire tiyospaye, and people within the tiyospaye aligned and cooperated together for the good of all of its members. And even though several leaders headed each tiyospaye, there was still a sense of equality among all people.

Affinity

Lakota life was also based on **affinity**, which to the Lakota involved:

living in harmony with others

having a sense of belonging to one's community

valuing interpersonal relationships

AND

trusting one another

The ideal of affinity was so strong in the Lakota society that it even went outside the boundaries of one's tiyospaye and extended to the entire Lakota nation.

Generosity

The Lakota also adhered to an emphasis on **generosity**. For the Lakota, **resources were shared** freely among people, in times of good and bad. And the sharing was not just limited to possessions. It also extended to the **sharing of emotions** such as **sympathy, compassion, understanding,** and **kindness**; and the sharing of **personal time.**

The Lakota believed that their generous acts and **support** for each other made them better people, and also helped them build **communal harmony.**

Cooperation

All the above-mentioned qualities of Lakota communities allowed them to build tremendously **effective cooperation and teamwork**. The Lakota properly **synergized their efforts,** and reaped benefits for the good of the entire tiyospaye and its individual members.

A Lakota proverb says:

It is observed that in any great endeavor, it is not enough for a person to depend solely on himself.

Valuing Children

In the Lakota tiyospayes, **children** were regarded as sacred and of primary importance, and received much of the tiyospaye's attention. For the Lakota, the responsibility of raising a child was given to the entire community, and not just limited to a child's mother and father. In fact, uncles and aunts also had parental duties to their nieces and nephews (especially in the case aunts on the mothers' side and uncles on the fathers' side).

A Lakota proverb says:

The ones that matter the most are the children.

Black Elk (a Lakota holly man who lived from 1863 to 1950) said:

Grown men can learn from very little children—for the hearts of little children are pure. Therefore, the Great Spirit may show them many things that older people miss.

A Lakota man named Robert High-Eagle said:

… A child is the greatest gift from Wakan Tanka [*the Great Spirit, the supreme spiritual power in Sioux belief*].

The Lakota Ideal of Strength

The Lakota also adhered to an ideal of having **physical and mental strength,** which also extended to having **composure, determination, self-confidence, self-control,** and **self-belief**. The Lakota were expected to face challenges with all these traits, and to find **solutions** to problems that would benefit everyone.

Lakota strength also applied to **courage**, in the sense of acknowledging the existence of fear, yet maintaining one's resolve, and controlling and mastering fear.

Lastly, the Lakota ideal of strength was also about **practice**, **patience,** and **perseverance**. In the case of practice, the Lakota often gained skills and abilities from certain games and drills.

The Lakota's emphasis on strength was particularly evident in their hunting and warrior activities, which they were both tremendously proficient at.

Viewpoint of Goals, Success, and Role Models

For the Lakota, a person who was more advanced at a skill than others was viewed as a role model, and not regarded as competition. The Lakota did not view achievement as a means to be superior to others. Instead, they viewed achievement and success in the scope of **elevating oneself and one's tiyospaye**.

Lakota Symbols

Like many Native American groups, the Lakota base much of their culture on symbolism, especially the number four and the circle.

Circle

Lakota spirituality is based on the **circle.** The Lakota saw the journey of life and death as a circular process. They also interacted with one another in a circular fashion, rather than in a struggle for domination.

The Lakota even used the circle's symbolism in their architecture. Their houses (which are known as *tipis*) had circular foundations.

Some circle-related Lakota Proverbs are:

Everything the Power does, it does in a circle

Creation is continuous.

I am standing at the Earth's center.

Black Elk said:

A man's life is a circle from childhood to childhood, and thus it is in everything where the power moves.

The power of the world always works in circles.

The center of the universe is everywhere.

Four

Lakota culture is also based on the **number four,** which the Lakota used symbolically to apply to such things as:

The elements: earth, fire, air and water

The seasons: winter, spring, summer and fall

The directions: north, south, east and west

<u>More Lakota Proverbs</u>

Knowledge is rooted in all things—the world is a library.

Touching the earth equates to having harmony with nature.

When a man moves from nature, his heart becomes hard.

If you continue to contaminate your own home, you will eventually suffocate in your own waste.

True peace between nations will only happen when there is true peace within people's souls.

No matter how hidden a force is, it will attract some kind of resistance.

Confucianism

Confucianism is a philosophy that has had a tremendous impact on China for over two thousand years, and has also influenced the cultures of many other East Asian regions. Confucianism has its foundations in the teachings of a Chinese man named Confucius (or Kung Fu Tzu, originally Kung Chiu), who lived from 551 BC to 479 BC.

Confucius

Confucius was a man who **loved learning**, and studied the numerous Classical Chinese texts enthusiastically. He formulated his teachings based on those texts (which he also revised and edited), and on his experiences with other teachers.

Confucius hoped to use his ideas in a position with the government, but despite his efforts, he only served briefly as a government official. However, he did end up becoming a renowned teacher in China, and spread his ideas to many people.

Confucius's Teachings and the Spread of Confucianism

Confucius's teachings were based on **self-improvement**, as well as other subjects such as social issues, government, ethics, rituals, music, history, math, and art.

By the time of his death, his teachings became popular among several thousand followers, and formed the foundation of a philosophy now known as Confucianism. After Confucius's death, Confucianism continued to attract many more people, and was developed further by various other Confucian scholars.

By the 100s BC, the Chinese government adopted Confucianism in their policies. From then on, Confucianism has had a tremendous impact throughout China on-and-off for centuries, and has also caused the Chinese Classical Texts to become ingrained in the country's educational system, and various Confucian writings to be added to those texts. Many variations of Confucianism also sprang up during the years.

The Analects

Confucian scholars collected many of Confucius's teachings and mannerisms, and wrote them in a text now known as *The Analects* (of Confucius), or in Chinese, *Lun Yu*. Some parts of *The Analects* also contain some sayings and mannerisms of a few other Confucian scholars.

It is not certain when exactly *The Analects* was written, but it has become the core text in Confucian philosophy, and has also been integrated into the Chinese Classical texts. For many centuries up until the early 1900s, *The Analects* has also been a main focus of the Chinese educational system.

The Analects is mainly concerned with self-improvement and learning, which to Confucius usually went hand in hand, i.e. **learning is to be used primarily as a means of self-improvement**. *The Analects* also deals with social subjects, politics, morals, and rituals.

Passages From *The Analects*

Note: These are a clarified adaptation based on several translations. Each passage is followed by a number identifying where it occurs in The Analects (i.e. 1:14 means Part 1, Section 14). Some versions of The Analects have different numbering systems, so certain passages here have been labeled to reflect that.

Note: In this translation, the commonly used Chinese term "chun tzu" has been translated to "superior person." In the Analects, it generally refers to the Confucian concept of the ideal / perfected / advanced / virtuous / balanced / developed person.

Confucius said: "Isn't it a pleasure to consistently study, and apply what you have learned?" (1:1)

Confucius said: "The superior person does not try to stuff himself when he eats... [and] is diligent in his work and careful in speech... Such a person is someone who can definitely be considered to love learning." (1:14)

Confucius said: "I will not fret over being unknown to others; I will fret that I do not know them." (1:16)

Confucius said: "He who governs by way of virtue [/ *excellence*] can be compared to the [North] Pole Star, which keeps its place while all the other stars position themselves around it." (2:1)

Confucius said: "There are 300 verses in the *Book of Odes* [*a Classical Chinese text of poetry*], but they can be summed up in one phrase: 'Don't have bad thoughts.'" (2:2)

Confucius said: "If you govern people with laws and control them by punishment, they will seek to avoid punishment, but have no sense of shame. If you govern them by virtue and control them with properness, they will have their own sense of shame, and guide themselves into doing good." (2:3)

Confucius said: "See a person's actions. Observe his motives. Examine in what things he rests. How can a person conceal his character? How can a person conceal his character?" (2:10)

Confucius said: "He who reviews old knowledge and continues to learn new knowledge is fit to teach others." (2:11)

Confucius said: "The superior person is not a utensil [that exists just to be used]." (2:12)

Tzu Kung asked about the character of the superior person, and Confucius said: "He does something [that he would talk about] first, and then speaks according to his actions." (2:13)

Confucius said: "The superior person is perceptive and not biased. The lesser person is biased and not perceptive." (2:14)

Confucius said: "Learning [/ *studying*] without thinking is useless; thinking without learning [/ *studying*] is dangerous." (2:15)

Confucius said: "Committing oneself to unsuitable teachings [/ *methods*] is no good." (2:16)

Confucius said: "Yu, shall I teach you what knowledge is? When you know something and know that you know it; and when you don't know something and know that you don't know it; —this is knowledge." (2:17)

Confucius said: "When the superior person deals with the world, he does not prejudice his mind for or against anything—he just follows what is right." (4:10)

Confucius said: "The superior person is concerned with his character; the lesser person cares only about his wealth." (4:11)

Confucius said: "Don't be concerned that you have no position; be concerned how you may fit yourself to occupy one. Don't be concerned with being unknown; be concerned with being worthy of being known." (4:14)

Confucius said: "When you see good [qualities] in a person, think of how to rise to that level. When you see bad [qualities] in a person, reflect inwards and examine your weak points." (4:17)

…[Confucius said:] "At first, my method with others was to listen to what they said, and expect them to act accordingly. Now, my method is to listen to what they say, and then observe what they do." (5:9 or 5:10)

When Tzu Lu heard a teaching and had not put it into practice yet, he was uneager to hear about some other teaching in the meantime. (5:13 or 5:14)

Chi Wen Tzu thought three times before acting. Confucius heard of this and said: "Twice is enough." (5:19 or 5:20)

Confucius said: "In a district of ten families, there must be someone as honorable and sincere as I, but none as fond of learning." (5:27 or 5:28)

Yen Ch'iu said: "It's not that I don't enjoy your teaching, but I am not strong enough."
Confucius said: "The person who is not strong enough gives up at the halfway point—but you are limiting yourself before even starting." (6:10)

Confucius said: "When raw nature dominates training, you will be rustic. When training dominates raw nature, you will be clerical. When raw nature and training are combined well, you will be a superior person." (6:16)

Confucius said: "Knowing the truth is not as good as loving it; loving it is not as good as delighting in it." (6:18)

During Confucius's leisure time, he was relaxed and enjoyed himself. (7:4)

Confucius said: "I don't teach the student who isn't eager to learn, nor do I help anyone who isn't eager to express himself. If I present one corner of a subject and the student cannot use it to learn the other three, I won't repeat my lesson." (7:8)

Confucius said: "I am not someone born with wisdom—but I love teachings, and have diligently sought them." (7:19 or 7:20)

Confucius said: "When I am with others, they are my teachers. I can select their good points and follow them, and select their bad points and avoid them." (7:21 or 7:22)

Confucius said: "My students, do you think I conceal things from you? I don't conceal anything from you—there is nothing that I do that is not made known to you. This is the real me." (7:23 or 7:24)

...Confucius said: "Consider people based on the way they come to you, not what they will do when they leave [based on their past experiences]... If someone purifies his mind to approach me, I accept his [current] pureness, without becoming a sponsor of his past." (7:28 or 7:29)

When Confucius was in company of a person who was singing well, he [Confucius] always had the song repeated, and joined the harmony with his own singing. (7:31 or 7:32)

Confucius said: "The superior person is calm and composed; the lesser person is continuously worried and distressed." (7:36 or 7:37)

Confucius was pleasant yet dignified, authoritative yet not overbearing, and respectful yet relaxed. (7:37 or 7:38)

Confucius said: "You can successfully force people to follow a certain course, but you cannot force them to understand it." (8:9)

Confucius said: "I have yet to find a person who loves virtue as much as sex." (9:17)

Confucius said: ... "When you have faults, do not stop yourself from abandoning them." (9:24 or 9:25)

This can also be translated as:

Confucius said: ... "When you make a mistake, do not stop yourself correcting it." (9:24 or 9:25)

Confucius said: "There are some we can study with, but cannot go along with in principles. There are some we can go along with in principles, but cannot establish ourselves with. There are some we can establish ourselves with, but cannot agree with on decision-making." (9:29 or 9:30)

Lu said: "May I ask about death?"
Confucius said: "If you don't understand life, how can you understand death?" (11:11 or 11:12)

The men of Lu were rebuilding the Main Treasury. Min Tzu Ch'ien observed this and said: "Why don't we retain some of what is already there? Why should we reconstruct it entirely?"
Confucius said: "This man doesn't talk that much, but when he does, he is right on the mark." (11:13 or 11:14)

Confucius said: "I can preside over lawsuits as good as anyone else, but what's best is to have no lawsuits at all." (12:13)

Confucius said: "The superior person seeks to further the good points in others, and not their bad qualities. The lesser person does the opposite." (12:16)

Confucius said: "If someone can recite the 300 Odes [*poems from the Classical Chinese text*], but when given a governing position he can't put them to effective practical use, or when sent on a mission he can't answer questions unassisted, then although the person's knowledge is extensive, of what use is it?" (13:5)

Zan Yu was driving for Confucius on a trip to Wei.
Confucius said: "This is a very populous place."
Zan Yu said: "Yes, the number of people is ever increasing—what should be done for them?"
Confucius said: "Enrich them."
Zan Yu said: "And after that, then what?"
Confucius said: "Educate them." (13:9)

Confucius said: "The superior person is in harmony, but does not follow the crowd. The lesser person follows the crowd, but is not in harmony." (13:23)

Confucius said: "The superior person is easy to work for and difficult to please. If you try to please him in any devious way, he will not be pleased. And in his employment of people, he uses them according to their capacity. The lesser person is difficult to work for, yet is easy to please. If you try to please him even in a devious way, he may be pleased. And in his employment of people, he expects them to be fit for everything." (13:25)

Confucius said: "I won't be concerned with other people not knowing me; I will be concerned with my lack of ability." (14:31 or 14:32)

Confucius said: "If a person is not in the habit of asking, 'What is this? What is this?' then I cannot do anything for him." (15:15 or 15:16)

Confucius said: "The superior person is dignified but does not fight for it. He is sociable, but not exclusive to one social clique." (15:21 or 15:22)

Confucius said: "The superior person does not appreciate a person solely on account of his words, nor does he disregard a person's words solely on account of the person." (15:22 or 15:23)

…Confucius said: "A lack of patience in trifling matters might lead to the disruption of great project." (15:26 or 15:27)

Confucius said: "When everyone hates something, it is necessary to examine it. When everyone likes something, it is necessary to examine it." (15:27 or 15:28)

Confucius said: "To make a mistake and not correct it—that, indeed, is a mistake." (15:29 or 15:30)

This can also be translated as:

Confucius said: "To have a fault and not correct it—that, indeed, is a fault." (15:29 or 15:30)

Confucius said: "I spent the whole day without eating and the whole night without sleeping so that I could think—but it was useless. It is better to learn [/ *study*]." (15:30 or 15:31)

Confucius said: "The superior person is adequately resolute, but not recklessly inflexible." (15:36 or 15:37)

Confucius said: "In speaking, it is best to be clear and say just enough to convey the meaning." (15:40 or 15:41)

Confucius said: "There are three mistakes to avoid when speaking to noble people:
Speaking when it is not time to speak—which is careless;
Not speaking when it is time to speak—which is unexpressive;
And speaking without studying the expression of the person—which is unobservant." (16:6)

Confucius said: "Yu, have you ever heard of the six good phrases and the six things that obscure them?"
Yu said: "No."
Confucius said: "Then sit down and I will tell you.
Love of kindness without a love of learning will be obscured by foolishness.
Love of wisdom without a love of learning will be obscured by excessive speculation.
Love of honesty without a love of learning will be obscured by deception.
Love of straightforwardness without a love of learning will be obscured by misdirected judgment.
Love of boldness without a love of learning will be obscured by lack of control.
Love of persistence without a love of learning will be obscured by stubbornness." (17:8)

Tzu Hsia said: "Someone who day by day gains awareness of his deficiencies, and month by month does not forget what he has become proficient in, can really be called a lover of learning." (19:5)

Tzu Hsia said: "Learning widely, steadying the will, questioning and investigating earnestly, and personal reflecting—virtue [/ *excellence*] lies in all of this." (19:6)

Tzu Hsia said: "The lesser person always embellishes [/ *"sugarcoats"*] his mistakes." (19:8)

MENCIUS

Mencius (a.k.a. Meng Tzu), who lived from c372 BC to c289 BC, is the most notable Confucian scholar other than Confucius. As a young scholar, Mencius studied under the tutelage of Confucius's grandson Ssu Tzu.

Like Confucius, Mencius became a teacher, and also served briefly as a government official. Many of Mencius's teachings, conversations, and doings are recorded in a book titled the *Mencius*.

Mencius Passages

Note: These are a clarified adaptation of the James Legge translation

The duke Wan of T'ang asked Mencius about the proper way of governing a kingdom.

Mencius said: "The business of the people must not be neglected... The way of the people is this: If they have a certain livelihood [*they have steady and satisfying careers*], they will have a fixed heart. [But] If they do not have a certain livelihood, they will not have a fixed heart. And if they do not have a fixed heart, they will participate in any kind of self-abandonment, moral deflection, depravity, and wild license. And then when they have thus been involved in crimes and you respond by punishing them, all you have done is trapped them [in the trap you set up by not ensuring that they have a certain livelihood]."

Mencius said: "Of all the parts of a person's body, there is none more excellent [in showing a person's nature] than the pupil of the eye. The pupil cannot hide someone's wickedness. If within the [person's] heart everything is proper, the pupil is bright. If within the heart everything is not proper, the pupil is dull. To [truly] listen to a person, listen to his words and look at the pupil of his eye. How can a person conceal his character?"

Mencius said: "People are eager to comment on something when they themselves are not in the situation of doing it."

Mencius said: "The evil of people can come from their like of being teachers of others."

Mencius said: "Only when someone refuses to do certain things will he be capable of doing great things."

Mencius said: "Confucius did not do extreme things."

Mencius said: "Great is the person who has not lost his childlike heart."

Mencius said: "Anybody who wishes to cultivate the t'ung [tree] or the tsze [tree], which may be grasped with both hands or perhaps with one [*because they are small and young trees*], knows by what means to nourish them. Yet in the case of their own selves, people do not know by what means to nourish them. Is it to be supposed that their regard of their own selves is inferior to their regard for a t'ung [tree] or tsze [tree]? These people [who place more regards on nourishing trees than themselves] really need to rethink things."

Mencius said: "The desire to be honored is common in the minds of all people. And all people have within themselves that which is truly honorable—but they often do not realize it. The honor that people confer is not authentic honor. Those whom Chao the Great honors [at one time], he can criticize again [at another time]."

Mencius said: "People for the most part err, and are afterwards able to reform. They are distressed in mind and perplexed in their thoughts, and then they arise to vigorous reformation."

Mencius said: "All things are already complete in us. There is no greater delight than to be conscious of sincerity on self-examination."

Mencius said: "The principle of Yang Chu was 'Each person for himself.' Even if he could have benefited the whole kingdom by plucking out a single hair [from himself], he would not have done it.

"Mo Tzu [, on the other hand,] loves all equally. If he could have benefited the kingdom by rubbing smooth his whole body from the crown to the heel, he would have done it.

"Tsze-mo holds a medium between these. By holding that medium, he is nearer the right. But by holding it without leaving room for the pressing needs of circumstances, it becomes like their holding their one point.

"The reason why I hate holding to one point is the hindrance it does to the [proper / suitable] Way. It takes up one point and disregards a hundred others."

Mencius said: "A person with definite aims to be accomplished may be compared to the process of digging a well. To dig the well to a depth of seventy-two cubits and stop without reaching the spring, is after all, throwing away the well."

Mencius said: "There are five ways in which the superior person effects his teaching.
He descends influence on people, just like seasonable rain.
He perfects people's virtue.
He assists the development of people's talent.
He answers people's inquiries.

And he also privately cultivates and corrects himself [and thus sets a good example]."

Mencius said: "The wise embrace all knowledge, but they are most earnest about what is of the greatest importance. The benevolent embrace all in their love, but they place the most importance on cultivating an earnest affection for the virtuous. Even the wisdom of Yao [*a legendary and highly exalted early ancient Chinese Emperor*] and Shun [*another legendary and highly exalted early ancient Chinese Emperor*] did not extend to everything, but they attended earnestly to what was important."

Mencius said: "It would be better to be without the *Book of History* than to believe it entirely. In the "Completion of the War" [chapter], I only accept only two or three portions [/ *strips of bamboo they were written on*]."

Mencius said: "A bad year cannot prove the cause of death to him whose stores of gain are large. An age of corruption cannot confound him whose equipment of virtue is complete."

Mencius said: "To nourish the mind, there is nothing better than to make the desires few. For the person whose desires are few, there will be some things he may not be able to keep his heart, but they will be few. To the person whose desires are many, there will be some things he may be able to keep his heart, but they will be few."

Note: More passages from the Mencius are contained in later sections of this chapter

HSUN TZU

Besides Confucius and Mencius, the other most notable Confucian scholar in ancient times was Hsun Tzu (not to be confused with the ancient Chinese war strategist Sun Tzu, who is covered in another chapter of this book).

Hsun Tzu lived from c312 BC to c230 BC. His writings are referred to as the *Hsun Tzu*, and are considered to have been originally written by him and unaltered over time. The *Hsun Tzu* is written in essay format (rather than in a format of recorded sayings, conversations, and mannerisms like the *Analect*s and the *Mencius* are written in), and is comprised of 32 essays / chapters.

Hsun Tzu Passages

I once tried thinking for an entire day, but I found it less valuable than one moment of study. I once tried standing up on my toes to see far out in the distance, but I found that I could see much farther by climbing to a high place.

There is a kind of bird in the south called the meng dove. It constructs its nest with feathers that are tied together with hair, and it hangs the nest on the ends of stems. But if wind comes, then the stems break, the eggs are destroyed, and the baby birds die. And this is not because the nest is flawed. Rather, it is the thing that it is hanging from that is flawed.

There is a kind of tree in the west called the yekan. Its trunk is only a few cun [*a measurement slightly more than an inch*] high. It grows at the top of mountains, and can see all the way down to incredibly deep valleys. It is not the height of its trunk that gives it this view; it is the place where it stands that does this…

We make the chih fragrance with the root of a type of flower. But if that root is immersed in urine, no rich person would get close to it, and no commoner would choose to wear it. And it is not the root that deters people from it; it is what it is soaked in that makes it flawed.

Thus, the superior person will prudently pick the community he will live within, and will choose the proper people to associate with.

When a person is imprudent, lackadaisical, and neglecting of himself, it makes him highly vulnerable to harm.

The basis of accomplishment is in never quitting.

The person attempting to travel two roads at once will get nowhere.

The superior person is committed to focus.

The superior person's learning goes in his ear, attaches to his heart, expands to the end of his limbs, and is established in his actions. Even in his smallest word or slightest action, he sets an example.

The lesser person's learning goes into his hear, and goes directly out of his mouth. With only a few cun [*a measurement slightly more than an inch*] between his ear and his mouth, how can it become rooted in him in that short time throughout his entire body?

The superior person uses learning as a means of self-improvement. The lesser person uses learning as a means of showing off.

Do not answer the person whose questions are vile. Do not question a person whose answers are vile.

When you locate good in yourself, approve of it with determination. When you locate evil in yourself, despise it as something detestable.

Wisdom is treating right as right, and wrong as wrong. Foolishness is treating right as wrong, and wrong as right.

… The old saying says: "The superior person uses things; the lesser person is used by things."

In order to properly understand the big picture, everyone should fear becoming mentally clouded and obsessed with one small section of truth.

… It is said that if the mind is sidetracked, it will lack understanding; if it is unbalanced, it will lack discernment; if it is split up, it will become subject to doubt and false conclusions.

Note: Also see other sections of this chapter for more passages from the Hsun Tzu

MORE CONFUCIAN THEMES

The World of Individuals Making up a Community

Confucianism is known for emphasizing society / community. However, Confucian ideals of making a harmonious community begin with the individual. In the *Mencius*, it says:

Mencius said: "The basis of the country is found in the state, the basis of the state is found in the family, and the basis of the family is found in the individual."

In the *Ta Hsueh* (a.k.a. the *Great Learning*, a well known Confucian text written around the same time as *The Analects*), it says:

Things have their root and their branches. Affairs have their end and their beginning. To know what is first and what is last will lead near to what is taught in the Great Learning.

Those ancients who wanted to illustrate illustrious virtue throughout the country would first bring order to the states. Those who wanted to bring order to the states would first regulate their families. Those who wanted to regulate their families would first cultivate their personal aspects. Those who wanted to cultivate their personal aspects would first rectify their minds [/ *hearts*]. Those who wanted to rectify their minds [/ *hearts*] would first make their thoughts sincere. Those who wanted to make their thoughts sincere would first further their knowledge. The furthering of knowledge consists of the investigation of things.

When things are investigated, knowledge is furthered. When knowledge is furthered, thoughts are sincere. When thoughts are sincere, minds [/ *hearts*] are rectified. When minds [/ *hearts*] are rectified, personal aspects are cultivated. When personal aspects are cultivated, families are regulated. When families are regulated, states are orderly. When states are orderly, the whole country is peaceful and happy.

…All and everyone must consider cultivation of personal lives as the root or foundation of everything else. There is never a case when the root is in disorder and that which springs from it is well ordered.

Is Human Nature Good or Bad?

After Confucius's death, debate persisted among Confucian scholars on whether people are naturally (unobstructed by refinement / training / experience) good or bad. Many Confucian scholars such as Mencius felt that people were good by nature. In the *Mencius,* it says:

Mencius said: "The tendency of human nature to good is like the tendency of water to flow downwards. All people have this tendency to good, just as all water flows downwards. Now, by striking water and causing it to leap up, you may make it go over your forehead, and, by damming and leading it, you may force it up a hill; —but are such movements according to the nature of water? It is just the force applied that causes them. When people are made to do what is not good, their nature is being dealt with in this same way."

Mencius said: "When people are allowed to follow their natural selves, they inherently do good—and that is why I conclude that human nature is good. If someone becomes evil, his inherent nature is not to be blamed. Everyone has the capacity for mercy, the capacity for shame, the capacity for respect, and the capacity for having a conscience… However, some people neglect those things…"

[Mencius said: "I believe everyone has the capacity of sympathy, and here's why]: If someone notices a child about to fall in a well, he will definitely feel alarmed and compassionate. This is not caused by the person's desire to be rewarded by the child's parents, nor is it caused by the desire to be applauded by the community, nor is it caused by the dread of guilty feelings. So therefore, it can be concluded that no person is [naturally due to their human nature] without the feeling of compassion, no person is without the feeling of shame, no person is without the feeling of courtesy, and no person is without the feeling of having a conscience."

Mencius said: "Let a person not do what his own sense of righteousness tells him not to do, and let him not desire what his sense of righteousness tells him not to desire; —to act thus is all he has to do."

Other Confucian scholars, particularly Hsun Tzu, felt that people were by evil by nature, which is similar to what the doctrines of most Western religions currently preach. Hsun Tzu felt that in order to deal the people's evil nature, they should be vigorously educated. He said:

Mencius said that human nature is good. I disagree with that.

Human nature is evil, and goodness is caused by intentional [/ *aware*] activity.

A person is born with a liking for profit. If he gives way to this, it will lead him to quarrels and conflicts, and any [acquired] sense of courtesy and humility will be abandoned.

A person is born with feelings of envy and hate. If he gives way to them, they will lead him to violence and crime, and any [acquired] sense of loyalty and good faith will be abandoned.

A person is born with desires of the eyes and ears, and a liking for beautiful sights and sounds. If he gives way to them, they will lead him to immorality and lack of restriction, and any [acquired] ritual principles and propriety will be abandoned.

Thus, anybody who follows this nature and gives way its states will be led into quarrels and conflicts, and go against the conventions and rules of society, and will end up a criminal.

Therefore, a person should first be changed by a teacher's instructions, and guided by principles of ritual. Only then can he observe the rules of courtesy and humility, obey the conventions and rules of society, and achieve order.

If people do not have teachers to guide them, they will have a tendency to follow evil, and not uprightness.

Whether children are born among the Han or Yueh people from the south, or among the Mo barbarians from the north, they all cry with the same voice at their birth. But as they live and are influenced, they follow different ways. It is education that makes them become different.

The superior person trains his eyes so that they only want to see what is right, his ears so that only want to hear what is right, and his mind so that it only wants to think what is right—until he has really learned to love [/ enjoy] what is right… When he has come to such a stage, he cannot be taken off course by power or the love for profit, he cannot be influenced by the masses, and he cannot be swayed by the world.

Around 0 AD, a poet and philosopher named Yang Hsiung, who is a figure in both Taoism (see Taoism chapter for more info on Taoism) and Confucianism, offered a middle ground point of view. He said:

Human nature is a combination of good and evil. The person who cultivates the good will become a good person, and the person who cultivates the bad will become a bad person. Chi [*the Chinese term for vital life force energy*] is the driving force that leads one to good or evil…

Morals, Rites, Etiquette, Family, Benevolence, and Government

Confucianism is highly concerned with morals, rites, proper etiquette, benevolence, and family (particularly good relationships between parents and children). Confucian philosophy sees all of these things as a key theme to maintaining order in society. It promotes and sets standards of behavior to follow, and strongly encourages the government to intently emphasize these ideals.

These ideals are also generally the most evident subjects where Confucianism differs with Taoism (another main philosophy that flourished in China and had a tremendous influence on the Chinese. Taoism is covered in detail in a separate chapter of this book).

Unlike Confucianism, Taoism emphasizes the individual more than society, and is opposed to heavily involved governments. Taoism is also opposed to rigid codes of behavior, and contends that people who are in harmony with the world will naturally follow good actions on their own without needing deliberate external influences.

Despite their differences in these subjects, both Confucianism and Taoism have had a tremendous impact on Chinese people and government for much of Chinese history, and have often alternated on which one had the dominant influence on Chinese government at a particular time period.

Music

Confucianism also embraces music, which extends to listening to music, singing, playing an instrument, and dancing. Early Confucian scholars such as Confucius and Hsun Tzu have praised the virtue of music.

This was in contradiction to another popular philosophy of that time called Mohism / the Mo-ist philosophy (based on the teachings of Mo Tzu, who lived from c470 BC to c390 BC), which was opposed to music, and viewed it as a waste of public resources / money that could be used to benefit society in other aspects of life.

In the *Hsun Tzu*, Hsun Tzu attacks the Mo Tzu's opposition to music, and says:

Music is a joy. It is an emotion that people naturally feel at times... [and thus,] it is necessary for this joy to be expressed and have a manifestation in voice and movement...

... [Music has so many virtues; so] why does Mo Tzu criticize it?

When someone listens to odes or hymns being sung, it expands his mind and will.

Music is a fantastic peacekeeper of the world, it is integral to harmony, and it is a required fundamental of human emotion.

More Confucian Sayings

Note: Most of these are based on various teachings attributed to Confucius.

Everything has its beauty, but not everyone sees it.

Our greatest glory is not in never falling, but in rising every time we fall.

Be not ashamed of mistakes and thus make them crimes.

Don't complain about the snow on your neighbor's roof when your own doorstep is dirty.

Life is simple, but some people insist on complicating it.

We often put more concern in convincing others that we are happy than we do in endeavoring to be so ourselves.

When anger arises, first think of the consequences.

The practice of archery is somewhat like the principle of a superior person's life: When the archer misses the center target, he turns and looks within himself for the cause of his miss.

The more a person meditates on good thoughts, the better his world will be, and the better the entire world will be.

While practicing virtue during normal situations, the superior person always makes further effort when there is a deficiency, and never goes over the limit where excess is approaching.

Choose a job that you like, and you will never have to work a day in your life.

The *I Ching*

The *I Ching* (*Classic-Book of Changes*) is among the most well known of the Classical Chinese texts that Confucius studied and commentated on. It dates back to very early times, perhaps as early as the 2900s BC.

Here are some *I Ching* Passages:

Do not be too fixed and inflexible; be in touch with time and change with it.

A circumstance becomes positive when you adapt to it.

Excessive dependence on words leads to poor results.

In your self-development, seek to eliminate bad habits and tolerate harmless ones.

The superior person can be emotionally joyful yet thoughtfully concerned.

To know someone, observe what he cares about and which of his own personal aspects he tries to develop and promote.

If you try to do too much, you will not achieve anything.

When facing impossible conditions, sometimes it is in your best interests to retreat.

Do not let a leader lead you on a bad path.

If you let your happiness become completely tied on your relationships, then your happiness will fluctuate as your relationships do.

Perseverance is not the only ingredient to winning. You can stalk a field forever and not get any game if the field does not contain any.

The superior person gathers his weapons together in order to provide against the unforeseen.

Taoism

Taoism is a Chinese philosophy deriving from ancient times. Although it is said to originate around the 600s BC, Taoism is based on teachings that were passed down throughout China for thousands of years prior to that time.

Taoism is known for being **spiritual** and **profound,** as well as **practical** and **useful**.

A Brief Look at Chinese Philosophy

Throughout Chinese history, various philosophies and ideas developed, ancient texts were written, and rituals were created. Dozens and dozens of philosophies existed at certain points, and some combined, some borrowed from each other, and others disappeared.

Taoism and Confucianism are the two main philosophies that emerged from all of these processes. Additionally, another philosophy known as Buddhism (which came from India) also flourished in China. (See the Confucianism and Zen Buddhism chapters for more info Confucianism and Buddhism).

Taoist Texts

Much of Taoist philosophy is based on several ancient Taoist texts written around 600 BC to 200 BC; most notably the *Tao Te Ching,* as well as the *Chuang Tzu,* the *Lieh Tzu,* and several others.

Central to Taoist texts and the Taoist philosophy is a concept known as *Tao* (usually pronounced "Dao").

Tao

Since the term Tao is a unique concept, it cannot be translated directly. The most common translations for the Tao are the *Way* or the *Path*. The concept of Tao was derived from **observing nature**. It is a concept that cannot be truly grasped, contained, or experienced with words, because it is **beyond words**. The *Tao Te Ching* says that "the tao that can be described is not the real Tao, and the name that can be named is not the real name."

According to Taoist philosophy, Tao is the basis of everything. The *Chuang Tzu* says, "Tao makes things what they are, but is not itself a thing [nor is it nothing]." The *Chuang Tzu* also says the "Tao is present by and through itself," or the "Tao is its own roots."

Some describe the Tao as the **mystical force and source of the universe, the unnamable "essence,"** or "God-nature." (Note: the philosophical Taoism described throughout this chapter is not a religion, and does not teach a system of religious beliefs.)

Tao is considered beyond such ideas such as good and bad, hot and cold, long and short, space and no space, existence and non-existence, etc. It has a **paradoxical** nature.

Te

Taoist philosophy also teaches of the Tao's *Te*—its **power / virtue / characteristics / excellence**.

Note: The terms Tao and Te are also used to denote slightly different concepts in the general Chinese language outside the scope of Taoism, with Tao meaning the general concept of a proper / suitable way, and Te meaning virtue / excellence / integrity. The words Tao and Te in this chapter refer to the Taoist concepts of Tao and Te, not the general Chinese words Tao and Te. However, note that even in Chinese outside of Taoism, the use of the words Tao and Te often relate somewhat to the Taoist concepts of Tao and Te.

Abiding by Tao

According to Taoist philosophy, the best way to accomplish anything is through Tao. The Taoist concept of an exemplary person is one who lives "abiding by Tao," "in harmony with the Tao," and "by being a person of Tao."

To the Taoists, Tao is an inexhaustible source that has the supreme effectiveness.

The Individual

Taoist is known for emphasizing the individual instead of society. According to Taoist philosophy, there is a uniqueness to each individual, and a person who abides by Tao is in harmony with his/her own self.

Many Taoists also extend this to saying that just as the Tao has its Te (power / characteristics / virtue / excellence), so does an individual have his/her own unique Te.

Keeping it Tao

Taoism also preaches that a person's harmony with the Tao can be hindered by such things as social conformity standards, unnatural rules of behavior, and "deliberate effort." In the case of deliberate effort, Taoist philosophy says that the Tao is already there, so why should you go looking or "striving," and thus neglect the inexhaustible Tao that can get everything done.

Wu Wei

Since Taoism preaches that a person's harmony with the Tao can be hindered by "deliberate effort," there is a unique Taoist concept of doing things. This concept is known as *Wu Wei*, which is literally "non-action" or "inaction," but more accurately defined as:

to **"do without doing"**

unattached action

action that transcends action

effortless action, or action that is outside the scope of effort and non-effort

using **action produced by Tao and its Te**

avoiding using a lower source of power, and thus leaving the way so that you can effortlessly use the **highest source** of power instead

having experiences **based on the actual experience** instead of on expectations
(Similar to what American basketball coach Phil Jackson said: "Winning is important to me, but what brings me real joy is the experience of being fully engaged in whatever I'm doing.")

advantageous and harmonious action

only using **naturally flowing effort**

using the **natural flow of nature / Tao / energy for one's benefit** rather than against one's efforts.
(Similar to what American philosopher R. Buckminster Fuller wrote: "Don't fight forces; use them.")

being in **control** by **being in harmony with nature / Tao / energy**, rather than trying and bend nature / Tao / energy at one's will

(Similar to what English philosopher Francis Bacon wrote: "Nature, to be commanded, must be obeyed.")

not forcing, or not forcing what does not need forcing

not taking effort to the point where it becomes counterproductive

letting yourself win / succeed

getting **out of your own way**

not making things more difficult than they are

doing without overdoing or underdoing

doing less, but getting more done

being **in the "zone"**

not veering, and keeping to the fine line that keeps you in the "zone"

being **"on"**

being **"in the flow"**

using smart and **useful** effort

being supremely **efficient**, and not wasting effort and energy

Sounds Like Wu Wei

Legendary discus thrower Mac Wilkins once said that he sometimes reached a "rhythmic hole" known as the "effortless throw," which allowed him to perform many of his best throws. Boxer Buster Douglas described his shocking win over Mike Tyson by saying, " I was just in that zone" and "It was my time to shine."

According to the Taoist viewpoint, these are both examples that correspond with Wu Wei. (Note: You don't necessarily need to have studied Taoism to use the principles of Wu Wei, because it is simply a natural principle that was created by observation of the world and people.)

Of course, Wu Wei does not just apply to sports—it applies to any type of experience.

The Simplicity of the Unfinished / Uncarved Block of Wood

To illustrate certain points, Taoist philosophy commonly uses the idea of the simplicity of an uncarved / unfinished block of wood. The Taoists feel that we should be like the simplicity of the uncarved / unfinished wood. This is in contrast to the finished piece of wood that has been smoothed out or made into something.

Taoists contend that the rough edges and formlessness of the uncarved / unfinished wood acts in accordance with the Tao, and **yields** the source of its and our own **true being and power** (Te).

A Tale of Three Men

A great way to illustrate points of the Taoist individual and the simplicity of the uncarved / unfinished block of wood, is to observe the ways of the three most dominant heavyweight boxers in the last twenty years: Mike Tyson, Evander Holyfield, and Lennox Lewis. (*Note: Mike, Evander, and Lennox are not known to have studied Taoism; I am just using their ways as an example to illustrate principles of Taoism.*)

It is very interesting to observe how all three of these men have very few similarities in their physical dimensions, training habits, fighting styles, and personalities; yet despite their dramatic differences, they all became legendary heavyweight champions.

According to the Taoist viewpoint, this is because they were in harmony with Tao, and each expressed their own unique Te and found what works for them. They did not strictly pattern themselves after rigid standards and rules that did not conform to their own personal uncarved / unfinished block of wood.

More About the Taoist Individual

Many Taoists feel that the ideal individual is **simple**, **creative**, spontaneous, **appreciative of life and the universe but not attached to things, and harmonious / expressive of his/her unique and self / realness.** Keep in mind, however that Taoist philosophy also advocates using **cautiousness** along with spontaneity and expressiveness.

Leadership

Taoism also offers views on leadership—whether it is leadership of a state, family, or anything else. According to the *Tao Te Ching*, the best kind of leadership is to **abide by the harmony of the Tao**, which will cause everything to **automatically and naturally follow**. This type of leadership will be in harmony with people's own individuality, without trying to make them conform to unnatural influences. Taoist philosophy is emphatically against any rigid standards and rules that do not abide with people's individuality and the Tao.

The *Tao Te Ching* also says the best leaders do **as little as possible** to effectively lead, **do not meddle with irrelevancies**, and often **remain almost unnoticed**. It also says that good leadership involves **letting those that you lead feel responsible for their own success**.

The *Tao Te Ching* also says that knowing and gaining mastery of yourself is superior to knowing and gaining mastery over others, and that the entire world cannot be ruled and controlled.

Government & Society

Since Taoist leadership is about doing as little as possible, it is also opposed to heavily involved governments or social standards. Taoist philosophy feels that it is unnecessary and counterproductive for the government or society to institute rigid codes of behavior. Taoists contend that people who are in harmony with the Tao will naturally follow good actions on their own without needing deliberate external influences.

Taoism and Confucianism

The Taoist viewpoints described above on leadership, society, and government are the main subjects where Taoism differs from Confucianism (another highly influential Chinese philosophy. Confucianism is covered in detail in a separate chapter of this book.)

Despite their differences in these subjects, both Confucianism and Taoism have had a tremendous impact on Chinese people and government for much of Chinese history, and have often alternated on which one had the dominant influence on the government at a particular time period.

Concept of Opposites / Polarity (Yin and Yang)

The concept of **opposites / polarity** plays an integral role in Taoism. In fact, this theme of opposites is prevalent in virtually all Chinese philosophies, and predates Taoism in the chronology of Chinese philosophy.

The Chinese often refer to this concept of opposites as **yin** and **yang**— yin representing one opposite, and yang representing the other.

In general Chinese philosophy, opposites are considered a key theme of the nature of the universe, and are used to describe much of the universe's activity, including the phenomenon of **change, balance,** and **cycles**. Taoist philosophy also extends opposites to apply to "being" and "nonbeing."

Additionally, Taoist philosophy says that things have a tendency to **balance out** and return to a natural balance that is inevitable.

The concept of opposites is also used to point out that the **distinction of each opposite exists because of the other opposite's existence**. For instance, there can be no concept of long without short, left without right, good without bad, etc—but their distinction is made apparent through the coexistence and relation of each other, and when they are measured against one another.

Also, the opposites are used to point out that most things are a matter of **degree** and **severity**, and are on the scale between both extremes, and are not necessarily either one absolute or the other.

Taoist philosophy also points out the usefulness of **living a balanced life that avoids extremes and excesses**.

TAOIST TEXTS

Here is a look at the Taoist texts the *Tao Te Ching*, the *Chuang Tzu,* and the *Lieh Tzu.*

TAO TE CHING

The title *Tao Te Ching* roughly translates to the *Classic-Book of the Tao and Its Te (Power / Characteristics / Virtue / Excellence)*. The purported author of the book is Lao Tzu (alternate spellings include Lao Tse, Lao Tze, Lao Tsu, Laozi, or Laotze), which roughly translates to "Old Master." He is said to have lived around the 600s BC, and is considered the founder of Taoism.

It is uncertain, however, if Lao Tzu really existed, or if he authored the *Tao Te Ching*. Some people speculate that Lao Tzu is a mythical and legendary figure, and that the *Tao Te Ching* was actually written by one or several contributors significantly later than the 600s BC, and perhaps as late as the 200s BC.

Whatever the case many be of its authorship, the *Tao Te Ching* has become the centerpiece text in Taoist thought, and one of the most notable texts in world philosophy and literature. The book is comprised of about 5000 Chinese characters (words), and is split into 81 chapters.

Since the *Tao Te Ching* is written in Classical Chinese (a very ambiguous language) and is also written in a unique format, it has been subject to many interpretations and dozens of different English translations.

(Note that the *Tao Te Ching* is also known as the *Dao De Jing*, or the *Lao Tzu*.)

Tao Te Ching Passages

Note: Each passage below is followed by the chapter number it is contained in. This translation is a clarified adaptation based primarily on the translations of James Legge and JH McDonald. In these translations, I have alternated using masculine and feminine pronouns, which is just an arbitrary choice.

The tao that can be "tao-ed" [*described / distinguished / followed*] is not the real [*true / eternal / enduring*] Tao. The name that can be named [*/ spoken*] is not the real [*true / eternal / enduring*] name. (1)

... [Tao] is the nameless [*/ unlimited*] source of all things that are nameable [*/ limited*]. (1)

Darkness [*/ mystery*] within darkness [*/ mystery*]—the beginning of all understanding. (1)

When people see things as beautiful, [the concept of] ugliness is created. When people see things as good, bad is created. Existence and non-existence give birth to one another. Difficult and easy produce each other. Long and short form the figure of one another. High and low arise from the contrast with each other. The musical notes and tones become harmonious through the relation with one another. Before and after come from the idea of following one another.

Therefore, the master can mange affairs without doing anything [*wu wei*], and teach without saying anything. Things change, and she does not deny it. She has things without possessing things, and she does things without expecting [*/ counting on*] things.

Work is accomplished, and she does not become fixated [in his past work]. Work is done, and she does not wallow in its credit. That is why the power will last forever. (2)

The Tao is [like] the emptiness of a container; and in our use of it, we cannot fill it all the way up. Infinitely deep and immeasurable, it is the source of all things. (4)

Stay at the center. (5)

The spirit of emptiness is immortal. It is called the Mystic Female. It is the root of Heaven and Earth. It is always here. Use it effortlessly, and it will never finish. (6)

Heaven and Earth are long enduring. This is because they do not live fixated on their selves. So the Master puts herself last, and thus finds herself first. She detaches herself from all things, and thus is united with all things. She is not fixated on her self, and thus is fully fulfilled. (7)

The supreme excellence is like water, which benefits all things without striving to compete. It gathers in unpopular places. Thus, it is like the Tao. (8)

Filling all the way up is not as good as stopping at the right amount. If a knife is sharpened too much, it will wear away. (9)

When your work is accomplished and your name is being distinguished, simply walk away. This is the pathway to harmony [/ realness]. (9)

Clay is molded into containers, but it is the empty hollowness inside that makes the containers useful. We cut and arrange material in order to make houses, but it is the empty space inside of the houses that makes them useful. We work with and adapt the tangibly existing material, but to experience them as useful we must use what is not there. (11)

Bring both aspects of your soul in harmony and in oneness—it can be maintained without unbalanced dispersion. Focus on the vital breath until you bring it to a level of a newborn's suppleness.

Cleanse your inner vision, and become flawless [/ clear] ... Open your heart, and you will become accepted. Accept experiencing, and you can step back from it and enter the path of experiencing.

Producing and nourishing, producing and not possessing, doing all and not clinging to the doing, presiding over all and not controlling it— this is the [Tao's] mysterious harmony. (10)

Who can make the muddy water [clear] by letting it be still, so it will gradually become clear by itself? Who can secure the condition of rest by letting movement go on, so that the condition of rest will gradually arise by itself? (15)

The supreme leaders are those who the people hardly even know are there. The next best are those who are loved and praised. Next are those who are feared. And next are those who are despised. (17)

The best leaders valued their words, and used them accordingly. And when work was done and undertakings were successful, the people [being led] said, "We have done it all by ourselves!" (17)

When Tao is abandoned, that is when people start to distinguish concepts of benevolence and righteousness. (18)

Conventional people have their role and place [in society]. As for me, I am flowing and natural. (20)

Who can tell of the Tao's nature? We can't see it or even touch it— yet we are able to know it exists. Eluding sight, eluding touch—yet it is has a semblance. It is profound, secluded, and dark—but it has vitality, a genuineness and pureness we can feel.

It exists and it existed since time began—it transcends time and no-time, it transcends existence and non-existence.

How do I know of it? I experience it. (21)

To be in harmony, speak just enough [to express yourself / communicate sufficiently]. (23)

Abide by Tao, and it will abide by you. Abide by Te, and it will abide by you. (23)

People follow Earth, Earth follows Heaven, Heaven follows Tao, and Tao follows itself. (25)

The Master can live surrounded by lavishness, but does not attach herself to it. (26)

Be an example for the world. If you are an example for the world, you are clear and excellent, and will return to limitless [*like the simplicity of the uncarved / unfinished block of wood*]. (28)

To those who wish to conquer and control the world, I don't believe they can do it. The world is a sacred thing, and it cannot be controlled. He who would take it over would only worsen it; he who would hold it in his hands would only lose [grip of] it.

[Thus,] Sometimes you lead, sometimes you follow; sometimes you are intense, sometimes you take it easy; sometimes you are rigid, sometimes you are flexible; sometimes you advance, sometimes you retreat.

[Thus,] The master does without excesses, overdoing, and extremities. (29)

The Master knows what is necessary to be done, does it, and then stops. (30)

The Tao is nameless and simple [*like the uncarved / unfinished block of wood*]. Although in its simplicity it appears insignificant, nothing in the world can embody and minister it.

If a ruler would abide by its harmony, everything will automatically follow him. Heaven would unite with earth and send down the sweet dew. People would have no need for lawful direction, because they would naturally follow proper actions on their own.

When standards begin, that's when names begin. Don't get caught up in names. When you avoid getting caught up in names, this brings security.

Everything in the universe leads to Tao just like various waters flow into the great seas. (32)

He who knows others is perceptive; he who knows himself is supremely wise [/ *enlightened*]. He who masters others is strong; he who masters himself is supremely powerful. (33)

…   The use of it [*Tao*] is inexhaustible (35)

The master abides in the substance, and not the surface. She dwells in the fruit [*Tao*], and not the flower. Not taking one, she chooses the other. (38)

The Tao is hidden and has no name, yet it is the Tao that is skilled at nourishing and completing everything. (41)

The Tao gave birth to One; One gave birth to Two; Two gave birth to Three; and Three gave birth to all things. (42)

Knowing what is enough avoids dishonor. Knowing where to stop avoids danger and is conducive to being long-lasting. (44)

The greatest fullness seems empty, yet is inexhaustible. (45)

He who knows when he has had enough will always have enough. (46)

Without going outside your door, you can understand the world. Without looking out from your window, you can understand the way of the Tao. The farther you stray, the less you will understand. The Master understands without straying, identifies things properly without looking, and accomplishes things without deliberately acting [*wu wei*]. (47)

One who is devoted to increasing knowledge seeks to learn new things each day. One who is devoted to Tao seeks to unlearn new things each day; less and less remains for him until arriving at non-action [/ *non-purpose* / *wu wei*].

Having arrived at non-action [/ *non-purpose* / *wu wei*], nothing will be left undone. Mastery of the world is achieved by letting things take their natural course. If one seeks to change the natural way, one cannot truly master the world. (48)

Everything honors the Tao and exalts its Te. This honor of the Tao and exalting of its Te occurs naturally [/ *spontaneously*], and is not the result of any ordination. (51)

… [The Master says: As a leader,] Do nothing, and the people will be transformed on their own. Seek tranquility, and the people will become correct on their own. Do not meddle [with irrelevancies], and the people become prosperous. Do not identify with greediness, and the people will attain the state of harmony [/ *simplicity of the uncarved / unfinished block of wood.*] (57)

For self-control and service to harmony [/ *realness*], there is nothing like moderation. Through moderation, one is already on the path to purity [/ *Tao*]. Those who follow this path as soon as possible will have a repeated accumulation of virtue. With a repeated accumulation of virtue, there will be a natural control. Where there is natural control, we know not of its limit. And when one knows not of the limit, then the kingdom is grasped. (59)

Act without acting; conduct affairs without troubling; taste the flavorless; consider the greatness in the small… Anticipate difficult things while they are still easy; do easy things before they become difficult. All difficult things in the world are sure to arise from a previous state in which they were easy, and all great things from one in which they were small.

Therefore the Master, while never becoming overwhelmed, is able to accomplish the greatest things… The master foresees difficulty even in what seems easy, and thus avoids any difficulties. (63)

Take [preventive] action before [problems] arise. Secure order before disorder has begun. The tree that fills the arms grows from a small sprout; the tower of nine levels starts with a single heap of dirt; the journey of a thousand li [*a Chinese unit of measurement equal to about 0.3 miles*] begins with a single step.

If you overact [in unnatural-excessive ways], you will hinder performance. If you over-hold, you will lose your grip. The Master does not over-act, and thus prevents failure. She does not over-hold, and thus does not lose things.

People sometimes err when they are on the verge of closing in on success, and this is often due to their overbold [/ *over-relentless*] conduct. If they were as concerned [/ *careful*] about the end as they are about the beginning, then they would be less likely to err. (64)

In governing the state, the person who uses simplicity [*of the uncarved / unfinished block of wood*] is a blessing to the state. (65)

You can't be cured until you know you are sick. (71)

When people don't fear the things they should fear, this opens a possibility for misfortune. (72)

Do not over-meddle with people. Just let them be, and then they will respond well to you. (72)

The Master knows herself but is not annoying about it. She loves herself but does not assign a set value on herself. This helps her make good decisions. (72)

Excessively bold daringness can result in death. Prudent cautiousness can protect life. One of these is the way to self-preservation; the other is a way to danger. But when chance [/ *probability* / *fate*] results in one's death, who can know what to place blame on? (73)

The way of Heaven [/ *Tao*] can be compared to the bending a bow. What was high is brought low, and what was low is raised up. It diminishes where there is too much, and supplements where there is not enough. It is the way of Heaven to diminish where there is too much, and to supplement where there is not enough. (77)

There is nothing in the world more soft and yielding than water, yet there is nothing better [than water] for attacking things that are firm and strong; there is nothing that can preside over it [*water*] or compete with it… Words that are true can seem paradoxical [/ *contradictory*]. (78)

CHUANG TZU

The *Chuang Tzu* is a collection of essays based on the teachings of a sage named Chuang Tzu, who lived from 369 BC to 286 BC. It is considered the most notable Taoist text other than the *Tao Te Ching*.

Chuang Tzu Passages

Note: These are a clarified adaptation based on the James Legge translation.

Where Does Tao Exist?

Tung Kuo Tzu: "Where does the Tao exist?"
Chuang Tzu: "It is everywhere—there is no place it does not exist."
Tung Kuo Tzu: "Come on now; you must be more specific."
Chuang Tzu: "It is in the ant."
Tung Kuo Tzu: "As low as that?"
Chuang Tzu: "It is in the weeds.
Tung Kuo Tzu: "And as low as that?"
Chuang Tzu: "It is in the broken pottery."
Tung Kuo Tzu: "Can it be so low?"
Chuang Tzu: "It is in the piss and sh--."

There Was a Beginning?

There was a beginning; and there was a beginning before there was a beginning. And there was a beginning before there was a beginning before there was the beginning.

Since there is existence, then there had been a non-existence. And there was a non-non-existence [when even non-existence didn't exist] before the beginning of the non-existence. And there was a non-non-non-existence before there was non-non-existence before there was non-existence.

If non-existence suddenly sprang up, we don't know whether it was really something existing, or really not-existing. Now I have just communicated what I just communicated—but I don't know if I have just communicated anything or not.

Butterfly

Once, Chuang Tzu dreamt he was a butterfly, a butterfly freely fluttering around and having fun, not knowing he was Chuang Tzu. Suddenly, he woke up and found himself to be Chuang Tzu. He did not know whether he was Chuang Tzu who dreamt he was a butterfly, or a butterfly who dreamt he was Chuang Tzu. Between Chuang Tzu and the butterfly there must be some distinction. This is what is meant by the transformation of things.

Words

Fish traps are employed to catch fish; but when the fish are taken, people forget the traps. Snares are employed to catch rabbits, but when the rabbits are got, people forget the snares. Words are employed to convey ideas; but when the ideas are apprehended, people forget the words. I would love to find and talk to such a person who has forgot the words!

Wen Hui and the Cook

Wen Hui's cook was cutting up an ox. Wen Hui was mesmerized by the cook's superb and trancelike actions and movements, which were not only precise, but were also beautifully rhythmic, and produced music that the cook's cutting movements danced to.

Wen Hui remarked, "It's unbelievable how your skill [/ *method*] is so perfected!"

The cook put down his knife and replied, "Tao is what this is about—Tao goes beyond skill [/ *methods*]. When I first began cutting up oxen, I could see nothing but the entire ox's carcass. After three years, I could see beyond the entire mass, and I could see its distinctions. And now, I deal with the ox through my whole being and spirit instead of with just my eyes.

"My spirit is free since my perception and senses have been transcended. Observing natural principles, my knife goes through everything in a natural path and avoids the ligaments or bones.

"A great cook cuts, and needs a new knife each year. An ordinary cook cuts rather carelessly, and needs a new knife every month. As for me, I have been using this knife for 19 years—it has cut up thousands of oxen, but is still sharp as when it was first made.

"There are small interval spaces in the joints. And since the blade's edge has no significant thickness, it also has plenty of room to easily move about and wander.   That is why it is still as fresh as when it first came from the grindstone.

"However, in my cutting, I sometimes come up to a complicated point. That is when I inspect the difficulties and prepare myself, and with caution, I focus and see what I am doing and working on, and move my knife with delicacy and subtleness.

"With a slight and sudden movement of the knife, the difficult part comes apart like clumps of dirt crumbling back to earth. And then I stand there holding my knife, looking all around me, leisurely content and satisfied, and enjoying my success. And then I wipe my knife clean and put it away."

Wen Hui remarked, "Excellent! Listening to my cook speak, I have learned how to nurture life."

Other *Chuang Tzu* Passages

Tao is beyond words and beyond things. It is not expressed in word or in silence.   Where there is no longer word or silence, Tao is apprehended.

Tao makes things what they are, but is not itself a thing [*nor is it nothing*].

Tao is present by and through itself.

Another variation of this:

Tao is its own roots.

Tao exists beyond the highest point—yet you cannot call it lofty. It exists beneath the limit of directions—yet you cannot call it deep. It existed before heaven and earth—yet you cannot say it has existed for a long time. It existed before the earliest time—yet you cannot call it old.

We cling to our own point of view as though everything depended on it—yet our opinions have no permanence. Like fall and winter, they gradually pass away.

The greatest person is nobody.

When the perfect person employs his mind, it is a mirror. It conducts nothing and assumes nothing; it responds [to what is before it], but does not retain it. Thus he [*the perfect person*] is able to deal successfully with all things, and injure none.

LIEH TZU

The *Lieh Tzu* is another notable Taoist text, written around 300 BC by a sage named Lieh Tzu.

Lieh Tzu Passages

Note: These are a clarified adaptation of the Lionel Giles translation.

Suspicious

A man could not find his axe, and suspected that his neighbor's son stole it. As the man inspected the boy's demeanor—the way he moved, the look on his face, and the way he spoke—everything seemed to point to the boy's guilt. The man was convinced that the boy stole his axe.

However, just hours later, the man was digging in a dell and came across his missing axe.

The next day, he looked at his neighbor's son again. This time, he could not spot all those cues that pointed to the boy's guilt the previous day.

[*Lieh Tzu commentary*]: "The man whose mind is filled with suspicion will let himself be carried away by distorted and disproportional impressions, until he sees white as black, and detects squareness in a circle."

Gold Theft

There was a young man in Chi State who had an intense lust for gold. One morning, he got up early, got dressed and went to the bazaar. As he walked through the bazaar, he spotted gold at a moneychanger's stand. Overcome by the sight of it, he proceeded to grab it and run off—but just seconds later, he was easily caught an arrested by the police.

As they took him away, they curiously asked him why he committed the theft when everyone was around, since it seemed so obvious that he would get caught. The young man replied, "When I was taking the gold, I did not see anybody at all—I only saw the gold, and nothing but the gold."

The Sailor and the Seagulls

There was a sailor who loved seagulls. Each morning he went into the sea and swam, and over one hundred seagulls would flock around him.

[*Lieh Tzu commentary*]: "Creatures do not fear those whom they perceive to be in mental and bodily harmony with themselves."

One day, the sailor's father told him, "I have heard about how seagulls swarm around you in the water. I want you to catch a couple for me so I can make them my pets."

The next day, the sailor went into the sea as usual. But this time, however, the seagulls only flew around in the air, and would not join him.

[*Lieh Tzu commentary*]: "There was disturbance in his mind and a change in his outward behavior; thus the birds became aware that he was a human being. How could their reaction be deceived?"

The Jade Mulberry Leaf

A man from Sung carved a mulberry leaf out of jade for the prince. It took the man three years to complete the leaf, and it looked just like a real one, down to its glossiness, shape, color, proportion, and symmetry—in fact, it was indistinguishable from a real mulberry leaf. The government rewarded his skill with great sums of money.

Lieh Tzu heard about this, and remarked, "If it took Nature three years at a time to make a single leaf, then there would be very few trees with leaves on them. The sage should not rely on human science and skill as much as he does on the carrying on of Tao."

White Outfit, Black Outfit

One day, Yang Chu's brother Yang Pu was outside wearing a white outfit. Then it began raining intensely. Yang Pu went inside, changed his clothes, and came back outside with a black outfit. Then Yang Pu's dog saw him, but could not recognize him in the black suit, and began barking and rushing at him.

Yang Pu became enraged, and was about to give the dog a beating. But Yang Chu stopped him and said, "Do not beat him—you are no wiser than he. Suppose your dog went away white and came home black—do you mean to tell me that you would not think it was strange?"

The Practical Joke

There was once a man who, though born in Yen, was brought up in Ch'u, and it was only in his old age that he went to return to his native country [of Yen].

On the way there [*traveling from Ch'u to Yen*], as he was passing through the Chin State, a fellow traveler played a practical joke on him. Pointing to the city he said, "Here is the capital of the Yen State"; whereupon the old man flushed with excitement. Then pointing out a certain shrine, he told him that it was his [*the old man's*] own village altar, and the old man heaved a deep sigh.

Then he showed him a house, and said, "This is where your ancestors lived," and the tears welled up into the old man's eyes. Finally, a mound was pointed out to him as the tomb where his ancestors lay buried, whereupon the old man could control himself no longer, and wept aloud. But his fellow traveler burst into roars of laughter. "I have been hoaxing you," he cried; "this is only the Chin State."

His victim was greatly mortified; and when he arrived at his journey's end and really did see before him the city and altars of Yen, with the actual abode and tombs of his ancestors, his emotion was much less acute.

Pigeon Festival

The good people of Han-tan were in the habit, every New Year's day, of presenting their Governor Chien Tzu with a number of live pigeons. This pleased the Governor very much, and he liberally rewarded the donors.

A stranger asked the meaning of the custom, and Chien Tzu explained, "We release living creatures on New Year's Day as a sign of a us having a benevolent disposition."

The stranger replied, "But the people, being aware of your Excellency's whim, no doubt exert themselves to catch as many pigeons as possible, and large numbers must get killed in the process. If you really wish to let the birds live, the best way would be to prohibit the people from capturing them at all. If they have to be caught first in order to be released, the kindness does not compensate for the cruelty."

Chien Tzu acknowledged that he was right.

Boy Refutes Tien

Tien of the Ch'i State was holding a banquet with over 1000 guests. As Tien sat among the guests, many of them presented him with gifts of fish and game. Tien looked at them approvingly, and exclaimed,

"Nature is indeed generous to man. It makes the five kinds of grain for us to grow, and creates the fish and fowl, especially for our benefit."

Tien's guests applauded the statement, but Pao's 12-year-old son came forward and said, "I respectfully disagree with you, Mr. Tien. All of the universe's living creatures are in the same category as us, and none have greater intrinsic value than the others. It is only by attributes of cunning, strength, and size that a one species masters or prays on another.

"None of them are produced just for others to use them. Man catches and eats certain creatures that are suitable for food, but how can it be deduced that Nature creates these solely for man's use? After all, mosquitoes and gnats suck man's blood, and tigers and wolves eat man's flesh; yet we do not use this to conclude that Nature created man just for the benefit of mosquitoes and gnats, and to provide food for tigers and wolves."

The Superlative Horse

Duke Mu of Ch'in said to Po Lo [*a famous judge of horses*], "You are now advanced in years. Is there any member of your family whom I could employ, as a replacement for you, to look for horses?"

Po Lo replied, "A good horse can be picked out by its general build and appearance. But the superlative [*of the highest excellence*] horse— one that raises no dust and leaves no tracks—is something evasive and fleeting, elusive as thin air. The talent of my sons lies on a lower plane altogether: they can tell a good horse when they see one, but they cannot tell a superlative horse. I have a friend, however, one Chiu-fang Kao, a seller of fuel and vegetables, who in things appertaining to horses is at my level. You should go see him."

Duke Mu did so, and subsequently sent Chiu-fang Kao on the quest to locate a great horse. Three months later, he returned with the news that he had found one, and said "It is now in Sha-ch'iu."

"What kind of a horse is it?" asked the Duke.

"Oh, it is a dun-colored mare," replied Chiu-fang Kao.

However, when someone was sent to go get it, the animal turned out to be a coal-black stallion! Much displeased, the Duke sent for Po Lo, and said, "That friend of yours whom I commissioned to look for a horse, has made a nice mess of it. Why, he cannot even distinguish a beast's color or sex! What on earth can he know about horses?"

Po Lo heaved a sigh of satisfaction. "Has he really got as far as that?" he cried. "Ah, then he is worth a thousand of me put together. There is no comparison between us.

"What Kao keeps in view is the spiritual mechanism. In making sure of the essential, he forgets the homely details. Intent on the inward qualities, he loses sight of the external. He sees what he wants to see, and not what he does not want to see. He looks at the things he ought to look at, and neglects those that need not be looked at. So clever a judge of horses is Kao, that he has it in him to judge something better than horses."

When the horse arrived, it turned out indeed to be a superlative horse.

Other *Lieh Tzu* Passages

Mr. Shih said: "Success consists in hitting off the right moment, while missing it means failure...

"[When a method is identical to another's that succeeds, yet it fails, this] is not due to any flaw in the action itself, but simply because it was not well timed.

"Nothing, in the ordering of this world, is either at all times right or at all times wrong. What was formerly used may nowadays be rejected; what is now rejected may by and by come into use again. The fact that a thing is in use or in disuse forms no criterion whatever of right or wrong. There is no fixed rule for seizing opportunities, hitting off the right moment, or adapting oneself to circumstances..."

There is a Creative Principle which is itself uncreated; there is a Principle of Change which is itself unchanging. The Uncreated is able to create life; the Unchanging is able to effect change. That which is produced cannot but continue producing; that which is evolved cannot but continue evolving. Hence there is constant production and constant evolution. The law of constant production and of constant evolution at no time ceases to operate. So is it with the Yin and the Yang, so is it with the Four Seasons.

The Yellow Emperor said: "If my spirit returns through the gates whence it came, and my bones go back to the source from which they sprang, where does the Ego continue to exist?"

Zen Buddhism

Zen Buddhism is a philosophy that is popular in both the Eastern and the Western worlds. The main themes of Zen include **mastering your mind** and **releasing a distorted sense of reality**.

Intro to Zen

Zen is a unique branch of Buddhism that developed in China, was later popularized in Japan, and then also spread to the West. It has many principles in common with Taoism (see the Taoism chapter for more info). Before we get into specific Zen teachings, here is a look at Buddhism.

Background of Buddhism

Buddhism is a philosophy based on the teachings of an Indian man named Siddhartha Gautama. Siddhartha was born a wealthy prince on the India- Nepal border in the 500s BC (it is estimated that he lived from 568 BC to 488 BC).

At some point in his life (probably around the age of 29), Siddhartha renounced his lavish and luxurious life of royalty, and went on a search for spiritual meaning. After about seven years, he is said to reach a mental state of understanding / experience called enlightenment / awakening.

Siddhartha then became a spiritual leader. His teachings became known as Buddhism, and he became known as the *Buddha*, or enlightened / awakened one. The term *Buddha* is not used to specifically refer to Siddhartha, but is instead used to describe the state of mind he experienced.

(Note: In its basic principles, Buddhism is not a religion or a system of religious beliefs.)

Buddhist Proverbs and Teachings

Note: Almost all of these are based on the sayings and teachings of the Buddha Siddhartha Gautama, and are contained in various Buddhist texts such as the Dhammapada and several others

All we are is the result of what we have thought.

The mind is very subtle, difficult to perceive, and restless. The wise person should guard it, since a guarded mind is conducive to joyfulness.

A controlled mind is conducive to joyfulness.

If you find someone with wisdom, good judgment, and good actions; make him a companion.

Irrigators guide water; arrow-makers straighten arrows; carpenters bend wood; wise people shape themselves.

A single meaningful and calming statement is better than one thousand pointless ones.

Overcoming yourself is better than overcoming a million enemies in battle.

Overcoming yourself is better than overcoming everyone else, because then the victory is yours, and cannot be taken from you by anyone...

Be master of mind rather than mastered by mind.

You are your own master.

You are the master and the way.

You are your own master and your own vacation resort; control yourself.

The virtuous control themselves.

The person who masters himself through self-control and discipline is truly undefeatable.

Those who are determined and control their mind, body, and tongue are indeed well controlled.

If you have done good, set your mind upon it so that it may be repeated over and over again. Allow yourself to be pleased by good. Accumulating good is joyful.

If you hold yourself dear, protect yourself well.

Do not neglect your own needs for someone else's... and recognize your needs so you will know what to do.

First direct yourself to what is right; and then teach others.

Even if you explore the whole universe, you will never find somebody who is more deserving of your love and affection than you are.

They criticize one who remains silent, they criticize one who talks a lot, and they even criticize one who talks in moderation. There is no one in the world who is not criticized. There is not, never was, and never will be a person who lives life on earth and is either always praised or always criticized.

People often see the faults of other people before they see their own faults. People often intently examine for other people's faults, and hide their own just as intently.

Practice love, and give joy.

Be loving and kind.

In doing good, consider not just yourself, but also all of the universe's beings.

Cultivate loving-kindness.

Cultivate good.

They regard the essential as essential, and they regard the unessential as unessential—those who nurture such right thoughts experience the essence.

Your enemy can be your greatest teacher.

Do not live in the past, do not live in the future; concentrate the mind on the present moment.

The pathway to liberation is to live in the present and free yourself from desiring to become anything.

To know your past and what has caused you, observe yourself in the present, since it is the effect of the past. To know your future, observe yourself in the present, since it is the cause the future.

Words have the power to both destroy and heal.

An idea that is developed and put into use is much different than an idea that only exists as an idea.

No matter how many good words you read and speak of, what good will they do you if you do not put them into practice and use them?

Peace comes from within; do not seek it without.

The person who envies others does not obtain peace of mind.

It is better to speak of what you know than to speculate foolishly.

We do not learn by experience, but by our capacity for experience.

Cease grasping, and you will be freed.

The awakened [/ *enlightened*] mind is everywhere all the same, and cannot be attained or grasped—but it can be realized.

All beings in the world transcend the scope of words, and their supremely pure and true nature is like the infiniteness of space.

When appearances and names are put away… what remains is the true nature and essence of things…

Even those who are ignorant are still searching for the way to reality—yet in their search, they often misinterpret what they come across. They are looking for names and categories, but they should look beyond names and go to realness.

The no-mind not-thinks no-thoughts about no-things.

Purify your mind.

Notice your thoughts.

You must be your own lamps.

Mindful attention makes advantageous thoughts that have not happened yet happen, and makes unadvantageous thoughts that already exist disappear.

I know what should be known. I have cultivated what should be cultivated. I have abandoned what should be abandoned. Thus, I am awakened.

If your mind becomes firm like a rock, and does not shake anymore in a world where things are shaking, your mind will be your best friend.

[*Paraphrased*] [A method of meditation:] Go somewhere where you will be alone, and develop yourself with this method: While you inhale, experience inhalation. While you exhale, experience exhalation. If you appreciate and engage in this, it will produce splendid fruit. Whatever you do and wherever you are, you can experience stableness, calm, and focus by having awareness on your breathing.

[A method of meditation:] Develop a meditation that is like water. In this process, you experience that thoughts and conceptions will flow away… This water meditation will bring you peace.

[*Paraphrased:*] Don't believe anything just because it is the public opinion or common rumor; don't believe in anything just because you heard it; don't believe in anything just because of the authoritiveness of your teachers and elders, don't believe in anything just because of longtime traditions; don't believe in anything just because of the use of strict logic or strict inferences; don't believe in anything just because of arguments about methods; don't believe in anything just because you like an opinion; and don't believe in anything just because of your reverence for a teacher and the idea that he must be followed.

[*Paraphrased:*] Just because you used a boat to cross a river [and thus the boat was useful to you], it doesn't mean you should pick up the boat after you reached land, and carry it with you wherever you go. And just like that boat example, sometimes you should consider using teachings [/ *methods*] the same way.

[*Paraphrased:*] Imagine a goldsmith that is using tongs and putting gold in a furnace to melt it. If he constantly makes the fire too hot, the gold will get too hot. If he constantly sprays too much water on it, the gold will not be hot enough. If he constantly takes it out to examine it, it will never become refined. However, if he does all these things but each at their suitable time when needed, and he is knowing of the way gold is, he will have no problem at all in molding and refining it.

Just like that example, any practitioner needs to attend to these three qualities: focus, determination, and composure. If he properly attends to these things at the right time and circumstance, his mind will become pliant, brilliant, and pure, just like gold.

[*Paraphrased*:] A young single father who was a widower had a young son that he loved and cared about very much. One day while the father was away, some plunderer came to his village and burned most of the village down, and also kidnapped the little boy.

When the father came back to the village and inspected the burnt down town, he mistook one of the burnt corpses of a child as his son. The man was devastated, and had the body cremated, and put the ashes in a bag that he always carried around.

Days later, his son escaped from the plunderers and ran back home and knocked on the door of the house that his father rebuilt. His father asked who it was. When the boy answered, "It is me, your son—please let me in," the father, who was still holding the bag of ashes, assumed it was some other boy playing a cruel joke. The father shouted back, "Go away."

The boy continued to knock and plead to the father, but the father continued to tell him to leave. Finally, the boy left, and never came back again.

And just like that example, if a person is intently holding to an idea as the absolute and unmodifiable truth, then he won't be able to open the door and accept the actual truth when it comes firsthand knocking on his door.

[*Paraphrased*:] If someone is wounded by a poisoned arrow, he would not delay taking it out so he could first find out the exact details of who shot it, the reason that person shot it, where the arrow was manufactured, etc. If he attended to understanding all these matters before he pulled out the poisonous arrow, he would probably die.

In this same way, the teachings of the Buddha Siddhartha Gautama are not concerned about understanding things [such as religious and metaphysical issues] as much as they are about dealing with the life situations that people experience at hand.

Suffering [/ *impermanence*] exists in this world… Thirst [/ *cravings* / *desires* / *attachment* / *preferences*] mixed with a passion for greed causes suffering [/ *impermanence*].

There is a middle path [between self-deprivation and indulgence / extremes; between not enough and too much] to control [/ *deal with*] thirst [/ *cravings* / *desires* / *attachment* / *preferences*] and to end suffering [/ *impermanence*]

[The Noble Eightfold Path / Middle Path that the Buddha Siddhartha Guatama taught consists of:] right understanding, right thought, right speech, right action, right livelihood, right effort, right mindfulness, and right meditation.

[*Paraphrased:*][The Middle Path as it applies to food and drink:] ... Eat and drink naturally corresponding to your body's needs. When you cling to the appetite and your appetite is deprivating or excessive, it becomes like slavery. However, satisfying your day-to-day needs is not wrong. In fact, it is a duty to maintain health of the body, because if you don't, this will limit the mind's maintenance of strength and clearness.

Zen Buddhism Emerges From Buddhism; and the Spread of Zen

Buddhism spread from India to China slowly beginning around the 00s AD, and around the year 500 AD, an Indian sage named Bodhidharma is said to have brought the foundation of a new branch of Buddhism to China that became known as Chan Buddhism. (Bodhidharma is considered the 28th Patriarch of a line of people passing down teachings starting with the Buddha Siddhartha Gautama. Bodhidharma is also considered the first of a line of six early Chan Buddhism Patriarchs.)

Chan teachings had a minor presence in Japan as early as the 600s, where it was known as Zen. In the 1200s, Zen became popularized in Japan, and while flourishing there, it particularly appealed to the Samurai warrior class due to its self-discipline and creative spontaneity. Zen also influenced Japanese culture, and particularly Japanese arts, which many Zen practitioners feel are ways of spontaneously expressing "Buddha-nature."

Zen later spread to other parts of the world, and currently has a large following in the United States, among other places. It has also influenced many marital arts practices.

Achieving a New State of Mind

According to Zen Buddhist teachings, conventional thought and reason attempt to *grasp* reality, and gives people a distorted sense of reality. The person who achieves "Zen mind," however, **observes, accepts, and acknowledges reality**.

Zen practitioners use various methods to relinquish and **release a distorted view of reality**, and reach a state of **enlightenment** known as *satori*, which can be loosely defined as a state of

recovering your original mind

freeing yourself from your mind and your thoughts

avoiding self-conscious oriented thinking

no-thought

Keep in mind that Zen enlightenment is not about *attaining* enlightenment. Instead, it is about **allowing** it to happen, and about **realizing** that you already have it, or realizing what is in the way of it.

According to Zen philosophy, everyone already has the enlightened nature, but needs to realize it, acknowledge it, or let themselves experience / be it.

Words and Ideas in Zen

According to Zen teachings, the deep essence of Zen **does not specifically lie in or depend on words or conventional ideas**. But since people use words and ideas in their lives, it becomes necessary that Zen teachings use words and ideas to subvert the ordinary use of words and ideas, and to **relinquish** the inaccuracy caused by them. Or to put it another way, although words and ideas might hinder enlightenment, they can also lead to enlightenment as well.

But the essence of Zen lies more in **experience**. The essence of Zen **circumvents words** and goes **directly into one's true nature**.

Opposites

Like most Eastern philosophies, Zen emphasizes the phenomenon of opposites. For more info on opposites, see the Taoism chapter in this book.

Living in the Present Moment

Zen teachings emphasize focusing on the present moment, and having everything in life experienced with the mind oriented in the present.

The Total Zen Experience

In Zen philosophy, the Zen experience is based on but not limited to specific Zen practices. Zen extends to everything one does. In Zen philosophy, eating, working / playing, and resting are all considered Zen experience / activities / practice.

Soto and Rinzai Schools of Zen Buddhism

When Zen was popularized in Japan, two sects of Zen emerged (which were based on two of the sects of Chan Buddhism in China): Soto and Rinzai.

Soto

The Soto believe that enlightenment can be achieved gradually through long-term experience, particularly of *zazen*, which is Zen meditation.

In zazen, the practitioner sits and practices "non-thinking," "emptying," or a achieving a mind devoid of purpose.

Here is a selection about zazen from the *Shobogenzo*, which written by Dogen (lived from 1200 to 1253), the founder of Japanese Soto Zen:

After you have selected [/ *settled*] a posture, you should regulate your breathing. Whenever a thought comes up, acknowledge it, and as soon as you do, it will go away. If you become forgetful of objects for a long time, you will naturally become unified. This is the essence of zazen…

After you have regulated your mind and body, take a breath and fully exhale. Sitting fixedly, think of not thinking. How do you think of not thinking? Nothinking. This is the art of zazen.

Rinzai

The other group of Zen Buddhists is the Rinzai. They believe that enlightenment can be triggered instantly and experienced at any time. The Rinzai usually use a master and disciple setting, where the master guides the disciple in attaining enlightenment. However, a Master is not a teacher, because Zen cannot be taught. Masters are experienced guides who put students in situations that will be conducive for them to experience Zen mind on their own.

KOANS

Rinzai monks also meditate upon Zen koans, which are any dialogues, riddles, stories, or sayings that can be used to make a person think spontaneously, to think outside the box, and trigger enlightenment. The master and disciple often have conversational exchanges and tests related to koans.

Koans are not exclusive to Rinzai Zen, and Soto Zen practitioners also include koans in their Zen studies as well.

(Note: The term koan can also be used to describe most Zen-related writings, sayings, proverbs, quotes, etc.)

Of the thousands of Zen koans, here are some of them:

Everything Is

Banzan overheard a conversation between a customer and a butcher.
Customer: "Give me the best piece of meat you have."
Butcher: "Everything in my shop is the best. You cannot find any piece of meat that is not the best."
Upon hearing this, Banzan was enlightened.

What is Moving?

Two monks were arguing about a flag, and the Sixth Chan / Zen Patriarch [Hui Neng] overheard them.
First monk: "The flag is moving."
Second monk: "The wind is moving."
The Sixth Patriarch: "Not the wind, not the flag. Mind is moving."

They Were Like

Disciple: "What did ancient masters attain when they entered the ultimate level?"
Master: "They were like crooks stealthily moving into a vacant home."

Perfect Understanding

Disciple: "Tell me about a person who has a perfect understanding of things?"
Master: "It is a great practice."
Disciple: "It is unclear to me—do you practice?"
Master: "I wear clothes and I eat food."
Disciple: "Those are standard behaviors. It is still unclear to me—do you practice?"
Master: "Tell me this—what do I do everyday?"

Can I Do It?

Disciple: "I plan to carve a stone into a Buddha. Can I do it?"
Master: "Yes, you can do it."
Disciple: "Can I not do it?"

Master: "No, you cannot do it."

A Million Objects

Disciple: "If a million objects come to you, what do you do?"
Master: "A green object is not yellow. A long object is not short. Each object conducts its own fate. Why should I interfere with them?"

The One Man Dialogue

Ruiyan is talking to himself.
Ruyain: "Master... Yes, sir... Be alert... Yes, sir... And also, do not be deceived by other people... Yes, sir; yes, sir."

Path

Disciple: "What is the clear path?"
Master: "Awakening your mind, and seeing your nature."

The Jewel

Disciple: "Does the bright jewel in my hand posses any illumination?"
Master: "Yes—but what are you calling a jewel?"

Energy

Disciple: "How about if I aim to be Buddha?"
Master: "What an immense waste of energy!"
Disciple: "How about if I am not wasting my energy?"
Master: "In that case, you are Buddha!"

What is the Buddha?

Dabai: "What is the Buddha?"
Baso: "The very mind is the Buddha."

What is the Buddha? II

Monk: "What is the Buddha?"
Baso: "Not the mind, not the Buddha"

What is the Buddha? III

Disciple: "What is the Buddha?"
Tozan: "Three pounds of flax!"

Who is Buddha?

Disciple: "Who is Buddha?"
Master: "Who is asking?"

Mind / Knowledge

Nansen: "Mind is not the Buddha; knowledge is not the Way [/ *Tao*]."

Unspoken

Monk: "Is there a truth unspoken to people?"
Nansen: "Yes."
Monk: "What is the truth unspoken to people."
Nansen: "Not the mind, not the Buddha, not a thing."

Nansen's Farming Tool

Nansen was working on the mountain, and a monk walked up to him
Monk: "What way leads to Nansen?"
Nansen: (Raising up his farming tool) "I bought this farming tool for 25 cents."
Monk: "I'm not asking about the farming tool you bought for 25 cents. What way leads to Nansen?"
Nansen: "It feels good when I use it."

What is the Way?

Joshu: "What is the Way [/ *Tao*]?"
Nansen: "Ordinary [/ *everyday*] mind is the Way."
Joshu: "How do I try to get it?
Nansen: "The more you pursue it, the more you will be separated from it."
Joshu: "Well, if I don't pursue it, then how can I know it?"
Nansen: "The Way is not about knowing, nor is it about not-knowing. Knowing is an illusion, and not-knowing is disorientation. The Way is vast, free, and boundless like outer space—so where is there room in that for good and bad, or right and wrong?"
Upon hearing this, Joshu was enlightened.

Tell Me a Summary of Buddhism

A young disciple felt that he had realized much of Zen, and he left his master's monastery to travel all over China. Many years later, he returned to the monastery to visit his old master.
Master: "Tell me the summary of Buddhism."
Disciple: "If a cloud does not float over the mountain, the moonlight will go through the waves of the lake."
Master (angrily): "After all these years, you still have such an idea of Zen!"
The Disciple was very upset to hear this from his Master. After a few minutes had passed, he inquired to the Master.
Disciple: "Please tell me the summary of Buddhism."
Master: "If a cloud does not float over the mountain, the moonlight will go through the waves of the lake."
Before the Master completed his statement, the Disciple was enlightened.

What is the Meaning of Buddhism?

Disciple: "What is the meaning of Buddhism?"
Master: "Wait until no one is around, and I will tell you."
The Next Day
Disciple: "OK. No one is around now. Please tell me."
The Master took the disciple to a bamboo orchard, and did not say anything. Some time passed and the disciple did not appear to understand, so the Master spoke.
Master: "Here is a tall bamboo; there is a short one."

Who Constricts You?

Master: "Who constricts you?"
Disciple: "No one."
Master: "Then why seek liberation?"

Inside Outside

Disciple: "What is your practice?"
Master: "Have nothing inside, search for nothing outside."

Leaving Home

Disciple: "What is leaving home?"

Master: "Not yearning for approval, not searching for impurities."

Leaving Home II

Disciple: "It is still unclear to me—what is it when someone asserts to leave home and search for paramount wisdom?"
Master: "When you have not left home yet, wisdom uses you. After leaving home, you can use wisdom."

Other Than Words

Disciple: "Other than words, please say something."
Master: (coughs)

What is Your Way?

Disciple: "What is your Way?"
Master: "What is right now?"

ZEN PROVERBS AND SAYINGS

If you understand, things are just as they are. If you do not understand, things are just as they are.

The infinite is in the finite of every moment.

Hide your body in the Big Dipper.

Everything the same; everything different.

When I eat, I eat. When I sleep, I sleep.

When sitting, sit. When walking, walk. Above all, don't wobble [unless you are wobbling].

The obstacle is the path.

Sitting quietly, doing nothing, spring comes and the grass grows by itself.

Only when you can be extremely flexible and soft can you be extremely hard and strong.

The tighter you squeeze, the less you have.

Flowing streams do not compete with one another.

Sometimes you need to slow down so that the thing you are chasing will come around and catch you.

To find your true self, release your illusory self.

This is *it*, but as soon as you distinguish it definedly, then it is not *it* anymore.

Know yourself, and be it.

If enlightenment is not where you are standing, where will you look?

When asking a question, ask yourself: who wants to know?

What is the color of wind?

Two mirrors facing each other. There is no image in between.

What is the sound of one hand clapping?

What is your original face, before your mother and father were born?

Learning Zen is a circumstance of gold and sh--. Before you understand it, it's like gold; after you understand it, it's like sh--.

With Zen, everyday is a good day.

ZEN QUOTES

Bodhidharma
(Lived in 400s and 500s) First Chan / Zen Patriarch

All know the way, but few actually walk it.

The Way is wordless.

Don't cling to appearances, and you will break through all barriers.

Not depending on words and letters;

A special transmission [from mind-to-mind] outside the scriptures;
Directly pointing to the soul [/ *mind* / *heart*]
Seeing into one's own nature, and attaining Buddhahood

Seng Ts'an
(Lived in 500s and 600s) Third Chan / Zen Patriarch

The Great Way is not difficult for people who have no preferences.

The Way is perfect like vast space, where nothing is lacking and nothing is in excess.

To return to the root is to find the meaning, but to pursue appearance is to miss the source.

Do not seek truth; simply stop cherishing [your own] opinions.

Living in the Great Way is neither easy nor difficult.

Hui Neng
(Lived in 600s and 700s) Sixth Chan / Zen Patriarch

The mind's capacity is as great as space's. It is infinite, and neither round nor square, neither big nor small, neither green nor yellow, neither red nor white, neither above nor below, neither long nor short, neither angry nor happy, neither right nor wrong, neither good nor evil, neither first nor last.

Look within! ... What I tell you is not secret. The secret is in you.

Just like one light drives away one thousand years of darkness, so does one flash of wisdom destroy ten thousand years of ignorance.

Shitou Xiqian
(700-790) Chinese Chan / Zen Master

Release hundreds of years and relax.

Rinzai Gigen Zenji
(?-866) Chinese Chan / Zen Master whose teachings later formed the foundation of Rinzai Zen

When I'm hungry, I eat; when I'm tired, I sleep. The foolish people ridicule me, but the wise people understand.

Joshu (a.k.a. Chao-Chou)
(778-897) Chinese Chan / Zen Master

If I meet a hundred-year-old man and I have something to teach him, I will teach; if I meet an eight-year-old boy and he has something to teach me, I will learn.

Ta-hui
(1088-1163) Zen Master who promoted Koan meditation

If you want to know the state of buddhahood, make your mind as clear as empty space. Release any false thinking and grasping, and then your mind will be unimpeded wherever it may turn. The state of buddhahood is not an external world containing a formal Buddha. It's the state of the wisdom of a self-awakened sage.

Wu-Men
(Lived in 1200s) Rinzai Zen master known for his collection and commentary of Koans

If your mind is not clouded by unnecessary things, this is the best season of your life.

One instant is eternity; eternity is in the now. When you see through the one instant, you see through the one who sees.

Search back into your own perspective; think back to the mind that thinks. Who is it?

The Great Way has no gate; there are a thousand different paths.

With realization, all things are one unity; without realization, all things are distinct. Without realization, all things are one unity; with realization, all things are distinct.

Dogen
(1200-1253) Founder of Japanese Soto Zen

To study the Way is to study the self. To study the self is to forget the self. To forget the self is to be enlightened by all things. To be enlightened by all things is to abandon our own body and mind, and those of others. No trace of enlightenment remains, and this traceless enlightenment continues endlessly.

Master Takuan Sono
(1573-1645) Zen master

This day will not come again. Each minute is worth a priceless gem.

Zen is to have the heart and soul of a little child.

Suzuki Roshi
(1905-1971) Japanese-American Zen teacher and author of *Zen Mind, Beginners Mind*

Each of us must make our own true way, and when we do, that way will express the universal way.

Seung Sahn
(1927-) Korean Zen Master

Zen mind is not Zen mind.

Cyrus The Great & *The Human Rights Charter*

Cyrus The Great (a.k.a. Kourosh Eh Kabir), who lived from 580 BC to 529 BC, is one of the most notable emperors in world history. He united the original Medes and Persian tribes to form the first equally unified and united Persian (Iranian) Empire, and after many other conquests, he created one of the largest empires ever. (The Persian Empire was later extended even further by successive Emperors.)

The Tolerant Emperor

What really makes Cyrus stand out in history is the **tolerant** and **respectful** attitude he had towards all people in his empire, including those he had just defeated. This was a vast contrast to virtually every other notable leader before him, most of who had oppressive reigns and commonly forced their ways and cultures into conquered people.

Cyrus had his own cultural background and was a follower of the Zoroastrian religion (which is covered in detail in a separate chapter of this book), yet he showed great respect for the religious beliefs and cultural traditions of all other races. His tolerant actions earned him the devotion, respect, and admiration of his citizens.

Although Cyrus is known today as a great conqueror, he was actually more like a liberator. His **understanding** and gracefulness towards others was truly ahead of his time. Even in modern times, most people in the world do not enjoy such freedoms as the ones Cyrus granted to the citizens of his empire over two and a half millennium ago.

Origins of Cyrus's Charter

When Cyrus conquered Babylon in 539 BC, he issued a special charter at his coronation that outlined his beliefs in the rights of nations and humankind. For most of history after Cyrus's reign, the charter was lost, and only excerpts of it remained in other historical texts. However, in 1878, an excavation in Babylon uncovered the original Charter, which was written in Ancient Persian cuneiform (wedge-shaped characters) on a baked clay cylinder.

Cyrus's charter is considered the first ever document on human rights. In 1971, the United Nations published and distributed translations of the charter in all the official UN languages in order to promote peace.

Excerpts From *The Human Rights Charter*

Cyrus begins his charter by proclaiming:

> I am Kourosh [*Cyrus*], King of the World, Great King, Mighty King, King of Babylon...

He goes on to list his kingdom and ancestry in detail. He then describes his humane treatment of the inhabitants of Babylonia after the Persian conquest:

> When I, well inclined, entered Babylon, I set up a seat of government in the royal palace amidst celebration and rejoicing... My numerous troops moved about calmly in Babylon... I did not let anyone terrorize the land...
>
> I considered the needs of Babylon and all its sacred places to further their prosperity... I took off their [*the citizens of Babylon*] unflattering yoke [*a yoke is a bar connected to animal collars to control them*]... I restored their deteriorated dwellings. I ended their misfortunes... [I allowed them to] live peacefully in their homes...

Cyrus then proclaims his policies of human rights:

> As I put the crown of the kingdom of Iran, Babylon, and the nations of the four directions on the head with the help of Mazda [*he is referring to Ahura Mazda (Wise Lord / Lord Wisdom), the supreme god of the Zoroastrian belief*], I proclaim that I will respect the traditions, customs and religions my empire's nations, and will never let any of my governors and deputies look down on or insult them while I am alive.
>
> From now on, until Mazda grants me and my kingdom the favor, I will not force my monarchy on any nation. Each [nation] is free to accept it, and if any one of them rejects it, I will never decide on letting war prevail.
>
> While I am the king of Iran, Babylon, and the nations of the four directions, I will never let anyone oppress anyone else, and if it does happen, I will restore the oppressed person's right, and punish the oppressor. And while I am king, I will never let anyone take possession of the movable or fixed properties [*real estate*] of others by force or without compensation.
>
> While I am alive, I will prevent unpaid, forced labor. Today, I announce that everyone is free to choose a religion. People are free to live anywhere and take up a job as long as they never violate other people's rights.

No one should be punished for his or her relatives' faults. I will prevent slavery, and my governors and deputies are required to outlaw the slave trade within their own ruling areas. Such a practice [*slavery*] should be abolished throughout the world.

I request Mazda to make me successful in fulfilling my obligations to the nations of Iran [*Persia*], Babylon, and the ones of the four directions.

Sun Tzu & *The Art of War*

The Art of War is a legendary Ancient Chinese book of military strategy. Although most people today are not military strategists engaging in warfare, *The Art of War* is widely read and studied by all types of people due to the principles it describes on general **strategy** and **leadership**.

Origins and History of the Book

Many scholars estimate that *The Art of War* was written around 500 BC. Like any book that old, the exact origins of it remain somewhat uncertain. Most scholars agree that it was written primarily by a military advisor of that era named Sun Tzu (originally named Sun Wu). He most likely formulated and wrote down a military text based on sacred oral teachings that were secretly transmitted and memorized by various military people, mixed in with his own input.

In all likelihood, after he wrote the text, it continued to exist in both oral and written forms, and was regarded as a series of profound information that was closely guarded by those who knew it. It passed down to various leaders and generals, and eventually, the information became more widely known throughout China and then the rest of the world.

The text is generally referred to as *Sun Tzu on the Art of War*, and is usually called the *Sun Tzu* by the Chinese, while most non-Chinese speakers refer to it as *The Art of War*. It is considered the first text of its kind in world history, and despite its early age, many readers feel that it is still among the best.

Sun Tzu has also become a legendary figure in Chinese history, although the earliest biographical information written about him dates from around the 00s AD, and probably contains mostly fictionalized material.

Main Themes

The Art of War is based on running a highly **effective**, **efficient**, and **harmonious** operation. Main themes of the book include:

adapting and responding to circumstances—including your **environment** and your **opponents**

basing your strategy on **unpredictableness, secrecy,** and **deception**

capitalizing on opportunities, including the vulnerabilities of opponents (i.e. exploiting their weaknesses and attacking where they are unprepared)

avoiding the opponents' strengths

making your opponents vulnerable by causing disorder and disharmony among them, and by **holding out baits** to manipulate them

minimizing your own vulnerability

getting the best out of those you command by **picking the right people to do the right job,** instituting **proper communication** methods, and **utilizing combined energy**

using spies to gather information

knowing when it is the best time and situation to do battle, and **avoiding unnecessary battle or battle where your odds of wining are low**

The Art of War Passages

Note: These are a clarified adaptation of the Lionel Giles translation

Modify plans according to when circumstances are favorable. [And know that] All warfare is based on deception. Thus, when you are able to attack, appear unable; when using forces, appear inactive. When you are near, make the enemy believe you are far; and when far, make him believe you are near.

Hold out baits to entice the enemy. Feign disorder, and crush him. If he is secure at all points, be prepared for him. If he is in superior strength, evade him. If your opponent is vulnerable to being annoyed, seek to irritate him.

Pretend to be weak, so he may become excessively arrogant. If he is taking his ease, make things difficult for him. If his forces are united, separate them. Attack him where he is unprepared; appear where you are not expected.

These military devices, leading to victory, must not be divulged beforehand. (1:17-25)

…In war, let your chief aim be victory, not lengthy campaigns. (2:19)

In the practical art of war, it is best to take the enemy's country whole and intact. To shatter and destroy it is not as good. And it is better to recapture an army whole than to destroy it, and to capture a regiment, detachment or company whole than to destroy them.

Thus, fighting and conquering in all your battles is not supreme excellence; supreme excellence consists of breaking the enemy's resistance without fighting.

Therefore:

The highest form of generalship is to thwart the enemy's plans;

The next best is to prevent the synergy of the enemy's forces;

The next in line is to attack the enemy's army in the field;

And the worst policy of all is to attack walled cities. (3:1-3)

...

Therefore, the skillful leader subdues the enemy's troops without any fighting; he captures their cities without surrounding [/ *attacking*] them; he overthrows their kingdom without any long lengthy field operations.

With his forces intact, he will dispute the mastery of the Empire, and thus, without losing a man, his triumph will be complete. This is the method of attacking by stratagem [*clever / deceiving maneuver*]. (3:6-7)

Thus we may know that there are five essentials for victory:

He will win who knows when to fight and when not to fight.

He will win who knows how to handle both superior and inferior forces.

He will win whose army is animated by the same spirit throughout all its ranks.

He will win who, having prepared himself, waits to take the enemy unprepared.

He will win who has military capacity, and is not interfered with by the sovereign.

Victory lies in the knowledge of these five points—hence the saying:

If you know the enemy and know yourself, you need not fear the result of a hundred battles. If you know yourself but not the enemy, you will win some and lose some. If you know neither the enemy nor yourself, you will be vulnerable to being overwhelmed in every battle. (3:17-18)

...The good fighters of early times first put themselves beyond the possibility of defeat, and then waited for an opportunity of defeating the enemy.

To secure ourselves against defeat lies in our own hands, but the opportunity of defeating the enemy is provided by the enemy himself.

Thus, the good fighter is able to secure himself against defeat, but cannot make certain of defeating the enemy. Hence the saying: One may *know* how to conquer without being able to *do* it. (4:1-4)

Security against defeat implies *defensive* tactics; ability to defeat the enemy means taking the *offensive*. Being totally fixed on the defensive is too passive; being totally fixed on the offensive is too aggressive.

The general who is skilled in defense hides in the most secret recesses of the earth; he who is skilled in attack flashes forth from the topmost heights of heaven. Thus, on the one hand we have ability to protect ourselves; on the other, a victory that is complete. (4:5-7)

To the ancients, a clever fighter is one who not only wins, but also excels in easily winning [when it was easy to win]. Hence, his victories bring him neither reputation for wisdom, nor credit for courage... (4:11-12)

The skillful fighter puts himself into a position that makes defeat impossible, and does not miss the moment for defeating the enemy. Thus, in warfare, the victorious strategist first wins, and then seeks to do battle; whereas the defeated strategist first fights, and then afterwards looks for victory. (4:14-15)

...The control of a large force is the same principle as the control of a few men—it is merely a question of sufficiently organizing their numbers. Fighting with a large army under your command is no different from fighting with a small one—it is merely a question of [having proper communication by] instituting signs and signals. (5:1-2)

Understanding direct [*sometimes translated as "common" or "straightforward"*] and indirect [*sometimes translated as "uncommon" or "surprise"*] maneuvers can be used to ensure that your whole host may overcome the brunt of the enemy's attack and remain unshaken. The science of weak points and strong points can be used to make the impact of your army be like a grindstone dashed against an egg.

In all fighting, the direct method may be used for joining battle, but indirect methods will be needed in order to secure victory. Indirect tactics, efficiently applied, are inexhaustible as the heavens and earth, and unending as the flow of rivers and streams. Like the sun and moon, they end but to begin anew; and like the four seasons, they pass away to return once more.

There are not more than five musical notes, yet the combinations of these five give rise to more melodies than can ever be heard. There are not more than five primary colors [*blue, yellow, red, white, and black*], yet in combination they produce more hues than can ever been seen. There are not more than five cardinal flavors [*sour, acrid, salt, sweet, bitter*], yet combinations of them yield more flavors than can ever be tasted.

In battle, there are not more than two methods of attack—the direct and the indirect—yet these two in combination give rise to an endless series of maneuvers. The direct and the indirect lead on to each other in turn like moving in a circle—you never come to an end. Who can exhaust the possibilities of their combination?

The onset of troops is like the rush of a torrent that will even roll stones along in its course. The quality of decision is like the well-timed swoop of a falcon that enables it to strike and destroy its victim. Therefore, the good fighter will be effective in his onset, and precise in his decisions [/ *timing*].

Energy may be likened to the bending of a crossbow; decision [/ *timing*] to the releasing of a trigger. Amid the turmoil and tumult of battle, there may seem to be disorder, and yet no real disorder at all. Amid confusion and chaos, your array may be [circling] without head or tail, yet it will be guarded against defeat. (5:3-16)

…One who is skillful at keeping the enemy on the move maintains deceitful appearances, according to which the enemy will act. He sacrifices something, so that the enemy may snatch at it. By holding out baits, he keeps him on the march; then with a body of picked men he lies in wait for him. (5:19-20)

The clever combatant looks to the effect of combined energy, and does not require too much from individuals; hence his ability to pick out the right men and utilize combined energy.

When he utilizes combined energy, his fighting men become as it were like unto rolling logs or stones; for it is the nature of a log or stone to remain motionless on level ground, and to move when on a slope; if four-cornered, to come to a standstill, but if round-shaped, to go rolling down. Thus the energy developed by good fighting men is like the momentum of a round stone rolled down a mountain thousands of feet in height. So much on the subject of energy. (5:21-23)

Appear at points where the enemy must move quickly to defend; move quickly to places where you are not expected. An army may march great distances without distress if it marches through country where the enemy is not. (6:5-6)

You can ensure the success of your attacks if you only attack places that are undefended. You can ensure the safety of your defense if you only hold positions that cannot be attacked. Therefore, that general is skillful in attack whose opponent does not know what to defend; and he is skillful in defense whose opponent does not know what to attack. (6:7-8)

...[Through the art of subtlety and secrecy,] we learn to be invisible and inaudible; and hence we can hold the enemy's fate in our hands. You may advance and be absolutely irresistible if you make for the enemy's weak points; you may retire and be safe from pursuit if your movements are more rapid than those of the enemy. (6:9-10)

If we want to fight, we can force the enemy to take us on, even if he is sheltered behind a high rampart and a deep ditch. All we need do is attack some other place that he will be obliged to relieve.

If we don't want to fight, we can prevent the enemy from taking us on, even if the lines of our encampment are merely traced out on the ground. All we need do is to throw something odd and unaccountable in his way. (6:11-12)

By discovering the enemy's dispositions and remaining invisible ourselves, we can keep our forces concentrated, while the enemy's must be divided. We can form a single united body, while the enemy must split up into fractions.

Hence, there will be a whole pitted against separate parts of a whole, which means that we shall be many to the enemy's few; and if we are able thus to attack an inferior force with a superior one, our opponents will be in vulnerable positions.

The spot where we intend to fight must not be made known. Thus, the enemy will have to prepare against a possible attack at several different points; and since his forces will then be distributed in many directions, the numbers we shall have to face at any given point will be proportionately fewer. For should the enemy strengthen his front, he will weaken his rear; should he strengthen his rear, he will weaken his front; should he strengthen his left, he will weaken his right; should he strengthen his right, he will weaken his left. If he sends reinforcements everywhere, he will be weak everywhere.

Numerical weakness comes from having to prepare against possible attacks; numerical strength, from compelling our adversary to make these preparations against us. Knowing the place and the time of the coming battle, we may concentrate from the greatest distances in order to fight... (6:13-19)

Even if the enemy is stronger in numbers, we may prevent him from fighting. Scheme so as to discover his plans and the likelihood of their success. Disturb him, and learn the principle of his activity or inactivity. Force him to reveal himself, so as to find out his vulnerable spots. Carefully compare the opposing army with your own, so that you may know where strength is superabundant and where it is deficient. (6:22-24)

How victory may be produced for them out of the enemy's own tactics—that is what the multitude cannot comprehend. All men can see the tactics by which I conquer, but what none can see is the strategy out of which victory is evolved.

Do not repeat the [exact same] tactics just because they have gained you one victory—instead, let your methods be regulated by the infinite variety of circumstances. Military tactics are like unto water; for water in its natural course runs away from high places and hastens downwards. So in war, the [effective] way is to avoid what is strong and to strike at what is weak. Water shapes its course according to the nature of the ground over which it flows; the soldier works out his victory in relation to the foe that he is facing.

Therefore, just as water retains no constant shape, so in warfare there are no constant conditions. He who can modify his tactics in relation to his opponent and thereby succeed in winning, may be called a harmoniously powerful captain.

The five elements [*water, fire, wood, metal, earth*] are not always equally predominant; the four seasons make way for each other in turn. There are short days and long; the moon has its periods of waning and waxing. (6:26-34)

Having collected an army and concentrated his forces, he [*the general*] must blend and harmonize the different elements thereof before pitching his camp. After that, comes tactical maneuvering...

The difficulty of tactical maneuvering consists in turning the devious into the direct, and misfortune into gain. Thus, to take a long and circuitous route after enticing the enemy out of the way, and though starting after him, to contrive to reach the goal before him, shows knowledge of the trick of deviation.

Maneuvering with an army is advantageous; with an undisciplined multitude, most dangerous. (7:2-5)

We cannot enter into alliances until we are acquainted with the designs of our neighbors. (7:12)

In war, practice deception and you will succeed. (7:15)

Whether to concentrate or to divide your troops must be decided by circumstances. (7:16)

…[A clever general] avoids an army when its spirit is keen, but attacks it when it is sluggish and inclined to return. This is the art of studying moods. Disciplined and calm, awaiting the appearance of disorder and confusion amongst the enemy—this is the art of retaining self-possession. (7:29-30)

It is a military axiom not to advance uphill against the enemy, nor to oppose him when he comes downhill. (7:33)

There are roads that must not be followed, armies that must be not attacked, towns that must not be surrounded, positions that must not be contested, and commands of the sovereign that must not be obeyed. (8:3)

The art of war teaches us to rely not on the likelihood of the enemy's not coming, but on our own readiness to receive him; not on the chance of his not attacking, but rather on the fact that we have made our position unassailable. (8:11)

There are five dangerous faults that may affect a general:
    Recklessness, which leads to destruction;
    Cowardice, which leads to capture;
    A hasty temper, which can be provoked by insults;
    A delicacy of honor [/ *morals*], which is sensitive to shame;
    Over-solicitude for his men, which exposes him to worry and trouble.
These are the five besetting sins of a general, ruinous to the conduct of war… Let them be a subject of meditation. (8:12-14)

If the enemy sees an advantage to be gained and makes no effort to secure it, the soldiers are exhausted. (9:31)

If soldiers are punished before they have grown attached to you, they will not prove submissive; and, unless submissive, then will be practically useless. If, when the soldiers have become attached to you, punishments are not enforced, they will still be useless.

Therefore, soldiers must be treated in the first instance with humanity, but kept under control by means of iron discipline. This is a certain road to victory. (9:42-43)

When the general is weak and without authority; when his orders are not clear and distinct; when there are no fixed duties assigned to officers and men, and the ranks are formed in a slovenly haphazard manner, the result is utter disorganization. (10:18)

Regard your soldiers as your children, and they will follow you into the deepest valleys. Look upon them as your own beloved sons, and they will stand by you even unto death.

If, however, you are lenient, but unable to make your authority felt; kind-hearted, but unable to enforce your commands; and incapable, moreover, of quelling disorder; then your soldiers must be likened to spoilt children—they are useless for any practical purpose. (10:25-26)

If we know that our own men are in a condition to attack, but are unaware that the enemy is not open to attack, we have gone only halfway towards victory. If we know that the enemy is open to attack, but are unaware that our own men are not in a condition to attack, we have gone only halfway towards victory. If we know that the enemy is open to attack, and also know that our men are in a condition to attack, but are unaware that the nature of the ground makes fighting impracticable, we have still gone only halfway towards victory.

Thus, the experienced soldier, once in motion, is never bewildered; once he has broken camp, he is never at a loss. Hence the saying: If you know the enemy and know yourself, your victory will not stand in doubt; if you know Heaven and know Earth, you may make your victory complete. (10:27-31)

On dispersive ground [*on your own territory*], do not fight.
On facile ground [*in hostile territory, but not deep into it*], do not stop.
On contentious ground [*advantageous to both sides*], do not attack.
On open ground [*where both sides can move around freely*], do not try to block the enemy's way.
On intersecting highway ground [*where the key to the boundaries of three states meet, and thus whoever occupies it first has most of the Empire at his command*], form alliances.

On serious ground [*in the heart of a hostile country, with reinforced cities in its rear*], gather in plunder.

On difficult ground [*where there is terrain difficult to travel through, such as mountains, forests, rugged steeps, marshes and fens*], keep steadily on the march.

On hemmed-in ground [*that you entered through narrow gorges, and can only be exited by difficult paths that would make your troops vulnerable*], be prepared to deceive and surprise.

On desperate ground [*where we can only be saved from destruction by fighting without delay*], fight. (11:11-14, with bracket info based on 11:1-10)

Those who were called skillful leaders in early times knew how to drive a wedge between the enemy's front and rear; to prevent cooperation between his large and small divisions; to hinder the good troops from rescuing the bad, the officers from rallying their men. When the enemy's men were united, they managed to keep them in disorder. When it was to their advantage, they made a forward move; when otherwise, they stopped still.

If asked how to cope with a great host of the enemy in orderly array and on the point of marching to the attack, I should say: "Begin by seizing something which your opponent holds dear; then he will be obedient to your will."

Rapidity is the essence of war: take advantage of the enemy's unreadiness, make your way by unexpected routes, and attack unguarded spots. (11:15-19)

Carefully study the well-being of your men, and do not overtax them. Concentrate your energy and hoard your strength... (11:22)

The skillful tactician may be likened to the shuai-jan. Now the shuai-jan is a snake that is found in the Chung Mountains. Strike at its head, and you will be attacked by its tail; strike at its tail, and you will be attacked by its head; strike at its middle, and you will be attacked by both its head and tail. (11:29)

By altering his arrangements and changing his plans, he [*the skillful general*] keeps the enemy without definite knowledge. By shifting his camp and taking circuitous routes, he prevents the enemy from anticipating his purpose. (11:37)

We cannot enter into alliance with neighboring princes until we are acquainted with their designs. We are not fit to lead an army on the march unless we are familiar with the face of the country—its mountains and forests, its pitfalls and cliffs, its marshes and swamps. We shall be unable to turn natural advantages to account unless we make use of local guides. (11:52)

Success in warfare is gained by carefully adapting ourselves to the enemy's purpose. By persistently hanging on the enemy's flank, we shall succeed in the long run in killing the commander-in-chief. This is called ability to accomplish a thing by sheer cunning.

On the day that you take up your command, block the frontier passes, destroy the official tallies, and stop the passage of all emissaries. (11:60-63)

If the enemy makes a mistake [/ *leaves himself vulnerable*], capitalize on it. Take measures to hinder your opponent by seizing what he holds dear, and subtly plan to time his arrival on the ground. Walk in the path defined by rule, and adapt yourself to the enemy until you can determine to fight the decisive battle.

At first, then, exhibit the coyness of a maiden, until the enemy gives you an opening; afterwards, emulate the rapidity of a running hare, and it will be too late for the enemy to oppose you. (11:65-68)

Unhappy is the fate of one who tries to win his battles and succeed in his attacks without cultivating the results of his initiative; for that causes a waste of time and general stagnation. Hence the saying: The enlightened ruler lays his plans well ahead, and the effective general cultivates his resources. (12:15-16)

Move not unless you see an advantage; use not your troops unless there is something to be gained; fight not unless the position is critical. No ruler should put troops into the field merely to gratify his own self; no general should fight a battle simply out of pride. If it is to your advantage, make a forward move; if not, stay where you are. (12:17-19)

Hostile armies may face each other for years, striving for the victory that is decided in a single day. This being so, to remain in ignorance of the enemy's condition simply because one grudges the expenditure of a hundred ounces of silver in honors and salaries, is the height of inhumanity. One who acts like that is no leader of men, no present help to his sovereign, no master of victory.

Thus, what enables the wise sovereign and the good general to strike and conquer, and achieve things beyond the reach of ordinary men, is foreknowledge. Now, this foreknowledge cannot be elicited from spirits; it cannot be obtained inductively from experience, nor can it be gotten by any deductive calculation. Knowledge of the enemy's dispositions can only be obtained from other men. Hence the use of spies... (13:2-7)

Be subtle! Be subtle! And use your spies for every kind of business. (13:18)

The enemy's spies who have come to spy on us must be sought out, tempted with bribes, led away, and comfortably housed. Thus they will become converted spies and available for our service. (13:21)

Opportunities multiply as they are seized.

Resources are to be structured strategically based on what is advantageous.

Leonardo da Vinci

Italian Leonardo da Vinci, who lived from 1452 to 1519, is considered one of history's greatest geniuses and most versatile people. He was an artist, architect, inventor, scientist, engineer, mathematician, and philosopher. Leonardo revolutionized almost every one of those fields, and his work was truly ahead of its time.

Notable Traits

One of Leonardo's most effective habits was his use of **objective observation**. Leonardo observed all things around him with an objective mind, and thus experienced life and approached his work in a way that contributed to his **understanding**, and aided his success in virtually all the fields he covered.

Some other productive aspects of Leonardo included his:

ability to look at the **big picture** while also paying careful attention to very **specific and relevant details**

belief in the effectiveness of using **common sense**

intense **curiosity**

Scientific Methods

In his scientific work, Leonardo covered such topics as anatomy, zoology, botany, geology, optics, aerodynamics, and hydrodynamics (the motion of fluids). He used a systematic approach to **investigate** his observations and make conclusions. Leonardo also repeatedly **tested** his work, and **recorded** much of it in numerous volumes of notes and illustrations in notebooks, most of which still exist today.

Leonardo's methods were in deep contrast to the vast majority of scientists before him, most of who were often unprofessional and biased in their work, and frequently jumped to error-filled conclusions without proper testing.

In the field of science, Leonardo made many important discoveries on topics such as the details of human anatomy, the formation of fossils, the mysteries of flight, and the nature of the sun, moon and stars. He also made many geological observations and theories that foreshadowed later breakthroughs in many fields.

Leonardo truly elevated the field of science by leaps and bounds, and laid the foundation for a much more **accurate** scientific approach than what was previously used.

The Innovator, Inventor, Engineer and Architect

Leonardo often worked for various people and Italian governments as an engineer and architect. He designed and coordinated the construction of many structures, and at several times he also worked as a military engineer and weapons designer.

Leonardo also enjoyed studying machines, and was particularly interested in mechanical gears and levers. In his sketches, he outlined the basic structure of such things as bicycles, automobiles, and even helicopters. However, he never got around to producing them, and their structure existed primarily in the form of his sketches and notes. As we know, these ideas became prophetic and inspirational for many inventions that occurred centuries later.

Leonardo also had a great interest in the mechanics of water. Since he lived before electricity had been harnessed, water was the best source for power in his time. Leonardo sketched plans for a device to measure humidity, a cannon powered by steam, a waterwheel, and many other water-powered machines. He also sketched devices similar to scuba gear.

The Artist

Leonardo's art style was realistic and lifelike, which is not surprising considering his traits mentioned earlier. Leonardo preferred following the laws of nature in his works. He observed and studied light, shadow, spatial dimensions, color, detail, depth, and atmosphere to add to his artistic accuracy and realism. He also drew upon his scientific knowledge of nature and human anatomy to further the realism of his works.

Leonardo's most well known art works include the *Mona Lisa*, *Madonna of the Rocks*, and *The Last Supper*. Strangely enough, Leonardo left many of his paintings unfinished, and although he was one of the greatest artists of the Italian Renaissance time period, he only a produced a handful of completed paintings.

A Major Flaw

One major **flaw** of Leonardo was his tendency of leaving work **unfinished**. This not only included most of his artwork, but it also included many of his sketches for new inventions. Additionally, evidence shows that Leonardo planned to turn his 4000+ pages of notes and sketches into a published encyclopedia, but like many of Leonardo's other projects, he left that unfinished, too.

Leonardo da Vinci Quotes

Note: These are a clarified adaptation of the Jean Paul Richter translation of Leonardo da Vinci's notebooks / encyclopedia.

Every once and a while, go away and take a relaxing break, and then when you come back to your work, your judgment will be better—because remaining constantly at work will hinder your power of judgment. Move some distance away, because then your work will appear smaller, and more of it can be taken in at a glance, and any lack of harmony or portion… will be more effortlessly seen.

Anyone who debates by appealing to authority is not using his intelligence—he is just using his memory.

The grandest pleasure is the joy of understanding.

[The three classes of people are]: those who see, those who see when they are shown [what to see], and those who do not see.

You do evil if you praise what you do not understand, but worse if you condemn it.

To speak well of a vulgar man is much the same as speaking ill of a good man.

Men of elevated genius, when they are doing the least work, are the most active.

Common sense is what judges the things given to it by other senses.

When you are identifying science of the motion of water, remember to include under each subject its application and use, so that the science will be useful.

He is a poor disciple who does not excel his master.

Nature has beneficently provided that throughout the world, you may find something to imitate.

Just as courage endangers life, fear protects it.

I [will now] reveal to men the origin of the first, or perhaps second cause of their existence. Lust is the cause of procreation. Appetite is the support of life. Fear or timidity is the prolongation of life and preservation of its instruments.

Necessity is the mistress and guide of nature.

Necessity is the theme and the inventress, the eternal curb and law of nature.

I teach you to preserve your health, so that you will succeed better in proportion as you avoid doctors…

Every action needs to be prompted by a motive.

The knowledge of past times and of places on the earth is both an ornament and nourishment to the human mind.

The water you touch in a river is the last of what has passed, and the first of what is coming. Thus, it is with present time.

You can have no greater or lesser dominion than the one over yourself.

The greatest deception men suffer is from their own opinions.

Experience does not make mistakes. Only your judgments make mistakes by expecting from her what is not in her power.

Men wrongly complain of Experience. With great abuse, they accuse her of leading them astray. But they [actually] set Experience aside, turning from it with complaints as to our ignorance, causing us to be carried away by vain and foolish desires to promise ourselves, in her name, things that are not in her power; [and] saying that she is deceptive [/ *fake*]. Men are unjust in complaining of innocent Experience, constantly accusing her of error and of false evidence.

Wisdom is the daughter of experience.

…My works are the issue of pure and simple experience, which is the one true mistress.

Those who are in love with practice without knowledge [/ *science*] are like the sailor who gets into a ship without rudder or compass, and who never can be certain where he is going.   Practice must always be founded on sound theory; and with this perspective is the guide and the gateway; and without this, nothing can be done well in the matter of drawing.

...Be curious to listen with patience to the opinions of others. Consider and weigh well whether those who find fault [with your work] have ground or not for blame, and, if they do, make the adjustment; but, if not, just act like you didn't hear [the criticism]; or if he [*the criticizer*] happens to be someone you esteem, communicate with him to show the cause of his mistake [in judgment].

Ask advice [/ *opinions*] from he who rules himself well.

We know very well that errors are better recognized in the works of others than in our own; and that often, while criticizing little faults in others, you may ignore great ones in yourself.
    ...[To avoid such behavior, first] make yourself a master of perspective.   Then acquire supreme knowledge of the proportions of men and other animals, and also, study good architecture, as far as it concerns the forms of buildings and other objects that are on the face of the earth.   These forms are infinite, and the better you know them, the better your work will be.   And in cases where you lack experience, do not stop yourself from drawing them from nature.
    But, getting back to the point I initially started, I say that when you paint, you should have a flat mirror, and frequently look at your work as reflected in it.   When you see it reversed, it will appear to you like some other painter's work, and you will be better able to judge of its faults than in any other way.

Historical pictures should not be crowded and confused with too many figures.

The figure that is most admirable is the one that by its actions best expresses the passion that animates it.

We know for certain that sight is one of the most rapid actions we can perform. In an instant, we see an infinite number of forms; still, we only take in thoroughly one object at a time.
    Suppose that you, Reader, were to glance rapidly at this entire written page. You would instantly perceive that it was covered with

various letters; but you could not, in that [short] time, recognize what the letters were, or what they were meant to tell. Therefore, you would need to see them word-by-word, line-by-line, to be able to understand the letters. Again [, as another example], if you wish to go to the top of a building, you must go up step by step; otherwise, it will be impossible for you to reach the top.

Thus I say to you, whom nature prompts to pursue this art, if you wish to have a sound knowledge of the forms of objects, begin with the details of them, and do not go on to the second [step] until you have the first [step] well fixed in memory and in practice. And if you do otherwise, you will throw away your time, or certainly greatly prolong your studies.

[*A Fable*:] A rat was surrounded in his little house by a weasel, who with unrelenting alertness, waited for surrender while watching his imminent peril through a little hole. Meanwhile, a cat came by and suddenly seized the weasel, and immediately ate it.

Then the rat offered up a sacrifice to Jove [*a.k.a. Jupiter, the supreme God of Roman mythology*] of some of his store of nuts, humbly thanking His providence, and came out of his hole to enjoy his lately won liberty. But he was instantly deprived of it, together with his life, by the cruel claws and teeth of the lurking cat.

[*A Fable*:] An old man was publicly casting contempt on a young one, and boldly showing that he did not fear him. In response to this, the young man replied that his [*the old man's*] advanced age served him better as a shield than either his tongue or his strength [did].

[*An interesting illusion*:] We are two brothers; each of us has a brother. Here the way of saying makes it appear that the two brothers have become four.

Niccolo Machiavelli & *The Prince*

Note: All passages from The Prince used in this chapter are clarified adaptations of the W.K. Marriott translation.

Italian Niccolo Machiavelli is arguably the most notable political theorist-philosopher of all time. He lived from 1469 to 1527. His theories not only concerned government, but also analyzed such things as general human nature and behavior. They are still studied today, and are considered valuable yet also controversial.

Life & Works

Niccolo Machiavelli received a typical middle class education and then worked for a banker for many years. By age 29 in 1498, he was named head of the second chancellery of the Florentine Republic, and became a notable person in Italian politics and government.

However, his career as a statesman and diplomat came to an abrupt end in 1512 when the Medici family (who ruled right before Niccolo was initially appointed work with the government) regained power and dismissed Niccolo. Shortly later, he was accused of conspiring against the Medici government, and was jailed and tortured.

Niccolo was found innocent of the charges several weeks later, but the Medici government still viewed him with suspicion. He was unable to secure any work with them, so he left Florence and went to a small town called Sant Andrea.

Reflecting on his career with the government and his dealings with various leaders, Niccolo turned to political advisory writing. By 1513, he came out with a brief book called *The Prince*, which is now considered one of the most notable literary works ever, and a classic of political philosophy.

His other works included *The Life of Castruccio Castracani, Discourses on the First Ten Books of Titus Livius, The Art of War* (not to be confused with another work of the same title by Sun Tzu, which is covered in another chapter in this book), a history of Florence, and several other various writings.

Niccolo died in Florence in June of 1527.

The Prince

Niccolo wrote *The Prince* at a time when Italian politics was marred with blackmail, violence, and conflict. In *The Prince*, Niccolo gives advice on how to be an effective and successful ruler, and how to stay in power.

The book was written as a **practical** guide to ruling that uses simple and straightforward descriptions in order to provide easily understandable advice.

The Prince was **groundbreaking** because Niccolo described the world as he saw it. This was much unlike earlier political writers who treated politics as an extension of morals, and whose theories had little practical use.

Niccolo's theories are based on the premise that a ruler must **base policies on people's true nature**.

Widespread Insights and Application of *The Prince*

Although *The Prince* is intended advice for a monarch, its informative value and application extends well beyond the realm of political governing. *The Prince* is not just a political essay, but also one on sociology, human nature, psychology, philosophy (including concepts such as free will and probability), and leadership.

OVERVIEW AND THEMES OF *THE PRINCE*

Human Nature

In *The Price,* Niccolo went at great depths to analyze **human nature** in order to formulate his advice for rulers. In the book, he points out a number of traits that he believes are common in people. Niccolo believes that **in general**, **most people**:

have a **primary interest in themselves**, and basically carry the mindset of "what's in it for me."

are mainly concerned with their **property** and **honor**. (In *The Prince*, Niccolo wrote: "...When neither their property nor their honor is touched, the majority of men live content...")

are motivated by their financial **greed,** but are usually **content** with the overall existing state of affairs, although those who have achieved some power are usually much more aspiring

often **remain content and uncomplaining unless something horrible happens** to them.

might sometimes be trustworthy in good times or due to various motives, but are almost always very dishonest in times of distress

admire and praise qualities such as integrity, mercy, honesty, humaneness, religiousness, and generosity in other people, but **rarely ever foster those characteristics in themselves**

are often **herd-minded, cling to the general opinion,** and **judge from appearances.** (In *The Prince*, Niccolo wrote: "In general, men judge more from appearances than from realness. All men have eyes, but few have perception. Everyone sees what you seem to be, few know what you really are, and those few do not dare take a stand against the general opinion.")

can become very loyal to another through receiving acts of **goodwill,** but even one's strong sense of **loyalty is not absolute,** and can be won or lost.

can have their feelings towards others changed; i.e. with certain catalysts, they can turn against someone they favored, or they can have their favor won towards someone they used to view negatively.

are **inconstant**

can have their friendship bought, but **friends that are bought with money are not reliable.** (In *The Prince*, Niccolo wrote: "… Friendships that are obtained by payments, and not by greatness or nobility of mind, may indeed be earned, but they are not secured, and in time of need cannot be relied upon…")

Virtu and *Fortuna*

In *The Prince*, Niccolo acknowledges the existence of two factors that play a role in determining success:

Virtu, which can be described as skill, prowess, wisdom, strength, cunning, good decision making, and using one's free will

AND

Fortuna, which refers to chance, luck, random variations, probability, and external factors outside of one's control

In *The Prince*, Niccolo attempts to determine how much of a role these two factors play in success or failure. He concludes that as they apply to the control of human actions and events, each factor carries nearly equal significance and controls approximately half of the outcome.

Niccolo then asserts that through **foresight**, one can hope to deal with random variations of fortuna, and thus **maximize one's success.** Niccolo then emphasizes the importance of **adapting behavior to suit the times, and making timely and appropriate adjustments to circumstances.**

(Note that at Niccolo's time period, any idea of free will was very uncommon. Most other writers and thinkers considered almost everything beyond the power of humans. They looked to religion and ancient ideas to explain most events, and believed almost exclusively in divine destiny.)

In *The Prince*, Niccolo wrote:

> ...I believe that fortuna is the settler of one half of our actions, but that she still leaves us [by virtu] to direct the other half, or perhaps a little less.

> I compare her [*fortuna*] to a raging river, which when in flood overflows the plains, sweeps away trees and buildings, and moves the soil from place to place. Everything flies before it, and everything yields to its violence without being able in any way to withstand it.

> But despite its nature, it can be said that when the weather becomes calmer, people can make provisions with defenses and barriers in such a way that if the waters rise again, they may pass away by canal, and their force will not be as out of control or as dangerous.

> And in the same way it happens with fortuna, who shows her power only where overboldness has not prepared to resist her, and [shows her power] in that direction she directs her forces where she knows that barriers and defenses have not been raised to constrain her...

> ...I assert that a prince can be seen happy today and ruined tomorrow even without having shown any change of [his] mood or character. I believe this happens mainly because... the prince who relies exclusively on fortuna is lost when it [*fortuna*] changes. I also believe that he who suits his action to fit the times will prosper, but he whose actions do not accord with the times will not be successful.

> Consider that people are [often] observed using a variety of methods to reach possibilities they have before them such as glory and riches: one [reaches such goals] with caution, another with haste; one by force, another by skill; one by patience, another by its opposite; and each one succeeds in reaching the goal by a different method. One can also observe instances of where in a group of two cautious men, one attains his goal and the other fails; and similarly, [one can also observe]

two men using different methods who become equally successful, [such as when] one is cautious and another is rash.

All this arises from… whether or not they conform in their actions to the spirit of the times. This all corresponds to what I have said: that two men working differently can bring about the same effect, and of two working similarly, one [can] attain his goal while the other does not.

Changes in prosperity also arise from this [principle], for if one governs himself with caution and patience, and [then] times and affairs move in such a way that his administration is successful, his wealth is made; but if times and affairs change, he is ruined if he does not change his course of action.

But a man is not often found to be prudent enough to know how to adapt himself to the change … [usually] because having always prospered by acting one way, he cannot be persuaded that it is a good idea to leave it. Thus a cautious man, when it is time to turn adventurous, does not know how to do it, hence he is ruined; but had he changed his conduct with the times, his fortune would not have changed…

[I conclude that]… since fortune is changeful, and mankind [is usually] steadfast in its ways, as long as the two [*man's actions and change / fortuna*] are in agreement, men are successful, but when they fall out, [they are] unsuccessful.

Lion and Fox

To develop one's virtu, Niccolo recommends that a monarch should **study other people and learn from their effective points.** Additionally, Niccolo also recommends that a monarch should **study and learn from the effective points of certain animals**, as well. In particular, Niccolo recommends that one should balance

the ways of a **lion (strength, ferocity)**

WITH

the ways of a **fox (cunning, slyness, understanding, outmaneuvering of enemies)**

In *The Prince*, Niccolo wrote:

…[Of the animals, a prince should be compelled to choose to emulate the effective points of] the fox and the lion, because the lion cannot defend himself against traps, and the fox cannot defend himself against wolves. Therefore, it is necessary to be a fox to discover the traps, and [to be] a lion to terrify the wolves. Those who rely simply on the [effective points of a] lion do not understand what they are about.

Should a Leader be Loved, Feared, and/or Hated?

Niccolo is well known for his controversial assertion that **it is better to be feared than loved if you cannot be both**.

In *The Prince*, he wrote:

Here arises the question: whether it is better to be loved than feared, or feared than loved. Obviously, it can be answered that one should choose to be both, but since the two rarely come together for one person... [anyone who must choose between the two] will find it safer to be feared than to be loved...

Love is preserved by an obligatory link in which men, being mean [/ *scoundrels / dishonest*] [especially when things are not going good for them], may break whenever it is advantageous for them to do so. But fear is preserved by the dread of punishment, which never fails.

...Men love according to their own will, and fear according to the will of the prince. [Thus,] A wise prince should establish himself on that which is in his own control, and not in that of others.

Despite his belief in the effectiveness of being feared, however, Niccolo feels that a leader should definitely **avoid being hated**, and wrote: "Nevertheless, a prince ought to inspire fear in such a way that, if he does not win love, he avoids hatred; because he can endure very well being feared whilst he is not hated."

To back up and further explain his theory on avoiding hatred, Niccolo describes the importance of having people's **goodwill and support**, which in a monarch's case can defend against both domestic revolutions (like widespread political activism) as well as foreign attacks.

Niccolo points out several **ways to avoid people's hatred**:

don't confiscate or even mess with people's private property
(Niccolo goes so far as to write, "above all things, he [*the prince*] must keep his hands off the property of others, because people forget the death of their father before they forget the loss of their inheritance.")

respect people's traditions

don't appear to be **greedy**

don't appear to be **bland or lacking in character**

direct people's energies into **private pursuits**.

promote **material prosperity**

when giving, **give gradually** (In *The Prince*, Niccolo wrote: "Benefits should be awarded gradually—that way, they will taste better.")

show off "praiseworthiness" and hide "evilness"

Showing Off "Praiseworthiness" and Hiding "Evilness"

In *The Prince*, Niccolo says that a ruler should prioritize doing **what needs to be done** to keep power, and should avoid doing things just for the sake of pursing certain morals or ideals. This theme turns out to be the source of much of the book's **controversy,** and is based on Niccolo's recommendation to adopt cunning foxlike qualities (which were described earlier in this chapter).

Niccolo says that a monarch should always attempt to **appear good and praiseworthy**, which he defines as having qualities such as being **merciful, loyal / trustworthy, moral, humane, and religious.**

But the key word in this equation is *appear*. Niccolo recommends that any of these good acts should be done strictly for a leader's own benefit, and most of the time should be done to be **noticed** and to **build goodwill and a good reputation** with his subjects. (Niccolo also notes that while generosity is usually considered praiseworthy, a monarch still needs to be financially responsible and overall stingy. He feels that this will cause him to be considered generous through lower taxes levied on the people, especially in times of war.)

Niccolo believes that behavior should suit the occasion, and not ideals of propriety. Niccolo takes his theory a step further by saying that the leader should use deceit and similar vices when necessary as long as they remain **unknown** to the subjects, and they are done to aid the monarch's power and contribute to the state. (He even recommends that rulers should calculatingly use violence whenever necessary.)

In *The Prince*, he wrote:

Therefore it is unnecessary for a prince to have all the good qualities I have enumerated, but it is very necessary to appear to have them. And I shall dare to say this also, that to have them and always to observe them is injurious, and that to appear to have them is useful—to appear to be merciful, loyal [/ *trustworthy*], moral, humane, and religious—and to be so, but with a mind so framed that should you require not to be so, you may be able and know how to change to the opposite.

Hence, it is necessary for a prince wishing to hold his own to know how to do wrong, and to make use of it or not according to necessity.

Everyone admits how praiseworthy it is in a prince to keep faith, and to live with integrity and not with craft. Nevertheless our experience has been that those princes who have done great things have held good faith of little account, and have known how to circumvent the intellect of men by craft, and in the end have overcome those who have relied on their word.

Therefore a wise lord cannot and should not remain loyal when doing so may be used against him, and when the reasons that caused him to pledge it [*loyalness*] do not exist anymore.

Niccolo attempts to justify the use of deceit and other vices by pointing out that other people are often dishonest and evil, and thus it is a prince's only choice to also be dishonest and not adhere to strict codes of propriety.

In *The Prince*, he wrote:

> This principle [I have just outlined about being foxlike and deceptive] would not hold if men were all good [/ *having integrity / honest*], but because they are [generally] bad [/ *lacking integrity / dishonest*] and will not keep faith with you, you too are not bound to observe it with them…
> But it is necessary to know well how to disguise this [foxlike deceptive] characteristic, and to be a great pretender and concealer…
> [And also observe that due to principles of human nature], anyone who seeks to deceive will always find someone who will allow himself to be deceived.

Employing the Right People, Getting Advice, and Dealing with Opinions

Niccolo feels that that rulers should **hire quality** ministers and servants who will be **dependent** on and **look out for** and the well being and interest of the state and the ruler. He also recommends that rulers should **study** servants and ministers, and do things to make them feel **encouraged**.

In *The Prince*, he wrote:

> As for the ways a prince can form an opinion of his servant, there is one test that never fails. When you see the servant thinking more of his own interests than of yours, and seeking inwardly his own profit in everything, such a man will never make a good servant, nor will you ever be able to trust him. He who has the state of another in his hands ought never to think of himself, but always of his prince, and never pay any attention to matters in which the prince is not concerned.
>
> On the other hand, to keep his servant honest, the prince ought to study him, honoring him, enriching him, doing him kindnesses, sharing with him the honors and cares; and at the same time let him see that he cannot stand alone, so that many honors not make him desire more, many riches make him wish for more, and that many cares may make him dread changes. When, therefore, servants and princes are this way, they can trust each other; but when it is otherwise, the end will always be disastrous for either one or the other.

Niccolo also points out that employing quality people will make the prince look wise to his subjects.

As far as taking advice from others goes, Niccolo recommends that the prince should take advice from only a **small and trusted group of advisors**, and only on matters the prince inquires about. However, he emphasizes that it is the prince who should **use his own brain**, and **make the final decisions of importance**.

In *The Prince*, he wrote:

> …[The only way to guard oneself from flatterers is by] letting men understand that telling you the truth doesn't offend you. However, when every one is allowed to tell you the truth, the respect for you lessens.
>
> Therefore, a wise prince should hold a third course by choosing the wise men in his state, and giving only them the freedom of speaking the truth to him, and only on those things that he inquires of, and of none others. But he [*the prince*] should question them upon everything, listen to their opinions, and then form his own conclusions.
>
> With these councilors… [the prince] should carry himself in a way that will let each one of them understand that the more freely he [*the councilor*] speaks, the more he will be preferred. Outside of these

[councilors], he [*the prince*] should listen to no one, and pursue what is resolved on, and be firm in his resolutions. He who does otherwise is either overthrown by flatterers, or is so frequently changed by varying opinions that he falls into being disrespected [by the people].

A prince, therefore, ought always to seek guidance, but only when he wishes and not when others wish; he ought rather to discourage every one from offering advice unless he asks it. However, he ought to be a constant inquirer, and afterwards a patient listener concerning the things of which he inquired. And additionally, on learning that any one, on any consideration, has not told him the truth, he should let his anger be felt.

In his information-getting advice in *The Prince*, Niccolo also wrote:

There are three kinds of intelligence: one understands things for itself, the second appreciates what others can understand, and the third understands neither for itself nor through others. This first kind is excellent, the second is good, and the third is useless.

Other Themes of *The Prince*

Niccolo's belief in the effectiveness of having a sound military and sound laws

an outline of how to have a strong military and engage in war

a call for Italian unity and nationalism

a dedication to Lorenzo de Medici, the ruler of Florence

Niccolo's attempts to justify his theories with historical evidence and examples (Note that most modern scholars feel Niccolo's examples are more like assumptions than observations.)

Legacy, and the Word "Machiavellian"

Since the publication of *The Prince*, the term **Machiavellian** has been used both in and out of politics to denote a cunning, deceptive, and deceitful kind of resourcefulness. This stems from many of the controversial recommendations outlined in *The Prince*.

The term Machiavellian has become so commonly used, that my computer spell check program recognizes the word *Machiavellian*, but it doesn't recognize the word *Machiavelli* or *Niccolo*!

Niccolo Machiavelli is not Totally Machiavellian

Although Niccolo Machiavelli is associated with *The Prince* and so-called Machiavellian tactics, it is interesting to note, however, that other political works written by him have different messages.

Most notably is *Discourses on the First Ten Books of Titus Livius*, which is aimed at republics (states controlled by politically active citizenry), not monarchies, and preaches themes of patriotism and civic excellence, as well as the use of open political participation and debate.

Michel de Montaigne & *Essays*

French writer Michel (Eyquem) de Montaigne, who lived from 1533 to 1592, is considered the pioneer of the modern essay. His works set the foundation for popularizing the essay form of writing, especially those that deal with philosophical and wisdom-related subjects.

Life

Michel studied classical texts as a youth, and later became a French court official and lawyer. By 1571, he retired and began work on the *Essais,* or *Essays* in English, which were published together in 1580 and added to in 1588. Besides writing, Michel also served as a mediator on various disputes, and as the mayor of Bordeaux (a city in Southwestern France) from 1581 to 1585.

Essays

The *Essays* is a collection of essays covering a variety of topics, drawing upon the perspective of Michel's own personal character, life, and observations. The *Essays* was fueled by Michel's curiosity and interest in the world.

In the book, Michel observes and analyzes human nature, himself, society, and various philosophical topics on the human experience. The *Essays* also shares information on various aspect's of Michel's time era in France.

Michel de Montaigne Quotes

Note: Most of these are from Essays

There is nothing that Nature seems to have inclined us to as much as society.

Truly, man is a spectacularly vain, diverse, and fluctuating subject. It is hard to establish a specific and uniform judgment on him.

There is as much difference between us and ourselves as there is between us and others.

I quote others in order to better express myself.

I know well what I am fleeing from, but not what I am in search of.

A person is bound to lose when he talks about himself; if he belittles himself, he is believed; if he praises himself, he isn't believed.

I don't care as much for what I am to others as I do for what I am to myself.

Wise men have more to learn of fools than fools do of wise men.

What he did by nature and accident, he cannot do by design.

[There is a] difference between memory and understanding

How many things are there that we regarded as articles of faith yesterday and that we tell as fables today?

Not being able to govern events, I govern myself, and apply myself to them if they will not apply themselves to me.

The strength of any plan depends on the time. Circumstances and things eternally shift and change.

When I play with my cat, who knows whether or not she is amusing herself with me more than I am with her?

The desire for riches is more sharpened by their use than by their need.

Pleasing all: a mark that can never be aimed at or hit.

One can say too much even on the best of subjects.

When we have got it, we want something else.

Desires increase as they are fulfilled.

[You can] become a fool by too much wisdom.

It's better to be alone than in foolish and troublesome company.

I lay no great stress upon my opinions, or on those of others.

It seems to me that the nursing mother of most false opinions—both public and private—is the excessively high opinion one places on oneself.

Souls that are regular and strong of themselves are rare.

Judge by the eye of reason, and not from common report.

Extremity of philosophy is hurtful.

Intelligence is required to be able to know that a man knows not.

Every day, I hear fools say things that are not foolish.

No man continues to do unfavorable things for long except by his own fault.

Things seem greater by imagination than they are in effect.

In true education, anything that comes to us is good as a book: a page-boy's prank, a servant's blunder, a bit of table talk—they are all part of the curriculum.

A wise man sees as much as he ought to, not as much as he can.

My art and profession is to live.

There is no man who is so good that if he were to submit all his thoughts and actions to the law, he would not deserve to be hung ten times throughout his life.

The word is half his that speaks, and half his that hears it.

The most universal quality is diversity.

Wise people are foolish if they cannot adapt to foolish people.

Knowing a lot is often the cause of doubting more.

Meditation is a powerful and deep study to those who can effectively taste and employ themselves to it. I would rather fashion my soul than furnish it. There is no employment, either weaker or stronger, than that of entertaining one's own thoughts according to as the soul is. The greatest people make it [*meditation*] their whole business...

My trade and art is to live.

[*Montaigne's motto*:] What do I know?

Essays Passages

Note: These are a clarified adaptation based on the Charles Cotton translation.

The Inconsistency of Our Actions

People who make it their business to analyze human actions do not find themselves as perplexed in anything as in making them [*a person's behaviors*] seem consistent, and putting them in perspective with the same luster and reputation; for they [*a person's behaviors*] so frequently and strangely contradict one another that it seems impossible they should come from one and the same person...

[Publilius Syrus wrote:] "A plan that cannot be modified is bad."

It seems reasonable to form a judgment of a man based on his most usual methods of life; but, considering the natural instability of our manners and opinions, I have often thought that even the best writers have been a little wrong in so stubbornly attempting to make any constant and solidly drawn-together conclusion of us.

They choose a general air of a man, and according to that, they interpret all his actions, of which, if they cannot bend some [of those actions] to a uniformity with the rest, they attribute them to [a person's use of] disguise...

Of the man you saw yesterday who was adventurous and brave, you must not think it strange to see him as great a coward the next day. Anger, necessity, company, wine, or the sound of the trumpet had roused his spirits. This is no valor formed and established by reason, but was accidentally created by such circumstances, and therefore it is no wonder if by contrary circumstances it appears quite another thing.

These readily changing variations and contradictions that so manifest in us have often made some believe that man has two souls, or two distinct powers that always accompany and incline us, one towards good and the other towards ill, according to their own nature and propensity; so abrupt a variety not being imaginable to flow from one and the same source.

For my part, the puff of every accident not only carries me along with it according to its own natural inclination, but moreover, I lose composure and I trouble myself by the instability of my own posture. And whoever looks narrowly into his own bosom will hardly find himself twice in the same condition.

I give to my soul sometimes one face and sometimes another, according to the side I turn her to. If I speak variously of myself, it is because I consider myself variously; all the contrarieties are there to be found in one corner or another after one fashion or another—bashful, arrogant; chaste, lustful; chattering, silent; laborious, delicate; ingenious, heavy; gloomy, pleasant; lying, truthful; knowing, ignorant; liberal, covetous, and prodigal—I find all this in myself, more or less, according as I turn myself about; and whoever will sift himself to the bottom, will find in himself, and even in his own judgment, this changeableness and disagreement.

I have nothing to say of myself entirely, simply, and solidly without mixture and confusion...

One gallant action, therefore, ought not to conclude a man valiant. If a man were brave indeed, he would always be so, and upon all occasions. If it were a habit of valor and not a sally, it would render a man equally resolute in all accidents; the same alone as in company; and the same in lists as in a battle.

For, let them say what they will, there is not one valor for the pavement and another for the field; he would bear a sickness in his bed as bravely as a wound in the field, and no more fear death in his own house than at an assault. And we should not then see the same man charge into a breach with a brave assurance, and afterwards torment himself like a woman for the loss of a trial at law or the death of a child; when, being an infamous coward, he is firm in the necessities of poverty; when he shrinks at the sight of a barber's razor, and rushes fearless upon the swords of the enemy, the action is commendable, not the man.

Solitude

If we can get them, we should have wives, children, goods, and above all, health; but we are not so to set our hearts upon them that our happiness must be entirely dependent on them. We must reserve a back-shop, wholly our own and entirely free, wherein to settle our true liberty, our principal solitude and retreat.

And in this we must for the most part entertain ourselves with ourselves, and so privately that no outside relationship or communication be admitted there; there to laugh and to talk, as if without wife, children, goods, followers, or attendance, to the end that when it shall so fall out that we must lose any or all of these, it may be no new thing to be without them.

We have a mind pliable in itself that will be company, that has wherewithal to attack and to defend, and to receive and give. Let us not then fear in this solitude to languish under an uncomfortable emptiness.

…

We have lived enough for others; let us at least live out the rest of our life for ourselves; let us now call in our thoughts and intentions to ourselves, and to our own ease and repose.

Profit and Honesty

No man is free from speaking foolish things; but the worst thing is when a man painstakingly labors to say them.

[Terence Wrote]: "Truly he, with a great effort, will say mighty trifles."

This does not concern me; mine slip from me with as little care as they are of little value, and it is the better for them. I would presently part with them for what they are worth, and neither buy nor sell them but as they weigh.

Miguel De Cervantes

Miguel De Cervantes is a legendary Spanish novelist, playwright, and poet who lived from 1547 to 1616. He is best known for his acclaimed novel *Don Quixote*.

Early Life

Miguel had a very interesting life. At one time, he was a soldier who fought in the naval battle of Lepanto in 1571. Although he received three gunshot wounds in the fight, one of which caused major and permanent damage to his left hand, Miguel continued to do battle in the army, and enjoyed talking about his army experiences throughout his life.

Captured and Enslaved

In 1575, Miguel and his brother were captured by Barbary pirates and sold as slaves in Algiers. At one point, his family sent only enough money to free one of them, and Miguel requested that his brother be freed. After several failed escape attempts by Miguel, his family collected enough money to ransom him five years after he was first captured, although the price was so high that it totally drained the family's finances.

Back to Spain

Upon arriving back in Spain, Miguel turned his efforts to writing and produced a novel named *La Galatea* in 1585, and many plays during the 1580s. By the mid 1580s, Miguel worked as a traveling government grain and oil collector and as a tax collector, although he was often in debt, and was even jailed two times for financial reasons. He also began writing again seriously at some point, although it is uncertain when.

Don Quixote

By 1605, Miguel released the first part of his masterpiece novel *Don Quixote* (Full title: *El Ingenioso Hidalgo Don Quixote de la Mancha*), which was partially based on his real life, and also drew upon his observations of the many people he encountered in his various duties as a traveling government worker.

The book became an immense success, but Miguel received little pay for it because he sold the rights to it in the publishing deal he made in 1604 before its release. In 1615, he released the second part to *Don Quixote* (Full title: *Segunda Parte del Ingenioso Cavallero Don Quixote de la Mancha*), and he died the next year.

Legacy and Other Works

Miguel's legacy as one of the world's greatest literary masters lies primarily in *Don Quixote*. His other notable works include *Novelas Ejemplares* (1613), *Ocho Comedias y Ocho Entremeses Nuevos* (1615), and *Los Trabaios de Persiles y Sigismunda: Historia Setentrional* (published posthumously in 1617).

Miguel De Cervantes Quotes

Note: Most of these are from Don Quixote

Take away the cause, and the effect ceases.

Let every man mind his own business.

It is good to live and learn.

The greatest enemies, and the ones we must mainly combat, are within.

There is no greater folly in the world than for a man to despair.

You are a king by your own fireside, as much as any monarch is in his throne.

The only comfort of the miserable is to have partners in their troubles.

Truth may be stretched, but it can't be broken, and will always get above falsehood as oil does above water.

Be slow of tongue and quick of eye.

Be brief, for no talk can please when too long.

Being prepared is half the victory.

Those who will with cats must expect to be scratched.

Make hay while the sun is shining.

One swallow alone does not make a summer.

All kinds of beauty don't inspire love; there is a kind that pleases only the sight, but does not captivate the affections.

I have other fish to fry.

Make yourself into honey, and the flies will eat you up.

Until death, all is life.

With life, many things are remedied.

Hunger is the best sauce in the world.

I never prod my nose into other men's porridge.

Make it your business to know yourself—which is the most difficult lesson in the world.

Baltasar Gracian & *The Art of Worldly Wisdom*

Spanish writer, scholar, and philosopher Baltasar Gracian was one of the most unique and innovative authors of his time. He lived from 1601 to 1658.

Life & Works

Baltasar entered the Jesuit order (a Roman Catholic missionary and scholarly organization) by age 18 in 1620, and soon became scholar, teacher, and priest. In 1637, he produced his first book, which was titled *El Heroe*, and in the 1640s he produced several works, including *Oraculo Manual y Arte de Prudencia,* or in English, *The Art of Worldly Wisdom*. Many bold messages contained in Baltasar's books caused him notoriety among the Jesuit order.

In the 1650s, he released a three part philosophical novel titled *El Criticon*, which caused even more controversy. By the late 1650s, his controversial works and defiance of others caused him to be sent to another mission, and then be exiled by the Jesuits authorities and regarded with aversion. Baltasar died in 1658.

His book *El Criticon* has become a highly notable work in the so-called "pessimist" branch of philosophy, while *The Art of World Wisdom* has been widely read throughout the years since its release.

The Art of Worldly Wisdom

The Art of Worldly Wisdom contains three hundred short pieces of life strategy advice, much of which relates to dealing with other people and establishing effective relationships.

The Art of Worldly Wisdom was considered bold compared to other writings on similar subjects at that time period, especially from a Jesuit priest. Certain portions of the book's advice border on the subject of strategies for gaining power and manipulating others, which made some consider *The Art of Worldly Wisdom* somewhat comparable to the ideas described in Niccolo Machiavelli's *The Prince* (which is covered in a separate chapter in this book).

The Art of Worldly Wisdom **Passages**

Note: These are a clarified adaptation of the translation by Joseph Jacobs. They are followed in parentheses by the section number they appeared in.

Cultivate relationships with those who can teach you. Let friendly interaction be a school of knowledge... Thus you make your friends your teachers, and combine the pleasures of conversation with the advantages of instruction... (11)

Keep helpful wits around you. It is a privilege of the powerful to surround themselves with champions of intellect...

It is a novel kind of supremacy—the best that life can offer—to use skill to make servants of those who by conditions are our masters...

There is remarkable cleverness in studying without effort, in getting much by means of many, and through them all to become wise... (15)

Vary your mode of action. In order to distract attention, do not always do things the same way, especially if you have a rival.

Do not always act on first impulse; people will soon recognize the uniformity and, by anticipating, frustrate your designs. It is easy to kill a bird on the wing that flies straight, but not one that twists and turns.

Nor should you always act on second thoughts; people will recognize the plan the second time. The enemy is on the watch; great skill is required to outwit him. The gamester never plays the card the opponent expects, still less the one he wants. (17)

...Some remain content with putting themselves confidently at the gate of fortune [/ *chance*], waiting until she opens it. Others do better, and press forward and profit by their clever boldness, reaching the goddess and winning her favor on the wings of their virtue and valor... (21)

Exercise [the proper] control of your imagination. You must sometimes correct it [and] sometimes assist it, for it is of all-importance in happiness and in balancing reason. The imagination... influences and even often dominates our life. It can make us happy or burden us... (24)

Find out each person's thumbscrew [*what they like, what motivates them to do things*]. It is the means of setting his wills in action...

You must know where to get at any one. Every choice has a special motive that varies according to taste. All people idolize something—for some it is fame, for others self-interest, for most it is pleasure. Skill consists in knowing these idols in order to bring them into play.

Know a person's mainspring of motive, and you have as it were the key to his will. Utilize [his] primary motives, which are not always the highest, but more often the lowest part of his nature, because there are more dispositions badly organized than well.

First guess a person's ruling passion, appeal to it with words, set it in motion by temptation, and you will always checkmate his freedom of will. (26)

Know how to withdraw. If it is a great lesson in life to know how to decline, it is even greater to know how to decline oneself to both affairs and persons. There are unnecessary occupations that eat away precious time; to be occupied in what does not concern you is worse than doing nothing.

It is not enough for a careful person to not interfere with others; he must [also] see that they do not interfere with him. One is not required to belong to others so much that he does not belong at all to oneself... (33)

Know your strongest quality. Know your preeminent gift— cultivate it, and it will assist the rest. Everyone would have excelled in something if he had known his strong point.

Notice in what quality you surpass, and take charge of that. In some people, judgment excels, and in others, valor. Most do violence to their natural aptitude, and thus attain superiority in nothing. Time enlightens us too late of what was first only a flattering of the passions. (34)

Use cunning, but do not abuse it. One ought not to delight in it, still less boast of it. Everything artificial should be concealed, most of all cunning, which is hated.

Deceit is common, so our caution has to be redoubled, but not in a way that it [*caution*] shows itself, for caution arouses distrust, causes annoyance, awakens revenge, and gives rise to more ills than you would imagine. To go to work with caution is of great advantage in action, and there is no greater proof of wisdom... (45)

Know how to say *no*. One should not give way in everything or to everybody. Thus, knowing how to refuse is as important as knowing how to consent. This is especially the case with people of power. Everything depends on how you do it. Some people's *no* is thought more of than the *yes* of others; for a gilded *no* is more satisfactory than a dry *yes*.

There are some who always have *no* on their lips, whereby they make everything distasteful. *No* always comes first with them, and when sometimes they give way after all, it does them no good on account of the unpleasant beginning…

Yes and *no* are soon said, but give much to think over. (70)

Know how to use evasion. That is how smart people get out of difficulties. They extricate themselves from the most intricate labyrinth by [using] some witty application of a bright remark. They get out of a serious contention by an airy nothing or by raising a smile. Most of the great leaders are well grounded in this art.

When you have to refuse something, often the most courteous way is to just change the subject. And sometimes, pretending that you don't understand proves to be the highest [form of] understanding. (73)

Take care when you get information. We live by information, not by sight. We exist by faith in others. The ear is the side door of truth, but [is also] the front door of lies.

The truth is generally seen, rarely heard. She [*truth*] seldom comes in elemental purity, especially if it has come from afar—for there is always something added to it by the moods of those through whom she [*truth*] has passed.   The passions tinge her, sometimes favorably, sometimes odiously.   She always brings out people's disposition; therefore, receive her with caution from him that praises, [and] with [even] more caution from him that blames.

Pay attention to the intention of the speaker; you should know beforehand on what footing he comes. Let reflection test for falsity and exaggeration. (80)

Make use of your enemies. You should learn to seize things not by the blade, which cuts, but by the handle, which saves you from harm—especially with the doings of your enemies.

A wise person gets more use from his enemies than a fool from his friends.   Their [*one's enemies'*] ill will often levels mountains of difficulties that one would otherwise not face. Many have had their greatness made for them by their enemies… The wise will turn ill will into a mirror more faithful than that of kindness, and remove or improve the faults referred to… (84)

Know yourself. Know your talents and capacity, in judgment and inclination. You cannot master yourself unless you know yourself.

There are mirrors for the face, but none for the mind. Let careful thought about yourself serve as a substitute. When the outer image is forgotten, keep the inner one to improve and perfect…   Keep your foundations secure and your head clear for everything. (89)

One half of the world laughs at the other, and fools are they all. Everything is good or everything is bad according to who you ask. What one pursues, another persecutes.

He is an insufferable ass who would regulate everything according to his ideas. Excellences do not depend on a single person's pleasure. So many people, so many tastes, all different. There is no defect that is not affected by some. We need not lose heart if something does not please someone, for others will appreciate it; nor should their applause turn our head, for there will surely be others to condemn it...

You should aim to be independent of any one opinion, of any one fashion, of any one century. (101)

Do not make mistakes about character. That is the worst and yet easiest error. Better be cheated in the price than in the quality of goods. In dealing with people, more than with other things, it is necessary to look within. Knowing people is different from knowing things. It is profound philosophy to study the depths of feeling and distinguish traits of character. People must be studied as deeply as books. (157)

Throw straws in the air to test the wind. Find how things will be perceived, especially from those whose reception or success is doubtful. One can thus be assured of its turning out well, and an opportunity is provided for going on in earnest or withdrawing entirely.

By trying people's intentions in this way, the wise person knows on what ground he stands. This is the great rule of foresight in asking, in desiring, and in ruling. (164)

Use the truth, but not the whole truth. Nothing demands more caution than the truth... It requires as much to tell the truth as to conceal it.

A single lie destroys a whole reputation for integrity. The deceit is regarded as treason and the deceiver as a traitor, which is worse. Yet not all truths can be spoken, some for our own sake, others for the sake of others. (181)

Do not stand on ceremony... To be punctilious [*strictly attentive to the minor and most trivial details*] is to be a bore, yet whole nations have this peculiarity. The clothing of folly is woven out of such things...

Neither affect nor despise etiquette. He cannot be great who is great at such trivial matters. (184)

...There is no one who cannot teach somebody something, and there is no one so excellent that he cannot be excelled. To know how to make use of everyone is useful knowledge.

Wise men appreciate everyone, for they see the good in each, and know how hard it is to make anything good. Fools depreciate everyone, not recognizing the good, and selecting the bad. (195)

...The greatest fool is he who thinks he is not one and all others are. To be wise, it is not enough to seem wise, and least of all to seem so to oneself... Though all the world is full of fools, there is no one who thinks himself one, or even suspects the fact. (201)

Do not turn one blunder into two. It is quite usual to commit four blunders in order to remedy one, or to excuse one piece of irrelevancy by still another...

A wise person may make one slip but never two, and that only in running, not while standing still. (214)

Be expressive—this is found not only on the clearness, but also on the vibrancy of your thoughts... (216)

Do not be the slave of first impressions. Some marry the very first account they hear, all others must live with them as concubines. But as a lie has swift legs, the truth with them can find no lodging.

We should neither satisfy our will with the first object, nor our mind with the first proposition—for that is superficial. Many are like new casks that keep the scent of the first liquor they hold, be it good or bad. If this superficiality becomes known... it then gives opportunity for cunning mischief. The evil-minded rush to color the mind of the gullible.

Always, therefore, leave room for a second hearing. Alexander always kept one ear for the other side. Wait for the second or even third edition of news... (227)

Know what is lacking in yourself. Many would have been great people if they had not had something lacking, and without which they could not rise to the height of perfection. It is remarkable that some people could be much better if they could be just a little better in something. They do not perhaps take themselves seriously enough to do justice to their great abilities... (238)

Make use of folly; the wisest person plays this card at times. Sometimes the greatest wisdom lies in seeming not to be wise. You need not be unwise, but merely pretend to be unwise.

To be wise with fools and foolish with the wise is of little use; speak to each in his own language. He is no fool who bluffs being foolish [when needed], but he is who suffers from it... (240)

...Alternate the cunning of the serpent with the openness of the dove.

Nothing is easier than to deceive an honest man. He who lies about nothing believes in much; he who does no deception has much trust in others. To be deceived is not always due to stupidity, it may arise from sheer goodness.

There are two sets of people who can guard themselves from injury: those who have learned by experiencing it at their own cost, and those who have observed it at the cost of others...

Combine in yourself the dove and the serpent, not as a monster, but as a prodigy. (243)

Create a feeling of obligation. Some [people] transform favors received into favors awarded, and seem—or let it be thought—that they are doing a favor when receiving one.

... [Some people] manage matters so cleverly that they seem to be doing others a service when receiving one from them. They reverse the order of obligation with extraordinary skill, or at least make it become doubtful as to who has obliged whom.

They buy the best by praising it, and make a flattering honor out of the pleasure they express. They oblige by their courtesy, and thus make people indebted for what they themselves should be indebted...

This is a subtle piece of finesse, but even greater is to perceive it... (244)

Do not follow up a folly. Many make an obligation out of a blunder, and because they have entered the wrong path, they think it proves their strength of character to go on in it.

Within they regret their error, while outwardly they excuse it. At the beginning of their mistake they were regarded as inattentive, in the end as foolish.

Neither an unconsidered promise nor a mistaken resolution is really binding; yet some continue in their folly and prefer to be constant fools. (261)

Do not become responsible for all or for everyone; otherwise, you become a slave—and the slave of all... Freedom is more precious than any gifts you may be tempted to give it up for.

Lay less stress on making many dependent on you than on keeping yourself independent of any. The sole advantage of power is that you can do more good... (286)

Live according to the moment—our acts and thoughts and all must be determined by circumstances. Act when you may, because time and tide wait for no one. Do not live by certain fixed rules... nor let your will pledge to fixed conditions, for you may have to drink the water tomorrow that you cast away today.

There are some [people] so absurdly stubborn in error, that they expect all the circumstances of an action should bend to their own eccentric whims, and not vice versa. The wise man knows that the very [North] Pole star of prudence is found in acting according to the current circumstances. (288)

Francois duc de La Rochefoucauld

French writer Francois duc de La Rochefoucauld, who lived from 1613 to 1680, has produced many unique ideas in philosophy, and many interesting insights on human nature.

Early Life

Francois was born in Paris, France. His family was of French nobility, and during those times, the unstable French government often alternated between aiding the nobility and posing a threat to them.

Much of Francois's life was spent as military figure and soldier. He served for the French army on-and-off from 1629 to 1646, and also was a notable fighter in the French civil war from 1648 to 1653. During his military career, Francois received major wounds several times before finally retiring around 1653.

Maxims

After retiring from the military, Francois joined an intellectual and scholarly group in Paris. During his time with them, he and the others often composed epigrams, which are concise statements and sayings that are often clever, witty, informative, and sometimes paradoxical or enigmatic.

Francois was very proficient at writing these epigrams, and by 1665, he collected many of them along with several of his essays, and put them in the first edition of *Reflexions ou Sentences et Maximes Morales*, which is more commonly known as *Maximes*, or *Maxims* in English.

Francois also produced various other writings throughout his life, but *Maxims* is by far and away the most famous and widely read of his works. He also produced several subsequent editions of *Maxims*.

Maxims contains mainly proverbial type statements, many of which are commentary about human nature and human interaction, and what Francois believes are the common inaccuracies of people's perceptions of themselves and of others. Francois's theories about human nature are based on such topics as self-interest & self-love, passions / emotions, vanity, relationships, love, conversation, insincerity, and trickeration. His writings are very concise, straightforward, and candid.

Francois's writings depict people as extremely self-interested and vain, and are often categorized under the "pessimistic" view of human nature. But despite this viewpoint, Francois enjoyed other people greatly throughout his life, and was also particularly noted for being very romantic.

Passages From *Maxims* and other Francois duc de La Rochefoucauld Writings

Note: These passages are a clarified adaptation of the J.W. Willis Bund & J. Hain Friswell translation. Maxim numbers are in parentheses.

Our virtues are usually just disguised vices.

What we call virtues are often just a collection of casual actions and selfish interests which chance or our own industry manages to arrange [in a certain way]. It is not always from valor that men are valiant, or from chastity that women are chaste. (1)

Now matter how many discoveries we make in the vast regions of self-love, undiscovered regions still remain there. (3)

Passion often makes the cleverest man foolish, and sometimes even makes the most foolish man clever. (6)

Many politician-type people represent certain great and dazzling actions as if they were results of carefully designed plans, when in actuality, they are usually the results of people's moods and passions… (7)

The passions are the most effective orators for persuading. They are a natural art that have infallible rules; and the simplest man with passion will be more persuasive than the most eloquent without it. (8)

No matter how much care we put into hiding our passions under the appearances of devotion and honor, they can always be seen to peer out through these covers. (12)

Not only are men susceptible to forget benefits and injuries, they can even grow to hate those who have done them a favor, and cease to hate those who have wronged them. The necessity of revenging an injury or of recompensing a benefit seems a slavery to which they are unwilling to submit. (14)

The clemency of princes is often just a policy to win the affections of the people. This clemency that is usually labeled virtue often arises from vanity, sometimes from idleness, often from fear, and almost always from all three combined. (15-16)

The constancy of the wise is only their art of concealing their inner annoyance. (20)

Philosophy easily triumphs over past and future evils; but present evils triumph over it. (22)

When great men let themselves be cast down by the succession of misfortune, it becomes apparent to us that they were only sustained by ambition, and not by their mind. So with *that* plus a great vanity, heroes are made like other men. (24)

Our evil actions do not attract as much persecution and hatred as our good qualities. (29)

We have more strength than will; and when we say things are impossible, it is often just excuses we make [for ourselves]. (30)

If we had no faults, we should not take so much pleasure in noting those [faults] of others. (31)

Pride is for the most part the same in everybody—the only difference is in the method and manner of showing it. (35)

When we criticize the faults of others, it is more because of our pride than our goodness. We reprove them not so much to correct [their faults], as we do to persuade them to believe that we ourselves are free from their faults. (37)

We promise according to our hopes; we perform according to our fears. (38)

Self-interest speaks all sorts of tongues and plays all sorts of characters—even that of self-disinterest. (39)

Self-interest blinds some people, and makes others see. (40)

Those who apply themselves too closely to trifling things often become incapable of great things. (41)

A man often believes he is leading when he is [actually being] led; while his mind seeks one goal, his heart unknowingly drags him towards another. (43)

The changes in our moods fluctuate even more than fortune [/ *chance*] does. (45)

The attachment or indifference to life that philosophers have shown is simply [a result] of their self-love style, which we cannot dispute about any more than [we can dispute over people's various] tastes in food or preferences of colors. (46)

We are never as happy or as unhappy as we suppose. (49)

Nothing should lessen our satisfaction with ourselves as much as when we notice that we disapprove of something at one time that we approve of at another time. (51)

To establish our position in the world, we will do anything to appear as if we established it. (56)

Although men flatter themselves with their great actions, these are more often a result of chance than of great design. (57)

The happiness or unhappiness of men depends no less on their dispositions as it does on fortune. (61)

Sincerity is an openness of heart that is found in very few people. What we usually see is only an artful disguise people put on to win the confidence of others. (62)

Truth does not do as much good in the world as the semblance of truth does evil. (64)

A clever man should handle his interests so that each will fall in suitable order [of their value]. Our greediness often brings trouble to this order, and makes us pursue so many things at the same time, that while we attend to the trifling too eagerly, we miss the great. (66)

What grace is to the body, good sense is to the mind. (67)

There is no disguise that can hide love for long where it exists, nor is there a disguise that can fabricate it where it does not [exist]. (70)

Love, like fire, cannot continue to exist without continual motion; both cease to live so soon as they cease to hope or to fear. (75)

True love is like a ghost: everyone speaks of it, but few have seen it. (76)

In most men, the love of justice is simply the fear of suffering injustice. (78)

Silence is the safest policy for he who distrusts himself. (79)

What makes us so changeable in our friendships is that it is difficult to know the qualities of the soul, but it is easy to know those of the mind. (80)

We can love nothing except what we base on our own selves, and when we prefer our friends to ourselves, we are just following our own taste or pleasure. Nevertheless, it is only by that preference that friendship can be true and perfect. (81)

Reconciliation with our enemies is simply a desire to better our condition, a weariness of war, or the fear of some unlucky thing from occurring. (82)

We often persuade ourselves to love people who are more powerful than we are; yet [it is] self-interest alone [that] produces the friendship. We do not give our hearts away for the good we wish to do [to them], but for what [good] we expect to receive [from them]. (85)

Men would not live long in society if they were not the dupes of each other. (87)

Self-love [either] increases or diminishes our measure of the good qualities of our friends, [and does so] in proportion to the satisfaction we feel with them; and we judge their virtue by way they act towards us. (88)

In the dealings of life, we please others more by our faults than by our good qualities. (90)

Old men delight in giving good advice as a consolation for the fact that they can no longer set bad examples. (93)

Even when a man acts ungrateful, it is often his benefactor who is more deserving of being labeled as disgraceful. (96)

Ideas often flash across our minds more complete than we could make them after much labor. (101)

The head is ever the dupe of the heart. (102)

Those who know their minds do not necessarily know their hearts. (103)

Men and things each have their proper perspective. To judge some of them rightly, it is necessary to see them at near, while to judge others rightly, we must see them at a distance. (104)

To boast that one never flirts is [actually] a kind of flirtation. (107)

The head cannot play the part of the heart for long. (108)

Nothing is given as plentifully [/ *liberally*] as advice. (110)

We are inconsolable at being deceived by our enemies and [being] betrayed by our friends, yet we are often content in be being treated like that by our own selves. (114)

It is as easy to unknowingly deceive yourself as [it is] to deceive others. (115)

Nothing is less sincere than the act of asking and giving advice. Although the asker seems to pay attention to the opinion of his friend, in reality he is just plotting to make the friend approve his [*the asker's*] own opinion and to make the friend responsible for his [*the asker's*] conduct.

The person giving the advice returns the confidence placed in him with a disinterested eagerness... and he is usually guided only by his own interest or reputation. (116)

Our subtlest act [of cleverness] is to simulate that we is not aware of traps that we know are set up for us. People are never deceived as easily as when they are in the act of trying to deceive [others]. (117)

The intention of never deceiving often exposes us to deception. (118)

We become so used to disguising ourselves to others, that we end up becoming disguised to ourselves. (119)

Our acts of betrayal are more from weakness than from a fixed motive. (120)

We frequently do good in order to enable us to do evil later with impunity [*exemption of punishment*]. (121)

If we never flattered ourselves, we should have but insufficient pleasure. (123)

The most deceitful people blame deceit in order to use it on some great occasion to promote a certain great self-interest. (124)

The true way to be deceived is to think of yourself as more knowing than others. (127)

It is sometimes necessary to play the fool in order to avoid being deceived by cunning men. (129)

It is far easier to be wise for others than to be wise for oneself. (132)

The only good examples are those that make the absurdity of bad originals become apparent. (133)

We sometimes differ more widely from ourselves than we do from others. (135)

When not prompted by vanity, we say little. (137)

A man would rather say evil of himself than say nothing. (138)

One reason that so few people that can carry on a rational and agreeable conversation is because virtually everyone puts more attention on what they want to say than they do on listening to what others are saying and answering them [accordingly].

[Even] the most clever and polite people are content with only appearing to be attentive... [but in truth], they are wandering from what is said, and really want to return to what they want to say...

The worst way to persuade or please others is to try thus strongly to please ourselves; and some of the greatest charms we can have in conversation come from listening well and answering well. (139)

As it is the mark of great minds to say many things in a few words, so it is that of little minds to use many words to say nothing. (142)

We exaggerate the good qualities of others more often due to the estimation of our own feelings than due to the actual virtue of others; [and] when we praise them, we wish to attract their praise. (143)

We often select envenomed praise which by a reaction upon those we praise shows faults we could not have shown by any other means. (145)

Usually, we only praise to be praised. (146)

There are few people wise enough to prefer useful criticism over treacherous praise. (147)

Some blames [actually] praise, and some praises [actually] blame. (148)

The refusal of praise is actually the wish to be praised twice. (149)

Our desire and urge to be praiseworthy of others strengthens our own good qualities; and praise that is given to wit, valor, and beauty, tends to increase them. (150)

It is easier to govern others than to prevent being governed. (151)

There are some people who only disgust with their abilities; [and] there are some people who please even with their faults. (155)

It is not enough to have great qualities; we should also have the management of them. (159)

No matter how brilliant an action, it should not be considered great unless [it was] the result of a great motive. (160)

A certain harmony should be kept between actions and ideas if we want to fully develop the effects they can produce. (161)

The art of using moderate abilities to advantage wins praise, and often acquires more reputation than actual brilliancy does. (162)

A countless number of acts that appear foolish [actually] have secret motives that are very wise and weighty. (163)

It is much easier to seem fitted for posts we do not fill, than for those we do. (164)

Ability wins us the appreciation of the true persons, and luck [wins] that of "the people." (165)

The world rewards the appearance of virtue more often than it rewards the virtue itself. (166)

There are different kinds of curiosity: one comes from self-interest, which makes us want to know everything that may be profitable to us; another from pride, which comes from a desire to know what others are ignorant of. (173)

It is much better to learn to deal with the ills we have now than to speculate on those that may befall us. (174)

Our repentance is not so much due to the sorrow for the ill we have already done, as [it is due to the] fear of the ill that may happen to us. (180)

There are both heroes of evil and heroes of good. (185)

We do not despise all who have vices, but we do despise all who do not have virtues. (186)

There are relapses in the diseases of the mind just like those of the body; what we call a cure is often merely an intermission or change of disease. (193)

The defects of the mind are like the wounds of the body: no matter how much care we take to heal them, the scars remain, and there is always the danger that they will reopen. (194)

What often prevents us from abandoning a single vice is [the fact that] we have so many. (195)

We easily forget the faults that are known only to ourselves. (196)

We exaggerate the glory of some men in order to detract from that of others… (198)

The desire to appear clever often prevents our being so. (199)

Virtue would not go far if vanity did not accompany her. (200)

Falsely honest men are those who disguise their faults to both themselves and others; truly honest men are those who know them [*their faults*] perfectly and acknowledge them. (202)

Folly follows us at all stages of life. If one appears wise, it is only because his folly is proportioned to his age and fortune [*/ circumstances*]. (207)

There are foolish people who know their folly and skillfully use it. (208)

In growing old, we become more foolish and more wise. (210)

Most people judge men only by success or by fortune. (212)

Love of glory, fear of shame, greed for fortune, the desire to make life agreeable and comfortable, and the wish to depreciate others [—all of these] are often the causes of the bravery that is spoken so highly of by men. (213)

Perfect bravery and total cowardice are two extremes that are rarely found. The space between them is vast, and embraces all other sorts of courage…
Some will freely expose themselves to danger at the beginning of an action, but diminish and become easily discouraged if it should last. Some are content to satisfy worldly honor, and beyond that will do little else. Some are not always equally masters of their timidity…
Some allow themselves to be overcome by panic, and others charge because they dare not remain at their posts. Some may be found whose courage is strengthened by small perils that prepare them to face greater dangers. Some are daring when facing swords but dread facing bullets; others dread bullets little but fear facing swords a lot.
These varied kinds of courage have this in common: darkness, by increasing fear and concealing both gallant and cowardly actions, allows men to spare themselves.
And there is another more general kind of discretion, for there is no man who does all he would have done if he were assured of getting off scot-free; thus, it is certain that the fear of death does somewhat subtract from valor. (215)

Perfect valor is to do without any witnesses what one would do before the entire world. (216)

Intrepidity is an extraordinary strength of soul that raises it above the troubles, disorders, and emotions that the sight of great perils can arouse in it. By this strength, heroes maintain a calm aspect and preserve their reason and liberty in the most surprising and terrible predicaments. (217)

Most men expose themselves in battle just enough to save their honor. Few are willing to do go any further than that to make sure that the purpose that they expose themselves for actually succeeds. (219)

What usually makes men brave and women chaste are vanity, shame, and most of all, disposition. (220)

Excessive hurriedness to fulfill an obligation is a kind of ingratitude. (226)

Lucky people are usually bad players when it comes to correcting their faults; they always believe that they are right when chance [/ *fortune*] backs up their vice or folly. (227)

It is great folly to wish only to be wise. (231)

Doing wrong to others is often less dangerous than doing them too much good. (238)

We often bore others when we think we cannot possibly bore them. (242)

Few things are impossible in themselves; application to make them succeed fails us more often than the means. (243)

Supreme resourcefulness consists in knowing the value of things. (244)

It is a great ability to know how to conceal one's ability. (245)

There is at least as much eloquence in the voice, eyes, and air [*individuality / personal bearing*] of a speaker as there is in his choice of words. (249)

True eloquence consists in saying all that should be [said], not all that could be said. (250)

All feelings have their distinct tone of voice, gestures and looks; and [it is] this harmony, as it is good or bad, and pleasant or unpleasant, [which] makes people agreeable or disagreeable. (255)

In all aspects of life, we take on a part and an appearance to seem to be what we wish to be [seen as]—and thus the world is merely composed of actors. (256)

What we call generosity is often just the vanity of giving, which we like more than what we give away. (263)

Pity is often a reflection of our own evils in the ills of others. It is a delicate foresight of the troubles into which we may fall. We help others [so] that on like occasions we may be helped ourselves; and these services that we render are in reality benefits we confer on ourselves by anticipation. (264)

Quickness in believing evil without having sufficiently examining it is the effect of pride and laziness. We wish to find the guilty, and we do not wish to trouble ourselves in examining the crime. (267)

We label judges with having the meanest motives, and yet we desire that our reputation and fame should depend upon the judgment of men, who are all, either from their jealousy or preoccupation or want of intelligence, opposed to us—and yet [despite their bias], just for the sake of making these men decide in our favor, we peril in so many ways both our peace and our life. (268)

No man is clever enough to know all the evil that he does. (269)

There are people who the world approves of who have no virtue besides the vices they use in social life. (273)

Absence lessens small passions and increases great ones, [just] as the wind will blow out a candle but blow in a fire. (276)

Women often think they are in love when they are not in love. [In actuality], it is the excitement of a love affair, the emotional reaction to sentiment, the natural wish to experience the pleasure of being loved, and the difficulty of saying no, [all of] which [combine to] persuade them that they have passion, when all they [really] have is playful [/ toying] flirting. (277)

When we exaggerate our friends' tenderness towards us, it is often less from gratitude than from a desire to exhibit our own virtue. (279)

Some lies are disguised so well to resemble the truth, that we should be poor judges of truth if not to be deceived by them. (282)

Sometimes there is equal or more ability in knowing how to use good advice than [there is] in giving it. (283)

There are wicked people who would be much less dangerous if they were totally without goodness. (284)

Fertility of mind is not what gives us with so many resources on the same matter. [In fact,] It is the lack of good discernment that makes us hesitate at each thing our imagination presents, and hinders us from at first discerning which is the best. (287)

There are some troubles and maladies that at certain times are made worse by attempted cures; and the real skill consists in knowing when it is dangerous to use them. (288)

The gratitude of most men is nothing more than a secret desire of receiving [even] greater benefits. (298)

There are follies as catching as infections. (300)

Many people despise wealth, but few know how to give it away. (301)

Only in trifling matters are we usually bold enough not to trust to appearances. (302)

The self-interest that is blamed for all our misdeeds should also often be praised for our good deeds. (305)

We find very few ungrateful people when we are able to confer favors. (306)

It is as suitable to be boastful alone as it is ridiculous to be so with others. (307)

Sometimes, occasions occur in life which demand you to be a little foolish in order to skillfully extricate yourself. (310)

If there are men whose folly has never appeared, it is only because it has never been looked for closely. (311)

The extreme delight we experience in talking about ourselves should warn us that those who listen do not share it. (314)

What commonly hinders us from showing the recesses of our heart to our friends is not the distrust we have of them, but that [*distrust*] we have of ourselves. (315)

If we take the liberty to dwell on the faults of our friends and benefactors, we cannot long preserve the feelings we should hold towards them. (319)

We are nearer loving those who hate us than those who love us more than we desire. (321)

Those only are despicable who fear to be despised. (322)

Ridicule dishonors more than dishonor itself [does]. (326)

We admit to small faults in order to persuade others that we don't have great ones. (327)

Sometimes we believe that we hate flattery, when in reality, we only dislike the method [of flattery]. (329)

When our hatred is too bitter, it places us below those whom we hate. (338)

To be a great man, one should know how to exploit advantages of every phase of chance [/ *fortune*]. (343)

Most men, like plants, possess hidden qualities that chance discovers. (344)

Opportunity makes us known to others, but more to ourselves. (345)

We rarely ever perceive others as being sensible, except for those who agree with us. (347)

When one loves, one doubts even what one most believes. (348)

The reason we bitterly hate those who deceive us is because they think they are cleverer than we are. (350)

We are almost always bored with people that we should not be bored with. (352)

There are certain defects, which [when] well mounted, glitter like virtue itself. (354)

Little minds are too much wounded by little things; great minds see all [these little things] and are not hurt. (357)

We are more humiliated by the least infidelity towards us, than by our greatest [infidelity] towards others. (360)

The evils we do to others give us less pain than those we do to ourselves. (363)

However we distrust the sincerity of those whom we talk with, we always believe them more sincere with us than with others. (366)

The greatest mistake of penetration is not to have fallen short, but to have gone too far. (377)

Chance [/ *fortune*] makes our virtues or our vices visible [just] as light does to objects. (380)

Our actions are like the rhymed ends of blank verses, where each one can be put in a way to mean whatever person wants [them to mean]. (383)

We should only be astonished at still being able to be astonished. (384)

No people are more often wrong than those who will not allow themselves to be wrong. (386)

Although we don't have the courage to say that in general, we have no faults and our enemies have no good qualities; in reality, we are not far from believing so. (397)

There is a kind of greatness that does not depend upon fortune: it is a certain manner that distinguishes us, and which seems to destine us for great things; it is the value we insensibly set upon ourselves; it is by this quality that we gain the esteem of other men, and it is this which commonly raises us more above them, than birth, rank, or even virtue itself. (399)

There may be virtue [/ *skill*] without position, but there is no position without some kind of virtue [/ *skill*]. (400)

Rank is to virtue what dress is to a pretty woman. (401)

It appears that nature has hid at the bottom of our hearts talents and abilities unknown to us. It is only the passions that have the power of bringing them to light, and sometimes give us truer and more perfect views than art [/ *resourcefulness*] could possibly make. (404)

We are [often] quite inexperienced as we reach the different stages of life, and we often lack experience even in spite of the number of our years. (405)

We should often be ashamed of our very best actions if the world only saw the motives that caused them. (409)

Almost all of our faults are more excusable than the means we take to hide them. (411)

Whatever disgrace we may have deserved, it is almost always in our power to reestablish our character. (412)

Idiots and lunatics see only their own wit. (414)

We often credit ourselves with vices the reverse of what we have, thus when weak we boast of our obstinacy. (424)

Nothing prevents our being natural as much as our desire to seem so. (431)

To praise good actions heartily is in some measure to take part in them. (432)

It is much easier to know men than it is to know a man. (436)

We should not judge a man's virtue by his great abilities, but by the use he makes of them. (437)

There is a certain kind of lively gratitude that not only releases us from benefits we received, but also becomes a return payment to our friends that makes them become indebted to us. (438)

We should earnestly desire but few things if we clearly knew what we desired. (439)

We try to make a virtue of the vices that we are unwilling to correct. (442)

What makes the grief of shame and jealousy so acute is that vanity cannot aid us in enduring them. (446)

Propriety is the least of all laws, but the most obeyed. (447)

It is easier for a well-trained mind to submit to an ill-trained mind than to guide it. (448)

In great matters, we should not try to create opportunities as much as we should utilize those opportunities that offer themselves. (453)

We should gain more by letting the world see what we are than by trying to seem what we are not. (457)

Our enemies come nearer to the truth in the opinions they form of us than we do in our opinion of ourselves. (458)

It would be beneficial for us to know what all our passions make us do. (460)

There is often more pride than goodness in our grief for our enemies' miseries; it is to show how superior we are to them that we bestow on them the sign of our compassion. (463)

Some bad qualities form great talents. (468)

However rare true love is, true friendship is rarer. (473)

The desire to be pitied or to be admired is often the main reason we confide in others. (475)

Imagination does not enable us to invent as many different contradictions as there are by nature in every heart. (478)

Only people who possess firmness can possess true gentleness. In those who appear gentle, it is usually only weakness that is readily converted into harshness. (479)

Timidity is a fault that is dangerous to blame in those we desire to cure of it. (480)

Nothing is rarer than true good nature [/ kindness]; those who are though to have it are usually just easily dominated, or weak. (481)

There are more people without self-love than [there are] without envy. (486)

The calm or disturbance of our mind does not depend so much on what we regard as the more important things of life, as [it does] in the prudent or impracticable arrangement [we make] of the little things of daily occurrence. (488)

However wicked men may be, they do not dare condemn virtue openly. Thus, when they want to attack virtue, they pretend it is false or charge it with crimes. (489)

What makes us see that men know their faults better than we imagine, is that they are never wrong when they speak of their conduct. The same self-love that usually blinds them also lets them see, and gives them such true views as to make them suppress or disguise the smallest thing that might be criticized. (494)

Quarrels would not last long if the fault was only on one side. (496)

Some people are so self-occupied, that [even] when in love, they find a way to be totally engrossed with the passion without being so with the person they love. (500)

The next selections are from the Sixth Edition of the Pensees De La Rochefoucauld, which was published after Rochefoucauld's death.

The labor of the body frees us from the pains of the mind, and thus makes the poor happy.

Few things are needed to make a wise man happy; nothing can make a fool content; that is why most men are miserable.

We concern ourselves less with becoming happy than [we do] to make others believe we are.

Wisdom is to the soul what health is to the body.

Before strongly desiring anything, we should examine the happiness of those who already posses it.

A true friend is the greatest of all goods, and that of which we think least of acquiring.

Lovers do not wish to see the faults of their mistresses until their enchantment is at an end.

The wise man finds it better not to enter the encounter than to conquer.

It is more necessary to study men than books.

There are certain faults, which [when] placed in a good light, please more than perfection itself.

The harm that others do to us is often less than that which we do to ourselves.

It is most difficult to speak when we are ashamed of being silent.

Those faults are always pardonable that we have the courage to avow [/ acknowledge].

The greatest fault of penetration is not that it goes to the bottom of a matter, but beyond it.

We give advice, but we cannot give the wisdom to profit by it.

Renewed friendships require more care than those that have never been broken.

A man who no one is pleasing is much unhappier than a man who pleases nobody.

We are quick to criticize other people's faults, but slow to use those faults to correct our own.

Most things are praised or condemned only because it is fashionable to praise or condemn them.

The next selections are from other various collections of Rochefoucauld writings.

Hope and fear are inseparable.

The power that the women we love have over us is greater than that which we have over ourselves.

What makes us easily believe that others have defects is [the fact] that we all easily believe what we wish.

The next selections come from epigrams that were included in the earlier editions of Maxims, but were taken out in later editions.

When we do not find peace of mind in ourselves, it is useless to seek it elsewhere.

Love is to the soul of him who loves, [as] what the soul is to the body that it animates.

When we are tired of loving, we are quite content if our mistress should become faithless, since it loosens us from our [responsibility of] fidelity.

In the adversity of our best friends, we always find something that is not wholly displeasing to us.

How shall we hope that another person will keep our secret if we do not keep it ourselves?

The most wise may be so in indifferent and ordinary matters, but they are seldom so in their most serious affairs.

Men only blame vice and praise virtue from [the perspective of] self-interest.

There are crimes that become innocent and even glorious by their brilliancy, number, or excess; [and] therefore, it happens that public robbery is called "financial skill," and the unjust capture of provinces is called "a conquest."

It is very hard to separate the general goodness [/ *kindness*] spread all over the world from great cleverness.

The confidence we have in ourselves arises in a great measure from that which we have in others.

There are fine things that are more brilliant when [they are] unfinished than when finished too much.

Magnanimity is a noble effort of pride that makes a man master of himself, to make him master of all things.

Women for the most part surrender themselves more from weakness than from passion; and by that reason, bold and pushing men succeed better than others, even though they are not so loveable.

Excerpts From Various Francois duc de La Rochefoucauld Essays

Air (Individuality / Personal Bearing) and Manner

There is an air that belongs to the figure and talents of each individual; we always lose it when we abandon it to assume another. We should try to find out what air is natural to us and never abandon it, but make it as perfect as we can.

This is the reason that the majority of children please—it is because they are wrapped up in the air and manner nature has given them, and are ignorant of any other. They are changed and corrupted when they quit infancy; they think they should imitate what they see, and they are not altogether able to imitate it. In this imitation, there is always something of falsity and uncertainty. They have nothing settled in their manner and opinions. Instead of being in reality what they want to appear, they seek to appear what they are not.

All men want to be different, and to be greater than they are; they seek for an air other than their own, and a mind different from what they possess; they take their style and manner at chance. They make experiments upon themselves without considering that what suits one person will not suit everyone, that there is no universal rule for taste or manners, and that there are no good copies.

Few men, nevertheless, can have unison in many matters without being a copy of each other, if each follows his natural turn of mind. But in general, a person will not wholly follow it. He loves to imitate. We often imitate the same person without perceiving it, and we neglect our own good qualities for the good qualities of others, which generally do not suit us.

I do not pretend, from what I say, that each should so wrap himself up in himself so as to not be able to follow example, or to add to his own, useful and serviceable habits which nature has not given him...

But yet, acquired qualities should always have a certain agreement and a certain union with our own natural qualities, which they imperceptibly extend and increase...

...Change of our fortune [/ *circumstances*] often changes our air and our manners, and augments the air of dignity, which is always false when it is too marked, and when it is not united and mixed with that which nature has given us. We should unite and blend them together, and thus render them such that they can never be separated.

...

Thousands of people with good qualities are displeasing; thousands pleasing with far less abilities. And why? Because they first wish to appear to be what they are not, the second are what they appear.

Some of the advantages or disadvantages that we have received from nature please in proportion as we know the air, the style, the manner, the sentiments that coincide with our condition and our appearance, and displease in the proportion they are removed from that point.

Society

In speaking of society, my plan is not to speak of friendship... For the present, I shall speak of that particular kind of interaction that gentlemen should have with each other. It would be idle to show how much society is essential to men—all seek for it, and all find it, yet few adopt the method of making it pleasant and lasting.

Everyone seeks to find his pleasure and his advantage at the expense of others. We always prefer ourselves to those with whom we intend to live [/ *interact*] with, and they almost always perceive the preference. This is what disturbs and destroys society.

We should discover a way to hide this love of selection, since it is too ingrained in us to be in our power to destroy. We should make our pleasure that of other persons, to humor, never to wound their self-love.

The mind is a major factor in such a great a work, but it is not merely sufficient for us to guide it in the different courses it should hold. The agreement we meet between minds would not keep society together for long if she was not governed and sustained by good sense, temper, and by the consideration which ought to exist between persons who have to live together...

To make society pleasant, it is essential that each should retain his freedom of action... [A man] should see himself without dependence, and at the same time, amuse himself. He should have the power of separating himself without that separation bringing any change on the society... He should share in what he believes to be the amusement of persons with whom he wishes to live [/ *interact with*], but he should not always be liable to the trouble of providing them.

Complying with others is essential in society, but it should have its limits; it becomes slavery when it is extreme...

There is a kind of politeness that is necessary in the interaction among gentlemen; it makes them comprehend playful teasing, and it keeps them from using and employing certain figures of speech too rude and unrefined, which are often used thoughtlessly when we hold to our opinion with too much warmth.

The interaction of gentlemen cannot subsist without a certain kind of confidence; this should be equal on both sides. Each should have an appearance of sincerity and of discretion...

There should be some variety in wit. Those who have only one kind of wit cannot please for long unless they can take different roads...

As we should stand at a certain distance to view objects, so we should also stand at a distance to observe society; each has its proper point of view from which it should be regarded. It is quite right that it should not be looked at too closely, for there is hardly a man who in all matters allows himself to be seen as he really is.

Conversation

The reason why so few people are agreeable in conversation is because each thinks more of what he desires to say than of what others say, and we make bad listeners when we want to speak.

However, it is necessary to listen to those who talk. We should give them the time they want... [and never] interrupt them. In fact, we should enter into their mind and taste, illustrate their meaning, praise anything they say that deserves praise, and let them see we praise more from our choice than from agreement with them.

To please others, we should talk on subjects they like and that interest them... The level of seriousness and of complexity we talk with should correspond to the temper and understanding of the persons we talk with, and should readily give them the advantage of deciding without obliging them to answer when they are not anxious to talk.

After having in this way fulfilled the duties of politeness, we can speak our opinions to our listeners when we find an opportunity [to do so]... Above all things, we should avoid frequently talking of ourselves and giving ourselves as an example. Nothing is more tiresome than a man who quotes himself for everything.

We cannot give too great a study to find out the manner and the capacity of those with whom we talk... Then we should fittingly use all the modes above mentioned to show our thoughts to them, and make them, if possible, believe that we take our ideas from them.

... [We should avoid] forced expressions, and never let the words be grander than the matter.

It is not wrong to retain our opinions if they are reasonable...

It is dangerous to seek to always be the leader of the conversation, and to push a good argument too hard when we have found one. Civility often hides half of its understanding, and when it meets with an opinionated man who defends the bad side, spares him the disgrace of giving way.

We are sure to displease when we speak too long and too often of one subject. And when we try to turn the conversation upon subjects that we think more instructive than others, we should enter indifferently upon every subject that is agreeable to others, stopping where they wish...

Every kind of conversation, however witty it may be, is not equally fitted for all clever persons. We should select what is to their taste and suitable to their condition, sex, and talents; and also choose the proper time to say it.

We should observe the place, the occasion, and the temper in which we find the person who listens to us, for there is equally much art in speaking to the purpose as there is in knowing when to be silent. There is an eloquent silence that serves to approve or to condemn; there is a silence of discretion and of respect.

In a word, there is a tone, an air, a manner, which renders everything in conversation agreeable or disagreeable, refined or vulgar. But it is given to few people to keep this secret well. Those who lay down rules too often break them, and the safest we are able to give is to listen much, to speak just enough, and to say nothing that will ever give ground for regret.

Difference of Character

...

One can be a fool with much wit, and one need not be a fool even with very little wit. To have much mind is a doubtful expression. It may mean every class of mind that can be mentioned, it may mean none in particular. It may mean that he talks sensibly while he acts foolishly.

We may have a mind, but a narrow one. A mind may be fitted for some things, not for others. We may have a large measure of mind fitted for nothing, and one is often inconvenienced with much mind; still of this kind of mind we may say that it is sometimes pleasing in society.

Though the gifts of the mind are infinite, they can, it seems to me, be thus classified:

There are some so beautiful that everyone can see and feel their beauty.

There are some lovely, it is true, but which are wearisome.

There are some which are lovely, which the entire world admire, but without knowing why.

There are some so refined and delicate that few are capable even of remarking all their beauties.

There are others that, though imperfect, are produced with such skill, and sustained and managed with such sense and grace, that they even deserve to be admired.

Death

Note: This essay comes from Maxims, and is Maxim 504

Thus having treated of the hollowness of so many apparent virtues [throughout *Maxims*], it appropriate to say something on the hollowness of the unconcern [some people show] for death…

…Everything that could be written has been written to persuade us that death is no evil, and the weakest of men, as well as the bravest, have given many noble examples on which to justify such an opinion; yet I still do not think that any man of good sense has ever yet believed in it. And the pains we take to persuade others as well as ourselves that such an opinion is true amply show that the task of convincing is far from easy.

For many reasons we may be disgusted with life, but for none may we despise it. Not even those who commit suicide regard it as a light matter, and are as much alarmed and startled as the rest of the world if death meets them in a different way than the one they have selected. The difference we observe in the courage of so many brave men is from meeting death in a way different from what they imagined when it shows itself nearer at one time than at another. Thus it ultimately happens that having despised death when they were ignorant of it, they dread it when they become acquainted with it.

If we could avoid seeing it with all its surroundings, we might perhaps believe that it was not the greatest of evils. The wisest and bravest are those who take the best means to avoid reflecting on it, as every man who sees it in its real light regards it as dreadful.

The necessity of dying created all the constancy of philosophers. They thought it but right to go with a good grace when they could not avoid going, and being unable to prolong their lives indefinitely, nothing remained but to build an immortal reputation, and to save from the general wreck all that could be saved.

To put a good face upon it, let it suffice not to say all that we think to ourselves, but rely more on our nature than on our fallible reason, which might make us think we could approach death with indifference.

The glory of dying with courage, the hope of being regretted, the desire to leave behind us a good reputation, the assurance of being freed from the miseries of life and being no longer dependent on the whims of fortune, these are all resources that should not be passed over. But we must not regard them as infallible.

They should affect us in the same proportion as a single shelter affects those who in war storm a fortress. At a distance they think it may afford cover, but when near they find it only a feeble protection. It is only deceiving ourselves to imagine that death, when near, will seem the same as at a distance, or that our feelings which are merely weaknesses, are naturally so strong that they will not suffer in an attack of the rudest of trials. It is equally as absurd to try the effect of self-esteem and to think it will enable us to count as naught what will of necessity destroy it.

And the mind [/ reasoning] that we trust to find so many resources will be far too weak in the struggle to persuade us in the way we wish. For it is this mind that betrays us so frequently, and which, instead of filling us with contempt of death, serves but to show us all that is frightful and fearful. The most it can do for us is to persuade us to avert our gaze and fix it on other objects. Cato and Brutus each selected noble ones. A lackey sometime ago contented himself by dancing on the scaffold when he was about to be broken on the wheel.

So however diverse the motives, they but realize the same result. For the rest it is a fact that whatever difference there may be between the noble and the peasant, we have constantly seen both the one and the other meet death with the same composure. Still there is always this difference, that the contempt the noble shows for death is but the love of fame which hides death from his sight; in the peasant it is but the result of his limited vision that hides from him the extent of the evil, and leaves him free to reflect on other things.

Blaise Pascal

Frenchman Blaise Pascal, who lived from 1623 to 1662, is one of history's most notable well-rounded people. He was a major figure in science, mathematics, writing, philosophy, and theology.

Early Life

Born and raised in Clermont-Ferrand and later in Paris, Blaise Pascal was noted early on as being highly brilliant and prodigious. As a teenager, he made several discoveries in the field of geometry, and around the age of twenty, he invented an early version of the digital calculator (which consisted of a wooden box with dials that could quickly add and subtract figures.)

(About twenty years earlier, a similar calculating device was built by German mathematician and scientist Wilhelm Schickard, although it was not widely used, and it remained in obscurity. Leonardo Da Vinci also sketched a design for a calculator device in the 1500s. Nevertheless, Blaise is often accredited as the inventor of the early-form calculator)

Early Notable Works

Blaise continued to make many strides in various fields of science and math. Among them, he discovered the principle in fluid mechanics that is now known as Pascal's law, he invented the hydraulic press and syringe, he did groundbreaking work in the mathematical subject of probability, and he helped develop a mathematical discovery now known as Pascal's triangle.

Blaise was also a notable writer, and was well known for a series of essays he wrote in defense of a persecuted friend. Those essays, known as *Les Provinciales*, were widely read throughout Europe, and had a tremendous impact on the literary style of many writers.

Later Life

In his later life, Blaise was heavily involved in philosophical and religious subjects, and also helped the poor. He struggled with health problems and lived in pain for most of his life, and he died of a stomach ulcer at age 39 in 1662. In 1670, his various writings on religion and philosophy were published in a work titled *Pensees*.

Personality

Blaise was often described as others as being tremendously gifted yet sometimes embarrassed of his talents; high strung and overbearing yet also sometimes trying to be the opposite; and highly intellectual, persevering, and curious.

Blaise Pascal Quotes

We are all something, but none of us are everything

All of man's troubles come from his inability to sit alone, quietly, in a room, for any length of time.

We like to be deceived.

If all men knew what others say of them, there would not be four friends in the world.

Imagination decides everything.

Habit is a second nature which destroys the first. But what is nature, and why is habit not natural? I am very fearful that nature itself is only a first habit, just as habit is a second nature.

Man's greatness lies in his power of thought.

When we encounter a natural style, we are surprised and charmed—for we expected to see an author, and we find a person.

Contradiction is not a sign of falsehood, nor is the lack of contradiction a sign of truth.

Art paintings are such a weird vanity—they attract admiration by resembling the original which we do not admire.

Going beyond the limits of moderation is an outrage to humanity.

The human soul's greatness is displayed by knowing how to stay within the proper bounds.

There are two extremes that are equally dangerous—shutting reason entirely out, and letting nothing in.

Nature is an infinite sphere whose center is everywhere and whose circumference is nowhere.

In general, we are convinced more easily by reasons we discover ourselves than by those that others have given us.

Can anything be stupider than for a man to have the right to kill me because he lives on the other side of a river and his ruler has a dispute with mine, even though I have not disputed with him?

Kind words do not cost much; yet they accomplish much.

It is the fight alone that pleases us, not the victory.

The heart has its reasons of which reason knows nothing. We know this in countless ways.

The multitude that is not organized to be a unity is confusion. The unity that does not originate from the multitude is tyranny.

It is not certain that everything is uncertain.

The more intelligent someone is, the more originality he finds of others. Average people find little difference between people.

I have made this letter longer because I didn't have the time to make it shorter.

The two types of men: the righteous who think they are sinners, and the sinners who think they are righteous.

The eternal silence of those infinite spaces frightens me.

Voltaire

Voltaire, who lived from 1694 to 1778, was a legendary French writer and philosopher. His life and works have had a tremendous impact on French, European, and world culture.

Early Life

Voltaire was born in Paris, France, with the name Francois-Marie Arouet. (Note: I will use the name Voltaire throughout this chapter for consistency). In 1710 at age 16, he ended his formal schooling and joined a Paris scholarly group, and shortly later began writing and distributing various verses. By 1717, Voltaire was accused of writing negatively about the French government, and was imprisoned for nearly a year. After he got out, he adopted the penname *Voltaire*, a term whose origin and meaning is uncertain.

In 1718, he released a play he wrote in prison named *Oedipe*, which became immensely popular and earned him great fame and acclaim. By the mid 1720s, Voltaire was very wealthy due to his writing success, as well as from an inheritance and several shrewd investments.

Duel Challenge and Exile

In 1726, Voltaire got into an argument with a French nobleman named Chevalier de Rohan. After receiving a beating from Rohan's men, Voltaire challenged Rohan to a duel (a formal and intense fight) three months later. Rohan used his influence to cause Voltaire to be imprisoned due to his duel challenge. Two weeks later, Voltaire accepted an option to be exiled from France rather than remain in jail.

England

Voltaire moved to England and spent three years there, which had a tremendous influence on him. He met writers such as Alexander Pope and Jonathan Swift, and also studied ideas of philosopher John Locke and scientist Isaac Newton.

Return to France

In 1729, Voltaire returned to France and came out with a variety of writings over the next few years, including an immensely popular play titled *Zaire*. He also issued a political work titled *Letters Concerning the English*

Nation (later named *Philosophical Letters*), which offended the French government and caused French authorities to condemn the book. This caused Voltaire to flee from Paris to the chateau of Mme du Chatelet, located in Champagne, France.

Voltaire continued his writing, producing a wide variety of other works, including plays, historical works, poetry, writings about Isaac Newton, a philosophical work called *Zadig,* and a science fiction philosophical story called *Micromegas*.

The Legend

Voltaire later moved about to Berlin, Switzerland, and then to the Swiss-French border, and continued producing a tremendous amount of material, including his most notable work, a philosophical fiction tale named *Candide*. He also wrote the *Philosophical Dictionary, Essay on the Manners and Spirit of Nations*, and countless other books, plays, and essays. He soon became a renowned figure and celebrity known throughout Europe.

Voltaire finally went back to Paris in the late 1770s, and was treated as a national hero. He died in Paris in 1778.

Voltaire Quotes

People hate others that they label greedy only because nothing can be gained from them.

It is forbidden to kill—and thus, all murderers are punished unless they kill in large numbers, and with the background of trumpets playing.

Our contemptible species is so made that those who walk on a commonly used path are sure to throw stones at those who are displaying a new road.

The best way to be boring is to include everything.

Many are destined to reason wrongly; others, not to reason at all; and others, to persecute those who do reason.

Self-love is the instrument of our preservation.

The multitude of books is making us ignorant.

It is much better to be silent than to merely increase the number of bad books.

Think for yourselves, and let others enjoy the privilege to do so, too.

Man is free at the moment he wishes to be.

Man is the creature of the era he lives in; very few can raise themselves above the ideas of the time.

Truth is a fruit that should not be plucked until it is ripe.

It is not enough to conquer; one must learn to seduce.

He must be very ignorant; for he answers every question he is asked.

…I like the people who say what they think.

The great consolation in life is to say what one thinks.

Common sense is not so common.

I know of no great men except those who have rendered great service to the human race.

Those who can make you believe absurdities can make you commit atrocities.

It is dangerous to be right when the government is wrong.

A long dispute means that both parties are wrong.

Judge others by their questions rather than by their answers.

For every author, let us distinguish the person from his works.

Is there anyone wise enough to learn from other people's experience?

When it comes to money, everyone is of the same religion.

We never live; we are always anticipating living.

[The Holy Roman Empire:] Neither Holy, nor Roman, nor an Empire.

If only the true and useful things were recorded, our huge historical libraries would be reduced to very narrow dimensions—but we would know more, and know it better.

… If you have two religions in your country, they will cut each other's throat; if you have thirty religions, they will live in peace.

History contains little beyond a list of people who have accommodated themselves with other people's property.

Friendship is the marriage of the soul, and this marriage is subject to divorce.

If you are want to gain a legendary name and found a sect or establishment, be completely mad [/ crazy]—but make sure that your madness corresponds with the turn and temper of your age. [And] in your madness, have enough reason to guide your extravagances; and do not forget to be excessively opinionated and forwarding. There is a definite chance that you may get hanged; but if you escape hanging, you will have altars built for you.

Excerpts from Voltaire's book *The Philosophical Dictionary*

Note: These are a clarified adaptation of the translation by H.I. Woolf

Prejudices

Prejudice is an opinion without judgment. Thus, all over the world, people inspire children with all the opinions they [*people*] desire, before the children can judge.

There are some universal and necessary prejudices that even form virtue. In all countries, children are taught to recognize a rewarding and revenging God; to respect and love their father and their mother; to look on theft as a crime and selfish lying as a vice, before they can guess what is a vice and what a virtue. Thus, there are some very good prejudices; they are those that are ratified by judgment when one reasons.

Sentiment is not a simple prejudice; it is something much stronger. A mother does not love her son because she has been told she must love him; she cherishes him happily in spite of herself. It is not through prejudice that you run to the help of an unknown child about to fall into a deep gap, or be eaten by a beast.

But it is through prejudice that you will respect a man clad in certain clothes, walking gravely, speaking likewise. Your parents have told you that you should bow before this man; you respect him before knowing whether he merits your respect. [Then] you grow in years and in knowledge; you perceive that this man is a charlatan steeped in arrogance, self-interest and artifice; you despise what you revered, and the prejudice cedes to judgment.

Through prejudice you have believed the fables with which your childhood was cradled; you have been told that the Titans made war on the gods, and Venus was amorous of Adonis. When you are twelve you accept these fables as truths; when you are twenty you look on them as ingenious allegories.

...

Historical Prejudices

Most historical stories have been believed without examination, and this belief is a prejudice. Fabius Pictor [*a Roman historian who lived in the c200s BC*] relates that many centuries before him, a vestal of the town of Alba, going to draw water in her pitcher, was ravished, that she gave birth to Romulus and Remus [*the founders of Rome according to Roman folklore*], that they were fed by a she-wolf, etc.

The Roman people believed this fable; they did not examine whether at that time there were vestals in Latium, whether it were probable that a king's daughter would leave her convent with her pitcher, whether it were likely that a she-wolf would suckle two children instead of eating them. The prejudice established itself...

Tolerance

What is tolerance? It is the consequence of humanity. We all have weaknesses and errors; let us mutually pardon each other's follies—it is the first law of nature.

It is clear that the individual who persecutes a man, his brother, because he is not of the same opinion, is a monster. That admits of no difficulty. But the government! But the magistrates! But the princes! How do they treat those who have another worship than theirs? If they are powerful strangers, it is certain that a prince will make an alliance with them...

...

...We ought to be tolerant of one another, because we all have weaknesses, inconsistencies, [and are] liable to inconsistency and error.

Shall a reed laid low in the mud by the wind say to a fellow reed fallen in the opposite direction, "Crawl as I crawl, wretch, or I shall petition that you be torn up by the roots and burned?"

General Reflection on Man

It takes twenty years to lead man from the… state in which he is within his mother's womb… to the state when the maturity… begins to appear. It took thirty centuries to learn a little about his structure. It might need eternity to learn something about his soul. It takes an instant to kill him.

Ancients and Moderns

The great debate over the [superiority of the] ancients and [*versus*] the moderns has not been resolved yet; it has been on the table since the silver age succeeded the golden age. Mankind has always insisted that the good old days were much better than the present day…

The Chevalier Temple, who has made it his business to demean all the moderns… [maintains with assurance] that there is nothing new in our astronomy, [and] nothing [new] in the knowledge of the human body, unless perhaps, he says, the circulation of the blood. Love of his own opinion… makes him forget the discovery of the satellites of Jupiter, of the five moons and the ring of Saturn… of the calculated position of three thousand stars, of the laws given by Kepler and Newton for the heavenly orbs, of the causes of the precession of the equinoxes, and of a hundred other pieces of knowledge that the ancients did not even suspect the possibility of. The discoveries in anatomy are as great in number.

[And additionally,] the tiny new universe discovered by the microscope was counted for nothing by the Chevalier Temple. He closed his eyes to the marvels of his contemporaries, and opened them only to admire ancient ignorance…

What is still stranger is that, having cultivated elegant literature throughout his life, he [*Chevalier Temple*] does not reason better about our good authors than about our philosophers [*/ scientists*]…

He [*Chevalier Temple*] was, however, a scholar, a courtier, a man of much wit, an ambassador, a man who had reflected profoundly on all he had seen. He possessed great knowledge—[yet] a prejudice was all it took to spoil all this merit.

There are beauties in Euripides [*an ancient Greek playwright who lived in the 400s BC*], and even more in Sophocles [*another ancient*

Greek playwright who lived in the 400s BC]; but they have many more defects...

Authority

Contemptible human beings—whether you wear green robes, turbans, black robes or surplices, cloaks and neckbands—[you should] never seek to use authority where it is only a question of reason...

Others have spoken to you a hundred times about the disrespectful absurdity that you condemned Galileo [*one of the world's greatest scientist ever*] with, and [now] I speak to you for the hundred and first, and I hope you will keep the anniversary of it forever.

I hope that on the door of your holy office, it is engraved: "Here seven cardinals, assisted by minor brethren, had Italy's master of thought [*Galileo*] thrown into prison at the age of seventy. And because of their own ignorance, [they] made him fast on bread and water because he instructed the human race."

There was pronounced a sentence in favor of Aristotle's [*an Ancient Greek philosopher and scientist who lived in the 300s BC*] categories, and there was decreed learnedly and equitably the penalty of the galleys for anyone who should be so daring enough as to have an opinion that differs from that of the Stagyrite [*a.k.a. Aristotle*], whose books were formerly burned by two councils...

In the neighboring schools, judicial proceedings were instituted against the circulation of the blood...

At the Customs of Thought, twenty-one folio volumes were seized, in which it was stated treacherously and wickedly that triangles always have three angles; that a father is older than his son; that Rhea Silvia [*a person from Roman folklore*] lost her virginity before giving birth to her child, and that flour is not an oak leaf...

In consequence, everyone thought themselves far superior to Archimedes [*a legendary Greek inventor and mathematician who lived in the 200s BC*], Euclid [*a Greek mathematician who lived in the c200s BC*], [and] Cicero [*a Roman writer, scholar, and statesman who lived from 106 BC-46 BC*]... and strutted proudly about the University quarter.

Connected Link of Events

It is said that the present delivers the future. Events are linked to each other... There is no effect without a cause... and the smallest cause often produces the greatest effects ...

Examine the position of all the peoples of the universe—they are established... on a sequence of facts which appear to be connected with nothing, and which are connected with everything. Everything is cog, pulley, cord, spring, in this vast machine. It is likewise in the physical sphere... The chain stretches from one end of the universe to the other.

But it seems to me that a strange abuse is made of the truth of this principle. From it, some people conclude that there is not a sole minute atom whose movement has not exerted its influence in the present arrangement of the world; that there is not a single minute accident, among either men or animals, that is not an essential link in the great chain of fate.

Let us understand each other: every effect clearly has its cause, going back from cause to cause in the abyss of eternity; but every cause has not its effect going forward to the end of the centuries.

I admit that all events are produced by each other—if the past delivers the present, the present delivers the future. Everything has father, but everything has not always children. Here it is precisely as with a genealogical tree; each house goes back, as we say, to Adam; but in the family, there are many persons who have died without leaving issue...

... Therefore, present events are not the children of all past events: they have their direct lines; but a thousand little collateral lines do not serve them at all....

Johann Wolfgang Von Goethe

Johann Wolfgang Von Goethe was a German poet, novelist, playwright, scientist, royal advisor, musician, and philosopher, who lived from 1749 to 1832. He is considered one of the top masters of Western writing, and one of the world's greatest geniuses.

Johann's vast number of novels, poems, and plays had an immense impact on German literature, and made him an important influence on German and European culture.

Writer

Johann's most notable literary work is a dramatic and philosophical poem called *Faust*, which is considered one of the most legendary writings in world history. Johann is also well known for his *Wilhelm Meister* series of novels, and for other novels such as *Sorrows of Young Werther,* and *Elective Affinities.*

Scientist

As a scientist, Johann made important discoveries in the fields of plant and animal life, and is well noted for his book *Metamorphosis of Plants.* Another scientific work of his called *Theory of Colors* is still being studied by modern physicists for the valuable observations it describes. Additionally, Johann's work in discovering human premaxilla jawbones was important in inspiring later studies by Charles Darwin.

Other Stuff

The well-rounded Johann knew French, English, Italian, Latin, Greek, and Hebrew. He translated many writings by foreign authors. He also served as chief minister of state at Weimar for ten years, and directed the state theater and the scientific institutions for several decades. And if that wasn't enough, he was even an accomplished amateur musician who conducted ensembles and directed operas.

Johann Wolfgang von Goethe Quotes

The right man is the one that seizes the moment.

Be he a king or a peasant, he is happiest who finds peace at home.

As soon as you trust yourself, you will know how to live.

The things that matter the most must never be at the mercy of things that matter the least.

Only learn to seize good fortune, for good fortune is always here.

Great abilities often announce themselves in youth in the form of awkwardness and peculiarity.

I respect the man who knows distinctly what he wants.

Common sense is the genius of humanity.

Against criticism a man can neither protest nor defend himself; he must act in spite of it, and then it will gradually yield to him.

One can be instructed in society; one is inspired only in solitude.

Nothing shows a man's character more than what he laughs at.

Progress has not followed a straight ascending line, but a spiral with rhythms of progression and declining, of evolution and dissolution.

Beware of wasting your powers; constantly strive to concentrate them.

Out of moderation, a pure happiness springs.

Every situation—nay, every moment—is of infinite worth, for it is the representative of a whole eternity.

The human mind will not be restricted to any limits.

The unnatural, that too is natural.

The most original of authors are not so because they advance what is new, but more because they know how to say something in a way it has never been said before.

All truly wise thoughts have already been thought thousands of times; but to make them truly ours, we must think them over again honestly, until they take root in our personal experience.

We usually lose today because there has been a yesterday and tomorrow is coming.

Nothing is worth more than this day.

There is nothing in the world more shameful than establishing one's self on lies and fables.

We are never deceived; we deceive ourselves.

Daring ideas are like chessmen moved forward. They may be defeated, but they may start a winning game.

Secrecy has many advantages. When you tell someone the purpose of any object right away, they often think there is nothing to it.

What you can do, or dream you can, begin it. Boldness has genius, power, and magic in it.

Everything in the world may be endured, except for a succession of prosperous days.

Knowing is not enough; we must apply!

One can be very happy without demanding that others agree with him.

Know yourself? If I knew myself, I would run away.

Ralph Waldo Emerson

Ralph Waldo Emerson, who lived from 1803 to 1882, is one the most notable people in the history of American philosophy. For many decades, he was a prominent lecturer, essayist and poet.

Known as the "Sage of Concord," Ralph was like the Tony Robbins (the current self-improvement teacher and guru) of the 1800s. Like Robbins, Ralph preached **personal empowerment**, and he gathered a devoted following of people.

Ralph was also the leading figure of a movement known as **transcendentalism**, which preached about a **level of reality and knowledge** that **transcends** the apparent reality of everyday life.

Life

Much of Ralph's early years were spent reading and studying. When Ralph's father died in 1811, his eccentric aunt Mary Moody Emerson became a close figure in his upbringing, and encouraged Ralph's independent thinking. She also instilled a love of nature in him.

Despite his family's lack of money, Ralph attended the Boston Latin School, and then went to Harvard College on a scholarship. At age 17, he began keeping a journal, which he continued for many decades. In 1826, Ralph began a career as a Unitarian (somewhat related to Christianity) minister, but by 1832 he resigned from his ministerial career.

Shortly later, he began a lecturing career. At that time, a system of lecturing known as the Lyceum had recently started in America, and was beginning to rise in popularity. Ralph quickly established himself among the best lecturers, and later started his own lecture courses to supplement his activity on the Lyceum.

His lectures soon grew into very popular essays and books. He became a very successful author, and also continued giving lectures throughout most of his life.

Main Philosophy and Beliefs

advocated the **integrity, reliance, and empowerment of the self**

proponent of **using imagination, creativity** and **vitality** in one's thinking instead of only relying on reasoning and rational power.

believed in **trusting yourself**.

rejected traditional authority.

believed in the **mystical unity of nature**, and encouraged people to **find "an original relation to the universe,"** and to **harmonize** their souls with the spiritual universe.

believed in a **sacredness of the natural world and humanity**, which he said was the highest source of knowledge.

emphasized **spirituality** over such things as materialism, but he also believed that they both corresponded symbolically. In his first published book, *Nature* (1836), he theorized the existence of the "Me" (the soul) and the "Not-Me" (the external world, including nature and one's body), and felt that the universe is designed to make the "Not-Me" a secondary representation of the "Me."

like other transcendentalists, Ralph was also a leading figure against slavery before the Emancipation Proclamation and subsequent Civil War that freed the slaves

Audience Reception

Ralph initially attracted a predominantly younger crowd, but his lectures and books eventually reached a more diverse audience. However, many of Ralph's views were considered controversial and revolutionary to some groups, and he met some opposition with various institutions throughout his career.

Helping Produce an American Identity and Culture

Ralph was one of the country's most prominent critics, but nevertheless, he held a firm belief in America, and was an integral figure in creating a distinguishable American culture.

He led the way through his writing as he encouraged others to produce a genuinely American identity through literature, music, and art.

Some of Ralph's most notable essays include *Self-Reliance, Nature, The Over-Soul, Spiritual Laws,* and *Compensation.*

Influence on Others

Ralph's influence is very widespread. He had a direct and personal impact on Henry David Thoreau (who is covered in the next chapter of this book), Amos Bronson Alcott, Theodore Parker, Margaret Fuller, and George

Ripley.   Ralph's writings and ideas also influenced the work of major American authors such as Emily Dickinson, Nathaniel Hawthorne, Walt Whitman, and Herman Melville.

Ralph Waldo Emerson Quotes

Nothing is rich but the inexhaustible wealth of nature.   She shows us only surfaces, but she is a million fathoms deep.

It is impossible for a man to be cheated by anyone but himself.

In every man there is something wherein I may learn of him, and in that I am his pupil.

The invariable mark of wisdom is to see the miraculous in the common.

Nothing astonishes men so much as common sense and plain dealing.

Common sense is genius dressed in its working clothes.

There is no one who does not exaggerate!

Money often costs too much.

All great masters are chiefly distinguished by the power of adding a second, a third, and perhaps a fourth step in a continuous line. Many a man had taken the first step. With every additional step you enhance immensely the value of your first.

In skating over thin ice, our safety is in our speed.

Beware what you set your heart upon. For it shall surely be yours.

Society is always taken by surprise at any new example of common sense.

The first wealth is health.

Write it in your heart that everyday is the best day of the year.

That which we persist in doing becomes easier to do; not that the nature of the thing itself is changed, but that our power to do is increased.

Character is higher than intellect. A great soul will be strong to live as well as think.

Nothing is at last sacred but the integrity of your own mind.

So far as a person thinks; they are free.

As long as a man stands in his own way, everything seems to be in his way.

Today is a king in disguise.

Man was born to be rich, or grow rich by use of his faculties, by the union of thought with nature. Property is an intellectual production. The game requires coolness, right reasoning, promptness, and patience in the players.

Real action is in silent moments.

Hitch your wagon to a star.

Without a rich heart, wealth is an ugly beggar.

We have more than we use.

To be great is to be misunderstood.

We acquire the strength we have overcome.

We boil at different degrees.

Talent for talent's sake is a bauble and a show. Talent working with joy in the cause of universal truth lifts the possessor to new power as a benefactor.

We learn geology the morning after the earthquake.

Do not be too timid and squeamish about your actions. All life is an experiment.

Respect the child. Be not too much his parent. Trespass not on his solitude.

I suffer whenever I see that common sight of a parent or senior imposing his opinion and way of thinking and being on a young soul to which they are totally unfit. Cannot we let people be themselves, and enjoy life in their own way? You are trying to make that man another you. One's enough.

Peace cannot be achieved through violence; it can only be attained through understanding.

The secret in education lies in respecting the student.

The man who can make hard things easy is the educator.

It is easy to live for others, everybody does. I call on you to live for yourselves.

Sincerity is the highest complement you can pay.

A man is what he thinks about all day long.

We are as much informed of a writer's genius by what he selects as by what he originates.

We are too civil to books. For a few golden sentences we will turn over and actually read a volume of four or five hundred pages.

I do not hesitate to read all good books in translations. What is really best in any book is translatable—any real insight or broad human sentiment.

There is then creative reading as well as creative writing. When the mind is braced by labor and invention, the page of whatever book we read becomes luminous with manifold allusion. Every sentence is doubly significant, and the sense of our author is as broad as the world.

Excerpts From *Nature*

To the body and mind which have been cramped by noxious work or company, nature is medicinal and restores their tone. The tradesman, the attorney comes out of the din and craft of the street, and sees the sky and wood, and is a man again. In their eternal calm, he finds himself. The health of the eye seems to demand a horizon. We are never tired, so long as we can see far enough.

...

To speak truly, few adult persons can see nature. Most persons do not see the sun. At least they have a very superficial seeing. The sun illuminates only the eye of the man, but shines into the eye and the heart of the child. The lover of nature is he whose inward and outward senses are still truly adjusted to each other; who has retained the spirit of infancy even into the era of manhood. His intercourse with heaven and earth, becomes part of his daily food.

...

To the attentive eye, each moment of the year has its own beauty, and in the same field, it beholds, every hour, a picture which was never seen before, and which shall never be seen again. The heavens change every moment, and reflect their glory or gloom on the plains beneath. The state of the crop in the surrounding farms alters the expression of the earth from week to week. The succession of native plants in the pastures and road-sides, which make the silent clock by which time tells the summer hours will make even the divisions of the day sensible to a keen observer.

Excerpt From *Spiritual Laws*

Each man has his own vocation. The talent is the call. There is one direction in which all space is open to him. He has faculties silently inviting him thither to endless exertion. He is like a ship in a river; he runs against obstructions on every side but one; on that side all obstruction is taken away, and he sweeps serenely over a deepening channel into an infinite sea.

This talent and this call depend on his organization, or the mode in which the general soul incarnates itself in him. He inclines to do something which is easy to him, and good when it is done, but which no other man can do. He has no rival. For the more truly he consults his own powers, the more difference will his work exhibit from the work of any other. His ambition is exactly proportioned to his powers. The height of the pinnacle is determined by the breadth of the base.

Every man has this call of the power to do somewhat unique, and no man has any other call. The pretence that he has another call, a summons by name and personal election and outward "signs that mark him extraordinary, and not in the roll of common men," is fanaticism, and betrays obtuseness to perceive that there is one mind in all the individuals, and no respect of persons therein.

By doing his work, he makes the need felt which he can supply, and creates the taste by which he is enjoyed. By doing his own work, he unfolds himself. It is the vice of our public speaking that it has not abandonment. Somewhere, not only every orator but every man should let out all the length of all the reins; should find or make a frank and hearty expression of what force and meaning is in him. The common experience is, that the man fits himself as well as he can to the customary details of that work or trade he falls into, and tends it as a dog turns a spit. Then is he a part of the machine he moves; the man is lost. Until he can manage to communicate himself to others in his full stature and proportion, he does not yet find his vocation.

He must find in that an outlet for his character, so that he may justify his work to their eyes. If the labor is mean, let him by his thinking and character make it liberal. Whatever he knows and thinks, whatever in his apprehension is worth doing, that let him communicate, or men will never know and honor him aright. Foolish, whenever you take the meanness and formality of that thing you do, instead of converting it into the obedient spiracle of your character and aims.

Henry David Thoreau

Henry David Thoreau is one of the most notable and influential American figures in thought and literature. He lived from 1817 to 1862, and is considered the top disciple of Ralph Waldo Emerson (see the prior chapter for more info on Emerson).

Transcendentalist Movement, and *The Dial*

Like his mentor Emerson, Henry was also part of the transcendentalist movement (see the Emerson chapter for more info). Along with Emerson and several others, Henry contributed to and co-edited the transcendental magazine *The Dial* in the early 1840s.

Life at Walden Pond

Perhaps the most profound part of Henry's life was a two-year span from 1845 to 1847. During that time, he lived primarily in a small cabin that he built on Emerson's land alongside Walden Pond. In Henry's words, he went there to be "living deep and sucking out all the marrow of life," and to "front only the essential facts of life."

While he was there, Henry lived free of materialistic pursuits, and supported himself by growing vegetables and doing odd jobs in the nearby village. He spent most of his time observing nature, reading, and writing. Much of the writing he did was in a journal that he had been keeping since around the age 20. Henry continued writing in his journal for the rest of his life, and the writings in it later became the basis for most of his essays and books.

WALDEN

Most notable among the works he later distilled from those journal entries of that time was a book titled *Walden*, which was not written and published until years later in 1854. In *Walden*, Henry uses his experience at Walden Pond to express his ideas on how people can become attune to the nature of themselves and of the natural world. *Walden* also outlines Henry's transcendentalist philosophy.

Some of the main points and underlining themes in *Walden* include:

Self-Reliance

Inspired by the ideals Emerson and transcendentalism, Henry points out the significance of including **independence** and **solitude** as a part of one's life, and living in with a sense of **self-sufficiency**. However, he also acknowledges the value of **social interaction** and **companionship**.

Henry encourages others to take part in enjoying their **inner selves** and **nature**, and acknowledge their right to be **different**, and to engage in **free thought and action** instead of falling into social conformity. He recommends that people avoid being too needy on other people or on society as a whole, or be overly concerned with social formalities.

Henry also explains his belief in economic self-reliance, and the ideas that one should be in charge of producing for oneself and managing expenditures.

Additionally, Henry deals with self-reliance in the spiritual sense. Transcendentalism teaches that the inner self is the center of reality, and Henry believes that the self-reliant attitude allows him to be **in harmony with nature**, and make it part of his soul

Simplicity

Henry believes in **simplicity** both economically and philosophically. He denounces materialism, and places an importance on minimizing consumer activity. Henry believes in **skipping irrelevancies** and sticking to what is truly **useful**.

Strangely enough, however, Henry's literary style in *Walden* is not very simplified at all.

Determining what is Genuine Progress and Improvement

Henry questions whether advances in technology, economy and territory should really be labeled as progress, especially since he feels that they don't contribute to finding inner peace. He points to the poor labor conditions that were a part of the industrial environment at that time. Henry feels that most types of progress are actually illusions of progress.

Henry focuses a lot of commentary on train traveling. He points out that many people who frequently travel often neglect to explore the wonders and intricacies that lie right in their own neighborhood.

Seasonal Cycles

The yearly cycle of the seasons is a recurring them in *Walden*, and Henry alludes that it corresponds to other facets of universal truth.

Passages from *Walden*

I learned this, at least, by my experiment; that if one advances confidently in the direction of his dreams, and endeavors to live the life which he has imagined, he will meet with a success unexpected in common hours.

What a man thinks of himself, that it is which determines, or rather indicates, his fate.

A lake is the landscape's most beautiful and expressive feature. It is Earth's eye; looking into which the beholder measures the depth of his own nature.

I would rather sit on a pumpkin and have it all to myself, than be crowded on a velvet cushion.

A man is rich in proportion to the number of things which he can afford to let alone.

Most men, even in this comparatively free country, through mere ignorance and mistake, are so occupied with the factitious cares and superfluously coarse labors of life that its finer fruits cannot be plucked by them. Their fingers, from excessive toil, are too clumsy and tremble too much for that. Actually, the laboring man has not leisure for a true integrity day by day; he cannot afford to sustain the manliest relations to men; his labor would be depreciated in the market. He has no time to be anything but a machine.

Let us spend one day as deliberately as Nature, and not be thrown off the track by every nutshell and mosquito's wing that falls on the rails.

I know of no more encouraging fact than the unquestionable ability of man to elevate his life by a conscious endeavor.

Simplicity, simplicity, simplicity! I say, let your affairs be as two or three, and not a hundred or a thousand; instead of a million count half a dozen, and keep your accounts on your thumb-nail.

To the sick the doctors wisely recommend a change of air and scenery.

Why should we live with such hurry and waste of life? We are determined to be starved before we are hungry.

Children, who play life, discern its true law and relations more clearly than men, who fail to live it worthily…

"ON THE DUTY OF CIVIL DISOBEDIENCE"

During his days at Walden Pond, Henry was jailed one night in 1846 because of his conscientious refusal to pay a poll tax that supported the Mexican War. He did that to protest the war, which he believed was part of the US government's efforts to extend slavery.

In 1849, Henry drew upon that experience and published an essay entitled "Resistance to Civil Government," which later was renamed "On the Duty of Civil Disobedience." It is considered one of the most influential writings in world history, and had had a wide-ranging impact throughout the world. It was an importance influence on events such as:

the early British Labor movement of the late 1800s

the Mahatma Gandhi-led passive resistance independence movement in India in the early to mid 1900s

AND

the Martin Luther King Jr. led nonviolent civil-rights movement in the US in the mid 1900s

It also had an impact on:

the Danish resistance in the 1940s

the opposition to McCarthyism in the 1950s

the struggle against the South African apartheid in the 1960s

AND

the US anti-war movement in the 1970s

Main Points of "On the Duty of Civil Disobedience"

recommends that people **prioritize their own conscience ahead of the government's laws**

points out that an individual isn't responsible for devoting himself to eliminating evils in the world, but **is responsible for choosing not to participate in those evils**

calls for a **passive resistance to unfair laws**

encourages people to **refuse to follow unfair laws**, and to **distance and disassociate themselves from unfair governments**

encourages others to use **civil disobedience** in order to **protest** against **unfair government actions**

comments that a government is usually not very useful, and its power from the majority does not necessarily indicate that it has a valid position

comments on the difficulty of trying to reform an unfair government within the unfair government, and argues that voting and petitioning are usually not very effective

criticizes American policy of slavery, as well as its role in the Mexican-American War and its overly aggressive military practices; and concludes that the US fits the criteria of an unjust government

uses Henry's own experiences as an example of how to deal with an unfair government; and points to his protest of slavery by refusing to pay taxes and spending a night in jail, which Henry believes was effective in dissociating himself from the government, and was an effective form of protest

Excerpts From "On the Duty of Civil Disobedience"

It is not a man's duty, as a matter of course, to devote himself to the eradication of any, even to most enormous, wrong; he may still properly have other concerns to engage him; but it is his duty, at least, to wash his hands of it, and, if he gives it no thought longer, not to give it practically his support.

The government itself, which is only the mode which the people have chosen to execute their will, is equally liable to be abused and perverted before the people can act through it.

Witness the present Mexican war, the work of comparatively a few individuals using the standing government as their tool; for in the outset, the people would not have consented to this measure.

I heartily accept the motto, "That government is best which governs least"; and I should like to see it acted up to more rapidly and systematically.

Governments show thus how successfully men can be imposed upon, even impose on themselves, for their own advantage.

There are nine hundred and ninety-nine patrons of virtue to one virtuous man.

Henry's Other Writings and Legacy

Henry's longtime journal was the source for most of his published work, including the aforementioned *Walden* (1854), and his first book *A Week on the Concord and Merrimack Rivers* (1849).

Strangely enough, those were his only two books that were published during his lifetime, and both were out of print when he died in 1862. It wasn't until decades later that Henry became regarded as one of among the most notable thinkers and writers in American history.

Henry lived out his final years knowing he had tuberculosis. He spent much of his time preparing his journals and manuscripts that ended up being published after his death, including *Excursions* (1863), *The Maine Woods* (1864), *Cape Cod* (1865), and *A Yankee in Canada* (1866).

A complete collaboration of his writings, including his journals, was published in 20 volumes in 1906, and contains (among others things) a great deal of outstanding poetry and prose.

Other Activities

Henry was also a naturalist, and was among the first American ecologists and conservationists. Additionally, he was a major proponent against slavery, and is noted for his effort and writings in defense of white abolitionist John Brown.

Henry David Thoreau Quotes

…All Nature is doing her best each moment to make us well. She exists for no other end. Do not resist her. Would you be well? See that you are attuned to each mood of Nature.

The greatest compliment that was ever paid me was when one asked what I thought, and attended to my answer.

As for conforming outwardly and living your own life inwardly, I do not think much of that.

We are constantly invited to be who we are.

Men are born to succeed, not to fail.

Knowledge does not come to us in details, but in flashes of light from heaven

Thought is the sculptor who can create the person you want to be.

Live in each season as it passes; breathe the air, drink the drink, taste the fruit, and resign yourself to the influences of each.

You must live in the present, launch yourself on every wave, find your eternity in each moment.

Our life is frittered away by detail.

It is not enough to be busy. So are the ants. The question is: What are we busy about?

Don't be too moral. You may cheat yourself out of much life so.

To have done anything just for money is to have been truly idle

Most men would feel insulted if it were proposed to employ them in throwing stones over a wall, and then in throwing them back, merely that they might earn their wages. But many are no more worthily employed   now.

Frederick Douglass

Frederick Douglass, who lived from 1818 to 1895, was one of the most notable social reformers in American history. He was an escaped slave who became a leader in speaking against slavery and fighting for African American rights. He believed deeply in the ideas of individual freedom.

Early Life

Frederick was born in Maryland with the name Frederick Augustus Washington Bailey. Although enslaved since birth, at age eight he began educating himself with the help of his master's wife.

At age twenty, Frederick fled from his master and went to Massachusetts, and changed his name to Frederick Douglass to avoid being caught. He had difficulty finding a good job due to his race.

Anti-Slavery Activist and Journalist

In the early 1840s, Frederick began speaking and protesting against slavery and discrimination. In one of his protests, he sat in a train car reserved for white passengers, and was pulled out by force. That protest foreshadowed similar protests that occurred over a century later in the American civil rights movement.

By 1845, Frederick published his autobiography, and moved to England to avoid being discovered as a runaway slave due to his book. While there, he continued his anti-slavery efforts, and was also able to raise enough money from friends to buy his freedom in the US.

He went back to the US in 1847, and started an antislavery newspaper called *The North Star*, based in Rochester, New York. His home was also part of the Underground Railroad—a secret organization that helped runaway slaves escape to freedom.

In the early 1860s, Frederick helped recruit African Americans to fight for the Union Army during the Civil War. He also corresponded many times with President Abraham Lincoln.

In the 1880s, Frederick was a recorder of deeds in the District of Columbia, and later became the US minister to Haiti. In 1855 and 1881, he wrote expanded versions of his autobiography, the last of which was titled *Life and Times of Frederick Douglass*.

Frederick Douglass Quotes

I prefer to be true to myself, even at the hazard of incurring the ridicule of others, rather than to be false and to incur my own abhorrence.

We have to do with the past only as we can make it useful to the present and the future.

Man's greatness consists in his ability to do and the proper application of his powers to things needed to be done.

Find out just what the people will submit to and you have found out the exact amount of injustice and wrong which will be imposed upon them.

Power concedes nothing without demand. It never did and it never will.

I know no class of my fellowmen, however just, enlightened, and humane, which can be wisely and safely trusted absolutely with the liberties of any other class.

To educate a man is to unfit him to be a slave.

To suppress free speech is a double wrong. It violates the rights of the hearer as well as those of the speaker.

Liberty is meaningless where the right to utter one's thoughts and opinions has ceased to exist. That, of all rights, is the dread of tyrants. It is the right which they first of all strike down.

[*On escaping slavery*:] I prayed for twenty years but received no answer until I prayed with my legs.

Excerpts From His Bold and Influential Speech on July 5, 1852, at an Event Celebrating the Declaration of Independence

Fellow Citizens, I am not wanting in respect for the fathers of this republic. The signers of the Declaration of Independence were brave men. They were great men... For the good they did, and the principles they contended for, I will unite with you to honor their memory...

...Fellow-citizens, pardon me, allow me to ask, why am I called upon to speak here today? What have I, or those I represent, to do with your national independence? Are the great principles of political freedom and of natural justice, embodied in that Declaration of Independence, extended to us [African Americans]? ...

I say it with a sad sense of the disparity between us: I am not included within the pale of glorious anniversary. Your high independence only reveals the immeasurable distance between us. The blessings in which you, this day, rejoice, are not enjoyed in common...

This Fourth July is yours, not mine. You may rejoice, I must mourn. To drag a man in fetters into the grand illuminated temple of liberty, and call upon him to join you in joyous anthems, is inhuman mockery and sacrilegious irony. Do you mean, citizens, to mock me, by asking me to speak today? ...

Fellow citizens, above your national, tumultuous joy, I hear the mournful wail of millions, whose chains, heavy and grievous yesterday, are, today, rendered more intolerable by the jubilee shouts that reach them... To forget them, to pass lightly over their wrongs, and to chime in with the popular theme, would be treason most scandalous and shocking...

My subject, then, fellow citizens, is American slavery. I shall see this day and its popular characteristics from the slave's point of view... Whether we turn to the declarations of the past, or to the professions of the present, the conduct of the nation seems equally hideous and revolting...

...[I will] dare to call in question and to denounce, with all the emphasis I can command, everything that serves to perpetuate slavery, the great sin and shame of America! ...

The feeling of the nation must be quickened; the conscience of the nation must be roused; the propriety of the nation must be startled; the hypocrisy of the nation must be exposed; and its crimes against God and man must be proclaimed and denounced.

What, to the American slave, is your 4th of July? I answer; a day that reveals to him, more than all other days in the year, the gross injustice and cruelty to which he is the constant victim.

To him, your celebration is a sham; your boasted liberty, an unholy license; your national greatness, swelling vanity; your sounds of rejoicing are empty and heartless; your denunciation of tyrants, brass fronted impudence; your shouts of liberty and equality, hollow mockery; your prayers and hymns, your sermons and thanksgivings, with all your religious parade and solemnity, are, to him, mere bombast, fraud, deception, impiety, and hypocrisy—a thin veil to cover up crimes which would disgrace a nation of savages.

There is not a nation on the earth guilty of practices more shocking and bloody than are the people of the United States, at this very hour...

...Allow me to say, in conclusion; notwithstanding the dark picture I have this day presented, of the state of the nation, I do not despair of this country. There are forces in operation which must inevitably work the downfall of slavery...

While drawing encouragement from The Declaration of Independence, the great principles it contains, and the genius of American Institutions, my spirit is also cheered by the obvious tendencies of the age.

Nations do not now stand in the same relation to each other that they did ages ago. No nation can now shut itself up from the surrounding world and trot round in the same old path of its fathers without interference. The time was when such could be done.

Long established customs of hurtful character could formerly fence themselves in, and do their evil work with social impunity. Knowledge was then confined and enjoyed by the privileged few, and the multitude walked on in mental darkness.

But a change has now come over the affairs of mankind. Walled cities and empires have become unfashionable. The arm of commerce has born away the gates of the strong city. Intelligence is penetrating the darkest corners of the globe. It makes its pathway over and under the sea, as well as on the earth. Wind, steam, and lightning are its chartered agents. Oceans no longer divide, but link nations together.

From Boston to London is now a holiday excursion. Space is comparatively annihilated. Thoughts expressed on one side of the Atlantic are distinctly heard on the other. The far off and almost fabulous Pacific rolls in grandeur at our feet. The Celestial Empire, the mystery of ages, is being solved...

No abuse, no outrage whether in taste, sport or avarice, can now hide itself from the all-pervading light.

Mark Twain

Mark Twain was a prolific writer who lived from 1835 to 1910. Among his many works, he produced several masterpiece novels that have become legendary in American literature.

Early Life

Mark Twain was born in Missouri with the name Samuel Langhorne Clemens. (Note: I will refer to him as Mark throughout this chapter for consistency). He spent most of his early life in the city of Hannibal, Missouri, which lay along the Mississippi River.

While growing up, Mark soaked up the colorful environment of the steamboat culture he was surrounded in, which included the immense variety of people that came and went along with the boats. It was those rich and diverse experiences that laid the foundation for much of Mark's later writings.

By the time Mark had reached his teens, his father died, and Mark began working in the printing and newspaper industry. By age 16, he began helping his older brother produce a local newspaper, and also contributed various pieces to the publication. A couple of years later, he scoured the country and worked in various print shops.

In his early to mid twenties, Mark trained for and became a riverboat pilot along the Mississippi River, and tremendously enjoyed dealing with the diverse array of people and situations he encountered.

Becoming Mark Twain

By the early 1860s, Mark decided to pursue a writing career, and began using the penname *Mark Twain*, which is a measuring term used by riverboat people. He wrote short stories for various newspapers and magazines, and his writing steadily grew in popularity.

Producing His Most Notable Works

Mark got married in 1870, and published his first novel *The Gilded Age* in 1873. Over the next eleven years, he produced many of his most notable works, including *The Adventures of Tom Sawyer* (1876), *Life on the Mississippi* (1883), and *The Adventures of Huckleberry Finn* (1884).

Most of Mark's books borrowed many various themes and characters from his diverse life growing up and working along the Mississippi River.

Mark's novels were noted for their colorful and lifelike dialogue and characters, as well as their humorous overtones.

Later Life and Career

After a operating a failed publishing company and pursuing a string of bad investments, Mark Twain began a worldwide lecturing career in the 1890s, and gained tremendous international acclaim. His lecturing also made him a very popular character, noted for his white suits, mustache, and cigar and pipe smoking.

Mark also continued writing a variety of novels and short stories. Unlike his earlier works, however, Mark's later works had a more serious tone to them, and also expressed some of his commentary on human nature (which he viewed as primarily selfish), and his various philosophical beliefs.

Over that time, Mark also endured several tragedies in his personal life, including the deaths of his daughter Susy in 1896, his wife Olivia in 1904, and his daughter Jean in 1909. Mark died of heart disease in 1910, and left behind several works that were published later.

Legacy

Mark Twain's work is considered among the preeminent material in modern American literature; and along with the works of several others writers, his writings helped define a distinct American flavor of literature.

Mark's vast volumes of works remain popular today, and have been a tremendous influence on numerous other American writers. *The Adventures Of Huckleberry Finn* is considered by many to be the greatest American novel ever written.

Mark Twain Quotes

The worst loneliness is to not be comfortable with yourself.

Keep away from people who try to belittle your ambitions. Small people always do that, but the really great ones make you feel that you too, can become great.

The secret of getting ahead is getting started. The secret of getting started is breaking your complex overwhelming tasks into small manageable tasks, and then starting on the first one.

The right word may be effective, but no word was ever as effective as a rightly timed pause.

The Pause; that impressive silence, that eloquent silence, that geometrically progressive silence which often achieves a desired effect where no combination of words, however so felicitous, could accomplish it.

Virtue has never been as respectable as money.

There are no grades of vanity; there are only grades of ability in concealing it.

Man will do many things to get himself loved; he will do all things to get himself envied.

A man is never more truthful than when he acknowledges himself a liar.

I am different from [George] Washington. I have a higher, grander standard of principle. Washington could not lie. I can lie, but I won't.

Why shouldn't truth be stranger than fiction? Fiction, after all, has to make sense.

Never tell the truth to people who are not worthy of it.

Honesty is the best policy—when there is money in it.

All generalizations are false, including this one.

Be careful about reading health books. You may die of a misprint.

It's not the size of the dog in the fight; it's the size of the fight in the dog.

We should be careful to get out of an experience only the wisdom that is in it—and stop there; lest we be like the cat that sits down on a hot stove-lid. She will never sit down on a hot stove-lid again—and that is well; but also she will never sit down on a cold one anymore.

We are always too busy for our children; we never give them the time or interest they deserve. We lavish gifts upon them; but the most precious gift, our personal association, which means so much to them, we give grudgingly.

Always do right. This will gratify some people, and astonish the rest.

Clothes make the man. Naked people have little or no influence on society.

I never let schooling interfere with my education.

Giving up smoking is the easiest thing in the world. I know because I've done it thousands of times.

I am an old man and have known a great many troubles, but most of them never happened.

I can live for two months on a good compliment.

There is nothing you can say in answer to a compliment. I have been complimented myself a great many times, and they always embarrass me—I always feel that they have not said enough.

I didn't attend the funeral, but I sent a nice letter saying I approved of it.

I thoroughly disapprove of duels. If a man should challenge me, I would take him kindly and forgivingly by the hand, and lead him to a quiet place and kill him.

Never put off till tomorrow what you can do the day after tomorrow.

Nothing so needs reforming as other people's habits.

October. This is one of the peculiarly dangerous months to speculate in stocks in. The others are July, January, September, April, November, May, March, June, December, August, and February.

Once you've put one of his [Henry James's] books down, you simply can't pick it up again.

A habit cannot be tossed out the window; it must be coaxed down the stairs a step at a time.

The best way to cheer yourself up is to try to cheer somebody else up.

The human race has one really effective weapon, and that is laughter.

Andrew Carnegie

US businessman and industrialist Andrew Carnegie, who lived from 1835 to 1919, is one of the richest people in history, and is also considered one of the greatest philanthropists ever. Throughout his lifetime, he gave away over $350,000,000 to charitable foundations, which at that time period was an enormous amount of money.

Early Jobs and Investments

The way Andrew built his vast fortune makes him a true example of **self-made** wealth. In fact, he and his family were virtually broke when they emigrated from their native Scotland to America when Andrew was about 13.

As a young man, Andrew went through various jobs. He also attended night school, and educated himself by reading and writing. At age 18 in 1853, he began working for the Pennsylvania Railroad Company, and six years later he became the company's superintendent.

Andrew used his money to make many smart investments in bridges, rail mills, railroad sleeping cars, iron mills, locomotives, and oil fields. In 1865, he became convinced that the iron and steel industries would flourish, so he left his Pennsylvania Railroad Company job to manage one of the companies he invested in, called the Keystone Bridge Company.

By 1873, he left that company and concentrated on manufacturing steel, and that is where Andrew built his fortune.

Building a Steel Fortune

Andrew's steel production business was based on **efficiency**. He sought out and adopted any processes, innovations and procedures that could maintain high quality while **reducing costs** and **streamlining operations**. As Andrew's business grew, he took this cost efficiency even further by purchasing coke-fields and iron-ore deposits so he could become his own supplier for those raw materials. He also purchased ships and railroads to transport the raw materials to his mills, and thus vertically **integrated** his entire business.

To ensure that his operations would continue smoothly, Andrew took great care in choosing his executive **employees**. Additionally, in order to ensure that his employees would be more interested in the company's profits than in their own salaries, Andrew made many of them shareholders who had a **direct stake** in the company's success.

Andrew was also an expert in **understanding people**, effectively **directing** his employees' energies into efficient use, and **synergistically combining** people's efforts.

Writer Napoleon Hill (see the Napoleon Hill chapter for more info about him) studied Andrew extensively and wrote about him and his methods. Here are several passages of Napoleon Hill's writings on Carnegie:

> Andrew Carnegie accumulated a gigantic fortune through the cooperative efforts of a small group of people numbering not more than a score.

> Andrew Carnegie easily dominated the steel business during his active connection with that industry, for the reason that he took advantage of the principle of organized, cooperative effort by surrounding himself with highly specialized financial men, buyers of raw materials, transportation experts, and others whose services were essential to that industry. He organized this group of "co-operators" into what he called a "Master Mind."

> Nearly twenty years ago I interviewed Mr. Carnegie for the purpose of writing a story about him. During the interview I asked him to what he attributed his success. With a merry little twinkle in his eyes he said:
> "Young man, before I answer your question will you please define your term 'success'?"
> After waiting until he saw that I was somewhat embarrassed by his request he continued: "By success you have reference to my money, have you not?"
> I assured him that money was the term by which most people measured success, and he then said:
> "Oh, well; if you wish to know how I got my money—if that is what you call success—I will answer your question by saying that we have a master mind here in our business, and that mind is made up of more than a score of people who constitute my personal staff of superintendents and managers and accountants and chemists and other necessary types. No one person in this group is the master mind of which I speak, but the sum total of the minds in the group, coordinated, organized and directed to a definite end in a spirit of harmonious cooperation is the power that got my money for me.
> "No two minds in the group are exactly alike, but each person in the group does the thing that he is supposed to do and he does it better than any other person in the world could do it."

Perhaps no person was ever associated with Mr. Carnegie who knew him better than did Mr. C. M. Schwab. In the following words Mr. Schwab has very accurately described that "subtle something" in Mr. Carnegie's personality which enabled him to rise to such stupendous heights.

"I never knew a man with so much imagination, lively intelligence and instinctive comprehension. You sensed that he probed your thoughts and took stock of everything that you had ever done or might do. He seemed to catch at your next word before it was spoken. The play of his mind was dazzling and his habit of close observation gave him a store of knowledge about innumerable matters.

"But his outstanding quality, from so rich an endowment, was the power of inspiring other people. Confidence radiated from him. You might be doubtful about something and discuss the matter with Mr. Carnegie. In a flash he would make you see that it was right and then absolutely believe it; or he might settle your doubts by pointing out its weakness. This quality of attracting others, then spurring them on, arose from his own strength.

"The results of his leadership were remarkable. Never before in history of industry, I imagine, was there a person who, without understanding his business in its working details, making no pretense of technical knowledge concerning steel or engineering, was yet able to build up such an enterprise.

"Mr. Carnegie's ability to inspire people rested on, something deeper than any faculty of judgment."

...

[*Back to Napoleon Hill's commentary*:] It is obvious that his [*Carnegie's*] success was due to his understanding of his own mind and the minds of other people, and not to mere knowledge of the steel business itself.

The Dominant Steel Company

In time, the Carnegie Steel Company became so well run and cost-efficient, that other steel companies could barely compete with it. Carnegie Steel soon became the dominant force in the US steel industry, and reaped huge profits for Andrew and its other shareholders for many years.

In 1901, Andrew decided to sell Carnegie Steel to JP Morgan's newly formed United States Steel Corporation for a whopping $250,000,000.

The Philanthropist

After the sale of Carnegie Steel, Andrew devoted himself to philanthropic work. He funded educational institutions, libraries, theatres, child-welfare centers, cultural institutions, scientific research, international peace-promoting foundations, medical research, law research, and economic research.

Andrew Carnegie Quotes

There is no use whatsoever in trying to help people who do not help themselves.

Surplus wealth is a sacred trust, which its possessor is bound to administer in his lifetime for the good of the community.

As I grow older, I pay less attention to what people say. I just watch what they do.

The man who acquires the ability to take full possession of his own mind may take possession of anything else to which he justly entitled.

Do not look for approval except for the consciousness of doing your best.

The first man gets the oyster; the second man gets the shell.

A man, to be in business, must be at least owner of the enterprise which he manages and to which he gives his attention, and is chiefly dependent on for his revenues not upon salary but upon its profits.

Men who reach decisions promptly usually have the capacity to move with definiteness of purpose in other circumstances.

I believe the true road to preeminent success in any line is to make yourself master in that line.

Put your eggs in one basket. And watch the basket. That's the way to make money.

No amount of ability is of the slightest avail without honor.

Immense power is acquired by assuring yourself in your secret reveries that you were born to control affairs.

The surest foundation of a manufacturing concern is quality.

The sole purpose of being rich is to give away money.

Whatever your wages are, save a little.

William James

William James, who lived from 1842 to 1910, was an American philosopher, psychologist, writer, and lecturer. He is considered one of the most innovative people ever in the history of psychology and philosophy.

William expressed many ideas concerning topics such as human thought, free will, themes of the universe, and spiritualism. He is most known for roles in a philosophical movement called Pragmatism, and a psychological movement called functionalism.

In accordance with the ideas of pragmatism, William's style was about using free observation and reflection, and not getting caught up in arguing preconceived conclusions.

Pragmatism

William was a leader of pragmatism, which is a philosophical movement based on experience, and used to apply to experience. He wrote a book called *Pragmatism: A New Name for Some Old Ways of Thinking*.

Themes and Outline of Pragmatism:

People should identify and investigate truth through their experiences. They can use this truth to improve experiences, and to gain practical knowledge.

Truth and practical knowledge come from:

actual experience

distinct, discoverable facts or actions

Truth and practical knowledge do not come from:

pure reasoning, or proofs based solely on logic

principles that are fixed, closed, or un-objective

"a priori" methods; i.e. deductive procedures that are made to work by using assumptions, hypotheses, or theories instead of by using experiences and observed facts

speculation

insufficiency

Truth is:

dynamic, not static

an event   (In *Pragmatism*, William wrote: "Truth happens to an idea.")

Truth is equivalent to (or is found in):

what works (i.e. the successful working of an idea)

usefulness

the process of verification (In *Pragmatism*, William wrote: "Truth for us is simply a collective name for verification processes.")

Our idea of anything is our idea of its observable effects.

True ideas:

have practical value and usefulness (i.e. they work when they are applied to experiences, and help us effectively deal with experiences)

can be shown to perform through examination and experiment under the light of doubt (In *Pragmatism,* William wrote: "True ideas are those that we can assimilate, validate, corroborate, and verify.")

have usefulness because of their truth, and have truth because of their usefulness.

can later become false ideas that need to be replaced

have their basis in the practical results from the use of the idea.
(In *Pragmatism,* William wrote: "Truth in our ideas means their power to work." He also wrote: "I am well aware how odd it must seem to some of you to hear me say that an idea is "true" so long as to believe it is profitable to our lives."

True ideas can be based on what is without physical presence, as long as they fit the criteria for truth.

False ideas:

> don't have practical value and usefulness

> cannot be validated and shown to perform

The possible (or a possibility):

> is something that is neither true nor false

> is something that may become a fact.

Emphasis should be placed on the particular instead of the universal

To understand experience, look at the world's totality (i.e. the world's unity as well as its disunity.) See the unity in the world, but don't rely on a philosophy where everything in life can be described by a single concept or system.

Functionalism

William also played a prominent role in the psychological movement of functionalism, which is concerned with the function of mental processes, and how they help an organism adapt and thrive in its environment.

Functionalism was unique when it was introduced because it studied the processes of the mind and how the mind operates, rather than only studying the structure of the mind.

In his groundbreaking book *Principles of Psychology*, William expressed ideas about such things as consciousness, attention, memory, habits, and emotions. The ideas of functionalism are now part of mainstream psychology.

William James Quotes

The greatest discovery of my generation is that human beings can alter their lives by altering their attitudes of mind.

Human beings, by changing the inner attitudes of their minds, can change the outer aspects of their lives

Be willing to have it so. Acceptance of what has happened is the first step to overcoming the consequences of any misfortune.

The deepest principle of human nature is the craving to be appreciated

I have often thought the best way to define a man's character would be to seek out the particular mental or moral attitude in which, when it comes upon him, he felt himself most deeply and intensely active and alive. At such moments there is a voice inside which speaks and says: "This is the real me!"

What every genuine philosopher (every genuine man, in fact) craves most is praise—although the philosophers generally call it "recognition"!

Nothing is so fatiguing as the hanging on of an uncompleted task.

If you believe that feeling bad or worrying long enough will change a past or future event, then you are residing on another planet with a different reality system.

Whenever two people meet there are really six people present. There is each man as he sees himself, each man as the other person sees him, and each man as he really is.

The most immutable barrier in nature is between one man's thoughts and another's.

Action seems to follow feeling, but really action and feeling go together; and by regulating the action, which is under the more direct control of the will, we can indirectly regulate the feeling, which is not.

Everybody should do at least two things each day that he hates to do, just for practice.

A great many people think they are thinking when they are merely rearranging their prejudices.

He who refuses to embrace a unique opportunity loses the prize as surely as if he had failed.

Men's activities are occupied into ways—in grappling with external circumstances, and in striving to set things at one in their own topsy-turvy mind.

Most people live, whether physically, intellectually or morally, in a very restricted circle of their potential being. They make very small use of their possible consciousness, and of their soul's resources in general, much like a man who, out of his whole bodily organism, should get into a habit of using and moving only his little finger.

There is but one cause of human failure. And that is man's lack of faith in his true Self.

Habit is second nature, or rather, ten times nature.

We must make automatic and habitual, as early as possible, as many useful actions as we can

In the acquisition of a new habit, or the leaving off of an old one, we must take care to launch ourselves with as strong and decided initiative as possible. Never suffer an exception to occur till the new habit is securely rooted in your life.

If you want a quality, act as if you already had it. Try the "as if" technique.

If you want a trait, act as if you already have the trait.

It is our attitude at the beginning of a difficult task which, more than anything else, will affect its successful outcome.

To be a real philosopher all that is necessary is to hate some one else's type of thinking.

Philosophy is at once the most sublime and the most trivial of human pursuits.

Man lives for science as well as bread.

I know that you, ladies and gentlemen, have a philosophy, each and all of you, and that the most interesting and important thing about you is the way in which it determines the perspective in your several worlds.

Each of us literally chooses, by his way of attending to things, what sort of universe he shall appear to himself to inhabit.

The art of being wise is the art of knowing what to overlook.

When you have to make a choice and don't make it, that in itself is a choice.

Faith means belief in something concerning which doubt is theoretically possible.

As a rule we disbelieve all the facts and theories for which we have no use.

Belief creates the actual fact.

Believe that life is worth living, and your belief will help create the fact

We never fully grasp the import of any true statement until we have a clear notion of what the opposite untrue statement would be.

It is wrong always, everywhere, and for everyone, to believe anything upon insufficient evidence.

Spiritual energy flows in and produces effects in the phenomenal world.

Why should we think upon things that are lovely? Because thinking determines life. It is a common habit to blame life upon the environment. Environment modifies life but does not govern life. The soul is stronger than its surroundings.

If merely "feeling good" could decide, drunkenness would be the supremely valid human experience.

We want all our friends to tell us our bad qualities; it is only the particular ass that does so whom we can't tolerate.

If you care enough for a result, you will most certainly attain it.

A new idea is first condemned as ridiculous and then dismissed as trivial, until finally, it becomes what everybody knows.

There is no more miserable human being than one in whom nothing is habitual but indecision, and for whom the lighting of every cigar, the drinking of every cup, the time of rising and going to bed every day, and the beginning of every bit of work, are subjects of express volitional deliberation.

Genius... means little more than the faculty of perceiving in an inhabitual way.

We have grown literally afraid to be poor. We despise anyone who elects to be poor in order to simplify and save his inner life. If he does not join the general scramble and pant with the money making street, we deem him spiritless and lacking in ambition.

The exclusive worship of the bitch-goddess Success is our national disease.

A difference which makes no difference is no difference.

The child will always attend more to what a teacher does than to what the same teacher says.

Any object not interesting in itself may become interesting through becoming associated with an object in which interest already exists. The two associated objects grow, as it were, together; the interesting portion sheds its quality over the whole; and thus things not interesting in their own right borrow an interest which becomes as real and as strong as that of any natively interesting thing.

Friedrich Nietzsche

German-Swiss philosopher and scholar Friedrich (Wilhelm) Nietzsche, who lived from 1844 to 1900, is one of the most unique, innovative, and influential philosophers of all time. Many of his ideas have had a profound impact on other philosophers, as well as on many psychologists, theologians, and writers.

Life

Friedrich was born in Germany in 1844. He studied a variety of literature in his early life, and he also loved music and dancing. Friedrich was in the military briefly, but left due to an injury and illness. He later worked as professor of classic texts in Switzerland beginning in 1868. In 1870, during a brief stint as a medical helper in the Franco-Prussian war, he contracted illnesses that continuously affected him from that point on.

In 1872, Friedrich produced his first book, *The Birth of Tragedy*, and continued teaching as he came out with several other philosophical writings, including a collection of essays titled *Thoughts Out of Season*, and a book of aphorisms titled *Human, All Too Human*.

In 1879, he retired from teaching due to health problems, and turned exclusively to a writing career. He lived a rather odd and usually solitary life, and was often in great pain due to his illnesses. Friedrich released such books as *Thus Spake Zarathustra, Beyond Good and Evil, The Genealogy of Morals*, and *Twilight of the Idols*, the last of which was published in 1889. That same year, he suffered an extremely severe mental and physical breakdown, which he never recovered from.

Friedrich lived in severe mental disorder from that point on. He spent time in an asylum and later under the care of relatives. Friedrich died in 1900.

Legacy

Throughout his life, Friedrich wrote about 14 books, some of which were published after his breakdown and after his death. Although his works were generally not popular or widely read before his breakdown, by the time of his death they were well known, and after his death they continued to increased in readership.

Friedrich's ideas and writing style have had a major impact on many people, including writers such as Hermann Hesse, William Butler Yeats, Andre Gide, and George Bernard Shaw; as well as on psychologists such as Carl Jung, Sigmund Freud, and Alfred Adler.

Misconceptions

Unfortunately, Friedrich has often been mistakenly linked to Nazism and Fascism. Much of this is due to various forgeries and changes to his writings that were made by his sister Elisabeth, and due to efforts by Nazi propagandists. Friedrich was actually emphatically against such things as nationalism. Additionally, his writings and behaviors were unquestionably against anti-Semitism.

PHILOSOPHY

The Will To Power, Self-Control, Self-Discipline, and the *Ubermensch*

In Friedrich's time, most people felt that human nature was predominated by the general desire to experience pleasure and avoid pain. Friedrich, however, countered that many people often are often willing to experience pain and tension in order to achieve goals that make them feel competent and **powerful**, and that the desire for feeling competent and powerful is a central theme of **human nature**.

Based on that human need for personal power, Friedrich theorized a concept of human nature he termed the ***will to power***. He felt that life is based on the inherent and natural tendency to feel powerful and grow and expand.

In his books, Friedrich wrote:

> [Anything that] is a living and not dying body... must be a bodily will to power. It will strive to grow, spread, embrace, become dominate—not from any morality or immorality—but because it is living, and because life simply is will to power.

> The will to power is just the will to live.

> He who humbles himself wants to be exalted.

> He who despises himself nevertheless esteems himself as a self-despiser.

Also note, however, that Friedrich did not feel that ruling others is necessarily part of the ideal of the will to power.

In his books, he wrote:

I have found strength where it usually has not been searched for—in simple, non-extreme, and pleasant people [who are] without the least desire to rule. And, at the other end, the desire to rule has often seemed to me an indication of inner weakness. They [*those who must rule others*] are scared of there own enslaved soul, and wrap it in a royal cloak...

In his theory of will to power, Friedrich also felt that people have a desire to gain power over their undisciplined behavior and tendencies. He theorized that **self-control** and **self-discipline**—although commonly labeled as moral or religious self-denial—is in reality a means of attaining a supreme form of power.

In his books, Friedrich developed the ideal of the *ubermensch* (overman), which he defined as a higher person (not through nature, but through development) who has discipline, acknowledges the chaos of the world and accepts / deals with it, develops control of his passions, and channels energy into a higher form of creative expression.

In his books, Friedrich wrote:

I teach you the ubermensch. Man is something that is to be surpassed [/ *overcome*]. What have you done to surpass [/ *overcome*] him?

...[The ubermensch] has organized the chaos of his passions, given style to his character, and is creative.

Some attend to their ideal with timid meekness, and want to deny it. They fear their higher self, because when it speaks, it speaks demandingly.

[A great man is] only an actor playing out his ideal.

The destiny of the higher man is to be a creator.

You shall become the person you are.

Whoever reaches his ideal transcends it eo ipso [*by that very act*].

He who cannot obey himself will be commanded. That is the nature of living creatures.

Let us stop thinking so much about punishing, criticizing, and improving others! ... Instead, let us rather raise ourselves that much higher. Let us color our own example with ever more vividness.

Help yourself; then everyone will help you.

It is very interesting to note that Friedrich's views on pain and some of the above subjects are very different than those of the writer who had the most influence on him—a German philosopher named Arthur Schopenhauer, who lived from 1788 to 1860. Unlike Friedrich, Schopenhauer believed that it is best for a person to base decisions from the viewpoint of avoiding pain at any cost, and that doing so would take care of everything else. (For quotes by Arthur Schopenhauer, see the More People / Quotes chapter of this book.)

Facts and Truth

In general, Friedrich believed that most or all facts / truth are constructs created by people. He also felt that the closest thing we have to genuine facts / truth is often missed by most people.

In his books, Friedrich wrote:

There are no facts, only interpretations.

All things are subject to interpretation; and whichever interpretation prevails at a given time is a result of power and not truth.

Every word is a prejudice.

More depends on what things are called than on what they are.

It matters little whether a thing is true, as long as it is effective.

Actually, all our senses have become rather obscured, because we always analyze after the reason—what it *means*, and no longer what it *is*... More and more, what is symbolic substitutes for what exists...

It is unlikely that a [distinct] duality of cause and effect ever exists; in truth, we are met by a continuous flow, and from it we extract two pieces, just like we perceive motion only as isolated points, and then conclude it without ever actually seeing it.

As important as it may be know the actual motives that caused human conduct up until now, it may be of even greater significance to know the made-up and imaginary motives that people attributed their conduct to.

Belief in truth begins with doubt of all truths in which one used to believe.

More Than Reasoning

In some of his writings, Friedrich also indicated that he felt that the world and mankind is not as based as on reasoning as much as people often say it is.

The misunderstanding of passion and reason: ...[as if reason] existed as an independent being, and not instead as a condition of the relations between different passions and desires; and as if every passion did not have within itself its own quantity of reason.

... Mankind would rather see gestures than listen to reasons.

Opinions

Related to his views on facts, truth, and reasoning, Friedrich also generally felt that people's opinions are sometimes gotten in an almost arbitrary manner, or in a way that is not based on objectively observing experiences of the world.

In his books, Friedrich wrote:

One often contradicts an opinion when what was really unpleasing was the tone it was conveyed in.

One often remains faithful to a cause only because its [*the cause's*] opponents do not cease to be dull.

If you can cause people to assert themselves in favor of something publicly, you have also usually caused them to assert themselves in favor of it inwardly; they want to be regarded as consistent.

Sometimes in the process of conversation, the sound of our own voice confuses [/ *embarrasses*] us and misleads us into making assertions that in no way match our opinions.

It is hard enough to remember my opinions without also remembering my reasons for them!

Public opinion—private laziness.

The struggle of opinions is not what has made history so violent; instead, [it was] the struggle of *belief* in opinions—that is, the struggle of convictions… Passions form opinions; mental indolence allows them to become convictions.

Manipulation

Based on Friedrich's theories of facts, truth, and opinions, he believed that people are open to being manipulated or influenced in certain ways.

In his book, Friedrich wrote:

People will always obey, as long as they can become intoxicated into doing so.

It is not true that "every man has his price." But for every one, there is bait [that exists] which he cannot resist biting. To win over certain people to something, it is only necessary to give it a shine of humaneness, nobleness, caring, self-sacrificing—and thus there is nothing you cannot get them to bite. To their souls, these are the icing… other kinds of souls have others.

People are deceived so much because they are always seeking a deceiver; that is to say, a wine to stimulate their senses. If they can have that, they are quite satisfied with bad bread.

One can entice brave people into doing something by representing it as being more dangerous than it is.

Good and Evil

In general, Friedrich argued that the ideas of good and evil were artificial constructs created by people, often to promote their own self-interests. He felt that labels of good and evil are temporary, and subject to being changed.

In his books, Friedrich wrote:

There are no moral phenomena; [there are] only moral interpretations of phenomena.

Morality is the herd-instinct in the individual.

History deals almost exclusively with wicked men who later become recognized as good men.

Anyone who has overthrown an existing law of custom has always at first been labeled a bad man. But when, as it has happened, the law could not afterwards be reinstated and this fact was accepted, the implication gradually changed.

Order and Chaos

In his book *The Birth of a Tragedy*, Friedrich analyzed Greek culture and used two Greeks gods symbolically to theorize the existence of two human drives. He termed one drive Apollonian—the drive for order; and the other Dionysian—the drive for the chaotic. In his philosophical career, Friedrich leaned towards the viewpoint that in reality, the order sought by the Apollonian drive is an illusion created in order to deal with the universe's true chaotic nature.

In his books, Friedrich wrote:

Whoever observes within himself as into vast space, and has galaxies in himself, also knows how strange all galaxies are. They lead into the chaos and maze of existence.

We have arranged for ourselves a world that we can live in, through the acceptance of bodies, lines, surfaces, causes and effects, motion and rest, form and content. Without these things we believe in, no one now would be able to [deal with] life. But by no means does this constitute a proof. Life is no argument. Among the conditions of life, error might be one.

It is unlikely that a [distinct] duality of cause and effect ever exists; in truth, we are met by a continuous flow, and from it we extract two pieces, just like we perceive motion only as isolated points, and then conclude it without ever actually seeing it.

Man conceives the existence of other things according to the analogy of his own existence... an illogical transmission.

...The concept of *thing* is a just reflex of the belief in the ego as cause. And to my dear mechanists and physicists, even your atom—how much error, how much simple psychology is still remaining in your atom!

Friedrich Nietzsche Quotes

In every real man, there is a child that wants to play.

No man lies as boldly as the man who is angered.

We are like store windows where we are constantly arranging, hiding, or setting out in front the qualities that others attribute to us, in order to deceive ourselves.

There is one thing notable in all great deceivers—their belief in themselves.

Talking a lot about oneself can also be a way to conceal oneself.

We are so fond of being out in Nature because it has no opinions of us.

People that give us their complete confidence also believe that they have a right to ours. [However,] the conclusion is false. A gift allots no rights.

A sick man lives more carelessly when he is under medical supervision than when he is attending to his own health.

During peaceful circumstances, the militant man attacks himself.

Many are stubborn in their pursuit of the path they have chosen...

The same emotions are in man and in woman, but in different *tempi* [pace]. Therefore, men and women never cease to misunderstand each other.

Why does man not see things? He himself is standing in the way—he conceals things.

The best weapon against an enemy is another enemy.

He who would learn to fly one day must first learn to stand and walk and run and climb and dance; one cannot fly into flying.

Let us beware of saying that death is the opposite of life. The living being is only a species of the dead, and a very rare species at that.

And if you gaze for long into an abyss, the abyss also gazes into you.

If life had a final purpose, it would have been reached by now.

Original minds are not distinguished by being the first to see a new thing, but instead by seeing the old, familiar thing that is overlooked as something new.

When we have found ourselves, we must then occasionally learn how to lose and find ourselves again. To a thinker, it is a drawback to always be tied to one person... A person must be able to lose himself occasionally if he wants to learn something from things other than himself.

Simplicity in style is ever the sign of genius. It alone has the entitlement of expressing itself naturally and honestly.

Every really productive thing is offensive.

The man of knowledge must not only be able to love his enemies, but also to hate his friends.

An excellent quotation may spoil whole pages, and even a whole book. It seems to warningly cry to the reader, "I am the precious stone, and around me is pale, worthless lead."

Those who know they are deep strive for clarity. Those who want to appear deep to the crowd strive for obscurity—for the crowd will consider anything deep if it cannot see to the bottom: the crowd is so timid and afraid of going in the water.

The misfortune of penetrating and clear authors is that people consider them shallow, and thus do not devote effort to them. The good fortune of obscure writers is that the reader makes an effort to understand them, and gives them credit for his own determination.

People regard the obscure and unexplainable more seriously than the clear and explainable... Something that becomes clear ceases to concern us.

He who has a *why* to live can bear almost any *how*.

The badly paired [couple] are the most revengeful. They make everyone suffer due to the fact that they are not single anymore.

Whenever I climb, I am followed by a dog called "Ego."

How is it that health is less contagious than disease—especially in matters of taste? Or are there epidemics of health?

It is my ambition to say in ten sentences what others say in a whole book.

Plato [*the ancient Greek philosopher*] was a bore.

The future influences the present just as much as the past.

Wisdom sets bounds even to knowledge.

The more abstract the truth is that you want to teach, the more thoroughly you must seduce the senses to accept it.

Most of the time in married life is taken up by talk.

Insanity in individuals is something rare—but in groups, parties, nations and eras, it is the rule.

There are no institutions that a man should value more than his own soul.

How can anyone glorify and revere an entire people? It is the individuals that count...

Self-admiration is healthy. Has a beautiful woman that knew she was well dressed ever caught a cold?

The desire to display more emotion than one feels taints style.

People that are very beautiful, very good, and very powerful, rarely ever learn the full truth about anything. In their presence, we involuntarily lie.

We ought to fear a man who hates himself, for we are at risk of becoming victims of his anger and revenge. Let us then try to lure him into self-love.

No thinker's thoughts give me as much pleasure as my own. Of course, this does not prove anything in their favor; but [on the other hand,] I would be foolish to neglect fruits that are tasteful just because they grow on my own tree.

...The worst enemy you can meet will always be you yourself; you lie waiting for yourself in caves and woods.

Without myth, every culture would lose its healthy creative power.

Valuing history beyond a certain [excessive] point damages and degrades life.

Excessive virtue can bring a nation to ruin just as much as excessive vice [can].

Hearing what is said about us everyday, or even endeavoring to discover what people think, will ultimately destroy even the strongest man.

Our body is simply a social structure made of many souls.

The one-eyed man will have a stronger one eye; the blind man will have deeper inner sight, and will definitely hear better. To this extent, to me, the famous theory of survival of the fittest does not seem to be the only perspective that can be used to explain the progress of strengthening of a man or a race.

In the past, one desired to acquire fame and to be talked about. [But] that is not sufficient anymore, because the market has grown too big—nothing less than screaming will do.

...One must need to be strong—otherwise, one will never become strong.

Helen Keller

American Helen Keller, who lived from 1880 to 1968, has one of the most extraordinary, amazing, and unique life stories in all of history. Despite being both blind and deaf, she learned to communicate with great effectiveness, and also wrote numerous books and articles.

Early Life

Helen was born in 1880, and at the age of just 19 months, she became blind, deaf and mute due to an illness (probably scarlet fever). As a child, Helen displayed many signs of frustration as she struggled to communicate.

Many years later in her 1905 autobiography *The Story of My Life*, Helen wrote:

> I do not remember when I first realized that I was different from other people; but I knew it before my teacher came to me. I had noticed that my mother and my friends did not use signs as I did when they wanted anything done, but talked with their mouths. Sometimes I stood between two persons who were conversing and touched their lips. I could not understand, and was vexed. I moved my lips and gesticulated frantically without result. This made me so angry at times that I kicked and screamed until I was exhausted.
>
> …
>
> Meanwhile the desire to express myself grew. The few signs I used became less and less adequate, and my failures to make myself understood were invariably followed by outbursts of passion. I felt as if invisible hands were holding me, and I made frantic efforts to free myself. I struggled—not that struggling helped matters, but the spirit of resistance was strong within me; I generally broke down in tears and physical exhaustion. If my mother happened to be near I crept into her arms, too miserable even to remember the cause of the tempest. After awhile the need of some means of communication became so urgent that these outbursts occurred daily, sometimes hourly.

Anne Sullivan

At the age of six, Helen was examined by Alexander Graham Bell (the man who invented the telephone in 1876, and who also was an expert on teaching various skills to the deaf), and he sent her to a teacher at the Perkins Institution for the Blind in Boston named Anne Sullivan.

The relationship between Helen Keller and Anne Sullivan, as teacher-pupil and also as friends, continued all the way until Sullivan's death in 1936.

Under Sullivan's tutelage, Helen quickly made great progress. Within months, she could make associations between objects that she touched and words that were spelled out with finger signals on her palm.

Years later in her 1905 autobiography *The Story of My Life*, Helen wrote:

> The most important day I remember in all my life is the one on which my teacher, Anne Mansfield Sullivan, came to me. I am filled with wonder when I consider the immeasurable contrasts between the two lives which it connects. It was the third of March, 1887, three months before I was seven years old.
>
> On the afternoon of that eventful day... I guessed vaguely from my mother's signs and from the hurrying to and fro in the house that something unusual was about to happen, so I went to the door and waited on the steps...
>
> I felt approaching footsteps. I stretched out my hand as I supposed to my mother. Some one took it, and I was caught up and held close in the arms of her who had come to reveal all things to me, and, more than all things else, to love me.
>
> The morning after my teacher came she led me into her room and gave me a doll... When I had played with it a little while, Miss Sullivan slowly spelled into my hand the word "d-o-l-l." I was at once interested in this finger play and tried to imitate it. When I finally succeeded in making the letters correctly I was flushed with childish pleasure and pride. Running downstairs to my mother I held up my hand and made the letters for doll. I did not know that I was spelling a word or even that words existed; I was simply making my fingers go in monkey-like imitation. In the days that followed I learned to spell in this uncomprehending way a great many words, among them pin, hat, cup and a few verbs like sit, stand and walk. But my teacher had been with me several weeks before I understood that everything has a name.
>
> One day, while I was playing with my new doll, Miss Sullivan put my big rag doll into my lap also, spelled "d-o-l-l" and tried to make me understand that "d-o-l-l" applied to both. Earlier in the day we had had a tussle over the words "m-u-g" and "w-a-t-e-r." Miss Sullivan had tried to impress it upon me that "m-u-g" is mug and that "w-a-t-e-r" is water, but I persisted in confounding the two. In despair she had dropped the subject for the time, only to renew it at the first opportunity. I became impatient at her repeated attempts and, seizing the new doll, I dashed it upon the floor. I was keenly delighted when I felt the

fragments of the broken doll at my feet. Neither sorrow nor regret followed my passionate outburst. I had not loved the doll. In the still, dark world in which I lived there was no strong sentiment or tenderness. I felt my teacher sweep the fragments to one side of the hearth, and I had a sense of satisfaction that the cause of my discomfort was removed. She brought me my hat, and I knew I was going out into the warm sunshine. This thought, if a wordless sensation may be called a thought, made me hop and skip with pleasure.

We walked down the path to the well-house, attracted by the fragrance of the honeysuckle with which it was covered. Some one was drawing water and my teacher placed my hand under the spout. As the cool stream gushed over one hand she spelled into the other the word water, first slowly, then rapidly. I stood still, my whole attention fixed upon the motions of her fingers. Suddenly I felt a misty consciousness as of something forgotten—a thrill of returning thought; and somehow the mystery of language was revealed to me. I knew then that "w-a-t-e-r" meant the wonderful cool something that was flowing over my hand…

I left the well-house eager to learn… I learned a great many new words that day… It would have been difficult to find a happier child than I was as I lay in my crib at the close of that eventful day and lived over the joys it had brought me, and for the first time longed for a new day to come.

Continuing Progress

Helen began learning to converse by finger signal. She also exploring nature and the world with Anne Sullivan, and also learned subjects such as math and science. She later began learning Braille.

Her teacher Sullivan incorporated a wide variety of lessons in a diverse learning experience for Helen.

In her 1905 autobiography *The Story of My Life*, Helen wrote:

For a long time I had no regular lessons. Even when I studied most earnestly it seemed more like play than work.

…I learned from life itself. At the beginning I was only a little mass of possibilities. It was my teacher [*Anne Sullivan*] who unfolded and developed them. When she came, everything about me breathed of love and joy and was full of meaning. She has never since let pass an opportunity to point out the beauty that is in everything, nor has she ceased trying in thought and action and example to make my life sweet and useful.

It was my teacher's genius, her quick sympathy, her loving tact which made the first years of my education so beautiful. It was because she seized the right moment to impart knowledge that made it so pleasant and acceptable to me.

Learning More Skills

Helen was later sent to a teacher named Sarah Fuller at the Horace Mann School for the Deaf in Boston, where Helen slowly learned to speak. She also learned lip-reading by putting her fingers on someone's lips and throat. At that time, such skills were considered totally revolutionary for a person with senses as limited as Helen's.

Schooling Advancement

By age 14, Helen began attending a school for the Deaf in New York City, and at age 16, she went to the Cambridge School for Young Ladies in Massachusetts. At age 20, she earned admission to Radcliffe College, and she graduated four years later.

Writer And Lecturer

Throughout her life, Helen wrote extensively about blindness and deafness in many major magazines. She also wrote many books and essays about her experiences and various other subjects, including *The Story of My Life* (1902), *Optimism* (1903), *The World I Live In* (1908), *The Song of the Stone Wall* (1910), *Out of the Dark* (1913), *My Religion* (1929), *Midstream: My Later Life* (1930), *Journal* (1938), *Let Us Have Faith* (1940), *Teacher* (1955, about Anne Sullivan), and *The Open Door* (1957)

Helen also gave many lectures with the help of an interpreter, most of which were for the American Foundation for the Blind. Her writing and lecturing had an enormous impact on improving treatment and resources for the deaf and the blind

The Miracle Worker

In 1959, Helen's childhood training experiences with Anne Sullivan were made into a Pulitzer Prize winning play called *The Miracle Worker*, and in 1962, that play was made into an acclaimed film.

Helen Keller Quotes

We can do anything we want to do if we stick to it long enough.

I am only one, but still I am one. I cannot do everything, but still I can do something; and [just] because I cannot do everything, I will not refuse to do the something that I can do.

The highest result of education is tolerance.

Although the world is full of suffering, it is full also of the overcoming of it.

Many people have the wrong idea of what constitutes true happiness. It is not attained through self-gratification, but through fidelity to a worthy purpose.

Your success and happiness lies in you. Resolve to keep happy, and your joy and you shall form an invincible host against difficulties.

Smell is a potent wizard that transports us across thousands of miles and all the years we have lived

Literature is my Utopia. Here I am not disfranchised. No barrier of the senses shuts me out from the sweet, gracious discourse of my book-friends. They talk to me without embarrassment or awkwardness.

It is not possible for civilization to flow backwards while there is youth in the world. Youth may be headstrong, but it will advance its allotted length.

The best and most beautiful things in the world cannot be seen or even touched. They must be felt with the heart.

Napoleon Hill

Legendary American writer and philosopher Napoleon Hill, who lived from 1883 to 1970, is consider among the greatest writers in the history of "success literature."

Writings

Napoleon diligently devoted much of his life to studying and analyzing hundreds of notable achievers such as Andrew Carnegie and John D. Rockefeller. From the observation of these people—many of which he interviewed first hand—as well as from lessons he based on his own personal experiences, Napoleon produced volumes of success literature that has a tremendous influence on millions of readers.

Most notable among them was *Think and Grow Rich*, which was published in its first original edition in 1937. He also published many other related works throughout his life, including a mammoth eight volume 1200+ page series released in 1928 titled *The Law of Success in Sixteen Lessons*.

Legacy

Napoleon is considered among the most influential American writers of all time. The ideas presented in his works have been hugely influential on American business philosophy. This business philosophy is often accredited with being an important part in taking America from its severe economic depression beginning in the late 1920s, all the way to becoming by far and away the premiere economic power in the world.

Themes

Napoleon's writings are based on gaining general and economic success, but also go beyond that and describe principles of mind control, psychology, philosophy, human nature, spirituality, and self-discovery.

Napoleon Hill Quotes

Note: All quotes are from The Law of Success in Sixteen Lessons (1928) and Think and Grow Rich (original 1937 edition). A few very minor changes on the original text have been made, such as comma placement, paragraph breakup, capitalization, and punctuation.

...Both success and failure are largely the results of habit!

Some people are successful as long as someone else stands back of them and encourages them, and some are successful in spite of Hell! Take your choice.

Ask the next ten people whom you meet why they have not accomplished more in their respective lines of endeavor, and at least nine of them will tell you that opportunity does not seem to come around their way.

Go a step further and analyze each of these nine accurately by observing their actions for one single day, and the chances are that you will find that every one of them is turning away the finest sort of opportunities every hour of the day.

Charles Chaplin makes a million dollars a year out of a funny, shuffling walk and a pair of baggy trousers, because he does "something different." Take the hint and "individualize" yourself with some distinctive idea.

The fear of criticism takes on many forms, the majority of which are petty and trivial.

If a person has built a sound character, it makes but little difference what people say about him, because he will win in the end.

…[Negative questioners] scoffed scornfully when Henry Ford tried out his first crudely built automobile on the streets of Detroit. Some said the thing never would become practical. Others said no one would pay money for such a contraption. Ford said, "I'll bet the earth with dependable motor cars," *and he did!* …

Let it be remembered that practically the sole difference between Henry Ford and a majority of the more than one hundred thousand people who work for him, is this—Ford has a mind and controls it, the others have minds which they do not try to control… You either control your mind or it controls you…

You have not only the power to think—but what is a thousand times more important still—you have the power to control your thoughts and direct them to do your bidding!

Concentration, itself, is nothing but a matter of control of the attention! … Learn to fix your attention on a given subject, at will, for whatever length of time you choose, and you will have learned the secret passage-way to power and plenty! This is concentration!

We do not have to wait for future discoveries in connection with the powers of the human mind for evidence that the mind is the greatest force known to mankind. We know, now, that any idea, aim or purpose that is fixed in the mind and held there with a will to achieve or attain its physical or material equivalent, puts into motion powers that cannot be conquered.

We have found that any idea or thought that is held in the mind, through repetition, has a tendency to direct the physical body to transform such thought or idea into its material equivalent.

We have found that any order that is properly given to the subconscious section of the mind... will be carried out unless it is sidetracked or countermanded by another and stronger order.

One of the most valuable things any person can learn is the art of using the knowledge and experience of others.

One of the outstanding tragedies of this age of struggle and money-madness is the fact that so few people are engaged in the effort which they like best... [Everyone should] find his or her particular niche in the world's work, where both material prosperity and happiness in abundance may be found.

[John D. Rockefeller] has one quality that stands out, like a shining star, above all of his other qualities; it is his habit of dealing only with the relevant facts pertaining to his life-work...

He not only recognized facts that affected his business, wherever and whenever he found them, but he made it his business to search for them until he was sure he had found them.

Note: For more writings of Napoleon Hill, see the chapter on Andrew Carnegie.

Eleanor Roosevelt

Eleanor Roosevelt, who lived from 1884 to 1962, was a diplomat, social reformer, political figure, peace advocate, and humanitarian. She was widely regarded as one of the world's most powerful and influential women during her time. As the wife of US President Franklin D. Roosevelt, Eleanor was the First Lady of America from 1933 to 1945, and she later served as a diplomat in the United Nations.

Early Life

Eleanor was the niece of Theodore Roosevelt, the 26th US President. Her early life was marked by the tragic losses of both of her parents and one of her brothers, all three of whom had died by the time Eleanor was 10 years old.

She and her surviving brother lived with other relatives. In her mid-teens, Eleanor attended a girls' boarding school near London. She later returned to New York and became active in community service.

Early Marriage

Several years later, Eleanor married her distant cousin Franklin D. Roosevelt, and within the next eleven years, she gave birth to six children (one of whom died in infancy). Franklin became a senator of New York State in 1911, and later became an assistant secretary of the navy, while Eleanor performed the traditional ceremonial roles of a "political wife." In 1917, the US entered World War I, and Eleanor became very actively involved in war-related volunteer work, which gave her a very satisfying feeling.

In 1918, Eleanor was devastated when she found out that Franklin was having an affair with another woman. She wanted a divorce, but Franklin convinced her that he would stop seeing the other woman. She and Franklin remained married, but their relationship lacked intimacy from that point on.

Eleanor's Early Political Involvement

Franklin's political career continued to progress, but in 1921, he was afflicted with polio, which soon crippled him. Eleanor began playing an integral part in his career. She also grew a personal interest in politics, and championed various causes and organizations such women's trade unions, women's voting, and the Democratic Party.

The First Lady

Franklin later became governor of New York City, and in 1933, he became President of the United States.

In her role as the nation's First Lady, Eleanor was extremely active: she pursued liberal causes, conducted White House press conferences for women in the media, represented Franklin and played many of his presidential roles, went on fact finding trips for him, and wrote a daily newspaper column.

Eleanor also went on lecture tours and spoke at various functions about child welfare, housing reform, and equal rights for women and minorities. Additionally, she also performed many bold actions to defend the rights of women, minorities, the underprivileged, and the youth.

United Nations Delegate

When Franklin died in 1945, new President Harry Truman made Eleanor a delegate to the United Nations (UN). She became the chairman of their Commission on Human Rights, and played an integral role in writing and instituting the Universal Declaration of Human Rights.

Eleanor also actively promoted the Democratic Party, and later served as chairman of President John F. Kennedy's Commission on the Status of Women for a year until her death in 1962.

Eleanor Roosevelt Quotes

One's philosophy is not best expressed in words; it is expressed in the choices one makes. In the long run, we shape our lives and we shape ourselves. The process never ends until we die. And, the choices we make are ultimately our own responsibility.

What one has to do usually can be done.

You gain strength, courage, and confidence by each experience in which you really stop to look fear in the face. You are able to say to yourself, "I have lived through this horror. I can take the next thing that comes along." You must do the thing you think you cannot do.

Do what you feel in your heart to be right—for you'll be criticized anyway. You'll be damned if you do, and damned if you don't.

Understanding is a two-way street.

Friendship with oneself is all-important, because without it one cannot be friends with anyone else in the world.

The future belongs to those who believe in the beauty of their dreams.

I cannot believe that war is the best solution. No one won the last war and no one will win the next.

All of life is constant education.

No one can make you feel inferior without your consent.

Excerpts From the "Universal Declaration on Human Rights"

Whereas recognition of the inherent dignity and of the equal and inalienable rights of all members of the human family is the foundation of freedom, justice and peace in the world... Whereas it is essential to promote the development of friendly relations between nations... Whereas the peoples of the United Nations have in the Charter reaffirmed their faith in fundamental human rights, in the dignity and worth of the human person, and in the equal rights of men and women; and have determined to promote social progress and better standards of life in larger freedom...

Now, therefore, The General Assembly proclaims This Universal Declaration of Human Rights:

Article 1: All human beings are born free and equal in dignity and rights...

Article 2: Everyone is entitled to all the rights and freedoms set forth in this Declaration, without distinction of any kind, such as race, color, sex, language, religion, political or other opinion, national or social origin, property, birth or other status...

Article 3: Everyone has the right to life, liberty and security of person.

Article 4: No one shall be held in slavery or servitude; slavery and the slave trade shall be prohibited in all their forms.

Article 5: No one shall be subjected to torture or to cruel, inhuman or degrading treatment or punishment.

Article 6: Everyone has the right to recognition everywhere as a person before the law.

Article 7: All are equal before the law and are entitled without any discrimination to equal protection of the law...

Article 9: No one shall be subjected to arbitrary arrest, detention or exile.

Article 10: Everyone is entitled in full equality to a fair and public hearing by an independent and impartial tribunal, in the determination of his rights and obligations and of any criminal charge against him.
...
Article 12: No one shall be subjected to arbitrary interference with his privacy, family, home or correspondence, nor to attacks upon his honor and reputation...
...
Article 15: (1) Everyone has the right to a nationality. (2) No one shall be arbitrarily deprived of his nationality nor denied the right to change his nationality.

Article 16...(3) The family is the natural and fundamental group unit of society and is entitled to protection by society and the State.

Article 17: (1) Everyone has the right to own property alone as well as in association with others. (2) No one shall be arbitrarily deprived of his property.

Article 18: Everyone has the right to freedom of thought, conscience and religion; this right includes freedom to change his religion or belief, and freedom, either alone or in community with others and in public or private, to manifest his religion or belief in teaching, practice, worship and observance.

Article 19: Everyone has the right to freedom of opinion and expression; this right includes freedom to hold opinions without interference and to seek, receive and impart information and ideas through any media and regardless of frontiers.

Article 20: (1) Everyone has the right to freedom of peaceful assembly and association. (2) No one may be compelled to belong to an association.

Article 21: ...(3) The will of the people shall be the basis of the authority of government...

...

Article 23: (1) Everyone has the right to work, to free choice of employment, to just and favorable conditions of work and to protection against unemployment. (2) Everyone, without any discrimination, has the right to equal pay for equal work...

Article 24: Everyone has the right to rest and leisure, including reasonable limitation of working hours and periodic holidays with pay.

Article 25: ...(2) Motherhood and childhood are entitled to special care and assistance. All children, whether born in or out of wedlock, shall enjoy the same social protection.

Article 26: (1) Everyone has the right to education. Education shall be free, at least in the elementary and fundamental stages... (2) Education shall be directed to the full development of the human personality and to the strengthening of respect for human rights and fundamental freedoms. It shall promote understanding, tolerance and friendship among all nations, racial or religious groups ...

Article 27: (1) Everyone has the right freely to participate in the cultural life of the community... (2) Everyone has the right to the protection of the moral and material interests resulting from any scientific, literary or artistic production of which he is the author.

Mary Kay Ash

Mary Kay Ash is the founder of cosmetics powerhouse Mary Kay Inc. She is one of the one of the greatest and most unique entrepreneurs in business history.

Early Life, and Experiences in Corporate America

Mary was born around 1918 (although throughout her life, she refused to tell her exact age). She got married at age 17, and soon began a part-time job of selling books door-to-door. She was instantly successful at the job, even though America was in the midst of a severe economic depression at that time.

Mary quickly moved on to selling house-wares for a direct sales company called Stanley Home Products, and soon became one of the company's most outstanding performers. Nevertheless, the company frequently neglected her because she was a woman—they underpaid her, under-promoted her, and ignored her ideas.

At age 27, Mary's husband left her, and she began working full time. After many years of giving great performance but receiving poor treatment at Stanley Home Products, in 1952 Mary went to work for an accessories company called World Gift. She proved to be an integral part of the company's success, and was even named to the Board of Directors—however, her ideas were ignored once again because she was a woman.

The Birth of a Business Plan

In 1963, Mary resigned from her job, and also remarried. For several weeks, she began writing notes for a planned book about her negative experiences in the male-dominated world of corporate America.

Her notes also detailed what companies should avoid doing, and how an ideal company should be run that would be attentive to the needs of career women and their families. As Mary wrote and studied her notes, it dawned on her that she had outlined a great plan to start a company of her own, and she decided to go into business.

Starting Mary Kay Cosmetics

Armed with her company plan, all Mary needed was a product! She remembered a fantastic skin product that she had bought for many years from the daughter of a hide tanner. She tracked down the supplier and bought the rights to this unknown product, and then sunk the rest of her $5,000 life savings to launch her company (originally called Mary Kay Cosmetics, and later known as Mary Kay Inc.) and rent a store.

One month before the store was scheduled to open, Mary's husband died from a heart attack. Mary's attorney and accountant both urged her to immediately liquidate the business and recover as much money as she could. Mary refused.

The first year of business was difficult; but by year two, she topped over a half a million dollars in sales! Throughout the next three and a half decades, Mary led her company into becoming one of the most recognizable brands in America, and to sales of over $1 billion a year by the late nineties. She also wrote several books, including *Mary Kay: You Can Have It All* (1995).

Mary died in 2001.

Themes of Mary Kay Inc. and of Mary Kay Ash

Effectively Filling an Untapped Need in the Working World

Mary reflected on her experiences in corporate America, and realized that the millions of working-women in America were not being attended to, and had to struggle and endure poor treatment in the male-dominated corporate atmosphere. Therefore, Mary based her company on this **glaring need** among the female workforce, and built a company that provided an **atmosphere** where women could flourish.

Most importantly, the company culture behind Mary Kay Inc was made to **understand** women who sought good jobs: it understood what women faced in traditional corporate America, it understood the unique lifestyles and needs of women that other companies overlooked, and it understood how to attend to those needs.

Effectively Filling an Untapped Need in the Marketplace

Although Mary built her company around strong products, it was the **unique** and **useful** way she marketed them that really led to her company's outstanding success. To this day, Mary Kay Inc. does not just offer women facial products—it also offers women the unique **service** of an individual consultant.

The consultant personally attends to each customer's needs in the privacy of their own home, and also teaches the customer about skin care. Additionally, the consultant **attentively** checks up on the customers' **satisfaction** with their products and services, and **builds strong goodwill** and **long-term relationships** with them through **regular care and communication**.

Creating a Unique and Premium Company Identity

Mary first chose to make her product containers pink simply so that they would blend well with white bathroom tile. But the color quickly became associated with her company, and Mary quickly **capitalized** on this.

She painted her house pink, and began driving a pink Cadillac. She even **rewarded** her sales consultants with pink Cadillacs after they met certain performance marks. She also rewarded them with other lavish gifts such as extravagant clothes and jewelry, which added to a glamorous company **image**.

Additionally, Mary built her company image and culture around herself. She is a **symbol** of what Mark Kay Inc. represents—her tremendous success story, her pink house and cars, her commitment to providing an environment for women to flourish, her dedication to the company, and her motivational and positive attitude.

Motivational and Positive Attitude

Mary's management style was about **motivation**, and about having a **positive attitude**. She was always focusing **on how and why things can be achieved**. She was constantly preaching various maxims (see the quotes section at the end of this chapter), and she was intent on supercharging the company with this attitude.

Offering Employees a Chance for Advancement

Mary Kay Inc is a multilevel marketing direct sales company, and has always offered sales consultants tremendous **opportunity** for advancement—which is in deep contrast to the companies that Mary worked for before starting her own business. Consultants at Mary Kay Inc have a **direct stake** in their production of sales, as well as in the number of recruits they bring in to join the company.

These policies are all a result of the principles Mary lay down in creating the company decades ago. They have **encouraged** people to work for Mary Kay Inc., and have also encouraged them to perform their jobs well, to recruit new employees, and to help expand the company.

Taking Initiative

When Mary first went into business, she took a very **assertive** step. Her husband had just died, and she poured over her entire life savings to start Mary Kay Inc. Many advisors told her that it would fail; but Mary was convinced that her business plan was sound and that it fit a glaring need—and she stayed **true to her dream**. She was willing to see it through under her own **reliance**, and she built one of the greatest business empires in American history.

Then in the mid eighties, some Mary Kay shareholders (the company had gone public in the late seventies) began questioning many of her methods, particularly the way she gave away pink Cadillacs as an incentive to employees.

Mary believed that doing such things formed the foundation for her company's culture and its motivational tools. Rather than fight it out with shareholders, she opted to take the company private by buying back all of the stock, and thus preserved the methods she felt contributed to her company's consistently strong performances.

Mary Kay Ash Quotes

A mediocre idea that generates enthusiasm will go farther than a great idea that inspires no one.

Fake it till you make it.

If you think you can, you can. And if you think you can't, you're right.

Those who are blessed with the most talent don't necessarily outperform everyone else. It's the people with follow-through who excel.

Aerodynamically the bumblebee shouldn't be able to fly, but the bumblebee doesn't know that so it goes on flying anyway.
Note: Mary was so enamored with the bumblebee that she made it her company logo.

We treat our people like royalty. If you honor and serve the people who work for you, they will honor and serve you.

Pretend that every single person you meet has a sign around his or her neck that says, "Make me feel important." Not only will you succeed in sales, you will succeed in life.

There are two things people want more than sex and money... recognition and praise.

Most people live and die with their music still unplayed. They never dare to try.

Hillary Rodham Clinton

Many people are waiting for the day that a women gets elected as President of the United States…but truth be told, the US has already had a woman co-president in Hillary Rodham Clinton. When her husband Bill ran for president in 1991, Hillary said, "If you vote for my husband, you get me—it's a two-for-one, blue plate special."

And in that campaign, Bill also pointed out, "If I get elected president, it will be an unprecedented partnership…   [Hillary and I will] do things together like we always have."

That "two-for-one" special enticed voters, and helped the Clintons win two consecutive presidential terms.   Bill's idea of an "unprecedented partnership" also turned out to be an accurate prediction for what was to come.

The word "unprecedented" is also a great way to describe the unique and fascinating Hillary, who became Senator of New York after Bill's presidency, and will most likely seek the presidency for herself at some point in the future.

In her various political roles, Hillary has shown that not only can she handle herself in a traditionally male-dominated US political environment, but also that she ranks among the strongest and most assertive leaders that America has ever known.

Early Life

Hillary Rodham was born in 1947, and grew up in Park Ridge, Illinois. She was a standout student, and was noted for her powerful personality. As a young child, she once came home crying to her mother complaining about how another child had bullied her. Hillary's mother told her to march right back out and confront the bully. Hillary did, and that experience is often accredited with starting her assertive nature.

Meeting Bill Clinton

Hillary attended Wellesley College, and then Yale Law School where she became active in political and social causes, and also met Bill Clinton in the Yale library. True to her assertive personality, it was Hillary who approached Bill, and soon established a close relationship with him.

Lawyer and Activist

At Yale, Hillary developed an interest in issues affecting families and children. After her graduation, she served as an advisor to the Children's Defense Fund in Cambridge. She later moved to Arkansas where Bill was starting a political career, and they got married in 1975. In Arkansas, Hillary became a very notable and influential lawyer, while Bill's political career flourished.

In 1978, Bill was elected governor of Arkansas. During Bill's twelve years in the position, Hillary served various public service functions to help disadvantaged children, improve education, and help families. She also maintained her flourishing law practice, and became one of the nation's most well known lawyers.

The First Lady

In 1993, Bill became President of the United States, thanks in great part to Hillary's advisory and her active role in making various public appearances. When Bill's term began, Hillary soon proved to be the most active First Lady in history, and even set up her own office in the White House's West Wing.

She advised Bill, she took an integral role in health care improvement and in numerous women's and children's issues around the world, and she expressed many of her views in a weekly newspaper column. In 1996, Hillary also wrote a best selling book called *It Takes a Village: And Other Lessons Children Teach Us*.

She later had to endure the difficult position of dealing with the attention from Bill's scandalous affair with White House intern Monica Lewinsky, and his subsequent impeachment and Senate trial where the Senate ultimately voted against his removal.

Senator Hillary Clinton

In 2000, shortly after Bill's second term ended, Hillary moved to New York with Bill, and she was decisively elected to the US Senate—the first time ever a woman was elected Senator of New York, and the first time ever a First Lady went on to hold public office.

President Hillary Clinton?

Hillary's strong leadership and popularity with voters makes her an ideal choice as candidate for President of the United States, and it is widely assumed that she will run in the 2008 election.

Character Study

Hillary is a truly unique and fascinating person. Most of her most notable traits can be split into several categories:

Self-Assured and Secure

The bottom line is that Hillary **believes in herself**. No matter what she's taking on, she maintains her **resolve and poise**, and breams with **self-confidence** and **assertiveness**. She also has a very **positive attitude**.

Direct, Authoritative and Assertive Communicator

Hillary **expresses** her nature and what she thinks. She is an **effective communicator** who presents her ideas with an **aura of strength**, and **carries herself with authority and dignity**.

Can Handle Controversy and Criticism

Just the fact that Hillary is an outspoken woman has made her draw criticism from many people. But no matter what the criticism is, Hillary is still **willing to be herself** and **keep it real**.

Additionally, when her husband Bill was in the midst of the much-publicized Monica Lewinsky scandal, Hillary didn't lose her cool. In fact, just years after the scandal, she captured a seat in the US Senate.

Resourceful

The intelligent and cunning Hillary is willing to experiment to **find solutions** and **overcome obstacles**. She is a very determined **tactician**, who remains **persistent** even when things don't seem to be going well.

Tough and Bold

Hillary is very **strong willed** and **tough minded**, and cannot be pushed around. In a world where men traditionally reign supreme, Hillary has shown that she can survive and thrive.

She often **carries an attitude that she is entitled to good things**. Her **self-discipline** and **resilience** have also made her a symbol of strength in American politics.

Creative

Hillary's successes as an author and speaker, as well as her reputation for being an idea-oriented person, are aided by her **creativeness**.

On a Quest For Social Progress

Hillary is truly concerned with the state of the world. She is heavily involved in humanitarian efforts, particularly those regarding efforts to strengthen the family structure and provide a positive environment for children.

Hillary Rodham Clinton Quotes

If you put me to work for you, I will work to lift people up, not put them down.

You can decide to be someone who brings people together, or you can fall prey to those who wish to divide us. You can be someone who educates yourself, or you can believe that being negative is clever and being cynical is fashionable. You have a choice.

There cannot be true democracy unless women's voices are heard. There cannot be true democracy unless women are given the opportunity to take responsibility for their own lives. There cannot be true democracy unless all citizens are able to participate fully in the lives of their country.

The challenges of change are always hard. It is important that we begin to unpack those challenges that confront this nation, and realize that we each have a role that requires us to change and become more responsible for shaping our own future.

Our lives are a mixture of different roles. Most of us are doing the best we can to find whatever the right balance is… For me, that balance is family, work, and service.

The challenge now is to practice politics as the art of making what appears to be impossible, possible.

I'm sick and tired of people who say that if you debate and disagree with this administration, somehow you're not patriotic. We need to stand up and say we're Americans, and we have the right to debate and disagree with any administration

[*In 1992, describing how she will be when she and Bill move into the White House:*] I hope I'm going to be myself.

Excerpts From Her 1996 Speech at the Democratic National Convention

...I decided to do tonight what I've been doing for more than 25 years. I want to talk about what matters most in our lives and in our nation: children and families...

For Bill and me, family has been the center of our lives. But we also know that our family, like your family, is part of a larger community that can help or hurt our best efforts to raise our child.

Right now, in our biggest cities and our smallest towns, there are boys and girls being tucked gently into bed, and there are boys and girls who have no one to call mom or dad, and no place to call home. Right now there are mothers and fathers just finishing a long day's work. And there are mothers and fathers just going to work, some to their second or third jobs of the day.

Right now there are parents worrying, "What if the baby sitter is sick tomorrow?" Or, "How can we pay for college this fall?" And right now there are parents despairing about gang members and drug pushers on the corners in their neighborhoods.

Right now there are parents questioning a popular culture that glamorizes... smoking and drinking, and teaches children that the logos on their clothes are more valued than the generosity in their hearts.

But also right now, there are dedicated teachers preparing their lessons for the new school year. There are volunteers tutoring and coaching children. There are doctors and nurses caring for sick children, police officers working to help kids stay out of trouble and off drugs.

Of course, parents, first and foremost, are responsible for their children. But we are all responsible for ensuring that children are raised in a nation that doesn't just talk about family values, but acts in ways that values families...

... Each one of us has value. Each child who comes into this world should feel special; every boy and every girl.

... One thing we know for sure is that change is certain; progress is not. Progress depends on the choices we make today for tomorrow, and on whether we meet our challenges and protect our values.

We can start by doing more to support parents and the job they have to do. Issues; issues affecting children and families are some of the hardest we face, as parents, as citizens, as a nation…

…Today, too many new mothers are asked to get up and get out after 24 hours, and that is just not enough time for many new mothers and babies… We have to do whatever it takes to help parents meet their responsibilities at home and at work…

You know, Bill and I are fortunate that our jobs have allowed us to take breaks from work not only when Chelsea was born, but to attend her school events and take her to the doctor. But millions of other parents can't get time off…

We all know that raising kids is a full-time job and since most parents work, they are, we are stretched thin. Just think about what many parents are responsible for on any given day. Packing lunches, dropping the kids off at school, going to work, checking to make sure that the kids get home from school safely, shopping for groceries, making dinner, doing the laundry, helping with homework, paying the bills, and I didn't even mention taking the dog to the vet...

My husband also understands that parents are their child's first teachers. Not only do we need to read to our children and talk to them in ways that encourage learning; we must support our teachers and our schools in deeds as well as words…

For Bill and me, there has been no experience more challenging, more rewarding, and more humbling than raising our daughter. And we have learned that to raise a happy, healthy and hopeful child, it takes a family, it takes teachers … it takes business people, it takes community leaders, it takes those who protect our health and safety, it takes all of us. Yes, it takes a village.

Oprah Winfrey

American media personality Oprah Winfrey just might be the most influential person in the world. Millions and millions of people all over the globe tune in to her talk show called *The Oprah Winfrey Show*, which airs every weekday, and has been a phenomenal success for nearly two decades.

Early Life

When Oprah was born in 1954, she was an illegitimate child who was basically unwanted by either of her parents. At a very young age, Oprah's mother left Oprah with her grandmother in rural Mississippi.

For many years, Oprah had no contact with her mother, did not know who her father was, and was hated by most of the kids in her school. She found her main joy in learning and reading, which continued throughout her life. She also had a knack and joy for speaking, especially public speaking. This, too, would be another theme that would continue throughout Oprah's life.

At age six, she went to live with her mother in an apartment in Milwaukee. While there, she received hardly any attention from her mother, who was busy with work, a new daughter, and a boyfriend. Oprah moved to Nashville to live with her father, but after less then a year, she moved back in with her mother.

At age nine, Oprah was raped by an older cousin, and for the next several years, she was sexually abused by several other male relatives and friends of her mother, but remained silent about it. Oprah also became very rebellious at that time, and her mother felt that she couldn't handle her anymore.

At age 14, Oprah was sent to Nashville to once again live with her father, and with her stepmother. They quickly became a very positive influence on her, and they helped form structure in Oprah's life. Oprah's outstanding schoolwork also caused a teacher to send her to a more challenging school.

Building a Career in Broadcasting

While Oprah was in high school, she began her broadcasting career as a newswomen for a Nashville radio station. In 1971, she entered Tennessee State University, and shortly later became a television news anchor for a Nashville station.

In 1976, Oprah went to Baltimore and briefly worked as a reporter and co-anchor for their ABC affiliate. However, she found that objective reporting was not her style, especially since she displayed so much emotion and personal involvement in her reporting.

She soon moved on to become co-host of a local talk show called *People Are Talking*. The show was very successful, and Oprah found her fit as a talk show host.

The Oprah Winfrey Show

In 1984, Oprah went to Chicago to host a struggling talk show called *A.M. Chicago*. She quickly turned the show into a phenomenon, and after less than one year it was renamed *The Oprah Winfrey Show*.

By 1986, the show entered national syndication, and it has been the number one talk show in America ever since. It currently draws over 20 million US viewers per week, and is also broadcast in over 100 other countries.

Other Pursuits

Through her production company Harpo Productions, Oprah owns and produces *The Oprah Winfrey Show* (which she bought the rights to in 1988), and is one of the wealthiest people in the media industry.

Among her other ventures, Oprah has had numerous television and movie roles, runs a magazine called *O*, is a cofounder of Oxygen media, produces films for ABC, is involved in many philanthropic activities, and speaks actively against child abuse.

Oprah and Her Show

So just what is it about Oprah and *The Oprah Winfrey Show* that give them such great appeal all over the world? Here are some aspects of the woman and the show:

Genuine

One thing that really stands out about Oprah is the **genuineness** and **sincerity** that she radiates both in and out of her show. Oprah **brings her heart and soul into her shows**, **keeps it real**, and **expresses her nature**. She is also **sincerely interested** in her show's topics and guests.

Oprah is even willing to honestly **share** her personal experiences to a television audience of millions, in hopes that viewers will **learn** from them. On many occasions, she has shared and expressed details of her past abuses, her former drug problem, and even her weight fluctuations.

Such personal topics would normally not even be mentioned by other talk show hosts or media personalities.

Empowering

Oprah not only preaches **self-empowerment**, she also **exemplifies and radiates** it herself. It was her self-empowering attitude that made her emerge from a frequently abusive and bleak looking upbringing to become one of the most influential people in the world. She developed such a **strong personality** that she was able to climb the rungs of broadcasting very quickly, even though very few African American women up to that time had become a major factor in the media.

Oprah even took everything a step further when she created Harpo Productions a few years after *The Oprah Winfrey Show* debuted, and later purchased sole ownership of the show, making her one of the top businesswomen the world has ever known.

When people tune into Oprah's show, they get a heavy dose of the empowering attitude that have made the woman and her show so successful for so many years.

Positive

Most people frequently encounter negative people in their lives and negative programming on television—which is exactly why so many people have opened their hearts to the **positive oriented** Oprah Winfrey and her show. Even when Oprah tackles negative issues, she **brings out a positive lesson or message** entailed in them.

Educational

When someone tunes in to an episode of *The Oprah Winfrey Show*, chances are that they are going to **learn something useful**. Oprah covers a wide **variety** of **informative topics**, ranging from how to improve relationships, how to strengthen families, instruction for crisis prevention and response, ways for children to protect themselves from danger, and much more. She also builds awareness of topics such as abuses occurring in different parts of the world, child sexual abuse, and many other matters that most people are not likely to know about.

Oprah has also spurned an increase in reading in the world through her show's Book Club segment, which has inspired millions of people to read the books she discusses, and has given a tremendous boost to book readership in America. Oprah's educational focus **stems from her own**

love of learning and knowledge that she has had ever since her childhood.

Fun

The greatest magic of Oprah's show is that it not only is informative and positive, but is also tremendously **entertaining** at the same time. Oprah has proven that you don't need to be focused on negative aspects of the world in order to bring in viewers.

On every show, Oprah isn't just doing a job—instead, she is **enjoying herself** and **being herself**. She has a playful and often humorous approach to her show, but is also willing to get serious during serious matters.

Innovative & Creative

Oprah has always been **willing to try new things** and **be creative**. If there is one thing that can be certain about the future of Oprah's media empire, it is that it will definitely continue bringing in **new innovations** and creative changes. Although not every one of these innovations becomes successful, looking at the big picture, Oprah's show has been getting better and better every year.

When Oprah began sharing painful aspects of her own life with millions of viewers, it was truly something that had never been done. Her innovativeness also made her take on many topics and show ideas that were uncommon before Oprah covered them. Her Book Club was also something very unique, since books had hardly ever been mixed with television up to that time.

And in 1998, Oprah began bringing a life strategist and psychiatrist named Dr. Phil onto her show, who quickly became an immense success with viewers. In fact, in 2001, his segment was spun off into a new show, which was created and is currently produced by Oprah's Harpo Productions.

Attentive

Through her genuine curiosity and interest in what she is doing, Oprah brings an engaging level of attentiveness to her show and her life, and is remarkably **attune** to both the major and minor details of what she is involved in. She **reads people well**, and is **attentive to what her guests are saying**, as well as **what her viewers are thinking and feeling**. Furthermore, Oprah is also **attentive to her own thoughts and feelings**.

Understanding and Synergistic

Oprah is great a building a **harmonious** and **synergistic** atmosphere. She covers **relevant** subjects, **asks good questions** (especially those that most people would want to know about), and **objectively listens** to answers.

And her warm, friendly, and **empathetic** attitude also allows her guests to open up to her. In many ways, Oprah is like a universal trustworthy and understanding friend. She also takes genuine care in what she is doing. This has also helped Oprah build **appeal** that can be appreciated by all kinds of people.

Oprah has also built her media empire by **hiring the right people** to work with her, and by knowing how to build synergy among them.

Trauma Doesn't Traumatize Her

Oprah has certainly experienced a lot of "traumatic" events in her life, but she has not allowed herself to remain "traumatized" by them. Of course, Oprah is not perfect, and certain events may have gotten to her at certain times. But overall, her **positive survivor attitude** has allowed her to **build herself up** from many of her traumatic experiences instead of letting them break herself down.

Oprah Winfrey Quotes

Be persistent in pursuing your dreams.

The whole path to success is not as difficult as some people would want you to believe. The process was the goal. I've taken great joy in the process.

Create the highest, grandest vision possible for your life, because you become what you believe.

I'm one of those people who lives for the moment.

Doing the best at this moment puts you in the best place for the next moment.

You do what you have to do to get through today, and that puts you in the best place tomorrow. (*Ladies Home Journal*, December 1988, Linden Gross)

If you live in the past and allow the past to define who you are, then you never grow. (*Woman's Day*, October 1, 1986; Lyn Torrnabene)

I'm finally ready to own my own power, to say, "This is who I am." If you like it, you like it. And if you don't like it, you don't. So watch out; I'm gonna fly. (*People Weekly,* January 10, 1994; Marjorie Rosen)

What I have learned in my life and work is that the more I am able to be myself, the more it enables other people to be themselves.

Don't live your life to please others.

Never give up your power to another person.

Athletes

Here is a look at the strategies and quotes of some incredible athletes:

MICHAEL JORDAN

Basketball legend Michael Jordan is a true international icon. He is considered by many to be the greatest basketball player of all time. But interestingly enough, Michael was not considered an NBA hopeful in his early teens—in fact, as a high school sophomore, he did not even make the cut for his school's varsity basketball team.

But Michael did not let that deter him from his passion for basketball. He **progressively developed** into a force to be reckoned with on the basketball court, and went on to win six NBA championships (the first in 1991), as well as ten NBA scoring titles.

Michael's extraordinary spirit is fueled by his **love for taking on challenges**, as well as his tremendous **self-discipline**, his **fierceness**, his **persistence**, his **step-by-step method of accomplishment**, and his philosophy of **having fun**.

Michael Jordan Quotes

Just play. Have fun. Enjoy the game.

Once I get the ball, you're at my mercy. There is nothing you can say or do about it. I own the ball

I'm all about challenges and seeing if I can go out and see if I can achieve something. If at the end of the day I do it, great. I f I don't, I can live with myself.

I never looked at the consequences of missing a big shot... When you think about the consequences you always think of a negative result.

I've failed over and over and over again in my life, and that is why I succeed.

You have to expect things of yourself before you can do them.

MIKE TYSON

Mike Tyson is perhaps the most exiting and explosive boxer of all time, and ranks among the legendary heavyweight fighters in the history of the sport. He is also noted for his very bizarre and unique behavior.

Mike was born in 1966, and raised in the notoriously tough neighborhood of Brownsville in Brooklyn, New York. At the age of thirteen, he became a disciple of legendary boxing trainer Cus D'Amato. Cus helped develop Mike's boxing skills, and also became his legal guardian.

In 1985, Mike turned pro at the age of 18, and was soon nicknamed "Iron Mike." Less than two years after his pro debut, he became the world heavyweight champion, and soon garnered a reputation as the "baddest man on the planet" for the vicious attitude he took to the ring.

The seemingly invincible Mike totally dominated and brutalized the heavyweight division in a four-year title reign before suffering his first pro loss in 1990. Many more various trials and tribulations persisted for Mike following the loss, as he had many ups and downs both in and out of the ring throughout his tumultuous life. This included two prison sentences, another title reign, and a long suspension from boxing for biting off a chunk of Evander Holyfield's ear in a 1997 fight. Mike is currently a contender for the title. In his spare time, he enjoys playing with pigeons, listening to rap music, and having romantic relationships with women.

One very notable contributor to Mike's boxing success is the way he uses **strategies that are specifically effective for him**. Mike is considered short for a heavyweight fighter, but he has developed a fight style that makes his height become an asset instead of a liability.

Mike is also well noted for being an outstanding **finisher**, who **capitalizes on opportunity** when his opponent is weakened.

Trial-and-error is another theme persistent in Mike's fight arsenal and his training habits. Mike finds what works against each opponent, and he uses those methods to gain an advantage over them.

And like other great boxers, much of Mike's success is dependent on how he is **responsive** to what his opponent does.

Mike Tyson Quotes

I have certain objectives, and I'm going to fulfill them.

I can deal with adversity.

I'm scared every time I go into the ring, but it's how you handle it. What you have to do is plant your feet, bite down on your mouthpiece and say "let's go."

There are nine million people who see me in the ring and hate my guts. Most of them are white. That's okay. Just spell my name right.

I'm Mike Tyson, and there is no one like me.

Everyone has a game plan until you get hit in the mouth.

I'm the best ever. I'm the most brutal and vicious and most ruthless champion there has ever been. No one can stop me... There's never been anyone like me... My style is impetuous, my defense is impregnable, and I'm just ferocious. I want his heart!

Am I an animal? If necessary—it depends on what situation am I in, what situation am I in to be an animal.

But how can somebody truly love a guy like me that has all this money? No, really, really, how could you ever get to know me in spite of everything I possess?

The one thing I know, everyone respects the true person and everyone's not true with themselves.

Fear is your best friend or your worst enemy. It's like fire. If you can control it, it can cook for you; it can heat your house. If you can't control it, it will burn everything around you and destroy you. If you can control your fear, it makes you more alert, like a deer coming across the lawn.
Note: This quote is also attributed to Tyson's former trainer Cus D'Amato.

WILMA RUDOLPH

Track legend Wilma Rudolph, who lived from 1940 to 1994, has one of sports' most incredible life stories. Born prematurely at under five pounds, she spent most of her childhood dealing with various ailments—pneumonia, scarlet fever, and then polio, which restricted the use of her left leg.

Many doctors wondered if Wilma would ever be able to walk normally. She hobbled around on leg braces as a child. She could not join the other kids in their activities, and was also home schooled, since her local school required that students be able to walk in order to attend.

Wilma grew up in a large family that was low on money, but high on morale and support. They all helped her with her numerous treatments, but none of them seemed to work. However, Wilma remained determined to escape her condition. At age nine, she finally took off her leg braces and began walking.

She continued to improve, and by age 11, she set a basketball hoop in her yard and grew very passionate about the game. She later became a high school basketball star and track standout. Wilma's incredible speed soon took her to the top of the sports world, and in the 1960 Olympics, she won three gold medals in track (the 100 meter race, 200 meter race, and 4 X 100 meter relay).

Wilma, who was African American, also helped promote racial harmony in America and the world, and was a role model for other African Americans.

Wilma Rudolph Quotes

Never underestimate the power of dreams and the influence of the human spirit... The potential for greatness lives within each of us.

I believe in me more than anything in this world.

BABE RUTH

George Herman "Babe" Ruth, who lived from 1895 to 1948, is almost unanimously considered the greatest baseball player of all time.

Babe began his major league baseball career as a dominant pitcher, who compiled an excellent 94-46 record. However, in 1918, he was switched over to outfielder so he could bat every day and take advantage of his superb hitting skills.

Babe soon revolutionized the game by becoming the first dominant home run hitter. He broke the single season home run record in 1919, and then broke that record three more times. He retired with a record 714 career major league home runs. To this day, only one other player (Hank Aaron) has surpassed that mark.

Babe Ruth Quotes

You just can't beat the person who never gives up.

The way a team plays as a whole determines its success. You may have the greatest bunch of individual stars in the world, but if they don't play together, the club won't be worth a dime.

What do I think about when I strike out? I think about hitting home runs.

OLGA KORBUT

Olga Korbut is an all-time legend in the sport of gymnastics. At age 17 in the 1972 Olympics, she turned heads with her spectacular performance that earned her three gold medals for the Soviet Union, and also displayed many innovative moves that have yet to be matched to this day.

Olga continued her outstanding gymnastics performances for several years, and then added another gold medal to her resume in the 1976 Olympics. She retired from active competition shortly later, but gymnastics enthusiasts still talk about her magnificent performances to this day.

Olga Korbut Quotes

It's better to have a rich soul than to be rich.

Don't be afraid if things seem difficult in the beginning. That's only the initial impression. The important thing is not to retreat; you have to master yourself.

I would like to do what I want to do. I don't want to do what do you tell me to do.

Sports Coaches

Here is a look at the coaching philosophies and quotes of several sports coaching legends:

PHIL JACKSON

The "Zenmaster" (as Phil is sometimes called) uses Zen philosophy (which is covered in a separate chapter in this book) and the ways of the Lakota Native Americans (also covered in a separate chapter in this book) in his basketball coaching efforts. He has been an NBA coach since 1989, and was also an NBA player from 1968 to 1980.

Phil's wizardry at building team **chemistry** and getting the best from his players has helped him win nine NBA championships as a head coach—with many more that are likely on the way.

Although he brings his own unique brand of wisdom to his job, Phil still **respects the individuality** of his players and does not force his ways and personality down their throat. In fact, he is well known for the way he builds and maintains **harmony and rapport** between himself and his players, and how he allows them to **express their natural creative efforts**.

Phil Jackson Quotes

Winning is important to me, but what brings me real joy is the experience of being fully engaged in whatever I'm doing.

Wisdom is always an overmatch for strength.

Approach the game with no preset agendas and you'll probably come away surprised at your overall efforts.

Always keep an open mind and a compassionate heart.

The ideal way to win a championship is step by step.

VINCE LOMBARDI

Arguably pro football's all-time greatest coach, Vince Lombardi compiled a phenomenal career head coaching record of 105-35-6 in 10 pro coaching seasons (9 with the Packers), with not one losing season. He led the Packers to five NFL championships in the 1960s, as well as wins in Super Bowl I and II (this was right before the NFL-AFL merger)

In his coaching, Vince emphasized such ideals as **commitment, will, dedication, preparation**, and **mental toughness**. Vince preached a simple philosophy that stressed **fundamentals** and the importance of blocking and tackling, yet he also brought innovations and trickeration into his game plan as well.

Sadly, Vince died of intestinal cancer at age 57 in 1970. The next year, The Super Bowl Trophy was renamed the Vince Lombardi Super Bowl Trophy—a true testament to his impact on the sport and his tremendous winning ways. To this day, his Packers team legacy and his coaching career are used as a measuring stick for other great teams and coaches.

Vince Lombardi Quotes

Winning is a habit. Unfortunately, so is losing.

It's easy to have faith in yourself and have discipline when you're a winner, when you're number one. What you've got to have is faith and discipline when you're not yet a winner.

You never win a game unless you beat the guy in front of you.

I've never known a man worth his salt who in the long run, deep down in his heart, didn't appreciate the grind, the discipline.

Mental toughness is essential to success.

It's not whether you get knocked down—it's whether you get up.

Confidence is contagious and so is lack of confidence, and a customer will recognize both.

[*Explaining why his game plan was so simple despite his vast array of talented players*:] It's hard to be aggressive when you're confused.

SCOTTY BOWMAN

The coaching style of pro hockey's Scotty Bowman can be summed up in four words: **taking care of business**. This is what Scotty did in his 30 seasons (over a span of 35 years) of NHL coaching that made him unquestionably the greatest coach in pro hockey history. Throughout his coaching career, Scotty was a true **professional** who was focused on **getting to the root** of games and **skipping the irrelevant details**.

Many people consider Scotty to be the winningest coach in team sports history. His NHL coaching accolades include 1244 wins and nine Stanley Cup Championships—the first of which was in 1973, and the last of which was in 2002. He retired after the 2001-2002 season.

Scotty Bowman Quotes

I found out that if you are going to win games, you had better be ready to adapt.

There is nothing so uncertain as a sure thing.

Statistics are for losers.

CASEY STENGEL

(Charles) Casey Stengel was a good baseball player in his major league career lasting from 1912 to 1925, but he is better known for his spectacular managing career, which lasted on-and-off for a span of three decades.

Most notable was his 1949 to 1960 stint with the Yankees where he led them to an amazing seven World Championships and ten pennants. By the latter part of his managing career, Casey was known as "The Old Professor," and his unique types of quotes were labeled "Stengelese."

Casey Stengel Quotes

Good pitching will always stop good hitting, and vice-versa.

The secret of managing is to keep the guys who hate you away from the guys who are undecided.

I don't like them fellas who drive in two runs and let in three.

[*After being fired by the Yankees for being too old to manage:*] I'll never make the mistake of being 70 again.

You gotta lose em some of the time. When you do, lose em right.

It's easy to get the players. It's getting them to play together that's the tough part.

More People / Quotes

Douglas Adams
(1952-2001) British writer most known for the science fiction novel *The Hitchhiker's Guide to the Galaxy* and the Hitchhiker series of books

> Human beings, who are almost unique in having the ability to learn from the experience of others, are also remarkable for their apparent disinclination to do so.

> I refuse to answer that question on the grounds that I don't know the answer.

Andre Agassi
(1970-) American tennis superstar

> You've got to believe you can win. But I believe respect for the fact that you can lose is what you always have to keep in your mind so that nothing surprises you.

Leo Aikman

> You can tell more about a person by what he says about others than you can by what others say about him.

Muhammad Ali
(1942-) Legendary three time heavyweight boxing champion who is arguably the greatest heavyweight fighter of all time

> It's lack of faith that makes people afraid of meeting challenges, and I believed in myself.

Alexander
(356 BC-323 BC) Macedonian ruler and conqueror of a vast empire

> There is nothing impossible to him who will try.

Saul Alinsky
(1909-1972) American social organizer and activist

> Always remember the first rule of power tactics: power is not only what you have, but also what the enemy thinks you have

The greatest enemy of individual freedom is the individual himself.

Woody Allen

(1935-) American movie director, actor, screenwriter, and author; he is most known for such films as *Annie Hall, Manhattan,* and *Crimes and Misdemeanors*

My one regret in life is that I am not someone else.

Some people want to achieve immortality through their work or their descendants. I intend to achieve immortality by not dying.

It's not that I'm afraid to die—I just don't want to be there when it happens.

Life is full of misery, loneliness, and suffering; and it's all over much too soon.

What if nothing exists and we're all in somebody's dream? Or what's worse, what if only that fat guy in the third row exists? (From his book *Without Feathers*)

Fred Van Amburgh

All the advice in the world will never help you until you help yourself.

There is no fool like the fool who will continue to kick the rubbish of his mistakes along the path ahead of him, and then be compelled to stumble over these mistakes a second time.

Dream big dreams, then put on your overalls and go out and make the dreams come true.

The most important wars in history were the result of trivial causes.

Those who know when they have had enough are wealthy.

To have a tranquil mind, a clean, calm, conscientious purpose, a few true friends, good health, a happy home, [and] a sufficient amount saved to guarantee against any embarrassment from want, means that you are wealthy.

Marian Anderson
(1897-1993) American opera singing legend who won the Grammy Award for Lifetime Achievement in 1991

As long as you keep a person down, some part of you has to be down there to hold the person down, so it means you cannot soar as you otherwise might.

U.S. Anderson

One does not decide in favor of one thing without deciding against another. Nothing is ever achieved or gained without giving up something.

Antisthenes
(Lived in 400s BC and 300s BC) Greek philosopher

The most useful piece of learning for the uses of life is to unlearn what is untrue.

Pietro Aretino
(1492-1556) Revolutionary Italian writer

I am indeed a king because I know how to rule myself.

Aristotle
(Lived in 300s BC) Greek scientist and philosopher who had a tremendous impact on Western culture

We are what we repeatedly do. Excellence them, is not an act, but a habit.

All human actions have one or more of these seven causes: chance, nature, impulse, habit, reason, passion, and desire.

It is the mark of an educated mind to be able to entertain a thought without accepting it.

The worst thing about slavery is that the slaves eventually get to like it.

Isaac Asimov
(1920-1992) American scientist and legendary writer of about 500 books

Those people who think they know everything are a great annoyance to those of us who do.

I am not a speed reader. I am a speed understander.

Never let your sense of morals get in the way of doing what's right.

Nothing interferes with my concentration. You could put on an orgy in my office and I wouldn't look up. Well, maybe once.

Self-education is, I firmly believe, the only kind of education there is.

If my doctor told me I had only six minutes to live, I wouldn't brood. I'd type a little faster.

It pays to be obvious, especially if you have a reputation for subtlety.

Susan B. Anthony
(1820-1906) American social activist who lead the way for giving women a right to vote

...The women of this nation [*the United States*] in 1876 have greater cause for discontent, rebellion and revolution than the men of 1776.

It was we, the people; not we, the white male citizens; nor yet we, the male citizens; but we, the whole people, who formed the Union

Louisa May Alcott
(1832-1888) American author noted for children's books such as *Little Women*

Love is a great beautifier.

It takes two flints to make a fire.

Rene Auberjonois
(1940-) American actor known for roles in *Star Trek* and *Benson*

Show me a guy who's afraid to look bad, and I'll show you a guy you can beat every time.

Kenneth Auchincloss
(1937-2003) Writer and editor for *Newsweek* magazine

It is one thing to learn about the past; it is another to wallow in it.

Saint Augustine (of Hippo)
(354-430) Philosopher and Christian bishop

Better to have loved and lost, than to have never loved at all.

Hear the other side.

Miracles are not contrary to nature; they are only contrary to what we know about nature.

To many, total abstinence is easier than perfect moderation.

If two friends ask you to judge a dispute, don't accept, because you will lose one friend. But if two *strangers* approach you with the same request, accept, because you will gain one friend.

The very perfection of a man is to find out his own imperfections.

The words printed here are concepts. You must go through the experiences.

Time never takes time off.

Marcus Aurelius
(121-180) Roman emperor known for his philosophical book *Meditations*

I have often wondered how each person loves himself more than everyone else, yet puts less value on his own opinions of himself than on that of others.

Our life depends on what our thoughts make it.

He who lives in harmony with himself lives in harmony with the universe.

The universe is change.

Constantly observe everything that takes place by change, and adapt yourself to consider that the universe's nature loves nothing as much as changing things that are, and making new things like them. In a way, everything that exists is like the seed of what it will be.

Richard Bach
(1936-) American author of books such as *Jonathan Livingston Seagull*

The simplest questions are the most profound. Where were you born? Where is your home? Where are you going? What are you doing? (From his book *Illusions*)

Francis Bacon
(1561-1626) English philosopher, statesman, and lawyer

Nature, to be commanded, must be obeyed.

A prudent question is one-half of wisdom.

Read not to contradict and confute, not to believe and take for granted, not to find talk and discourse, but to weigh and consider.

Some books are to be tasted, others to be swallowed, and some few to be chewed and digested—that is, some books are to be read only in parts, others to be read, but not curiously, and some few to be read wholly, and with diligence and attention.

Ivern Ball
(1926-) American writer

Most of us ask for advice when we know the answer but we want a different one.

Most of us can read the writing on the wall; we just assume it's addressed to someone else.

Lucille Ball
(1911-1989) American actress most known for her role in the sitcom *I Love Lucy*

One of the things I learned the hard way was that it doesn't pay to get discouraged.

I have an everyday religion that works for me. Love yourself first, and everything else falls into line.

Carl Bard

Though no one can go back and make a brand new start, anyone can start from now and make a brand new ending.

Auguste Barthelemy
(1796-1867) French poet

The absurd man is he who never changes.

Pierre Bayle
(1647-1706) French philosopher

It is pure illusion to think that an opinion that passes down from century to century and from generation to generation may not be entirely false.

Samuel Beckett
(1906-1989) Irish French writer who won the Nobel Prize for Literature in 1969

Nothing is more real than nothing.

Alexander Graham Bell
(1847-1922) Scottish American scientist, vocal physiologist, audiologist, teacher for the deaf, and inventor of the telephone

When one door closes another door opens; but we so often look so long and so regretfully upon the closed door that we do not see the ones which open for us.

Robert Benson

The heart sometimes finds out things that reason cannot.

Richard M. Bergland
(1932-) American scientific researcher

The stuff of thought is not caged to the brain, but is scattered all over the body...

Henri Bergson
(1859-1941) French philosopher who won the Nobel Prize for Literature in 1927

Think like a man of action, act like a man of thought.

There is nothing in philosophy that could not be said in everyday language.

Isaac Bickerstaff
Penname used by Jonathan Swift and also by Richard Steele

Health is the greatest of all possessions; a pale cobbler is better than a sick king.

Josh Billings
(1818-1885) American humorist and philosopher

As scarce as truth is, the supply has always been in excess of the demand.

Lawana Blackwell
Writer of books such as *The Dowry of Miss Lydia Clark* (1999)

Forgiveness is almost a selfish act because of its immense benefits to the one who forgives.

Patterning your life around other's opinions is nothing more than slavery.

Mary Bond

Sometimes the hardest habit to curtail is the habit of trying too hard.

Daniel Boone
(1734-1820) Well-known American frontiersman

I have never been lost, but I will admit to being confused for several weeks.

Napoleon Bonaparte
(1769-1821) French emperor who believed he was totally invincible

An order that *can* be misunderstood *will* be misunderstood.

The only one who is wiser than anyone is everyone.

The best cure for the body is a quiet mind.

The human race is governed by its imagination.

The people to fear are not those who disagree with you, but those who disagree with you and are too cowardly to let you know.

History is simply the version of past events that people have decided to agree on.

Take time to deliberate, but when the time for action has come, stop thinking and go in.

True heroism consists in being superior to the woes of life, in whatever shape they may challenge us to combat.

The surest way to remain poor is to be an honest man.

There is no place in a fanatic's head where reason can enter.

If you want a thing done well, do it yourself.

Never interrupt your enemy when he is making a mistake.

A man will fight harder for his interests than for his rights.

Men are moved by only two mechanisms: fear and self-interest.

Victory belongs to the most persevering.

A celebrated people lose dignity upon a closer view.

Men are lead by trifles.

The herd seek out the great, not for their sake but for their influence; and the great welcome them out of vanity or need.

A leader is a dealer in hope.

A throne is only a bench covered with velvet.

Men are more easily governed through their vices than through their virtues.

There is only one step from the sublime to the ridiculous.

You must not fight too often with one enemy, or you will teach him all your art of war.

The crowd that follows me with admiration would run with the same eagerness if I were marching to the guillotine.

Power is founded upon opinion.

Victor Borge
(1909-2000) Danish-American comedian and piano player

Laughter is the shortest distance between two people.

Christian Nevell Bovee
(1820-1904) American author and lawyer

A book should be luminous, not voluminous.

All men are alike in their lower natures; it is in their higher characters that they differ.

Our first and last love is...self-love.

The passions are like fire, useful in a thousand ways and dangerous only in one, through their excess.

Example has more followers than reason.

Nathaniel Branden
(1930-) Psychologist, psychotherapist, and author of books such as *Six Pillars of Self Esteem*

The tragedy is that so many people look for self-confidence and self-respect everywhere except within themselves, and so they fail in their search.

David Brinkley
(1920-2003) American broadcast journalist who won ten Emmy awards

> People have the illusion that all over the world, all the time, all kinds of fantastic things are happening; when in fact, over most of the world, most of the time, nothing is happening.

> A successful person is one who can lay a firm foundation with the bricks that others throw at him or her.

Charlotte Bronte
(1816-1855) English novelist who wrote *Jane Eyre*

> Feeling without judgment is a washy draught indeed; but judgment untempered by feeling is too bitter and husky a morsel for human deglutition. (From *Jane Eyre*)

Mel Brooks
(1926-) American comedian and movie actor, writer, and director

> I've been accused of vulgarity. I say that's bullsh--.

Larry Brown
(1940-) Pro basketball coach

> Don't be afraid to win.

Les Brown
American public speaker and author of books such as *Live Your Dreams* (1993)

> Someone's opinion of you does not have to become your reality.

> Some people would rather get even instead of get ahead.

> Live out of your imagination instead of out of your memory.

Harry Browne
(1933-) American author and Libertarian Presidential candidate

> You don't have to buy from anyone. You don't have to work at any particular job. You don't have to participate in any given relationship. You can choose.

Jean de la Bruyere
(1645-1696) French writer most known for his book *Les Caracteres de Theophraste, Traduits du Grec; Avec Les Caracteres ou les Moeurs de ce Siecle*

The pleasure we feel in criticizing robs us from being moved by very beautiful things.

There are only two ways of getting on in the world: by one's own diligence, or by other people's stupidity.

The great gift of conversation is less about displaying it ourselves than in drawing it out of others. Anyone who leaves your company pleased with himself and his own cleverness is very well pleased with you.

Generosity lies less in giving much than it does in giving at the right moment.

A person's worth in this world is estimated according to the value he puts on himself.

Two people cannot remain friends for long if they cannot forgive each other's little failings.

Men blush less for their crimes than for their weaknesses and vanity.

You think he is your dupe; but if he pretends to be so, then who is the greater dupe: him or you?

There are three stages in people's lives: birth, life and death. They are not conscious of birth, submit to death, and forget to live.

A slave has only one master; an enterprising man has as many masters as there are people who may serve useful in bettering his position.

Even the most well intentioned of great men should have several scoundrels nearby. After all, there are some things you cannot ask an honest man to do.

William Jennings Bryan
(1860-1925) American public speaker, journalist, and politician

Destiny is not a matter of chance; it is a matter of choice; it is not a thing to be waited for; it is a thing to be achieved.

George Earle Buckle
(1854-1935) English journalist

To simplify complications is the first essential of success.

Robert Jones Burdette

It isn't the experience of today that drives men mad. It is the remorse for something that happened yesterday, and the dread of what tomorrow may disclose.

Edmund Burke
(1729-1797) British politician and political theorist

We must all obey the great law of change. It is the most powerful law of the universe.

Leo Burnett
(1891-1971) American advertising genius

Make it [*an advertisement*] simple. Make it memorable. Make it inviting to look at. Make it fun to read.

George Burns
(1896-1996) American actor and comedian

I'd rather be a failure at something I love than a success at something I hate.

You've got to be honest—if you can fake that, you've got it made!

Everyday happiness means getting up in the morning, and you can't wait to finish your breakfast. You can't wait to do your exercises. You can't wait to put on your clothes. You can't wait to get out. And you can't wait to come home, because the soup is hot.

William Burroughs
(1914-1997) Best selling author and former drug addict

There isn't any feeling you can get on drugs that you can't get without drugs.

Leo Buscaglia
(1924-1998) American self-help guru and author

Too often we underestimate the power of a touch, a smile, a kind word, a listening ear, an honest compliment, or the smallest act of caring, all of which has the potential to turn a life around.

Happiness and love are just a choice away.

To deny change is to deny the only single reality.

(Edward) Robert Bulwer-Lytton a.k.a. Owen Meredith
(1831-1891) British poet and diplomat

Childhood and genius have the same master-organ in common— inquisitiveness.

Lord Byron
(1788-1824) British Poet

Truth is stranger than fiction. (From his epic poem "Don Juan")

Samuel Parkes Cadman
(1864-1936) Christian radio preacher

Earth is the lunatic asylum of the Solar System.

A little experience often upsets a lot of theory.

Saint Cadoc (of Llancarvan)
(Lived in 500s) Welsh bishop

There is no king like him who is king of himself.

Maria Callas
(1923-1977) American opera star

Don't talk to me about rules, dear. Wherever I stay, I make the goddamn rules.

I don't need the money, dear. I work for art.

Joseph Campbell
(1904-1987) American writer on mythology

People say that what we are all seeking is meaning for life. I think that what we're really seeking is an experience of being alive, so that our life experiences on the purely physical plane will have resonance within our innermost being and reality, so that we can actually feel the rapture of being alive.

Albert Camus
(1913-1960) French writer who won the Nobel Prize for Literature in 1957

Nobody realizes that some people expend tremendous energy merely to be normal.

Thomas Carlyle
(1795-1881) Scottish historian

The Present is the living sum-total of the whole Past.

Alexis Carrel
(1873-1944) French surgeon who won the Nobel Prize for Physiology or Medicine in 1912

One must train oneself, by small and frequent efforts, to dominate one's feelings.

Rosalynn Smith Carter
(1927-) American mental health advocate, and former first lady (wife of 39th US President Jimmy Carter)

You have to have confidence in your ability, and then be tough enough to follow through.

Pablo Casals
(1876-1973) Legendary Spanish cellist and conductor

The love of one's country is a splendid thing—but why should love stop at the border?

The child must know that he is a miracle, a miracle that there hasn't been since the beginning of the world, and there won't be another like him until the end of the world. He is a unique thing, from the beginning to the end of the world.

The world today is bad... because people don't talk to the children in the way that the children need.

You must work; we must all work to make the world worthy of its children.

Sebastien-Roch Nicolas Chamfort
(1740-1794) French writer and conversationalist

Most people who put together verses or quotes are like people who eat cherries and oysters: they start with the best, and end up eating everything.

Coco Chanel
(1883-1971) French fashion designer, innovator, and businesswoman

How many cares one loses when one decides not to be something, but to be someone.

Fashion is not something that exists only in dresses. Fashion is in the sky, in the street; fashion has to do with ideas, the way we live, what is happening.

Fashion has become a joke. The designers have forgotten that there are women inside the dresses.

Charlie Chaplin
(1889-1977) Legendary British comedian, actor, producer, director, and writer

I don't believe that the public knows what it wants; this is the conclusion that I have drawn from my career.

(Don) John Chapman
(1865-1934) Religious scholar and spiritual figure

My own habitual feeling is that the world is so extremely odd, and everything in it so surprising. Why should there be green grass and liquid water, and why have I got hands and feet.

Anton Chekhov
(1860-1904) Russian playwright and short story writer

Love, friendship, and respect do not unite people as much as a common hatred for something.

G.K. Chesterton
(1874-1936) English writer and theologian

There is a great man who makes every man feel small. But the real great man is the man who makes every man feel great.

Even among liars there are two classes, one immeasurably better than another. The honest liar is the man who tells the truth about his old lies; who says on Wednesday, "I told a magnificent lie on Monday." He keeps the truth in circulation; no one version of things stagnates in him and becomes an evil secret. (From *The Old Curiosity Shop*)

Shirley Chisholm
(1924-) Politician, first African-American female to be elected to US Congress

In the end, antiblack, antifemale, and all forms of discrimination are equivalent to the same thing: antihumanism.

Agatha Christie
(1890-1976) English writer of detective novels and plays

Every murderer is probably somebody's old friend.

Winston Churchill
(1874-1965) British prime minister and leader in World War II

All men make mistakes, but only wise men learn from their mistakes.

It is better to be frightened now than killed hereafter

There are a terrible lot of lies going about the world, and the worst of it is that half of them are true.

If you have an important point to make, don't try to be subtle or clever. Use a pile driver. Hit the point once. Then come back and hit it again. Then hit it a third time—a tremendous whack.

Democracy's the worst form of government except for all the others.

I always avoid prophesying beforehand, because it is much better to prophesy after the event has already taken place.

Marcus Tullius Cicero
(106 BC-43 BC) Roman statesman

It is the nature of every person to error, but only the fool perseveres in error.

Silence is one of the great arts of conversation.

A person does not have to believe everything he hears.

Mighty is the power of habit.

The wise man knows nothing if he cannot benefit from his wisdom.

Wisdom is not only to be acquired, but also to be utilized.

I believe that even if a thing is not foul in itself, it can become so when commended by the multitude.

Frank A. Clark

Modern man is frantically trying to earn enough to buy things he's too busy to enjoy.

There's nothing that can help you understand your beliefs more than trying to explain them to an inquisitive child.

It's hard to detect good luck—it looks so much like something you've earned.

Arthur C. Clarke
(1917-) English scientist and writer

Sometimes I think we're alone in the universe, and sometimes I think we're not. In either case, the idea is quite staggering.

Space is what stops everything from happening in the same place.

The mind has an extraordinary ability to "see" things that are hoped for.

Claudius
(10 BC-54 AD) Roman emperor from 41 AD to 54 AD

No one is free who is not master of himself.

Bill Clinton
(1946-) 42nd US President

There is nothing wrong with America that cannot be cured with what is right in America.

[*During his grand jury testimony in 1998*:]   It depends on what the meaning of the word *is* is.

Ty Cobb
(1886-1961) Legendary American baseball player known for his ferocious attitude

The great trouble with baseball today is that most of the players are in the game for the money and that's it, not for the love of it, the excitement of it, the thrill of it.

Johnnie Cochran
(1937-) American lawyer most known for his role in defending OJ Simpson

If it doesn't make sense, you should find for the defense.

If the glove don't fit, you must acquit.

Jean Cocteau
(1889-1963) French writer, artist, film director, and actor

The extreme limit of wisdom—that's what the public calls madness.

What the public criticizes in you, cultivate. It is you.

Nearly all societies have the instinct is to lock up anybody who is truly free. First, society begins by trying to beat you up. If this fails, they try to poison you. If this fails too, they finish by loading honors on your head.

Samuel Taylor Coleridge
(1772-1834) English poet and philosopher

Common sense in an uncommon degree is what the world calls wisdom.

To sentence a man of true genius to the drudgery of a school is to put a racehorse on a treadmill.

To most men, experience is like the stern lights of a ship which illumine only the track it has passed.

John Churton Collins
(1848-1908) English writer

To profit from good advice requires more wisdom than to give it.

Charles C. Colton

All excess brings on its own punishments.

Bill Cosby
(1937-) American actor, comedian, and producer most known for his roles in *I Spy* and *The Cosby Show*

I don't know the key to success, but the key to failure is trying to please everybody.

Frank Crane

It takes so little to make people happy. Just a touch, if we know how to give it, just a word fitly spoken, a slight readjustment of some bolt or pin or bearing in the delicate machinery of a soul.

Salvador Dali
(1904-1989) Spanish Surrealist artist

I do not take drugs—I am drugs.

Cus D'Amato
(1908-1985) Legendary boxing trainer most known for his roles training Floyd Patterson, Jose Torres, and Mike Tyson

> The punch that knocks a man out is the punch that he doesn't see. Have you ever seen the pea in the shell game? [*A street gambling game where the dealer puts a pea under one of three shells and shuffles the shells, and then the player has to guess which shell the pea is under*] The man who works the game must have the ability to direct attention to the wrong area. That's what happens in boxing.

Frank Dane

> The great American novel has not only already been written—it has already been rejected.

Dante
(1265-1321) Italian writer and philosopher

> I love to doubt as well as know.

Charles Darwin
(1809-1882) Legendary English naturalist and scientist who wrote the groundbreaking book *On the Origin of Species by Means of Natural Selection*

> It is not the strongest of the species that survive, nor the most intelligent, but the one most responsive to change.

> The highest possible stage in moral culture is when we recognize that we ought to control our thoughts.

Ram Dass (a.k.a. Richard Alpert)
(1931-) American spiritual leader

> When you are already in Detroit, you don't have to take a bus to get there.

> The spiritual journey is individual, highly personal. It can't be organized or regulated. It isn't true that everyone should follow one path. Listen to your own truth.

Laura Davies
(1963-) LPGA golf star

You've got to put those bad shots behind you. That's why some people win a lot more than others. They have the ability to forget about a bad swing and think about the good stuff.

Miles Davis
(1926-1991) Legendary American jazz musician

I'll play it first and tell you what it is later.

Rene Descartes
(1596-1650) Influential French philosopher, mathematician, and scientist

I think therefore I am.

Except our own thoughts, there is nothing absolutely in our power.

Whenever anyone has offended me, I try to raise my soul so high that the offense cannot reach it.

Divide each difficulty into as many parts as is practicable and necessary to resolve it.

To be a real seeker after truth, it is necessary that at least once in your life you doubt, as far as possible, all things.

John Dewey
(1859-1952) American philosopher, psychologist, and educator

The deepest human urge is the desire to be important.

Princess Diana a.k.a. Diana Frances Spencer
(1961-1997) English princess and social activist

Only do what your heart tells you.

I think the biggest disease the world suffers from in this day and age is the disease of people feeling unloved. I know that I can give love for a minute, for half an hour, for a day, for a month, but I can give. I am very happy to do that; I want to do that.

Charles Dickens
(1812-1870) Legendary British novelist who wrote books such as *Oliver Twist*, *A Christmas Carol*, and *A Tale of Two Cities*

A wonderful fact to reflect upon, that every human creature is constituted to be that profound secret and mystery to every other.

It was the best of times, it was the worst of times, it was the age of wisdom, it was the age of foolishness, it was the epoch of belief, it was the epoch of incredulity, it was the season of Light, it was the season of Darkness, it was the spring of hope, it was the winter of despair, we had everything before us, we had nothing before us, we were all going direct to Heaven, we were all going direct the other way—in short, the period was so far like the present period, that some of its noisiest authorities insisted on its being received, for good or for evil, in the superlative degree of comparison only. (From the beginning of his novel *A Tale of Two Cities*)

Walt Disney
(1901-1966) American animator and cofounder of Walt Disney Productions

If you can dream it, you can do it.

Benjamin Disraeli
(1804-1881) British statesman and writer

There are three kinds of lies: lies, damned lies, and statistics.

The secret of success in life is for a man to be ready for his opportunity when it comes.

Shannon Doherty
(1971-) American actress

To be a b---- or not to be a b----, that is the question. (*From her role as Brenda Walsh on the television show Beverly Hills 90210*)

Flirting is a universal language. (*as Brenda Walsh on Beverly Hills 90210*)

(Sir) Arthur Conan Doyle
(1859-1930) Scottish novelist most known for his detective character Sherlock Holmes

There is nothing as deceptive as an obvious fact.

Peter F. Drucker
(1909-) Austrian American business consultant and writer

The entrepreneur always searches for change, responds to it, and exploits it as an opportunity.

The most important thing in communication is to hear what isn't being said.

The successful person places more attention on doing the right thing rather than doing things right.

Until we can manage time, we can manage nothing else.

Hansell B. Duckett

What this country needs is more free speech worth listening to.

David Dunham

Efficiency is intelligent laziness.

Will Durant
(1885-1981) Best-selling American writer on philosophy and history

It may be true that you can't fool all the people all the time, but you can fool enough of them to rule a large country.

History is so indifferently rich, that a case for almost any conclusion from it can be made by a selection of instances. (From *The Lessons of History* by Will and Ariel Durant)

Shirin Ebadi
(1947-) Iranian lawyer and social rights activist who won the Nobel Peace Prize in 2003

We must not enable anyone to impose his personal view regarding religion on others by force, oppression, or pressure.

I maintain that nothing useful and lasting can emerge from violence.

Meister Eckhart
(Lived in 1200s and 1300s) German mystic and theologian

There exists only the present instant... a Now which always and without end is itself new. There is no yesterday, or any tomorrow, but only Now, as it was a thousand years ago, and as it will be a thousand years later.

Thomas Edison
(1847-1931) Legendary American inventor whose numerous inventions had a profound impact on technological innovations and the widespread use of electricity

To invent, you need a good imagination and a pile of junk.

If we all did the things we are capable of doing, we would literally astound ourselves.

Albert Einstein
(1879-1955) German Swiss American physicist who is recognized as one of the greatest scientists of all time

Imagination is more important than knowledge.

Everything should be made as simple as possible, but not simpler.

It should be possible to explain the laws of physics to a barmaid.

The important thing is not to stop questioning. Curiosity has its own reason for existing.

The attempt to combine wisdom and power has only rarely been successful, and then only for a short while.

Edwin Elliot

By being yourself, you put something wonderful in the world that was not there before.

Havelock Ellis
(1859-1839) British sex researcher and woman's right advocate

Dreams are real while they last. Can we say more of life?

Nathaniel Emmons

Habit is either the best of servants or the worst of masters.

Epictetus
(Lived in c500s BC) Greek potter and artist

No man is free who is not master of himself.

Is freedom anything else than the power of living as we choose?

Desiderus Erasmus
(1469-1536) Dutch priest and reformer

The fox has many tricks. The hedgehog has but one—but that is the best of all.

Milton Erickson
(1901-1980) American psychiatrist, psychologist, and hypnotherapist

Every person's map of the world is as unique as their thumbprint. There are no two people alike. No two people who understand the same sentence the same way... So in dealing with people, you try not to fit them to your concept of what they should be.

M.C. Escher
(1898-1972) Dutch artist known for his use of optical illusions

He who wonders discovers that this in itself is wonder.

Douglas Everett

There are some people who live in a dream world, and there are some who face reality; and then there are those who turn one into the other.

Harvey Fierstein
(1954-) American actor

Never be bullied into silence. Never allow yourself to be made a victim. Accept no one's definition of your life. Define yourself.

F. Scott Fitzgerald
(1896-1940) American writer of novels and short stories; his most noted work is *The Great Gatsby*

The test of a first-rate intelligence is the ability to hold two opposed ideas in mind at the same time and still retain the ability to function.

Either you think—or else others have to think for you and take power from you, pervert and discipline your natural tastes, civilize and sterilize you.

Genius is the ability to put into effect what is in your mind.

Vitality shows in not only the ability to persist but the ability to start over.

George Fernandez

One should learn from the past, but one should not live in the past. My concern is to look to the future, learn from the past, and deal with the present.

Lisa Fernandez
(1971-) Legendary softball player

I make my weaknesses my strengths and my strengths stronger.

Jane Fonda
(1937-) American actress and fitness personality

When you can't remember why you're hurt, that's when you're healed.

B.C. Forbes
(1880-1954) Scottish American publisher, founder of *Forbes* magazine

Real riches are the riches possessed inside.

Without self-respect there can be no genuine success. Success won at the cost of self-respect is not success—for what shall it profit a man if he gains the whole world and loses his own self-respect.

Malcolm S. Forbes
(1917-1990) Publisher of *Forbes* magazine, politician, and businessman

How to succeed: try hard enough. How to fail: try too hard

The biggest mistake people make in life is not trying to make a living at doing what they most enjoy.

People who matter are most aware that everyone else does, too.

Let your children go if you want to keep them.

Too many people overvalue what they are not and undervalue what they are.

Henry Ford
(1863-1947) American businessman, industrialist and engineer who co-formed Ford Motor Company; he is most noted for his manufacturing efficiency innovations and his eccentric business methods

There isn't a person anywhere that isn't capable of doing more than he thinks he can.

It doesn't matter to me if a man is from Harvard or Sing Sing [*a prison in New York*]. We hire the man, not his history.

Most people spend more time and energy going around problems than in trying to solve them.

When I can't handle events, I let them handle themselves.

If there is any one secret to success, it lies in the ability to get the other person's point of view and see things from his angle as well as yours.

Nothing is particularly hard if you divide it into small jobs.

There are no big problems; there are just a lot of little problems.

My best friend is the one who brings out the best in me.

One of the greatest discoveries a man makes, one of his great surprises, is to find he can do what he was afraid he couldn't do.

Many people think that by hoarding money they are gaining safety for themselves. If money is your hope for independence you will never have it. The only real security that a person can have in this world is a reserve of knowledge, experience, and ability. Without these qualities, money is practically useless.

A business absolutely devoted to service will have only one worry about profits. They will be embarrassingly large.

Whether you think you can or you can't, you're right!

I cannot discover that anyone knows enough to say definitely what is and what is not possible.

It is not the employer who pays wages—he only handles the money. It is the product and customer who pay the wages.

Business is never so healthy as when, like a chicken, it must do a certain amount of scratching around for what it gets.

It has been my observation that most people get ahead during the time that others waste.

Time and money spent in helping men to do more for themselves is far better than mere giving.

The best we can do is size up the chances, calculate the risks involved, estimate our ability to deal with them, and then make our plans with confidence.

You are not "saving" when you prevent yourself from becoming more productive. You are really taking away from your ultimate capital; you are taking away the value of one of nature's investments.

Anatole France
(1844-1924) French novelist

Nature, in her indifference, makes no distinction between good and evil.

Victor Frankl
(1905-1997) Psychologist and author of books, including *Man's Search for Meaning*

The last of the human freedoms is to choose one's attitudes.

Benjamin Franklin
(1706-1790) American statesman, writer, printer, scientist, and the guy on the hundred-dollar bill

All humanity is divided into three classes: those who are immovable, those who are movable, and those who move!

Men take more pains to mask than to mend.

Games lubricate the body and the mind.

Observe all men, thyself most.

"Smokin" Joe Frazier
(1944-) Heavyweight boxing champion from 1970 to 1973

When I go out there, I have no pity on my brother. I'm out there to win.

Cathy Freeman
(1973-) Australian track star who won the 2000 Olympic gold medal in the 400-meter race

Twenty seconds before a race, there's absolute focus. The key thing is to achieve relaxation, but at the same to have absolute total control. You've got to find the balance between being totally ready to go and being really at peace with yourself as well.

(Dr.) Sonya Friedman
Psychologist, television and radio host, and author of books such as *Take It From Here* (2004)

The way you treat yourself sets the standard for others.

Robert Fulghum
(1937-) American author and Unitarian clergyman

Be aware of wonder. Live a balanced life—learn some and think some and draw and paint and sing and dance and play and work every day some.

R. Buckminster Fuller
(1895-1983) American poet, philosopher, inventor, and architect

Nature is trying very hard to make us succeed, but nature does not depend on us. We are not the only experiment.

Don't fight forces; use them.

Faith is much better than belief. Belief is when someone else does the thinking.

I am convinced all of humanity is born with more gifts than we know. Most are born geniuses and just get de-geniused rapidly.

Now there is one outstanding important fact regarding spaceship earth, and that is that no instruction book came with it.

Thou mayest as well expect to grow stronger by always eating as wiser by always reading. Too much overcharges Nature, and turns more into disease than nourishment. Tis thought and digestion which makes books serviceable, and give health and vigor to the mind.

Thomas Fuller
(1608-1661) British public speaker and well-known writer

Be a friend to thyself, and others will be so too.

A wise man turns chance into good fortune.

Allen Funt
(1914-1999) American television personality who created and hosted the popular show *Candid Camera*

...[Children are] so original, so independent. They're everything you wish adults were. But adults are consistently herd-minded, conformant, subject to group pressure. They're moving in the wrong direction. They're moving away from the individual toward the herd.

Galileo Galilei
(1564-1642) Italian scientist and mathematician who made numerous groundbreaking discoveries

Doubt is the father of invention.

In questions of science, the authority of a thousand is not worth the humble reasoning of a single individual.

You cannot teach a man anything; you can only help him discover it within himself.

Indira Gandhi
(1917-1984) Indian Prime Minister from 1966 to 1977 and 1980 to 1984

The power to question is the basis of all human progress.

People tend to forget their duties, but remember their rights.

Mohandas K(aramchand) Gandhi a.k.a. Mahatma Gandhi
(1869-1948) Indian leader against British rule who successfully used a movement based on nonviolence to build social and political progress

Nonviolence is the greatest force at the disposal of mankind. It is mightier than the mightiest weapon of destruction devised by the ingenuity of man.

Freedom and slavery are mental states.

Non-cooperation with evil is a sacred duty.

You must be the change you wish to see in the world.

The music of life is in danger of being lost in the music of the voice.

Charles A. Garfield
Author of *Peak Performers* (1987) and other books

The fact is, the difference between peak performers and everybody else are much smaller than everybody else thinks.

Jose Ortega y Gasset
(1883-1955) Influential Spanish philosopher who focused on the individual perspective

Tell me what you pay attention to and I will tell you who you are.

Shakti Gawain
Writer of personal growth books such as *Creative Visualization*

Our bodies communicate to us clearly and specifically, if we are willing to listen to them.

We will discover the nature of our particular genius when we stop trying to conform to our own or to other peoples' models, learn to be ourselves, and allow our natural channel to open.

J. Paul Getty
(1892-1976) American oil tycoon, investor, and philanthropist

I would rather earn 1% off a 100 people's efforts than 100% of my own efforts.

The meek shall inherit the earth, but not the mineral rights.

The man who comes up with a means for doing or producing almost anything better, faster or more economically has his future and his fortune at his fingertips.

In times of rapid change, experience can sometimes be your worst enemy.

The individual who wants to reach the top in business must appreciate the might of the force of habit and must understand that practices are what create habits. He must be quick to break those habits that can break him and hasten to adopt those practices that will become the habits that help him achieve the success he desires.

My father said, "You must never try to make all the money that's in a deal. Let the other fellow make some money too, because if you have a reputation for always making all the money, you won't have many deals."

There are always opportunities through which businessmen can profit handsomely if they will only recognize and seize them.

Darcy E. Gibbons

Success is just a matter of attitude.

Jerry Gillies
American speaker and author of books such as *Moneylove* (1978) and *Psychological Immortality* (1981)

It takes a lot more energy to fail than to succeed, since it takes a lot of concentrated energy to hold on to beliefs that don't work.

Make sure you visualize what you really want, not what someone else wants for you.

You will recognize your own path when you come upon it, because you will suddenly have all the energy and imagination you will ever need.

Charlotte Anna Perkins Gilman
(1860-1935) American feminist, public speaker, writer, and publisher

Eternity is not something that begins after you are dead. It is going on all the time. We are in it now.

Life is a verb, not a noun.

Arnold H. Glasow

Success is simple. Do what's right, the right way, at the right time.

Laughter is a tranquilizer with no side effects.

Alfred Glossbrenner
American author of books such as *Google and Other Search Engines* (2004)

With so much information now online, it is exceptionally easy to simply dive in and drown.

Vincent Van Gogh

(1853-1890) Legendary Dutch artist; he is also noted for cutting off part of his ear and giving it to his friend at one point in his life, and committing suicide two years later

Great things are done by a series of small things brought together.

Samuel Goldwyn

(1879-1974) Legendary American filmmaker / producer who founded Goldwyn Pictures Corp., which later merged to form Metro Goldwyn Mayer (MGM). His various oxymoronic quotes are referred to as "Goldwynisms"

A verbal contract isn't worth the paper it's written on.

I hate a man who always says "yes" to me. When I say "no," I like a man who also says "no."

I don't want any yes-men around me. I want everybody to tell me the truth—even if it costs them their job.

I'm willing to admit that I may not always be right, but I am never wrong.

I read part of it all the way through.

[*After being told a script was full of old clichés*:] Let's have some new clichés.

If people don't want to go to the picture, nobody can stop them.

Our comedies are not to be laughed at.

Spare no expense to make everything as economical as possible.

The reason so many people turned up at his funeral is that they wanted to make sure he was dead.

Color television! Bah, I won't believe it until I see it in black and white.

We want a story that starts out with an earthquake and works its way up to a climax.

We're overpaying him, but he's worth it.

Gentlemen, include me out.

Let's bring it up to date with some snappy nineteenth century dialogue.

I'll give you a definite maybe.

If Roosevelt were alive, he'd turn over in his grave.

If I could drop dead right now, I'd be the happiest man alive.

Give me a couple of years and I'll make that actress an overnight success.

I never put on a pair of shoes until I've worn them five years.

A bachelor's life is no life for a single man.

Tell them to stand closer apart.

When I want your opinion, I will give it to you.

You are going to call him Sam? What kind of a name is that? Every Tom, Dick, Harry is called Sam.

Go see that turkey for yourself, and see for yourself why you shouldn't see it.

Never make forecasts, especially about the future.

In no time, it will be a forgotten memory.

If you can't give me your word of honor, will you give me your promise?

I don't think anyone should write their autobiography until after they're dead.

[*After his secretary asked to destroy the very old files*:] Certainly, but make copies of them.

Modern dancing is so old fashioned.

Gentlemen, for your information, I have a question to ask you.

Keep a stiff upper chin.

When someone does something good, applaud! You will make two people happy.

I think luck is the sense to recognize an opportunity and the ability to take advantage of it. The man who can smile at his breaks and grab his chances gets on.

Wayne Gretzky
(1961-) Hockey player widely considered the greatest ever in the sport

Every shot not taken is a goal not scored.

George Ivanovitch Gurdjieff
(1872-1949) Mysterious philosopher

Self-observation brings man to the realization of the necessity of self-change. And in observing himself a man notices that self-observation itself brings about certain changes in his inner processes. He begins to understand that self-observation is an instrument of self-change, a means of awakening.

It is the greatest mistake to think that man is always one and the same. A man is never the same for long. He is continually changing. He seldom remains the same even for half an hour.

Edward Everett Hale
(1822-1909) Teacher, author, Unitarian minister

Never bear more than one kind of trouble at a time. Some people bear three kinds of trouble—all they've had, all they have, and all they expect to have.

Thich Nhat Hanh
(1926-) Vietnamese Buddhist monk, teacher, and author

People deal too much with the negative, with what is wrong. Why not try and see positive things, to just touch those things and make them bloom?

Lorraine Hansberry
(1930-1965) American playwright

Never be afraid to sit awhile and think.

Barbara G. Harrison
American publicist and author of books such as *Off Center* (1981)

To have a crisis, and act upon it, is one thing. To dwell in perpetual crisis is another.

There is no way to take the danger out of human relationships.

Stephen Hawking
(1942-) Legendary English physicist who has written many best selling books including *A Brief History of Time*

My goal is simple. It is complete understanding of the universe, why it as it is and why it exists as all.

The eventual goal of science is to provide a single theory that describes the whole universe.

William Hazlitt
(1778-1830) English writer and humanist

He who undervalues himself is justly undervalued by others.

We often repent the good we have done as well as the ill.

Katherine Hepburn
(1907-2003) American actress

My greatest strength is common sense.

Abraham Heschel
(1907-1972) Jewish Polish American philosopher

The higher goal of spiritual living is not to amass a wealth of information, but to face sacred moments.

Self-respect is the fruit of discipline; the sense of dignity grows with the ability to say no to oneself.

Jascha Heifetz
(1901-1987) Legendary Russian American violinist

No matter what side of the argument you are on, you always find people on your side that you wish were on the other.

Ernest Hemmingway
(1899-1961) American writer who won the Nobel Prize for Literature in 1954

Never confuse movement with action.

Be fully in the moment, open yourself to the powerful energies dancing around you.

Robert Henri
(1865-1929) Influential American artist and art teacher

Cherish your emotions and never undervalue them.

Know what the old masters did. Know how they composed their pictures, but do not fall into the conventions they established. These conventions were right for them, and they are wonderful. They made their language. You make yours. All the past can help you.

Heracleitus
(Lived in 500s and 400s BC) Greek philosopher

There is nothing permanent except change.

You cannot step twice into the same river, for other waters are continually flowing on.

Man is most nearly himself when he achieves the seriousness of a child at play.

Don Herold
(1889-1966) American author, cartoonist, and humorist

Unhappiness is not knowing what we want, and killing ourselves to get it.

Hippocrates
(Lived in 400s BC and 300s BC) Greek physician; often considered the "father of medicine"

If we could give every individual the correct amount of nourishment and exercise—not too little and not too much—we would have found the safest way to health.

Everything in excess is opposed to nature.

Doing nothing is sometimes a good remedy.

Hitopadesa
An ancient Sanskrit text

Many can speak words of wisdom; few can practice it themselves.

Russell Hoban
(1925-) American writer

After all, when you come right down to it, how many people speak the same language even when they speak the same language?

Hans Hofmann
(1880-1966) Innovative German painter

The ability to simplify means to eliminate the unnecessary so that the necessary may speak.

Josiah Gilbert Holland
(1819-1881) American writer

The secret of man's success resides in his insight into the moods of people, and his tact in dealing with them.

There is no royal road to anything; one thing at a time, all things in succession.

The soul, like the body, lives by what it feeds on.

Ernest Holmes
(1887-1960) Founder of the Religious Science movement

We cannot lead a choiceless life. Every day, every moment, every second, there is a choice. If it were not so, we would not be individuals.

True teaching liberates the student from his teacher.

John Andrew Holmes

It is well to remember that the entire universe, with one trifling exception, is composed of others.

Oliver Wendell Holmes
(1809-1894) American writer and physician

What lies behind us and what lies ahead of us are tiny matters compared to what lives within us.

Life is an end in itself, and the only question as to whether it is worth living is whether you have had enough of it.

The great thing in the world is not so much where we stand, as in what direction we are moving.

Lou Holtz
(1937-) American college football coach

How you respond to the challenge in the second half will determine what you become after the game, whether you are a winner or a loser.

Life is ten percent what happens to you and ninety percent how you respond to it.

(Warrior) Evander "The Real Deal" Holyfield
(1962-) Three time undisputed heavyweight boxing champion

It is not the size of a man, but the size of his heart that matters.

When you have a sound mind, you can do what's necessary.

Admiral Grace Murray Hopper
(1906-1992) American Navy Admiral, computer engineer, and mathematician

One accurate measurement is worth a thousand expert opinions.

Horace (Flaccus)
(65 BC-8 BC) Roman philosopher and poet

Burdened with yesterday's excess, the body drags the mind down with it.

A person will gain everyone's approval if he mixes the pleasant with the useful.

Rule your mind, or it will rule you.

Karen Horney
(1885-1952) German American psychoanalyst

Fortunately, analysis is not the only way to resolve inner conflicts. Life itself still remains a very effective therapist.

We may feel genuinely concerned about world conditions, though such a concern should drive us into action and not into a depression.

Edgar Watson Howe
(1853-1937) American writer known for his non-conformist style

Don't abuse your friends and expect them to consider it criticism.

Kin Hubbard
(1868-1930) American journalist, cartoonist, and political commentator

The only way to entertain some folks is to listen to them.

Some folks can look so busy doing nothing that they seem indispensable.

I will say this for adversity: people seem to be able to stand it, and that is more than I can say for prosperity.

The fellow that agrees with everything you say is either a fool or he is getting ready to skin you.

It's pretty hard to be efficient without being obnoxious.

There's no secret about success. Did you ever know a successful man who didn't tell you about it?

Hugo of Fleury

There is a time to say nothing, and there is a time to say something, but there is not time to say everything.

Victor Hugo
(1802-1885) French writer known for such works as *Les Miserables*

Love is the reduction of the universe to a single being.

William Hung a.k.a. "Hong Kong Ricky Martin"
(1984-) Singer most known for his rendition of the song "She Bangs."

I already gave my best. I have no regrets at all.

Margaret Wolfe Hungerford
(1855-1897) Irish novelist

Beauty is in the eye of the beholder. (From her novel *Molly Bawn*)

Edmund Husserl
(1859-1938) German philosopher who founded Phenomenology

Merely fact-minded sciences make merely fact-minded people.

Aldous Huxley
(1894-1963) Famed English novelist and critic

There is only one corner of the universe you can be certain of improving, and that's your own self.

A child-like man is not a man whose development has been arrested; on the contrary, he is a man who has given himself a chance of continuing to develop long after most adults have muffled themselves in the cocoon of middle-aged habit and convention.

Thomas Henry Huxley
(1825-1895) English biologist and philosopher

> Every great advance in natural knowledge has involved the absolute rejection of authority.

Lee Iacocca
(1924-) American businessman most known for his time as CEO of Chrysler

> I have always found that if I move with seventy-five percent or more of the facts, that I usually never regret it. It's the guys who wait to have everything perfect that drive you crazy.

(Dean) William Ralph Inge
(1860-1954) British Christian philosopher and theologian

> When our first parents were driven out of Paradise, Adam is believed to have remarked to Eve, "My dear, we live in an age of transition."

Edgar N. Jackson
Writer of books such as *You and Your Grief* (1986)

> When dealing with the unknown, children are often bewildered by the fact that their parents do not know all the answers.

Michael Jackson a.k.a. "The King of Pop"
(1958-) American singer, dancer, performer, pop superstar, and frequent user of such expressions as *jah-mon*, *hee hee*, *hee hee hee*, and *dah*

> The power is in believing, so give yourself a chance… All you need is the will to want it and a little self-esteem. (From his song "Keep the Faith")

> Don't stop till you get enough. (From his song "Don't Stop Till You Get Enough")

Carol Heiss Jenkins
(1940-) Figure skater who won the Olympic gold medal in 1956

> You can want it too much. You can try too hard. There's a point where you just have to let your muscle memory kick in.

Shaikh 'Abd al-Qadir al-Jilani
(1075-1166) Muslim Iraqi writer

> Do not become a candle that gives light to others but remains in darkness itself.

Jimmy Johnson
(1943-) Pro football coach who won two Super Bowls with the Dallas Cowboys in the 1990s; he is currently a television football analyst

> A losing football team looks at excuses. A championship football team looks at solutions.

Samuel Johnson
(1709-1784) English writer

> We are inclined to believe those whom we do not know because they have never deceived us.

E(li) Stanley Jones
(1884-1973) Christian Evangelist

> Your capacity to say No determines your capacity to say Yes to greater things.

Franklin P. Jones
(1887-1929) American businessman

> Nothing makes you more tolerant of a neighbor's noisy party than being there.

> Honest criticism is hard to take, especially from a relative, a friend, an acquaintance, or a stranger.

> It's a strange world of language in which skating on thin ice can get you into hot water.

> One advantage of talking to yourself is that you know at least somebody's listening.

Erica Jong
American novelist known for such works as *Fear of Flying* (1973)

Advice is what we ask for when we already know the answer but wish we didn't.

Carl (Gustav) Jung
(1875-1961) Influential Swiss psychologist and psychiatrist

Everything that irritates us about others can lead us to an understanding of ourselves.

The shoe that fits one person pinches another; there is no recipe for living that suits all cases.

Who has fully realized that history is not contained in thick books, but lives in our very blood?

Nobody—as long as he moves about among the chaotic currents of life—is without trouble.

Nothing has a stronger influence psychologically on their environment and especially on their children than the unlived life of the parent.

The meeting of two personalities is like the contact of two chemical substances: if there is any reaction, both are transformed.

Observance of customs and laws can very easily be a cloak for a lie so subtle that our fellow human beings are unable to detect it.

It all depends on how we look at things, and not on how they are themselves.

The pendulum of the mind alternates between sense and nonsense, not between right and wrong.

The most terrifying thing is to accept oneself completely.

John Junor
(1919-1998) British journalist

An ounce of emotion is equal to a ton of facts.

Immanuel Kant
(1724-1804) Influential German philosopher

Men can never acquire respect by benevolence alone...

Science is organized knowledge. Wisdom is organized life.

Billie Jean King
(1943-) Female tennis star who won a much publicized 1973 "Battle of the Sexes" match versus male tennis player Bobby Riggs.

A champion is afraid of losing. Everyone else is afraid of winning.

Don King
(1920-) Legendary boxing promoter knows for his attention-getting personality, unique hairstyle, and mega event fight promotions; he has also popularized the use of such words as *splendiferous* and *trickeration*

I never cease to amaze myself. I can say this humbly.

Only in America!

(Dr.) Martin Luther King Jr.
(1929-1968) Social activist who led the civil rights movement in America, and won the Nobel Prize for Peace in 1964

People who have a stake in their society protect that society—but when they don't have it, they unconsciously want to destroy it.

He who passively accepts evil is as much involved in it as he who helps to perpetrate it

War is a poor chisel to carve out tomorrow.

Note: I would love to include more material of Martin Luther King, Jr., but King's family and heirs very strictly enforce copyrights on his material, including the famous "I Have a Dream" speech.

Thomas A. Kempis
(1379-1471) German Christian monk and theologian

Habit is overcome by habit.

Who has a harder fight than he who is striving to overcome himself.

Corita Kent
(1918-1986) American artist

Life is a succession of moments. To live each one is to succeed.

Love the moment and the energy of that moment will spread beyond all boundaries.

Chuck Knox
(1932-) NFL football head coach from 1973 to 1994

You can concede to an opponent something he hasn't earned. It's one thing to underestimate an opponent. But maybe the worst thing is to overestimate. You always play your strengths. But that doesn't mean you become predictable.

J(iddhu) Krishnamurti
(1895-1986) Indian spiritual teacher

Meditation is not a means to an end. It is both the means and the end.

(Swami) Kriyananda a.k.a. J. Donald Walters
(1926-) American spiritual teacher and musician

If you have just one or two spiritual friends with whom you can share your highest aspirations, you should consider yourself richly blessed.

Burt Lancaster
(1913-1994) American actor known for his roles as tough yet emotionally sensitive characters

Most people seem to think I'm the kind of guy who shaves with a blowtorch. Actually, I'm bookish and worrisome.

Tom Landry
(1924-2000) Legendary football coach of the Dallas Cowboys; he won two Super Bowls and had an incredible string of twenty consecutive winning seasons from 1966 to 1985

Leadership is a matter of having people look at you and gain confidence, seeing how you react. If you're in control, they're in control.

Estee Lauder

(1908-2004) American businesswoman, and co-founder of cosmetics and fragrance powerhouse Estee Lauder Inc

If you don't sell, it's not the product that's wrong—it's you.

Fran Lebowitz
(1951-) American author of such books as the 1970s release *Social Studies*

Food is an important part of a balanced diet.

Bruce Lee
(1940-) Martial arts legend

All fixed set patterns are incapable of adaptability or pliability. The truth is outside of all fixed patterns.

Aart van der Leeuw
(1876-1931) Dutch writer

The mystery of life is not a problem to be solved; it is a reality to be experienced.

Ursula K. LeGuin
(1929-) American science fiction author of such books as *The Left Hand of Darkness*

Almost anything carried to a logical extreme becomes depressing.

Herbert Henry Lehman
(1878-1963) American politician

I must respect the opinions of others even if I disagree with them.

John Lennon
(1940-1980) British musician, member of the legendary rock group The Beatles

Life is what happens while you're busy making other plans.

Eda LeShan
(1922-2002) American writer of books such as *When Your Child Drives You Crazy*

Depression occurs when you are not being yourself. You're probably doing things you don't want to do.

Aaron Levenstein

Statistics are like a bikini. What they reveal is suggestive, but what they conceal is vital.

Lennox Lewis
(1965-) Jamaican Canadian British two time undisputed heavyweight boxing champion

I am the best there is. I am at the top of the food chain…

Walter Lippmann
(1889-1974) Influential American political commentator and columnist

Where all men think alike, no one thinks very much.

Abraham Lincoln
(1809-1865) 16th US President

I don't know who my grandfather was; I am much more concerned to know who his grandson will be.

Anne Morrow Lindbergh
(1906-2001) American aviator and author of the best selling book *Gift From the Sea*

The most exhausting thing in life is being insincere. This is why so much of social life is exhausting.

If you surrender completely to the moments as they pass, you live more richly those moments.

Only in growth, reform, and change—paradoxically enough—is true security to be found.

Sonny Liston
(1917-1970) Heavyweight boxer who was world champion from 1962 to 1964

A boxing match is like a cowboy movie—there's got to be good guys, and there's got to be bad guys.

Georg Christoph Litchenberg
(1742-1799) German physicist and writer

Nothing is more conducive to peace of mind than not having any opinion at all.

Exercise, exercise your powers; what is difficult will finally become routine.

Rebecca Lobo
(1973-) Basketball superstar

Make it a point to be around those with positive energy—people who want what's best for you, people who understand your goals and priorities.

John Locke
(1632-1704) English philosopher who inspired the English and French Enlightenment periods, and also inspired the principles of the US Constitution

...Every man has a property in his own person. This nobody has a right to, but himself.

New opinions are always suspected, and usually opposed, without any other reason but because they are not already common.

Reading furnishes the mind only with material for knowledge; it is thinking that makes what we read ours.

...It is much easier for a tutor to command than to teach.

I attribute the little I know to my not having been ashamed to ask for information, and to my rule of conversing with all descriptions of men on those topics that form their own peculiar professions and pursuits.

Henry Wadsworth Longfellow
(1807-1882) Legendary American poet

If we could read the secret history of our enemies, we shall find in each man's life sorrow and suffering enough to disarm all hostility.

We judge ourselves by what we feel capable of doing, while other judge us by what we have already done.

Sophia Loren
(1934-) Legendary Italian actress

After all these years, I am still involved in the process of self-discovery.

Ronnie Lott
(1959-) One of the greatest pro football players of all time; he won four Super Bowl championships, and was named to the Pro Bowl team 10 times

If you can believe it, the mind can achieve it.

John Lust

The body is consuming energy when tense, and restoring energy when it is relaxed.

JC Macaulay

It takes a great man to give sound advice tactfully, but a greater to accept it graciously.

Elinor MacDonald

Too often we visit the well of divine abundance with a teacup instead of a bucket.

Madonna
(1958-) American singer, actress, and businesswoman

I am my own experiment. I am my own work of art.

Sometimes you have to be a bi--- to get things done!

… If you don't express yourself, if you don't say what you want, then you're not going to get it. And in effect, you are chained down by your own inability to say what you feel or go after want you want.

Poor is the person whose pleasures depend on the permission of another.

There is no such thing as normal.

(Sri) Nisargadatta Maharaj
(1897-1981) Indian spiritual leader

Whatever you consider yourself to be changes from moment to moment. Nothing is constant.

Ramana Maharshi
(1879-1950) Hindu yogi and philosopher

Mind control is not one's birthright. The successful few owe their success to their perseverance.

The degree of freedom from unwanted thoughts and the degree of concentration on a single thought are the measures to gauge spiritual progress.

Nelson Mandela
(1918-) Influential South Africa statesman, leader, and black civil rights advocate who won the Nobel Peace Prize in 1993

There is no passion to be found playing small—in settling for a life that is less than the one you are capable of living.

I learned that courage was not the absence of fear, but the triumph over it. The brave man is not he who does not feel afraid, but he who conquers that fear.

To be free is not merely to cast off one's chains, but to live in a way that respects and enhances the freedom of others.

A good head and a good heart are always a formidable combination.

We must use time wisely and forever realize that the time is always ripe to do right.

Katherine Mansfield
(1888-1923) Legendary New Zealand-born English writer of short stories

Act for yourself. Face the truth.

I must say I hate money, but it's the lack of it I hate most.

I want, by understanding myself, to understand others. I want to be all that I am capable of becoming.

Orison Swett Marden
(1850-1924) American writer on success

A good system shortens the road to the goal.

If you do not feel yourself growing in your work and your life broadening and deepening, if your task is not a perpetual tonic to you, you have not found your place.

When we are sure that we are on the right road there is no need to plan our journey too far ahead. No need to burden ourselves with doubts and fears as to the obstacles that may bar our progress. We cannot take more than one step at a time.

The waste of life occasioned by trying to do too many things at once is appalling.

The golden opportunity you are seeking is in yourself. It is not in your environment; it is not in luck or chance, or the help of others; it is in yourself alone.

The golden rule for every business man is this: "Put yourself in your customer's place."

Unless you are prepared yourself to profit by your chance, the opportunity will only make you ridiculous. A great occasion is valuable to you in proportion as you have educated yourself to make use of it.

Deep within man dwell those slumbering powers; powers that would astonish him, that he never dreamed of possessing; forces that would revolutionize his life if aroused and put into action.

There are powers inside of you which, if you could discover and use, would make of you everything you ever dreamed or imagined you could become.

We fail to see that we can control our destiny; make ourselves do whatever is possible; make ourselves become whatever we long to be.

Our destiny changes with our thought; we shall become what we wish to become, do what we wish to do, when our habitual thought corresponds with our desire.

You cannot measure a man by his failures. You must know what use he makes of them. What did they mean to him. What did he get out of them.

The beginning of a habit is like an invisible thread, but every time we repeat the act we strengthen the strand, add to it another filament, until it becomes a great cable and binds us irrevocably, thought and act

The Universe is one great kindergarten for man. Everything that exists has brought with it its own peculiar lesson.

Opportunities? They are all around us. There is power lying latent everywhere waiting for the observant eye to discover it.

Don Marquis
(1878-1937) American author of books such as *Archy and Mehitabel*

Successful people are the ones who think up things for the rest of the world to keep busy at.

An idea is not responsible for the people who believe in it.

Harriet Martineau
(1802-1876) English writer of various subjects who became prominent despite disabilities such as deafness

Readers are plentiful; thinkers are rare.

Groucho Marx
(1890-1977) American actor, comedian, and game show host

I must say I find television very educational. The minute somebody turns it on, I go into the other room and read a good book.

… I was born at a very early age.

I've had a perfectly wonderful evening. But this wasn't it.

Outside of a dog, a book is man's best friend. Inside of a dog, it's too dark to read.

A black cat crossing your path signifies that the animal is going somewhere.

I don't care to belong to a club that accepts people like me as members.

Next time I see you, remind me not to talk to you.

Quote me as saying I was misquoted.

Who are you going to believe—me or your own eyes?

Why was I with her? She reminds me of you. In fact, she reminds me more of you than you do!

Time flies like an arrow. Fruit flies like a banana.

He may look like an idiot and talk like an idiot but don't let that fool you. He really is an idiot.

Those are my principles. If you don't like them I have others.

A child of five could understand this. Fetch me a child of five.

Andrew Matthews
Motivational speaker, cartoonist, and author of books such as *Being Happy* (1990)

Even the people we most admire often feel inadequate.

W. Somerset Maugham
(1874-1965) English novelist and playwright

Dying is a very dull dreary affair. My advice to you is to have nothing to do with it.

Andre Maurois
(1885-1967) French writer on a variety of subjects

Conversation would be vastly improved by the constant use of four simple words: I do not know.

Our minds have unbelievable power over our bodies.

William James Mayo
(1861-1931) Medical doctor who confounded the Mayo clinic

Lord, deliver me from the person who never makes a mistake, and also from the person who makes the same mistake twice.

Willie Mays
(1931-) Arguably the greatest baseball player of all time

They throw the ball, I hit it. They hit the ball, I catch it.

Mignon McLaughlin

Society honors its living conformists and its dead troublemakers.

Margaret Mead
(1901-1978) American anthropologist

It may be necessary temporarily to accept a lesser evil, but one must never label a necessary evil as good.

Herman Melville
(1819-1891) American writer most known for his novel *Moby Dick*

We cannot live only for ourselves. A thousand fibers connect us with our fellow men.

H.L. Mencken
(1880-1956) Influential American writer

Immorality: The morality of those who are having a better time.

Karl A. Menninger
(1893-1990) American psychiatrist and author of *The Human Mind*

One of the most untruthful things possible, you know, is a collection of facts, because they can be made to appear so many different ways.

Attitudes are more important than facts.

Thomas Merton
(1915-1968) French Catholic monk and writer on spiritual and social themes

> Happiness is not a matter of intensity but of balance and order and rhythm and harmony.

Michelangelo
(1475-1564) Legendary Italian artist, architect, and poet known for such works as the ceiling of the Sistine Chapel, and the sculpture *David*

> [*Michelangelo's motto*:] I am still learning

John F. Milburn

> Men's actions depend to a great extent upon fear. We do things either because we enjoy doing them or because we are afraid not to do them.

> Fear is like fire: if controlled it will help you; if uncontrolled, it will rise up and destroy you

John Stuart Mill
(1806-1873) British philosopher and economist

> Ask yourself whether you are happy, and you cease to be so.

> That so few now dare to be eccentric marks the chief danger of the time.

> Human nature is not a machine to be built after a model, and set to do exactly the work prescribed for it, but a tree, which requires to grow and develop itself on all sides, according to the tendency of the inward forces which make it a living thing.

Henry Miller
(1891-1980) American writer of such books as *Tropic of Cancer* and *Tropic of Capricorn*

> The moment one gives close attention to anything, even a blade of grass, it becomes a mysterious, awesome, indescribably magnificent world in itself.

Olin Miller

You probably wouldn't worry about what people think of you if you could know how seldom they do.

If you want to make an easy job seem mighty hard, just keep putting off doing it.

Wang Yang-Ming
(1472-1529) Influential Chinese philosopher

A person's greatest virtue is his ability to correct his mistakes and continually make a new person of himself.

Charles Mingus
(1922-1979) Legendary American jazz musician

Making the simple complicated is commonplace; making the complicated simple, awesomely simple, that's creativity.

Mo Tzu
(Lived in 400s BC and 300s BC) Influential Chinese philosopher and humanist whose teachings are the foundation of the Mo-ist philosophy (a.k.a. Mohism)

When conditions are prosperous, those people who are worthy must be promoted [by the government or leader]. When conditions are not prosperous, those people who are worthy must be promoted.

Honoring the worthy is the basis of good government.

If someone trespasses into an orchard and steals nectarines and plums, people who find out about this will condemn the person. And if government officials catch him, they will punish him. This is because the person is harming others and acting with a lack of benevolence in order to advance himself.

And in the case of stealing dogs, pigs, chickens, and piglets, such an act is considered even more wicked than trespassing into an orchard and stealing nectarines and plums. This is because there is even greater harm to others, and this indicates a further lack of benevolence, and is a more serious transgression.

And in the case of trespassing into a stable and stealing someone's horses and cows, the act is considered even more wicked than stealing dogs, pigs, chickens, and piglets. This is because the loss is greater, and indicates a further lack of benevolence, and is a more serious transgression.

And in the case of murdering an innocent person, taking his clothes, and stealing his spear and sword, this act is considered even more wicked than trespassing into a stable and stealing someone's horses and cows. This is because the injury to others is even greater, and indicates a further lack of benevolence, and is a more serious transgression.

All of the proper people of the world know enough to condemn such acts and label them as wicked. Yet, when it comes to the more serious transgression of offensive warfare against other states, people do not know enough to condemn such an act. In fact, they praise it and call it virtuous...

If someone saw little bit of black and called it black, and then saw a lot of black and called it white, we would conclude that he did not properly differentiate between white and black.

Or, if someone tasted a little bit of bitter and called it bitter, and then tasted a lot of bitter called it sweet, we would conclude that he did not properly differentiate between sweet and bitter.

Yet when an atrocity is committed and a state is attacked, people do not know enough to condemn it. Instead, they praise it.

When the world's people praise something as good, what is their reason?

... [People sometimes do ineffective or wrong things] because they mix up what is habitual with what is appropriate, and what is customary with what is right.

(Charles de Secondat,) Baron de Montesquieu
(1689-1755) French political philosopher

It would be easy if we only wanted to be happy; but we want to be happier than others, which is difficult, since we think they are happier than they are.

Sun Myung Moon
(1920-) Korean religious leader who founded the Unification Church

If you want to criticize someone, first criticize yourself more than three times.

The spiritual world is connected with the physical world. The common factor connecting all things is true love.

Archie Moore
(1913-1998) Legendary boxer nicknamed "The Old Mongoose," he had 194 wins over his career and was light heavyweight champion from 1952 to 1962, and is also well known for his role as Jim in the movie *The Adventures of Huckleberry Finn*

In this game [*boxing*], you have to be a good finisher. I call it finishing, and you don't learn it in Miss Hewitt's School for Young Ladies.

Charles Langbridge Morgan
(1894-1958) English playwright and writer

The art of living does not consist in preserving and clinging to a particular mood of happiness, but in allowing happiness to change its form without being disappointed by the change.

One cannot shut ones eyes to things not seen with eyes.

Marlo Morgan
Author of books such as the 1990s release *Mutant Message Down Under*

If you go to bed at night and think about your day and you haven't laughed very much, then you must jump out of bed and go do something fun.

Akio Morita
(1921-1999) Japanese cofounder, CEO, and chairman of global electronics powerhouse Sony

Curiosity is the key to creativity. (From his book *Made in Japan*)

Toni Morrison
(1931-) American writer who won the Nobel Prize for Literature in 1993

There is really nothing more to say except why. But since why is difficult to handle, one must take refuge in how.

If there's a book you really want to read, but it hasn't been written yet, then you must write it.

Hermann Joseph Muller
(1860-1967) American geneticist who won the Nobel Prize for Physiology or Medicine in 1946

> Life as a whole is a ceaseless change... There is no sign of a physical limit yet.

Puck Axel Munthe
(1857-1949) Swedish physician

> A man can stand a lot as long as he can stand himself.

Iris Murdoch
(1919-1999) British writer most known for her novels that contain philosophical points as well as humor

> He led a double life. Did that make him a liar? He did not feel a liar. He was a man of two truths.

George Jean Nathan
(1882-1958) American writer, editor, and drama critic

> The test of a real comedian is whether you laugh at him before he opens his mouth.

Patricia Neal
(1926-) Actress who recovered from three major strokes, and later opened a stroke rehabilitation center to help stroke victims around the world

> A strong positive mental attitude will create more miracles than any wonder drug.

Jawaharlal Nehru
(1889-1964) Indian leader and prime minister from 1947 to 1964

> It is far better to know our own weaknesses and failings than to point out those of another.

> What we really are matters more than what other people think of us.

A.S. Neil
(1884-1973) Educational theorist and author of *Summerhill School*

Take from others what you want, but never be a disciple of anyone.

Dorothy Nevill
(1826-1913) British writer

The real art of conversation is not only to say the right thing at the right place, but to leave unsaid the wrong thing at the tempting moment.

Isaac Newton
(1642-1727) Arguably the greatest scientists ever

If I have ever made any valuable discoveries, it has been due to patient attention more than to any other talent.

Charles Nodier
(1780-1884) French writer

To believe everything is to be an imbecile. To deny everything is to be a fool.

Jessye Norman
(1945-) American opera star

Problems arise in that one has to find a balance between what people need from you and what you need for yourself.

Novalis
(1772-1801) German poet and philosopher

We are close to waking up when we dream that we are dreaming.

Abe Oheb
(1942-) Iranian American California real estate investor / developer, and *jadval* (Persian crossword puzzle) grandmaster

Get your priorities in the proper order.

The most important aspect of success—whether it is in business or in the overall scope one's life—is to recognize needs based on their order of importance, and to handle matters based on that order. In a word, it is *prioritization*.

Prioritization is the supreme attribute that engulfs everything else— it is more important than determination, perseverance, persistence, or patience; and it is usually more important than just having skills. Like La Rochefoucauld wrote, "It is not enough to have great qualities; we should also have the management of them."

And ultimately, prioritization isn't about handling the year, month, day, hour, minute, or even the second. Prioritization is about establishing priorities at every moment. Oprah Winfrey once said, "Doing the best at this moment puts you in the best place for the next moment."

And when we face the moment, and establish our priorities as we live in each situation, it is then—and only then—that we have truly mastered the management of our lives, and ended the threat of disorder in our souls.

Identifying your priorities is an effective way of preventing procrastination.

Kakuzo Okakura
(1862-1913) Japanese writer

The art of life is a constant readjustment to our surroundings.

P. J. O'Rourke
(1947-) American political satirist

You know your children are growing up when they stop asking you where they came from and refuse to tell you where they're going.

Leonard Orr
New Age spiritual leader

If you are willing to discipline yourself, the physical universe won't need to discipline you.

Osho
(1931-1990) Indian Mystic

If you are in the future, then ego seems to be very substantial. If you are in the present, the ego is a mirage; it starts disappearing.

Camille Paglia
(1947-) Controversial Italian American writer and social figure

Pursuit and seduction are the essence of sexuality. It's part of the sizzle.

Satchel Paige
(1906-1982) Arguably the greatest baseball pitcher of all time

> When a batter swings and I see his knees move, I can tell just what his weaknesses are, and then I just put the ball where I know he can't hit it.

Mal Pancoast

> The odds of hitting your target go up dramatically when you aim at it.

Susan Partnow
Founder of Partnow Communications and author of *Everyday Speaking for all Occasions* (1998)

> Children learn about their world from their play.

Boris Pasternak
(1890-1960) Russian writer most known for his novel *Doctor Zhivago*

> Your health is bound to be affected if, day after day, you say the opposite of what you feel, if you grovel before what you dislike and rejoice at what brings you nothing but misfortune.

Jordan & Margaret Paul
Authors of books such as *Do I Have to Give Up Me To Be Loved by You?* (1989)

> Nobody has the answer for you. The truth lies in each person.

Cesare Pavese
(1908-1950) Italian writer

> We do not remember days; we remember moments.

Walter Payton
(1954-1999) Football running back who is arguably the greatest pro football player in history

> Don't worry about people who are ahead of you or behind you. Your concentration has to be on what you're doing. Once you lose that concentration, that's when things go awry.

Norman Vincent Peale
(1898-1993) American preacher and author

Change your thoughts and you change your world.

Joseph Chilton Pearce
Researcher of the human mind, and author of books such *The Biology of Transcendence* (2002)

Man's mind is a mirror of a universe that mirrors man's mind.

Harvey Penick
(1904-1995) Legendary golf teacher

Thinking too much about how you're doing when you're doing is disastrous.

H. Ross Perot
(1930-) American businessman, philanthropist, and Presidential candidate

If you can't stand a little sacrifice and you can't stand a trip across the desert with limited water, we're never going to straighten this country out.

Business is not just doing deals; business is having great products, doing great engineering, and providing tremendous service to customers. Finally, business is a cobweb of human relationships.

Failures are like skinned knees, painful but superficial.

Most people give up just when they're about to achieve success. They quit on the one-yard line. They give up at the last minute of the game, one foot from a winning touchdown.

The activist is not the man who says the river is dirty. The activist is the man who cleans up the river.

Irene Peter

Always be sincere, even when you don't mean it.

Thomas (Tom) Peters
Author of books such *In Search of Excellence* (1982)

Life is pretty simple: You do some stuff. Most fails. Some works. You do more of what works.

Michelle Pfeiffer
(1957-) American actress

Just standing around looking beautiful is so boring, really boring, so boring.

Mark Philippoussis
(1976-) Australian tennis star

I have nothing to prove to anyone. I only play for myself.

Pablo Picasso
(1881-1973) Legendary Spanish artist

I do not seek, I find.

Some painters transform the sun into a yellow spot; others transform a yellow spot into the sun.

Everything you can imagine is real.

My mother told me, "If you are a soldier, you will become a general. If you are a monk, you will become the Pope." Instead, I was a painter, and became Picasso.

Scottie Pippen
(1965-) Basketball superstar and 6 time NBA Champion

I visualize the game. I think about who I am guarding, the things he likes to do.

Plato
(Lived in 400s BC and 300s BC) Influential Greek philosopher

Nothing ever *is*, but is always becoming.

The first and best victory is to conquer self. To be conquered by self is, of all things, the most shameful and objectionable.

How can you prove if we are currently sleeping and our thoughts are a dream, or if we are awake and talking to each other in the waking state?

Rutherford Platt

We can see a thousand miracles around us every day. What is more supernatural than an egg yolk turning into a chicken?

Plutarch
(Lived in 00s AD and 100s AD) Greek writer on a large variety of topics

Character is long-standing habit.

Courage stands halfway between cowardice and rashness, one of which is a lack of courage, and the other an excess of it.

Alexander Pope
(1688-1744) English poet

A man should never be ashamed to own he has been in the wrong, which is but saying, in other words, that he is wiser today than he was yesterday.

Ezra Pound
(1885-1972) Influential American writer

Real education must ultimately be limited to men who insist on knowing. The rest is mere sheep-herding.

Herbert Prochnow
(1931-) Author of books such as *The Toastmaster's Treasure Chest* (1988)

A city is a large community where people are lonesome together.

Pythagoras
(Lived in 500s BC) Influential Greek philosopher and mathematician

No man is free who cannot command himself.

Above all things, love yourself.

Be satisfied with doing well, and leave others to talk of you as they will.

Swami Rama
(1925-1996) Indian Yogi, philosopher, writer, and artist

All of life is relationship.

Wilhelm Reich
(1897-1957) Revolutionary Viennese psychologist

Once we open up to the flow of energy within our body, we can also open up to the flow of energy in the universe.

Jules Renard
(1864-1910) French writer

I am not sincere, even when I say I am not.

Look for the ridiculous in everything, and you will find it.

The only man who is really free is the one who can turn down an invitation to dinner without giving an excuse.

Adrienne Rich
(1929-) American poet, scholar, and educator

Every journey into the past is complicated by delusions, false memories, [and] false naming of real events...

Sugar Ray Robinson
(1920-1989) Widely considered the greatest pound-for-pound fighter in boxing history

To be a champion, you have to believe in yourself when nobody else will.

Harriet Rochlin
Jewish American author of books such *Pioneer Jews* (1986)

Laughter can be more satisfying than honor; more precious than money; more heart cleansing than prayer.

John D. Rockefeller
(1839-1937) One of America's greatest businessmen, industrialists, and philanthropists

I do not think that there is any other quality so essential to success of any kind as the quality of perseverance. It overcomes almost everything, even nature.

I always tried to turn every disaster into an opportunity.

Charity is injurious unless it helps the recipient to become independent of it.

I know of nothing more despicable and pathetic than a man who devotes all the hours of the waking day to the making of money for money's sake.

Singleness of purpose is one of the chief essentials for success in life, no matter what may be one's aim.

It is wrong to assume that men of immense wealth are always happy.

I had no ambition to make a fortune. Mere moneymaking has never been my goal. I had an ambition to build.

The only question with wealth is: what do you do with it?

The ability to deal with people is as purchasable a commodity as sugar or coffee...and I will pay more for that ability than for any other under the sun.

Carl Rogers
(1902-1987) American psychologist known for promoting a client (patient) focused approach

The curious paradox is that when I accept myself as I am, then I can change.

The good life is a process, not a state of being. It is a direction, not a destination.

The only person who is educated is the one who has learned how to learn...and change.

Jim Rohn

Motivational speaker, business philosopher, consultant, and author of books such as *7 Strategies for Wealth & Happiness* (1996)

> Take advantage of every opportunity to practice your communication skills so that when important occasions arise, you will have the gift, the style, the sharpness, the clarity, and the emotions to affect other people.

> Success is not to be pursued; it is to be attracted by the person you become.

Frank Romer

> People will sit up and take notice of you if you will sit up and take notice of what makes them sit up and take notice.

Jean Jacques Rousseau

(1712-1778) Influential French philosopher and political theorist

> There are two things to consider with regard to any scheme. First: "Is it good in itself?" Second: "Can it be easily put into practice?"

> Those that are slowest in making a promise are the most faithful at performing it.

> Insults are the arguments used by those who are in the wrong.

> All of my misfortunes come from having thought too well of my fellows.

> It is not the criminal things that are hardest to confess, but the ridiculous and the shameful.

> Whoever blushes confesses guilt—true innocence never feels shame.

> As long as there are rich people in the world, they will be desirous of distinguishing themselves from the poor.

> Nature never deceives us; it is we who deceive ourselves.

> The world of reality has its limits; the world of imagination is boundless.

Man is born free, and everywhere he is in chains [due to governments].

Leo Rosten
(1908-1997) Polish American social scientist and writer

We see things as we are, not as they are.

Extremists think "communication" means agreeing with them.

Amy Ruley
(1955-) One of the greatest women's basketball coaches of all time

Everyone wants to win, but I think winners believe they deserve to win. They've made the commitment, they've followed the right path, and they've taken the right steps to be successful.

Dean Rusk
(1909-1994) American politician

One of the best ways to persuade others is with your ears, by listening to them.

John Ruskin
(1819-1900) English artist and writer

To give alms is nothing unless you give thought also.

A little thought and a little kindness are often worth more than a great deal of money.

Tell me what you like and I'll tell you what you are.

A thing is worth what it can do for you, not what you choose to pay for it.

The greatest thing a human being ever does is to see something and tell what he sees in a plain way.

Say all you have to say in the fewest possible words, or your reader will be sure to skip them; and in the plainest possible words or he will certainly misunderstand them.

The highest reward for a person's toil is not what they get for it, but what they become by it.

Do not think of your faults, still less of others' faults; look for what is good and strong, and try to imitate it. Your faults will drop off, like dead leaves, when their time comes.

Bertrand Russell
(1872-1970) English philosopher, mathematician, and social reformer who won the Nobel Prize for Literature in 1950

Aristotle maintained that women have fewer teeth than men; although he was twice married, it never occurred to him to verify this statement by examining his wives' mouths.

A life without adventure is likely to be unsatisfying, but a life in which adventure is allowed to take whatever form it will is sure to be short.

Democracy is the process by which people choose the man who'll get the blame.

Do not fear to be eccentric in opinion, for every opinion now accepted was once eccentric.

I would never die for my beliefs, because I might be wrong.

We know too much and feel too little. At least, we feel too little of those creative emotions from which a good life springs.

One should respect public opinion insofar as is necessary to avoid starvation and keep out of prison, but anything that goes beyond this is voluntary submission to an unnecessary tyranny.

The fact that an opinion has been widely held is no evidence whatever that it is not utterly absurd.

Conventional people are roused to fury by departures from convention, largely because they regard such departures as a criticism of themselves.

Man is a credulous animal, and must believe something; in the absence of good grounds for belief, he will be satisfied with bad ones.

Nolan Ryan
(1947-) Legendary baseball pitcher and all-time MLB career strikeouts record holder

Enjoying success requires the ability to adapt. Only by being open to change will you have a true opportunity to get the most from your talent.

Carl Sagan
(1934-1996) American astronomer and legendary science writer of books such as *Cosmos*

If you want to make an apple pie from scratch, you must first create the universe.

The universe is not required to be in perfect harmony with human ambition.

Somewhere, something incredible is waiting to be known.

Science is not only compatible with spirituality; it is a profound source of spirituality.

Virginia Sale
(1906-1992) American actress who appeared in about 200 movies and also performed her own one-woman show

Laughter is a great soul cleanser.

Saint Francis de Sales
(1567-1622) French Roman Catholic Bishop

There is no annoyance as great as the annoyance that is made up of many trifling but continuous worries.

Jonas Salk
(1914-1995) American medical researcher known for developing a polio vaccine

Life is an error-making and an error-correcting process...

Pete Sampras
(1971-) Arguably the greatest tennis player of all time

Anybody who plays sports and says they've never choked is lying to you.

Herbert Samuel
(1870-1963) British diplomat

No effect is ever the effect of a single cause, but only a combination of causes.

George Santayana
(1863-1952) Spanish-American philosopher

Habit is stronger than reason.

Virginia Satir
(1916-1988) American family therapist

We must not allow other people's limited perceptions to define us.

Arthur Schopenhauer
(1788-1860) Influential German philosopher

We forfeit three-quarters of ourselves in order to be like other people.

As a rule, a person's face says more things and more interesting things than his mouth does, for it [*his face*] is a compendium [*a short but thorough definition*] of everything his mouth will ever say, in that it is the monogram of all this person's thoughts and yearnings.

After your death, you will be what you were before your birth.

Just like an immense but disordered library is not as useful as a small but well arranged one, so is the greatest amount of knowledge that is not elaborated by our own thoughts worth much less than a much smaller amount that has been thoroughly utilized.

Money is human happiness in the non-concrete. Thus, he who cannot enjoy human happiness in the concrete devotes himself utterly to money.

In their search for [converting other materials into] gold, the alchemists discovered many other things of greater value.

The difficulty lies in trying to teach the multitude that something can be true and untrue at the same time.

The discovery of truth is not prevented as much by the current false appearance of things that mislead into error, or by the direct weakness of the reasoning powers, as it is by preconceived opinion, by prejudice.

Talent hits a target no one else can hit; genius hits a target no one else can see.

Change alone is eternal, perpetual, [and] immortal.

If we were not all so interested in ourselves, life would be so uninteresting that none of us would be able to endure it.

It is a clear gain to sacrifice pleasure in order to avoid pain.

… A person should never try to purchase pleasure at the cost of pain, or even at the risk of incurring it.

Care should be taken not to build the happiness of life upon a broad foundation—[which means] not to require a great many things in order to be happy. Happiness on such a foundation is the most easily undermined. It offers many more opportunities for accidents; and accidents are always happening.

Buying books would be a good thing if one could also buy the time to read them in; but as a rule, the purchase of books is mistaken for the allocation of their contents.

There is nothing that is too obvious of an absurdity to be firmly planted in the human head as long as you begin to instill before the age of five by constantly repeating it with an air of great seriousness [/ *impressiveness*].

    Most of the glories of the world are mere outward show, like the scenes on a stage: there is nothing real about them. Ships festooned and hung with pennants, firing of cannon, illuminations, beating of drums and blowing of trumpets, shouting and applauding—these are all the outward sign, the pretence and suggestion—as it were the hieroglyphic—of joy. But just there, joy is, as a rule, not to be found; it is the only guest who has declined to be present at the festival.

Where this guest [*joy*] may really be found, he comes generally without invitation; he is not formerly announced, but slips in quietly by himself *sans facon* [*"without way,"* / *unarranged* / *simple* / *free from ornament*], often making his appearance under the most unimportant and trivial circumstances, and in the commonest company—anywhere, in short, but where the society is brilliant and distinguished.

Joy is like the gold in the Australian mines—found only now and then, as it were, by the caprice of chance, and according to no rule or law; oftenest in very little grains, and very seldom in heaps. All that outward show which I have described, is only an attempt to make people believe that it is really joy which has come to the festival; and to produce this impression upon the spectators is, in fact, the whole object of it.

… A person should never let himself be mastered by the impressions of the moment, or indeed by outward appearances at all…

Most people are so thoroughly subjective that nothing really interests them but themselves. They always think of their own case as soon as ever any remark is made, and their whole attention is engrossed and absorbed by the merest chance reference to anything which affects them personally, be it never so remote: with the result that they have no power left for forming an objective view of things, should the conversation take that turn; neither can they admit any validity in arguments which tell against their interest or their vanity.

People are like children, in that, if you spoil them, they become naughty. Therefore it is well not to be too indulgent or charitable with anyone… There is one thing that, more than any other, throws people absolutely off their balance—the thought that you are dependent upon them. This is sure to produce an insolent and domineering manner towards you.

And it should be borne in mind that people, in their interaction with others are like the moon, or like hunchbacks: they show you only one of their sides. Every man has an innate talent for mimicry—for making a mask out of his physiognomy, so that he can always look as if he really were what he pretends to be; and since he makes his calculations always within the lines of his individual nature, the appearance he puts on suits him to a nicety, and its effect is extremely deceptive. He dons his mask whenever his object is to flatter himself into some one's good opinion; and you may pay just as much attention to it as if it were made of wax or cardboard…

No person is so formed that he can be left entirely to himself, to go his own ways; everyone needs to be guided by a preconceived plan, and to follow certain general rules. But if this is carried too far, and a person tries to take on a character which is not natural or innate in him, but it artificially acquired and evolved merely by a process of reasoning, he will very soon discover that Nature cannot be forced, and that if you drive it out, it will return despite your efforts.

You ought never to take any person as a [exact] model for what you should do or leave undone; because position and circumstances are in no two cases alike, and difference of character gives a peculiar, individual tone to what a person does. Two persons may do the same thing with a different result.

A person shows his character most in the way in which he deals with trifles—for then he is off his guard.

… [Some kind of material / financial interest] is the true foundation of almost all alliances: nay, most people have no notion of an alliance resting upon any other basis.

… We should never forget that the present is the only reality, the only certainty; that the future almost always turns out contrary to our expectations; that the past, too, was very different from what we suppose it to have been.

Our trust in other people often consists in great measure of pure laziness, selfishness, and vanity on our own part. I say *laziness*, because, instead of making inquiries ourselves, and exercising an active care, we prefer to trust others; *selfishness*, because we are led to confide in people by the pressure of our own affairs; and *vanity*, when we ask confidence for a matter on which we rather pride ourselves. And yet, for all that, we expect people to be true to the trust we repose in them.

If people insist that honor is dearer than life itself, what they really mean is that existence and well-being are as nothing compared with other people's opinions.

Nothing in life gives a man so much courage as the attainment or renewal of the conviction that other people regard him with favor; because it means that everyone joins to give him help and protection, which is an infinitely stronger defense against the ills of life than anything he can do himself.

Robert Schuller
(1926-) Christian American Reverend and author

Creative words generate energy; negative words drain out energy.

Charles M. Schwab
(1862-1939) American steel tycoon

Every one's got it in him, if he'll only make up his mind and stick at it. None of us is born with a stop-valve on his powers or with a set limit to his capacities.

There's no limit possible to the expansion of each one of us.

The person who does not work for the love of work but only for money is not likely to make money or to find much fun in life.

All successful employers are stalking men who will do the unusual, men who think, men who attract attention by performing more than is expected of them.

The first essential in a boy's career is to find out what he's fitted for, what he's most capable of doing and doing with a relish.

A man who trims himself to suit everybody will soon whittle himself away.

To carry on a successful business, a man must have imagination. He must see things as in a vision, a dream of the whole thing.

The hardest struggle of all is to be something different from what the average man is.

In my wide association in life, meeting with many and great men in various parts of the world, I have yet to find the man, however great or exalted his station, who did not do better work and put forth greater effort under a spirit of approval than he would ever do under a spirit of criticism.

Arnold Schwarzenegger
(1947-) Austrian American bodybuilder, movie superstar, businessman, and politician

The worst thing I can be is the same as everybody else. I hate that.

Tom Seeley

Life is the only game where the object of the game is to figure out what the rules are.

Seneca
(Lived in 00s BC and 00s AD) Roman playwright, philosopher, and statesmen

The most powerful one is he who has himself in his own power.

Life is neither a good nor an evil—it is simply a place where good and evil exist.

Lack of confidence is not the result of difficulty. Difficulty is a result of lack of confidence.

The sun shines even on the evil.

A man who suffers before it is necessary suffers more than necessary.

Little learning is needed to form a sound mind.

Johann G. Seume
(1763-1810) German writer

Nothing is more common on earth than to deceive and be deceived.

William Shakespeare
(1564-1616) Legendary British playwright who is widely considered among the greatest writers ever

Note: I have made minor revisions in line changing and capitalization on these quotes.

Your face, my thane, is as a book where men may read strange matters. (From *Macbeth*)

… What's done is done. (From *Macbeth*)

Present fears are less than horrible imaginings. (From *Macbeth*)

This above all: to thine own self be true... (From *Hamlet*)

To be or not to be, —that is the question (From *Hamlet*)

Though this be madness, yet there is method in 't. (From *Hamlet*)

Therefore, since brevity is the soul of wit... I will be brief. (From *Hamlet*)

...'tis the mind that makes the body rich; (From *The Taming of the Shrew*)

Frame your mind to mirth and merriment, which bars a thousand harms and lengthens life. (From *The Taming of the Shrew*)

How quickly nature falls into revolt, when gold becomes her object! (From *Henry IV*)

All things are ready, if our minds be so. (From *Henry V*)

For goodness' sake, consider what you do; how you may hurt yourself... (From *Henry VIII*)

For by his face straight shall you know his heart. (From *Richard III*)

All the world's a stage, and all the men and women merely players. (From *As You Like It*)

Shantidasa

Life is a series of choices, and sometimes your only choice is what your attitude will be.

I have discovered the ultimate goal in life is to be your own best friend—and only after you have befriended yourself, can you become a friend to others.

George Bernard Shaw
(1856-1950) Irish writer on a variety of subjects who won the Nobel Prize for Literature in 1925

The only man who behaved sensibly was my tailor; he took my measurement anew every time he saw me, while all the rest went on with their old measurements and expected them to fit me.

Patty Sheehan
(1956-) Female golf standout

Enjoy the successes that you have, and don't be too hard on yourself when you don't do well. Too many times we beat up on ourselves. Just relax and enjoy it.

Edgar A. Shoaff

A skeptic is a person who would ask God for his ID card.

A cynic is a person searching for an honest man with a stolen lantern.

Nigel Short
(1965-) British chess Grandmaster

Chess is ruthless. You've got to be prepared to kill people.

Homer Simpson
Character from the television show *The Simpsons*

You can't keep blaming yourself. Just blame yourself once, and move on.

Phfft! Facts. You can use them to prove anything.

Facts are meaningless. You could use facts to prove anything that's even remotely true!

Oh, people can come up with statistics to prove anything, Kent. 14% of people know that.

Isaac Bashevis Singer
(1904-1991) Jewish Polish American writer who won the Nobel Prize for Literature in 1978

We must believe in free will. We have no choice.

(Swami) Sivananda

(1887-1963) Indian yoga master

Life is a series of awakenings.

Emmitt Smith
(1969-) Football running back who leads the NFL in career rushing yards, and has won three Super Bowl Championships

Winning is something that builds physically and mentally every day that you train and every night that you dream.

Logan Pearsall Smith
(1865-1946) English American writer

Charming people live up to the very edge of their charm, and behave as outrageously as the world lets them.

How can they say my life is not a success? Have I not for more than sixty years got enough to eat and escaped being eaten?

There are two things to aim at in life: first, to get what you want; and after that, to enjoy it. Only the wisest if mankind achieve the second.

Baird Spalding
(1857-1953) Spiritual teacher and writer

Learn to thrill yourself... Make everything bright and beautiful about you. Cultivate a spirit of humor. Enjoy the sunshine.

Herbert Spencer
(1820-1903) British philosopher and sociologist

Life is the continuous adjustment of internal relations to external relations.

Charles Spurgeon
(1834-1892) Popular English Christian preacher

With children we must mix gentleness with firmness. They must not always have their own way, but they must not always be thwarted.

Adlai Stevenson
(1900-1965) American politician and Presidential candidate who also confounded the United Nations

The human race is a family. Men are brothers. All wars are civil wars.

Gerhard Staguhn
(1952-) American physicist

He who gazes at the stars unavoidably starts thinking.

Rex Stout
(1886-1975) American mystery novelist

There are two kinds of statistics: the kind you look up, and the kind you make up.

Annamalai Swami
(1906-1995) Indian spiritual figure

Virtually all people are a mixture of good and bad. It is very rare to find someone wholly good and wholly bad. If you have to come into contact with a lot of people, try to make yourself aware of their good points and don't dwell on their bad points.

Muni Swamy

No one can become another, even by following exactly what the other is doing.

Charles R. Swindoll
Christian pastor and author of books such as *Hand Me Another Brick* (1998)

Attitude, to me, is more important than facts. It is more important than the past, than education, than money, than circumstances, than failures, than successes, than what other people think or say or do. It is more important than appearance, giftedness, or skill. ... We cannot change our past... we cannot change the fact that people will act in a certain way... The only thing that we can do is to play on the one string we have, and that is our attitude...

Madame Ann Sophie Jeanne Soymonof Swetchine
(1782-1857) Russian mystic

We do not judge men by what they are in themselves, but what they are relatively to us.

Publilius (or Publius) Syrus
(Lived in 00s BC) Roman writer

No pleasure endures unseasoned by variety.

Powerful indeed is the empire of habit.

Good health and good sense are two of life's greatest blessings.

A plan is bad if it is not capable of being changed.

It is wise to learn what to avoid from the misfortunes of others.

Keep the golden mean between saying too much and too little.

We are interested in others when they are interested in us.

It is better to learn late than never.

Many receive advice; few profit by it.

A pleasant traveling companion on a journey is as good as a carriage.

Each day is the scholar of yesterday.

Every one excels in something in which another fails.

In excessive argument, truth is lost.

Everything is worth what its purchaser will pay for it.

Ryoko Tamura
(1975-) Japanese women's judo champion

I don't agree with the idea that you have to live in a bubble and sacrifice all your time to something if you want to succeed. I need to be interested in things outside my sport, and I need to meet new people. For me, judo is an expression of the harmony I achieve in my life.

Fran Tarkenton
(1940-) Pro football legend

If it's not fun, you are not doing it right.

Charles T. Tart
(1937-) American psychologist and writer

Your imaginings can have as much power over you as your reality, or even more.

Judy Tatelbaum
American psychotherapist and author of books such as *Courage to Grieve* (1984)

Appreciate life instead of resisting it.

Terence
(Lived in 100s BC) Roman writer of comedies

I consider it a principle rule of life not to be excessive in anything.

It is great to be clever and have common sense.

You are a wise person if you can easily direct your attention to whatever needs it.

It is possible for someone to be changed so much by love that he will hardly be recognized as being the same person.

Mother Teresa
(1910-1997) Albanian-Indian woman who devoted herself to helping the poor, and won the won the Nobel Prize for Peace in 1979

The biggest disease today is not leprosy or tuberculosis, but rather the feeling of being unwanted.

Margaret Thatcher
(1925-) Britain's first ever woman prime minister

Nothing is more obstinate than a fashionable consensus.

If you just set out to be liked, you would be prepared to compromise on anything at any time, and you would achieve nothing.

You may have to fight a battle more than once to win it.

James Thurber
(1894-1961) American cartoonist and writer

Seeing is deceiving. It's eating that's believing.

Roderick Thorp
Author of books such as *Nothing Lasts Forever* (a.k.a. *Die Hard*) (1979)

We have to learn to be our own best friend, because we fall too easily into the trap of being out worst enemy.

Leo Tolstoy
(1828-1910) Legendary Russian novelist who wrote *War and Peace*

Freethinkers are those who are willing to use their minds without prejudice and without fearing to understand things that clash with their own customs, privileges, or beliefs.

Paul Tournier
(1898-1986) Medical doctor who developed a psychiatric method he termed "medicine of the person"

Many ordinary illnesses are nothing but the expression of a serious dissatisfaction with life.
Most illnesses do not, as is generally thought, come like a bolt out of the blue. The ground is prepared for years through faulty diet, intemperance, overwork, and moral conflicts, slowly eroding the subject's vitality.

Brian Tracy
Public speaker and author of success books such as *Change Your Thinking, Change Your Life* (2003)

Successful people are simply those with success habits.

Donald J. Trump
(1946-) American real estate mogul known mainly for his high-end properties located in or near New York State

I try to learn from the past, but I plan for the future by focusing exclusively on the present. That's were the fun is.

What separates the winners from the losers is how a person reacts to each new twist of fate.

Sometimes your best investments are the ones you don't make.

I don't make deals for the money. I've got enough, much more than I'll ever need. I do it to do it.

Money was never a big motivation for me, except as a way to keep score. The real excitement is playing the game.

Liv Ullman
(1939-) Norwegian actress

The best thing that can come with success is the knowledge that it is nothing to long for.

Paul Valery
(1871-1945) French poet and essayist

The best way to make your dreams come true is to wake up.

The trouble with our times is that the future is not what it used to be.

Marquis De Vauvenargues
(1715-1747) French philosopher

Emotions have taught mankind to reason.

The most absurd and reckless aspirations have sometimes led to extraordinary success.

People often feel offended by praise because it designates a limit to their excellence. Few people are modest enough not to be offended by someone appreciating them.

Kurt Vonnegut, Jr.
(1922-) American science fiction novelist

We are what we pretend to be, so we must be careful about what we pretend to be.

Denis Waitley
Motivational speaker and author of books such as *The Psychology of Winning* (1984)

The essence of life is finding something you really love and then making the daily experience worthwhile.

Mary H. Waldrip

It's important that people know what you stand for. It's equally important that they know what you won't stand for.

Sam Walton
(1918-1992) American businessman who founded retail giant Wal-Mart

I have always been driven to buck the system, to innovate, to take things beyond where they've been.

There is only one boss—the customer. And he can fire everybody in the company from the chairman on down, simply by spending his money somewhere else.

Capital isn't scarce; vision is.

We let folks know we're interested in them and that they're vital to us— cause they are.

Outstanding leaders go out of the way to boost the self-esteem of their personnel. If people believe in themselves, it's amazing what they can accomplish.

I had to pick myself up and get on with it, and do it all over again—only even better this time.

An Wang
(1920-1990) Chinese American electronics engineer who founded Wang Laboratories

No matter how complicated a problem is, it usually can be reduced to a simple, comprehensible form that is often the best solution.

William Arthur Ward
(1812-1882) English writer and theologian

If you can imagine it, you can create it. If you can dream it, you can become it.

Flatter me, and I may not believe you. Criticize me, and I may not like you. Ignore me, and I may not forgive you. Encourage me, and I will not forget you.

Booker T. Washington
(1856-1915) African-American leader, reformer, educator, and presidential advisor

Character is power.

H.G. Wells
(1866-1946) English writer, historian, and sociologist; he is most known for science fiction novels such as *The Time Machine*

We must not allow the clock and the calendar to blind us to the fact that each moment of life is a miracle and mystery.

Mae West
(1892-1980) Innovative American actress

Your real security is yourself. You know you can do it, and they can't ever take that away from you.

T.H. White
(1906-1964) English writer and social historian

The best thing for being sad is to learn something.

Alfred North Whitehead
(1861-1947) English philosopher and mathematician

Familiar things happen, and mankind does not bother about them. It requires a very unusual mind to undertake the analysis of the obvious.

The art of progress is to preserve order amid change and to preserve change amid order.

Walt Whitman
(1819-1892) American writer

> Do I contradict myself?
> Very well then I contradict myself,
> (I am large, I contain multitudes.)

Elie Wiesel
(1928-) Jewish Romanian French American writer who won the Nobel Prize for Peace in 1986

> I don't believe in accidents. There are only encounters in history. There are no accidents.

Oscar Wilde
(1854-1900) Irish writer most known for works such as *Lady Windermere's Fan* and *The Importance of Being Earnest*

> To love oneself is the beginning of a life-long romance.

Thornton Wilder
(1897-1975) American novelist and playwright known for such plays as *The Matchmaker*

> We do not choose the day of our birth nor may we choose the day of our death, yet choice is the sovereign faculty of the mind.

Kelly Williams
American fencer who was women's Sabre champion in 1998

> When I'm in a bout and I stop fighting to win and start fighting not to lose, I'm almost guaranteed to lose because I quit taking chances.

Tennessee Williams
(1911-1983) American playwright known for such works as *A Streetcar Named Desire, The Night of the Iguana,* and *Cat on a Hat Tin Roof*

> Life is all memory, except for that one present moment that goes by so quickly you hardly catch it going.

Marianne Williamson
Author of *A Return to Love* (1996) and other books

Joy is what happens to us when we allow ourselves to recognize how good things really are.

Our deepest fear is not that we are inadequate. Our deepest fear is that we are powerful beyond measure... Your playing small does not serve the world. There is nothing enlightened about shrinking so that other people won't feel insecure around you. We are all meant to shine... And as we let our own light shine, we unconsciously give other people permission to do the same. (From *A Return to Love*)

Colin Wilson
(1931-) English author of a variety of subjects

When I open my eyes in the morning, I am not confronted by a world, but by a million possible worlds.

Henry Winkler
(1945-) American actor and producer most known for his role as Arthur "The Fonz" "Fonzi" Fonzarelli on the show *Happy Days*

Assumptions are the termites of relationships.

John Wooden
(1910-) Legendary American college basketball coach

Never mistake activity for achievement.

Tiger Woods
(1975-) American golf superstar who is considered one of the greatest golfers of all time

My mind is my biggest asset.

John Woolman
(1720-1772) British American Quaker-Christian leader and writer

Conduct is more convincing than language.

Orville Wright
(1871-1948) He and his brother Wilbur invented, built and flew the first airplane

If we all worked on the assumption that what is accepted as true is really true, there would be little hope of advance.

Jon Wynne-Tyson
(1924-) British writer

The wrong sort of people are always in power because they would not be in power if they were not the wrong sort of people.

Lin Yutang
(1895-1976) Chinese author on Chinese philosophy and other subjects

Besides the noble art of getting things done, there is the noble art of leaving things undone. The wisdom of life consists in the elimination of non-essentials.

If you can spend a perfectly useless afternoon in a perfectly useless manner, you have learned how to live.

The wise man reads both books and life itself.

This I conceive to be the chemical function of humor: to change the character of our thought.

Robert Zend
(1929-1985) Writer

People have one thing in common: they are all different.

Johann G. Zimmerman
(1957-) German scientist

The more you speak of yourself, the more you are likely to lie.

Zohar
Jewish mysticism (Kabbalah) text

If you wish to strengthen a lie, mix a little truth in with it.

Anonymous / Unknown

Times change, and we change with them.

A lie can go halfway around the world before the truth even has its shoes on.

Wisdom is the ability to correct mistakes.

A diamond is a chunk of coal that made good under pressure.

You gain power over another person by winning his heart or by breaking his spirit.

Anyone can count the seeds in an apple; no one can count the apples in a seed.

A friend is a person with whom you dare to be yourself

Many people would rather fight for their principles than live up to them.

Not respecting yourself is the same as committing suicide at a slow rate.

It isn't the mountains ahead that wear you out—it's the grain of sand in your shoe.

Think highly of yourself, because the world takes you at your own estimate

Sow a thought and you reap an action; sow an act and you reap a habit; sow a habit and you reap a character; sow a character and you reap a destiny.

Don't steal. The government hates competition.

You are unique, just like everyone else.

All "isms" are "wasms."

I've told you for the thousandth time—stop exaggerating!

It's not an optical illusion—it just looks like one.

Preface to Proverbs Section

The next section of chapters contains proverbs and background information of various countries or cultures.

Proverbs are short commonly used sayings based on people's observations and experiences. Example: "The sweetness of food doesn't last long, but the sweetness of good words do." (Thai Proverb)

There are tens of thousands of proverbs the world has produced throughout history. Before we get to some of the world's greatest proverbs, here are some various quotes and proverbs about proverbs:

Russian Proverb

Proverbs are the people's wisdom.

Miguel De Cervantes
(1547-1616) Legendary Spanish writer

Proverbs are short sentences drawn from long experience.

R. Buckminster Fuller
(1895-1983) American poet, philosopher, inventor, and architect

A proverb is much matter distilled into few words.

English Proverb

A proverb is the child of experience.

Thomas Carlyle
(1795-1881) Scottish historian

There is often more spiritual force in a proverb than in whole philosophical systems.

William Gilmore Simms
(1806-1870) American author of romances

The proverb answers where the sermon fails, as a well-charged pistol will do more execution than a whole barrel of gunpowder idly exploded in the air.

William R. Alger
(1823-1905) American writer

Proverbs are mental gems gathered in the diamond fields of the mind.

Nigerian Proverb

When an occasion arises, there is a proverb to suit it.

Arabic Proverb

Proverbs are the lamp of speech.

Zimbabwean Proverb

Proverbs can be applied to get what you want.

African Proverbs

Africa is one of the world's most abundant sources of proverbs. Before we explore some of them, here is a brief overview of the continent of Africa, which is widely considered to be the birthplace of humankind.

Note: Madagascar (an island country southeast of the mainland African continent) is covered towards the end of this chapter.

General Info

Africa is the second largest continent on Earth (Asia is first), and has a current population of over 800 million people. Much of the region is comprised of either deserts or forests. The population in Africa is very unevenly distributed—much of it is uninhabitable, while other parts are heavily populated.

Natural Wonders

Africa is noted for natural wonders such as its tropical rainforests, the Sahara Desert (the world's largest desert), and the Nile River (the world's longest river).

The continent also contains a wide range of animals, including leopards, lions, cheetahs, hyenas, jackals, wildcats, antelope, buffalo, rhinos, hippos, zebras, giraffes, elephants, foxes, chimpanzees, gorillas, monkeys, seals, whales, dolphins, and fish.

Birthplace of Humankind

Many archeologists and biologists consider Africa the birthplace of humankind. While numerous theories abound, many scientists believe that the earliest form of humans lived in Africa a few million years ago (the average estimate is about 3.5 million years ago) and spread throughout the world.

Most scientists also believe that the modern variation of human (*Homo sapiens sapiens*) also originated in Africa about 150,000 years ago, and later spread to the Middle East and Asia, and then to the rest of the world.

Cultural Groups

Africa has an immense variety of people and cultures. Just the Black Africans alone have over 1000 different distinct ethnic groups among them, most of which have different languages, traditions, and ways of life.

Cultural Backgrounds

Africa contains a vast number of cultural background and population groups. Northern parts of Africa contain predominantly Arab Africans and Berbers, while sub-Saharan Africa is inhabited predominantly by Black Africans, who make up most of Africa's population.

Other African ethnic groups include people of European dissent (most of which live in South Africa, Zimbabwe, and Kenya), and people of Asian ancestry (who are mainly of Indonesian and Indian backgrounds).

Early Empires and City-States

Africa was home to one of the world's first known empires, Ancient Egypt, which lay along the Nile River and existed primarily from 3200 BC to 0 AD.

Many other empires later originated or existed in Africa, including Carthage (700s BC-600 AD), the Ghana Empire (400s-1000s), the Mali Empire (1200s-1400s), the Songhai Empire (1400s-1500s), the Kongo Kingdom (1200s-1600s), and many other kingdoms in the 2nd Millennium. Regions in Northern Africa have also been part of foreign Empires at various times, such as the Roman Empire from the 100s BC to the 400s AD.

Many large city-states also developed in Africa, such as Lepcis Magna (900s BC-500s AD), Axum (100s AD-400s AD), Mogadishu (900s AD-Present Day), and Mombasa (1000s AD-Present Day).

Arabs and Islam

In the 600s AD, Muslim Arabs conquered much of Northern Africa and soon established trade with other parts of Africa. They also spread the Islamic religion throughout Northern Africa and parts of the rest of the continent, and caused the creation of an Arab / Bantu-African hybrid language known as Swahili.

Lifestyles

Besides its city dwellers, most Africans have lived in smaller communities throughout most of African history. Those societies generally had one of these five themes dominant in its peoples' lifestyles: hunting &

gathering, fishing, grain growing, nomadic animal herding, or tropical forest village farming.

Slavery

In the 1400s, Europeans (particularly the Spanish and Portuguese) established trading posts in Africa, and by the 1500s, they began taking Africans captive as slaves. (Slave labor had also existed in earlier times in Africa, particularly in Ancient Egypt, the Roman Empire, and in some African Islam states.)

The British (and the French and Dutch to lesser extents) soon became the main slave trading presence in Africa, and the slave trade grew steadily, particularly due to the plantation-based economy in the Southern United States that depended on slave labor. Some African cities later began capturing slaves to trade with the Europeans, and some of them also used slave labor within their own borders.

In the early 1800s, the British government issued laws making the slave trade illegal, but the trading continued to persist. By the 1860s, the United States had abolished slavery within its borders, and the slave trade lessened in Africa.

Colonialization

By the late 1800s, different European countries began competing for control of various African regions and resources, and began colonializing the continent. The European presence soon caused the slave trade to end.

By the early 1900s, Europeans (from Britain, Portugal, France, and Germany) controlled most of Africa (except Ethiopia and Liberia), and also caused Christianity to spread in the colonies. Some Europeans also settled in parts of Africa. For the most part, the European presence in Africa was to exploit the continent's resources, particularly its diamonds and gold.

Independence

Africans resisted the European rulers, and throughout the 1900s, all African nations gained their independence. The first was Egypt in 1922 and the last was South Africa in 1988; while most others happened in the 1950s and 1960s.

Current Africa

Most Africans today inhabit farms and have a lifestyle similar to Africans generations ago. Others live in cities and have a modern lifestyle.

African Themes

Although Africa varies greatly, some themes of Africa include religion (including traditional African religions as well as Christianity and Islam), textiles, sculptures, cultural ceremonies and festivals, rituals, music (especially drums), dancing, hot weather, folktales / storytelling, witchcraft, mineral and crop exporting, diamond and mineral mining, coffee, cotton, petroleum, fishing, poetry, spears, pottery, beadwork, poverty, famine, political turmoil, overcrowding, soccer, boxing, cricket, long distance running (particularly in Kenya), South African hero Nelson Mandela, Egyptian UN diplomat Boutros Boutros-Gali, and multiculturalism.

Countries

Most of the country divisions in current Africa are due cultural differences, political situations, and the effects of European colonialism.

The countries of Africa include Algeria, Angola, Benin, Botswana, Burkina Faso, Burundi, Cameroon, Cape Verde, Central African Republic, Chad, Comoros, Congo (Democratic Republic of the Congo, or Kinshasa—formerly known as Zaire), Congo Republic (Brazzaville), Cote d'Ivoire, Djibouti, Egypt, Equatorial Guinea, Eritrea, Ethiopia, Gabon, Gambia, Ghana, Guinea, Guinea–Bissau, Kenya, Lesotho, Liberia, Libya, Madagascar, Malawi, Mali, Mauritania, Mauritius, Morocco, Mozambique, Namibia, Niger, Nigeria, Reunion, Rwanda, Sao Tome e Principe, Senegal, Seychelles, Sierra Leone, Somalia, South Africa, Sudan, Swaziland, Tanzania, Togo, Tunisia, Uganda, Western Sahara, Zambia, and Zimbabwe.

African Proverbs

Note: It is difficult to pinpoint what specific countries many African proverbs are primarily from, especially due to the enormous number of different cultures that Africa is home to, as well as the varied factors responsible for African country divisions, many of which have very recently been created. However, for most of these proverbs, I have included a country of common use and origin.

Do not rush the night—the sun will always rise for its own sake.

Send a boy where he wishes to go, and you will see his best pace.

A man who pays respect to the great paves his own way for greatness.

Tomorrow belongs to the people who prepare for it today.

When the heart acts, the body is its slave.

He who has not traveled widely thinks that his mother is the best cook.

It takes a whole village to raise a child.

Do something at its (right) time, and peace will accompany it.

It is not what you are called, but what you answer to.

The key that unlocks is also the key that locks.

Honor a child, and he will honor you.

Repetition is the mother of knowledge.

The sun shines on those who are standing before it shines on the people kneeling under them.

Three things that a man must know to survive: what is too much for him, what is too little, and what is fitting.

The world does not make promises to anybody.

When there is no enemy within, the enemies outside cannot hurt you.

If you live next to the cemetery, you cannot cry for everyone.

A wise man doesn't know everything—only a fool does.

Anxiety will not let you die of hunger.

If you don't stand for something, you will fall for something.

A weapon that you don't have in your hand will not kill a snake.

Looking for something can get in the way of finding it.

The person who rides a donkey cannot avoid smelling its farts.

Indecision is like a stepchild: if he doesn't wash his hands, then he is called dirty; but if he washes his hands, then he is wasting water!

A leopard is chasing us, and you are asking me, "Is it a male or a female?"

A marketplace is not the pace for a husband and wife to argue.

However long the night may last, there will be a morning.

Daylight follows a dark night.

A secret for two is soon a secret for nobody. (Algeria)

Since we didn't say anything, he thought he could do whatever he wanted to. (Algeria)

A sensible enemy is better than a narrow-minded friend. (Algeria)

If you have not been to two different bazaars, then you do not know what the best value is. (Burkina Faso)

The unborn baby that fears criticism will never be born. (Burundi)

By trying repeatedly, the monkey learns how to jump from the tree. (Cameroon)

Lying can get you a wife, but it won't keep her. (Cameroon)

If you ask questions, you cannot avoid answers. (Cameroon)

No matter how fast a man is, he cannot outrun his shadow. (Cameroon)

The heart of a wise man lies quiet like clear water. (Cameroon)

If everyone is going to dance, then who will watch? (Cameroon)

If the fight is tomorrow, then why should you clench your fist today? (Cameroon)

A man with too much ambition cannot sleep in peace. (Chad)

He who does not like chattering woman will remain a bachelor. (Congo)

A day of hunger is not starvation. (Congo)

No matter how long the night is, the morning is sure to come. (Congo)

If you are too modest, then you will go hungry. (Congo)

He who talks continuously, talks nonsense. (Cote d'Ivoire)

Honorable is the person who is aware of his power, yet refrains from inflicting bad things onto others. (Egypt)

We let him in; but then he brought his donkey along, too! (Egypt)

A beautiful thing is never perfect. (Egypt)

The bullet that doesn't hit (anything) still makes a noise. (Egypt)

If you put a rope around your neck, many people will be glad to drag you by it. (Egypt)

The person who is not ashamed does whatever he wants. (Egypt)

Silence is more than just a lack of words. (Egypt)

They couldn't find any reason to criticize the roses, so they complained that they were red! (Egypt)

He has his own brain—he can solve his own problems. (Egypt)

Don't blame God for creating the tiger—instead, thank him for not giving it wings. (Ethiopia)

If you are going to go where corn grows, take a cutting tool with you. (Ethiopia)

Eat when the food is ready; speak when the time is right. (Ethiopia)

It is foolish for someone to remain thirsty when he is in the midst of water. (Ethiopia)

When the hyena is gone, that is when the dog barks. (Ethiopia)

Bad friends will prevent you from having good friends. (Gabon)

Heal yourself first before you heal others. (Gambia)

Several repeated visits to the mud pit enable the wasp to build its house. (Ghana)

Don't expect to be offered a chair when you are visiting a place where the chief sits on the floor. (Ghana)

If someone is walking towards you, you don't need to tell him "come here." (Ghana)

Bad luck for one man is good luck for another. (Ghana)

Only a fool tests the water's depth with both feet. (Ghana)

By coming and going, a bird constructs its nest. (Ghana)

When you are rich, you are hated; when you are poor, you are despised. (Ghana)

One lie spoils a thousand truths. (Ghana)

It is no disgrace at all to work for money. (Ghana)

When the hunter returns and is holding mushrooms, don't ask him about how his hunt went. (Guinea)

No matter how much milk a cow has, you cannot milk butter from it. (Guinea)

A man's actions are more important than his ancestry. (Kenya)

Crawling on hands and knees has never prevented anyone from walking upright. (Kenya)

The enemy you know is better than the one you do not know. (Kenya)

The day before yesterday and yesterday are not the same as today. (Kenya)

The always-hurrying person eats goat, but the one who takes his time eats beef. (Lesotho)
Note: In Lesotho and many other parts of Africa, cow meat is prized much more than goat meat.

An elephant never gets tired of supporting its tusks. (Liberia)

Don't look where you fell; look where you slipped. (Liberia)

Gossiping about the enemy can result in a war. (Liberia)

Every head must do its own thinking. (Liberia)

Each trip gives you its own uniqueness. (Libya)

If everyone thought the same way, no goods would ever be sold. (Libya)

A mad dog bites anything except itself. (Libya)

While the sun is shining, bask in it! (Malawi)

No matter how many house chores you complete, there are always more to be done. (Mali)

The hyena chasing two gazelles at the same will go to bed hungry. (Mali)

If the rabbit is your enemy, admit that he can sprint fast. (Mali)

The radiant and well-understood speech of one person is better than the speech of a thousand people that is not. (Morocco)

The cat and the mouse can't be neighbors for long. (Namibia)

The person who guards himself will not be destroyed. (Namibia)

Old people's speech is not to be dishonored—after all, they saw the sun first. (Namibia)

The zebra told the white horse, "I am white," and told the black horse, "I am actually black." (Namibia)

When the music changes, so does the dance. (Niger)

Every kind of love is love, but self-love is supreme among them. (Niger)

The man that won't marry a woman with other admirers won't marry a woman at all. (Nigeria)

Rain does not make friends with anybody—it falls on any person it meets outside. (Nigeria)

You can't use your hand to force the sun to set. (Nigeria)

Black goats must be caught early, before it gets dark. (Nigeria)

No matter how dark it is, the hand always knows the way to the mouth. (Nigeria)

The mouth that eats pepper is the one that the pepper influences. (Nigeria)

Being happy in one's home is better than being a chief. (Nigeria)

You know who you love, but you can't know who loves you. (Nigeria)

What is sensible today may be derangement at another time. (Nigeria)

Until lions have their own historians, accounts of the hunt will always celebrate the hunter. (Nigeria)

In the birds' court, a cockroach never wins his case. (Rwanda)

You can outrun what is running after you, but not what is running inside of you. (Rwanda)

If you are building something and a nail breaks, should you stop building altogether, or should you change the nail? (Rwanda)

Work is good, as long as you don't forget to live. (Rwanda)

If you wait for tomorrow, tomorrow comes. If you don't wait for tomorrow, tomorrow comes. (Senegal)

The house roof fights the rain, but the person who is sheltered ignores it. (Senegal)

Where there is negotiation, there is hope for agreement. (Somalia)

Moving water makes stagnant water move. (Somalia)

Even when there is no rooster, the morning will still start. (South Africa)

Don't meddle with a family feud. (South Africa)

A small shrub may grow into a tree. (Sudan)

A person who is not disciplined cannot be cautioned. (Tanzania)

I pointed out the stars and moon to you, but all you saw was the tip of my finger! (Tanzania)

Little by little, a little becomes a lot. (Tanzania)

Help me during the flood, and I will help you during the drought. (Tanzania)

Hunger is felt by a slave, and hunger is felt by a king. (Togo)

Rain wets the leopard's spots, but it doesn't wash them off. (Togo)

Respect yourself, and you will get it back. (Tunisia)

If you see someone riding a bamboo-cane [in a way that he is enjoying his imagination and fantasizing like he is riding an animal], tell him "What a lovely horse!" (Tunisia)

It is better to blush than to keep the concern in your heart. (Tunisia)

The hunter who is tracking an elephant does not stop to throw stones at birds. (Uganda)

If you have a dog, don't throw away bones. (Uganda)

The laughter of a child is the light of a house. (Uganda)

You can learn a lot about someone by observing him when he is hungry. (Zambia)

A roaring lion kills no game. (Zimbabwe)

MADAGASCAR

Madagascar is a large island and group of smaller islands all off of southeast coast of the African continent.   Despite its close proximity to Africa, Madagascar is a very unique land. The people are Malagasy, and have a primarily Indonesian culture combined with some Arab and Bantu-African influences and ethnicities mixed in.

The origins of Malagasy people are uncertain, but they are thought to derive from Indonesian navigators from the first millennium AD who settled there, and soon established trade with Arabs. The French later established settlements in Madagascar and took control of it by the late 1800s, but by 1960, the island gained full independence.

Malagasy themes include music, dancing, unique animal species, elaborate burial tombs, woodcarving, literature, festivals, rice, bananas, cassava, yams, and fruit.

Malagasy Proverbs

It is better to refuse to go than to accept and not go.

Don't be so in love that you can't tell when rain is coming.

A man who lets his problems get the better of him is like the man who divorces his wife the first time she makes him angry.

Distracted by what is far away, he does not see his nose.

A fortuneteller says, "If it is not a boy, it will be a girl."

Nothing is so difficult that diligence cannot master it.

Don't blame the axe for the noise made by the chicken you are about to slaughter.

Chinese Proverbs

Located in eastern Asia, China (the Chinese call it Zhongguo) is the most populous country in the world with well over one billion people, and is an abundant source of great proverbs.

China is considered one of the world's oldest civilizations. It has also had a tremendous impact on neighboring areas such as Japan and Korea.

Much of Chinese history has to do with various dynasties that ruled and various philosophies that flourished throughout the land. Before we explore its proverbs, here is a brief look at China.

Note: Tibet (a semi-independent region in China) and the Uighur (a Turkish speaking cultural group in China) are covered in separate sections towards the end of this chapter

Early Culture and Dynasties

The roots of China come from the early Yangshao and Longshan cultures, which later spurned China's first dynasty around 1700 BC, known as the Shang dynasty.

Zhou Dynasty

Around the 1100s BC, western Chinese people known as the Zhou overthrew the Shang, and they directly ruled northern China until 256 BC, and also indirectly ruled other parts of China

Confucius and Confucianism

Around 500 BC, a Chinese philosopher named Confucius (a.k.a. Kung Fu Tzu) popularized a code of moral principles now known as Confucianism, which shaped Chinese culture on-and-off for many centuries. (Confucianism is covered in a separate chapter of this book)

Around the same time, a school of thought known as Taoism began developing and flourishing throughout China, which also influenced China tremendously throughout its history. (Taoism is covered in a separate chapter of this book.)

Qin Dynasty—Legalism, Standardization, and the Great Wall

By 221 BC, the Qin dynasty began. It had a strong central government and used a philosophy called Legalism, which promoted ideals such as authority, efficiency, and lawmaking. Like Confucianism, Legalism also had a significant impact on China, although the Qin dynasty dissolved by 206 BC.

Other notable impacts of the Qin dynasty included an era of standardization in China, as well as the construction of the massive Great Wall (which joined earlier walls that existed, and was later added to and rebuilt in subsequent dynasties. The Great Wall is currently over 4500 miles long.)

Han & Xin Dynasties, Buddhism, and Foreign Rulers

The Han dynasty ruled China from 202 BC to 220 AD, but was interrupted from 8 AD to 25 AD during the Xin dynasty. During the Han and Xin periods, science, art, and writing flourished, and Confucianism also grew in popularity. Additionally, a school of thought known as Buddhism spread to China from India (see the Zen Buddhism chapter for more info on Buddhism).

From 220 AD to the late 500s, various foreign rulers controlled various parts of China, while Buddhism continued to spread and influence Chinese culture.

Sui and Tang Dynasties

In the late 500s, China was reunified by the Sui dynasty, which lasted for under four decades, and was replaced by the Tang in 618. The Tang ruled for nearly three centuries, and in that time, China experienced many scholarly and financial advancements.

Several offspring of Buddhism also developed in China, including Chan (known as Zen in Japan—see the Zen Buddhism chapter for more info)

Song Dynasty and Neo-Confucianism

The Tang Empire ended in 907, and China was later unified once again in 960 by the Song. The Song period marked the development of Neo-Confucianism, which combined aspects of Confucianism, Buddhism, and Taoism.

The Song period also marked a dramatic increase in rice production, as well as inventions such as gunpowder and movable type, an increase in literacy, and advancements in literature, history, philosophy, and art.

Mongol Rule

In 1279, Mongol warriors led by Kublai Kan established the Yuan dynasty. They ruled for nearly a century before being driven out, and in that time, the rest of the world became more aware of China.

Ming and Qing Dynasties

The Ming Dynasty ruled from 1368 to 1644, and marked a time when China was prosperous, and also when it rejected foreign influence and culture. In 1681, the Manchus (people from Manchuria—a region in northeastern China) took over China and began the Qing (Manchu) dynasty.

The early Qing period was marked by Chinese influence on countries such as Mongolia and Tibet, a dramatic increase in Chinese population, and an increase in foreign trade. The Qing gradually lost power throughout the 1800s and early 1900s.

Rebellions, Conflicts, Revolutions and Wars

China underwent many conflicts, rebellions, revolutions and wars from the late 1700s to the late 1900s.

In the late 1700s, Chinese production could not keep up with the growing population, and political corruption also brewed. This sparked a rebellion in 1796 that lasted until 1804.

In the 1800s, European traders began smuggling opium into China. This caused enormous problems in China, and led to The Opium War, where the United Kingdom defeated China. After that war, the UK, and later other European countries and the United States, began signing unfair treaties with China.

By the mid 1800s, the Qing still had some power, but many violent rebellions persisted in China. In the late 1800s, Japan defeated China in a war. Other foreign powers looked to turn China into colonies, but China remained unified, and the Western powers agreed to share equal trading rights with China.

In 1900, China had a rebellion against Western and Christian influences. In 1905, a revolutionary group formed, and by 1911, they defeated the Qing (Manchus) and officially ended the Qing dynasty. They established the Republic of China, but political unrest ensued. Communist, Nationalist, and Japanese groups struggled for power of China for many years.

Communism, and the People's Republic of China

In 1946, a civil war began, and in 1949, the Communist Party and army under leader Mao Zedong declared the establishment of the People's Republic of China. The government redistributed land from landlords to peasants, although this led to more bloodshed. More revolutionary activities also continued in China.

Mao Zedong died in 1976. Beginning in the 1970s, China's relations with the West began improving.

Current China

Most Chinese people currently live in small villages and towns, while others live in large cities such as Shanghais and Beijing. The eastern parts of China are very overcrowded, and the Chinese government encourages people to marry late and to have only one or two children.

China is home to many cultures, but most people belong to the Han nationality. Most people speak one of several variations of Chinese, although the government hopes to standardize the Northern Chinese language, which is known as Mandarin or Putonghua. Unlike spoken Chinese, written Chinese is mostly the same throughout the nation.

Lately, China's economy has been undergoing major transitions.

Chinese Themes

Some themes of China include philosophy (such as Confucianism, Buddhism, and Taoism), tai chi (a form of exercise), marital arts, communism, overcrowded populations, soybeans, cotton, low cost manufacturing, a recent influx of American culture (such as McDonalds and KFC), pirated movies, basketball superstar Yao Ming, ping pong, soccer, tennis, literature, textiles, coal, rice, soup, the consumption of many different kinds of animals, pottery, acrobatics & gymnastics, music, dancing, calligraphy, poetry, painting, and theatre.

Chinese Proverbs

The best time to plant a tree was 20 years ago. The second best time is today.

A hobbling cat is better than a fast horse when rats swarm the palace.

In a group of many words, there is bound to be a mistake somewhere in them.

Everything in the past died yesterday, and everything in the future is born today.

Patience is a bitter plant, but its fruit is sweet.

Listening well is as powerful as talking well, and is also as essential to true conversation.

Do not believe that you will reach your destination without leaving the shore.

If you ask for directions rudely, you might end up ten li [*a Chinese unit of measurement that is equal to about 0.3 miles*] from your destination.

If you are patient in one moment of anger, you will escape a hundred days of sorrow.

A clever person turns great troubles into little ones, and little ones into none at all.

Listen to all, pluck a feather from every passing goose, but follow no one absolutely.

Only one who can swallow an insult is a man.

The person who is his own master cannot tolerate another boss.

It's better to be without a book than to believe a book entirely.

When economy goes south, people get political.

The melon seller does not announce, "Bitter melons."

Distant water does not put out a nearby fire.

You can be cautious of the future, but not of the past.

If you want to find out about the road ahead, then ask about it from those coming back.

It is easy to open a store—the hard part is keeping it open!

Think about your own faults during the first half of the night, and the faults of others during the second half.

Genius can be recognized by its childish simplicity.

A hundred no's are less agonizing than one insincere yes.

Guessing is cheap, but guessing wrong can be expensive

There are two kinds of perfect people: those who are dead, and those who have not been born yet.

A man who cannot tolerate small misfortunes can never accomplish great things.

Solve one problem, and you keep a hundred others away.

If you want to avoid being cheated, ask for prices at three different stores.

The more acquaintances you have, the less you know them.

If a girl seems as shy as a mouse, you still have to look out for the tiger within her.

To be totally at leisure for one day is to be immortal for one day.

One beam, no matter how big, cannot support an entire house on its own.

Do everything at its right time, and one day will seem like three.

The best doctor prevents illness, a mediocre one treats illnesses that are about to occur, and an unskilled one treats current illnesses.

The people who talk the best are not the only ones who can tell you the most interesting things.

If you want your children to have a peaceful life, let them suffer a little hunger and a little coldness.

The people sitting in the free theatre seats are the first ones to boo.

Ripe fruit falls by itself—but it doesn't fall in your mouth.

He who cheats the earth will be cheated by the earth.

To know another is not to know that person's face, but to know that person's heart.

He who asks is a fool for five minutes, but he who does not ask remains a fool forever.

Better the cottage where one is merry than the palace where one weeps.

Give a man a fish, and you feed him for a day. Teach a man to fish, and you feed him for life.

A person of high principles is one who can watch an entire chess game without making a comment.

It is difficult to catch a black cat in a dark room—especially if the cat isn't there.

The person who has never been cheated cannot be a good businessman.

He who thinks too much about every step he takes will always stay on one leg.

No matter how tall the mountain is, it cannot block the sun.

Tenacity and adversity are old foes.

A wise man makes his own decisions, but an ignorant man mindlessly follows the crowd.

Of all female qualities, a warm heart is the most valuable.

Before preparing to improve the world, first look around your own home three times.

All things change, and we change with them.

Teachers open the door. You enter by yourself.

If you curse your wife in the evening, you will sleep alone at night.

A crisis is an opportunity riding the dangerous wind.

Never do anything standing that you can do sitting, or anything sitting that you can do lying down.

The person who says it cannot be done should not interrupt the person doing it.

Some prefer carrots while others like cabbage.

Do not do all you can, do not spend all that you have, do not believe all that you hear, and do not tell all that you know.

Do not tear down the east wall to repair the west wall.

A hasty man drinks his tea with a fork.

If you are standing upright, don't worry if your shadow is crooked.

If you want an audience, start a fight.

Life is partly what we make it, and partly what it is made by the friends we choose.

Everyone should carefully observe which way his heart draws him, and then choose that way with all his strength.

Wine does not intoxicate a man—a man intoxicates himself.

Learning is a weightless treasure you can always carry easily.

Married couples tell each other a thousand things without speech.

The best cure for drunkenness is to observe a drunken person when you are sober.

Two good talkers are not worth one good listener.

It is better to save your innocence at the cost of your honor, than to save your country at the cost of your life.

Jails are always closed yet full, while temples are always open yet empty.

An accidental meeting is more pleasant than a planned one.

It is foolish for someone to seek credit for his ancestor's achievements.

Some people want to be praised for the rest of their lives for what they did well for one day.

You always win by not saying the things you don't need to say.

A one hundred yard high tower still has its foundation on the ground.

TIBET

Tibet is an independent part of China. It is filled with many high mountains, including part of the Himalayas mountain chain. Tibet is a very cold region, and not very good for farming.

Tibetans derive from tribal people who have been mixed with neighboring cultures like Chinese and Mongolian people. The region's official language is Tibetan. There are about two million Tibetans in Tibet, and three million more Tibetans living in other regions of China.

Themes of Tibet include Tibetan Buddhism (which is headed by a spiritual leader known as the Dalai Lama), yoga, cold temperatures, dumo heat (body heat generated by visualization and breathing exercises), tankas (scroll paintings), holy songs & dances, the symbolic use of white scarves, holy flags, barley (including barley flour and barley beer), vegetables, tea, festivals, monks, monasteries, temples, superstition, farming, herding, and handicrafts.

Tibetan Proverbs

Who can say for sure that one will live to see tomorrow.

Landing a single punch on your enemies nose is more satisfying than hearing well-intentioned advice from your elders.

The person who gets stuck on trivial prosperity will not attain great prosperity.

With a resolute heart, a mouse can lift an elephant.

Spreading the news is also multiplying it.

The wise pursue understanding; fools follow the reports of others.

If your inner mind isn't deceived, your outer actions won't be wrong.

Knowing just one word of wisdom is like knowing a hundred ordinary words.

UIGHUR

The Uighur are cultural group who speak a variation of Turkish and mostly live in China, were they have had a presence for nearly two millenniums and used to have a Uighur kingdom in what is part of modern Mongolia.
There are nearly 8 million Uighur people currently in China, and about 500,000 in nearby countries.

Uighur Proverbs

The bad shooter blames his bullets.

If a guest doesn't want to stay, it is better to let him go.

A wife makes her husband a man, but she can also makes her husband an asshole.

The person who can control himself can control a city

Who do I to sue for my own faults?

Regret afterwards is your own enemy.

Even if the world is flooded, the duck feels safe.

If the boss is full, no one will care if the slave is hungry.

Eastern Asian (Oriental) Proverbs

(Also see the chapter on Chinese Proverbs)

Contents: Bhutan, Cambodia, Indonesia, Japan, Korea, Laos, Malaysia, Mongolia, Myanmar, Nepal, The Philippines, Singapore, Taiwan, Thailand, Vietnam

BHUTAN

Bhutan is a small country between China and India, and contains part of the Himalayan Mountains. Most people in the county are Tibetan, Nepalese, or Assamese. The country has been secluded for much of its history due to its location that is filled with mountains and forests. The British influenced the area beginning in the 1800s, and was replaced by India in the mid 1900s. The country still has strong ties with India.

Bhutan themes include Buddhism (including Tibetan Buddhism), agricultural exporting to India, modernization efforts, cultural variety, rice, chilies, potatoes, art, architecture, craftwork, and Hinduism.

Bhutanese Proverbs

If the thought is good, place and path are good; if the thought is bad, place and path are bad.

Whatever joy you seek, it can be found by yourself; whatever misery you seek, it can be found by yourself.

On the battlefield, there is no distinction between upper and lower class.

You must first walk around a little before you can understand the distance from the valley to the mountain.

CAMBODIA

Cambodia has its roots in the Khmer Empire (600s-1400s), and the main language in Cambodia is also called Khmer. Cambodia became under French influence in the 1800s, and Japanese influence during World War I before becoming independent in 1954.

Cambodia has been the site of much turmoil in the late 1900s, including many of the battles in the Vietnam War, as well as the brutally oppressive rule of Pol Plot in the late 1970s, and later civil conflicts that lasted until the late 1990s.

Themes of Cambodia include consistently hot temperatures, summer monsoon rainfall, tropical forestlands, many wild animals, Buddhism, Hinduism, and rice.

Cambodian / Khmer Proverbs

Don't trust a hungry man to watch your rice.

Plant rice when the ground is ready; pursue women when you feel passion.

Sow good and you'll reap good; sow bad and you'll reap bad.

You don't have to cut down a tree to get its fruit.

An elephant has enormous dung—don't try to defecate like an elephant.

Don't try to wipe someone else's ass if yours is unwiped.

INDONESIA

Indonesia is made up of nearly 14,000 islands, many of which have tropical rain forests and volcanoes, and about half of which are unpopulated. In those islands, there are about 300 different ethnic groups and languages. Indonesia has recently adopted and promoted an official language called Bahasa Indonesian.

Indonesia has a population of over 200 million people, many of whom derive from people who came from Asia to Indonesia about 3000 years ago. Indonesia has had various cultural ties with China and India throughout its history. The Dutch ruled Indonesia from the 1600s to the 1900s, and the country became independent in 1945.

Themes of Indonesia include rice, Islam, multiculturalism, music, dancing, ancient architecture, storytelling, puppet shows, fabric designing, clothing manufacturing, and poverty.

Indonesian Proverbs

Nothing is difficult when you get used to it.

Different men have different opinions—some prefer apples, some onions.

A hill is created little by little over a long time.

Most people don't announce their faults with a gong.
Note: A gong is a very popular instrument in Indonesia

Your mouth, your tiger.

JAPAN

Though small in land area, Japan has a population of over 130 million people, many of whom live in or near the capital city of Tokyo. The country is well known for being a giant in the industrial and technological worlds.

Japan is an island chain with four main islands plus about 4,000 other small islands. The country has lots of hills, mountains, active volcanoes, and plant and animal life. Almost all Japanese people have similar ethnic backgrounds, and speak Japanese.

Throughout much of Japanese history from 0 AD and on, the Japanese continuously made visits to China and observed, learned, and adopted aspects of their culture. Around the 1800s, Japan also began observing Western practices and adopted them as well. Around that time, Japan quickly became modernized and industrialized.

In the early to mid 1900s, Japan began warring with and trying to conquer many regions, including China. In the 1940s, they tried to take over the entire world, but were defeated in World War II due to atomic bomb attacks from America. They signed a peace treaty shortly thereafter. After World War II, Japan built itself into one of the world's premiere economic powers, with such corporate giants as Sony and Toyota.

Themes of Japan include rice, technology, business, apartment buildings, earthquakes, shopping, baseball, sumo wrestling, pachinko (a game similar to pinball), geisha women (female entertainers for male businessmen and friends), fishing, tea, vegetables, soy, Confucianism, Buddhism (including Zen Buddhism), Shinto (a native religion), poetry, painting, plays, sculptures, decorating, calligraphy, music, dancing, samurai warrior culture, and martial arts.

Japanese Proverbs

Note: Some of these proverbs are designated from Okinawa, which is a semi-independent region in Japan whose people are known for their longevity, and is also known for being the hometown of Mr. Miyagi from the movie The Karate Kid.

Note: Samurai (Japanese warrior class) proverbs are listed towards the end of this section.

Cold tea and cold rice are tolerable; cold looks and cold words aren't.

First the man takes a drink (*liquor*), then the drink takes a drink, and then the drink takes the man.

Because of their figure, vain women stay cold.

It is better to write down something once than read it ten times.

Character can be built on daily routine.

(Apply) fitting ability in the fitting place.

A single arrow is easily broken, but ten in a bundle aren't.

Poor is the person who does not know when he has had enough.

He who talks to a silent listener will soon stand naked.

Truth often comes out of a joke.

Instead of worrying, a strong man wears a smile.

It's better to lie a little than to be unhappy.

A few kind words can warm three winter months.

In strategy, secrecy is highly regarded.

A crying child thrives.

You can only endure the weaknesses of others by knowing your own.

Flattery is the best persuader.

Books are preserved (parts of) minds.

When someone is really hungry, then there is no such thing as "bad food."

The person who admits ignorance shows it once; the one who tries to hide it shows it often.

Ten men, ten minds.

If there is a lid that doesn't fit, then there is a lid that does.

To a person that does not wander, there is not enlightenment.

Fall seven times, stand up eight.

The reverse side also has a reverse side.

Advertising is the mother of trade.

It's better to not read at all than to believe everything you read.

The day you decide to do it is your lucky day.

An excess of courtesy is discourtesy.

Even a sheet of paper has two sides.

You can't see the whole sky through a bamboo tube.

The reputation of a thousand years may be determined by the conduct of one hour.

Even if you hide yourself from the world, don't lose sight of your real nature. (Okinawa)

We learn by watching and listening. (Okinawa)

Respect old people, and be gentle with children. (Okinawa)

Old people are everyone's treasures. (Okinawa)

The heart is the most essential human quality. (Okinawa)

Common sense is essential. (Okinawa)

One who eats plain food is healthy. (Okinawa)

Spend words as efficiently as money. (Okinawa)

If you respect others, others will respect you. (Okinawa)

To know and to act are one and the same. (Samurai)

Tomorrow's battle is won during today's practice. (Samurai)

Control your emotion or it will control you. (Samurai)

Conqueror the self and you will conquer the opponent. (Samurai)

Control of mental conduct, not skill, is the sign of a matured samurai. (Samurai)

I have no friends; I make my mind my friend. (Samurai)

I have no sword; I make no-mind my sword. (Samurai)

I have no (set) principles; I make adaptability to all circumstances my principle. (Samurai)

Put faith in your own abilities and not in the stars. (Samurai)
Note: Many samurai were highly superstitious, and this proverb was a warning against superstition.

KOREA

Korea is located between China and Japan. Though it is not large in size, it has a population of over 65 million people. Korean history has its roots in the Choson Kingdom, which started thousands of years ago by Chinese immigrants.

Korea has been often split into various kingdoms throughout its history, and has also come under rule by China, Mongolia, and Japan at various times. It became free of Japan in the mid 1900s, but was split into North and South territories, and became subject to a US involved War over Communism. The North and South parts of Korea currently operate under separate governments.

The country's main language is Korean, although English also has a significant presence in South Korea. The Korean language is uniquely different from languages in surrounding countries in Eastern Asia.

Themes in Korea include Confucianism, Buddhism, museums, music, dance, theatre, literature (particularly novels), pottery, painting, and communism (in the North).

Korean Proverbs

One moment is worth more than a thousand gold pieces.

Man's mind changes throughout the course of a day.

Anyone who goes hungry for three days will be inclined to steal.

The person who has many faults is usually the first to criticize others.

Put something off for one day, and ten days will pass.

Even though words have no wings, they can still fly a thousand miles.

Even if you encounter a stone bridge, tap it first before crossing.

Through old things, we learn new things.

A great river does not refuse any small streams.

The person who knows himself and his opponent will be invincible.

Carve a peg only after you have observed the hole.

Even children of the same mother look different.

To begin is to be half done.

Even if the sky falls on you, there is a hole that you can escape from.

LAOS

Most of Laos borders Vietnam and Thailand. The vast majority of Laos is comprised of mountains and forests. Most people in the country belong to one of several Lao ethnicities, and the country's official language is Lao.

Many Lao people derive from Chinese immigrants who arrived in the region around the 700s AD. The region developed a united kingdom in the 1300s, which split up in the 1700s, and became under French control in the late 1800s. Laos became independent in the 1950s, and its current government was instituted in 1991.

Themes of Laos include Buddhism, taking one's time, rice, sugarcane, opium, literature, art, music, dancing, and plays.

Lao Proverbs

When the water rises, the fish eat the ants; when the water falls, the ants eat the fish.

Although he who walks behind an elephant may feel very secure, he is likely to get splattered with elephant dung.

Learning means loving the country.

You know, you teach. You do not know, you learn.

MALAYSIA

Malaysia is made of two parts: one in mainland Asia, and the other on the Borneo island. There are lots of mountains and rainforests in Malaysia. There are about 20 million people in the country, the majority of which are natives, and the rest (about one third) are mostly Chinese and Indian. Malaysia has been under Dutch, British, Chinese, and Japanese rule at various times, and became independent in the mid 1900s. The county has many languages, including the official national language of Bahasa Melayu.

Common themes of Malaysia include rice, hot and rainy climates, Islam, Indian cultural influences, and exporting raw materials.

Malaysian Proverbs

Do not be tricked into thinking that there are no crocodiles just because the water is still.

If you are too shy to ask, you might lose your way.

When you go away, the conversation changes.

Don't use an axe to embroider.

If you plant grass, you won't get rice

No matter how big the whale is, a tiny harpoon can kill him.

To truly love your wife, leave her alone every once in a while.

MONGOLIA

Mongolia borders Northern China. Most Mongolians have Mongoloid / Asiatic ancestry, which is the same ancestry prevalent in most other Asian regions. Many Mongolians originate from the region's tribal people, as well as from Manchus (of Northern China), Huns, and Turks.

The Mongolians created a tremendous empire in the 1200s under the well-known leader Genghis (Chinggis) Khan. His successors continued the Empires dominance for several more generations, but in the 1400s the Mongols lost power, and in the 1600s Mongolia became part of China. In the 1900s, Mongolia became an independent country. Khalkha Mongol is the country's main language.

Themes of Mongolia include storytelling, *shatar* (a game like chess), rituals, horses, wrestling, archery, literature, poetry, temperature variances, widely varied plant and animal life, animal herding, and mineral exporting.

Mongolian Proverbs

Even foul water will put out a fire.

The distance between heaven and earth is no greater than one thought.

The supreme treasure is knowledge, the middle treasure is children, and the lowest treasure is material wealth.

The meat-biting tooth is in the mouth; the man-biting tooth is in the soul.

If you want to build high, you must dig deep.

If the mind is clean, the fate is good.

Each country's customs are different, (just as) each meadow's grass is different.

It is easier to catch an escaped horse than to take back an escaped word.

MYANMAR / BURMA

Much of Myanmar's population lives near the Irrawaddy River. The country is filled with forests, swamps, and mountains. Of the 40 million people living in Myanmar, most derive from people who migrated from China around 0 AD.

The nation of Myanmar is often referred to as Burma by English speakers. Burma is actually an ethic group in Myanmar that makes up the majority of the population. Burmese is the country's official language. Myanmar was under British control for many years until gaining independence in the mid 1900s.

Themes of Myanmar include rice, tribal life, Buddhism, metal and gem mining, woodcarving, literature (particularly biographies), and poor sanitary conditions.

Myanmar / Burmese Proverbs

Sparrows who mimic peacocks are likely to break a thigh.

Excessive talk is sure to include errors.

The excessively kind-hearted person becomes a slave.

If you really want honesty, then don't ask questions you don't really want the answer to.

When it rains, collect the water.

Don't use up your arrows before you go to battle.

NEPAL

Nepal is a highly isolated and mountainous country (it includes part of the Himalayas mountain chain), and the site of most "abominable snowman" accounts. The Nepalese ancestry is traced to groups such as the Tibetans, the native Newars, and to Indo-Aryan people who migrated from India. Nepali is the main language of Nepal.

Themes of Nepal include Buddhism, Hinduism, rice, timber, sculptures, architecture, paintings, poetry, music, and dancing.

Nepalese Proverbs

It is the mind that wins or loses.

Wealth is both an enemy and a friend.

To take revenge on an enemy, give him an elephant—first he must thank you for the gift, and then the elephant's appetite will deplete your enemy's resources.

If you only depend on others, you will soon go hungry.

Opportunities come, but do not linger.

THE PHILIPPINES

The Philippines is a chain of over 7,000 large and small islands, about a dozen of which make up 90% of the land area. Much of the country contains mountainous land and forests.

The majority of the Filipino population lives in farming communities, while about a third live in cities, especially in or near the capital Manila. There are many different ethnicities and language variations that have developed in the Philippines, but much of the culture and Filipino language is based on the Tagalog ethnic group and language. The Philippines is very westernized compared to other nearby countries, due to various control and influences throughout history by Spain and the United States.

Common themes of the Philippines include rice, corn, fishing, earthquakes, pleasant year round temperatures, art, storytelling, music, dancing, a strong emphasis on family and marriage, boxer Manny Pacquaio, Christianity, and timber production.

Philipino / Philippine / Filipino / Tagalog Proverbs

Where there is gossip, there will be arguing.

The person who is always criticizing others is usually the one who deserves criticism the most.

Avoiding danger is not cowardice.

Courage without discretion is no good.

Every community has its own customs and traditions.

If you buy things you don't need, you will soon be selling things you do need.

It is easier to dam a river than to stop the flow of gossip.

Alertness and courage are life's shield.

No matter how much care is taken, someone will always be misled.

The voluntary obedience of people depends on who is commanding them.

Many people count other people's faults and ignore their own.

If you like what you are doing, nothing is too far and no job is too hard.

The person who makes an error should be taught, and not made fun of.

A good character is more valuable than gold.

No child was ever born without having been conceived.

A good character is real beauty that never fades.

The child who is given everything he asks for usually won't succeed in life.

Even if the truth is buried for centuries, it will eventually come out and thrive.

Strength is defeated by (a strong) strategy.

Every road leads somewhere.

A diligent person will soon prosper.

Water can wear away even the hardest rock.

SINGAPORE

Singapore is one main island and sixty smaller islands, all located south of Malaysia. Many Singaporeans have Chinese ethnicity, and most others have Malay and Indian ethnicity.

Fisherman and pirates lived in Singapore for much of its early history. The region became part of several nearby empires beginning in the 1300s, and was then controlled by the Portuguese beginning in the 1500s, the Dutch beginning in the 1600s, and the British from 1819 until Singapore gained independence in the mid 1900s. The country's official languages include Malay, Chinese, English, and Tamil.

Themes of Singapore include cleanliness, Buddhism, Christianity, Islam, Taoism, Confucianism, hot temperatures, agriculture, international trade & finance, petroleum, music, art, and drama.

Singaporean / Malay Proverbs

Where there is a sea, there are pirates.

A given excuse that was not asked for implies guilt.

Clapping with only the right hand will not make a noise.

The person who can see a house in China is unaware of an elephant on his nose.

Incremental efforts have an impact as benefits accumulate.

Never take a quiet person for granted. He might have great qualities underneath his quiet nature.

TAIWAN

Taiwan is an island near China. Although mountainous, its climate conditions make it incredibly good for farming. Many Taiwanese have either Chinese and/or original tribal heritage, and the countries main languages are Mandarin Chinese and Taiwanese (Min). Taiwan has recently become a highly industrialized and heavily populated nation.

Themes in Taiwan include education, industrial manufacturing, technology, rice, art (including calligraphy and ceramics), and music.

Taiwanese Proverbs

It takes sweat to work on things, but it only takes saliva to criticize things.

It takes nine months to have a baby.

A husband and wife often fight intensely at one moment and then kiss intensely at the next moment.

A beautiful person might not have a beautiful life.

Something that looks good does not necessarily taste good.

Many students have become kings or queens, but no teachers have.

Even champions make mistakes—there is no one who does not mistakes.

"I will give you 1000 later" is worth less than "here is 800 (right now)."

Some people prefer liquor, others prefer tofu, and some even like rotten salmon.

Greed will cause pain.

If someone transports dung and does not eat it, it should not be concluded that he is an honest person.

THAILAND

Thai people call Thailand "Muang Thai," which means "Land of the Free." Thailand has a population of about 60 million people. The region has a rich cultural history, and many long-inhabited cities and regions, many of which have had people continuously living there for over 20,000 years.

Thailand was part of the Mon and Khmer Empires from the 800s AD-1200s AD, which also marked a period of Chinese immigration to the region. Two separate Kingdoms replaced the Mon and Khmer in the 1200s. In the mid 1700s, the Burmese, who were enemies with the Thai for many years, caused widespread destruction in Thailand.

The Chakri Dynasty took over in 1782, and by the mid 1800s had established the Siam Empire. By the 1930s, the Siam Empire was named Thailand, and converted into its current government. The country's main language is Thai. Unlike most other neighboring regions, Thailand has remained free of Western colonization throughout its history.

Themes of Thailand include Buddhism, rice, soybeans, pineapples, soccer, Thai kickboxing, kite flying, music, dancing, ceremonies, drama, porcelain, rubber, tourism, and tin production.

Thai Proverbs

Don't help the elephant carry its tusks.

Don't borrow someone else's nose to breathe with.

The sweetness of food doesn't last long, but the sweetness of good words do.

Wrapped within rags might be gold

(Don't) Escape from the tiger (in order to) meet the crocodile.

To eat is human, to digest—divine.

VIETNAM

Vietnam has a population of about 80 million people. The Vietnamese are descendants from Chinese and Thai people, and the country's most commonly used language is Vietnamese.

Vietnamese became a distinct culture around the 300s BC, and the Vietnam region was under Chinese control from about 100 BC to 1000 AD. After splitting into Northern and Southern regions in the 1600s, Vietnam was reunified in the 1800s.

The French took control of Vietnam in the mid 1800s until the Japanese occupied it during World War II. The French tried to take over again after that, but were defeated by Vietnamese troops in 1954.

Vietnam was soon split into a communist North led by Ho Chi Minh, and a US supported South led by Bao Dai. The division as well as US intervention led to the Vietnam War, which lasted until 1975 when the South surrendered. The country then united into the Socialist Republic of Vietnam, and resumed relations with the US in 1995.

Themes of Vietnam include Taoism, Buddhism, Confucianism, communism, strong family ties, rice, noodles, seafood, literature, dominoes, chess, soccer, wrestling, volleyball, musical comedy plays, and water puppet shows.

Vietnamese Proverbs

The buffalo that arrives late will have to drink muddy water and eat dry grass.

When you eat, it's vegetables; when you are sick, it's medicine.

It's better to have lots of children than to have lots of material goods.

Even if a mountain is high, there is always a way to reach the top—and although the way might be full of danger, there is always a way for someone to get through it.

No matter how sharp it is, a knife will never cut it's own handle.

A little food while hungry is like a lot of food while full.

Eating slowly is good for the stomach; plowing deeply is good for the fields.

A frog living at the bottom of the well thinks that the sky is as small as a cooking pot lid.

Make the amount of sauce you use correspond to the amount of rice you have.

Indian Ocean Proverbs (India, Bangladesh, Pakistan, and Sri Lanka)

Note: Since Bangladesh and Pakistan have been part of India for much of history, the proverbs and histories of the three countries have been consolidated in this chapter. References to India in this chapter generally refer to the greater India region that includes Bangladesh and Pakistan.

Note: Sri Lanka, an island country located near India, is also covered within this chapter.

India is the world's second most populous country (China is first). It contains a wide variety of people, lifestyles, languages, and landscapes. Here is a look at the history and proverbs of India (including the independent countries of Pakistan and Bangladesh that used to be part of India)

Early History

It is believed that people have been living in India for thousands and thousands of years, and much of India's current ethic heritage derives at least partly from those early natives of the region. Other groups that came to India in early times include Dravidian-speaking people, and Mongoloid people (who share common ancestry with such ethnicities as Chinese natives.)

By 2500 BC, ancient civilizations began sprouting in the Indus Valley region of India. Many people from central Asia known Aryans also migrated to India at various times, particularly around 1500 BC.

Over time, the Aryan Sanskrit language was popularized, and many ancient teachings and scriptures flourished in the area. Additionally, many people from nearby territories such as Persia, Arabia, Turkey, and Mongolia migrated to India. This has caused a rather mixed ancestry currently prevalent in India, and the wide variances of people in different regions of the land.

Spread of Buddhism and Hinduism

In the 500s and 400s BC, an Indian sage named Siddhartha Gautama, later also known as the "Buddha" (Enlightened One), preached a series of teachings that is known today as Buddhism. His teachings soon had a widespread impact on India, and later on much of the rest of the world. (See the Zen Buddhism chapter in this book for more info on Buddhism)

From around 500 BC to 0 BC, parts of India were ruled by various Empires, which caused Buddhism to spread to other lands, especially to

China. In India, however, a religion called Hinduism (which is based on various ancient teachings of the Indus Valley natives and the Aryan immigrants) spread in popularity and soon became dominant. (See the Hinduism chapter of this book for more info on Hinduism)

Hinduism led to a certain social system in India where people are placed into a specific caste (social level based on a certain hierarchy) due to their heredity. This caste system is still to some extent a prevalent theme in modern India.

Gupta Empire

In around 300 AD, Northern India was united under the Gupta Empire, which later spread its domain to other regions outside of India. The Guptas reigned for about 200 years, and in that time, Indian art, literature, mathematics, philosophy, and science flourished.

Mughal Empire

From the mid 400s to the early 1500s, many foreign armies invaded India, resulting in a great deal of turmoil. In 1526, a central Asian leader named Babur established the Mughal Empire.

His grandson Akbar later made the Empire among the most powerful in the world. He was also able to make Hinduism coexist with Islam, which had steadily gained in popularity throughout the Empire. (For more info on Emperor Akbar, see the chapter "Birbal Tales and Other Indian Folktales.")

British Rule

In the 1700s, the Mughal Empire had almost dissolved, and British groups who had been trading in India soon began gaining influence there. They began levying taxes and taking away land. This caused a major Indian rebellion against the British in the mid 1800s, which British troops defeated.

The British continued to rule and oppress India for many more decades.

Gandhi & Indian Independence

An Indian leader named Mohandas K. Gandhi led a nonviolent movement starting in the 1920s that slowly helped gain Indian independence from Britain. At the same time, a region now known as Myanmar (see the East Asian Proverbs chapter for more info about Myanmar) broke off from the British-Indian Empire in 1937.

In 1947, India became an independent nation, and was also split into two separate countries, Pakistan and India, in order to help quell conflicts between Muslims and Hindus. In the 1970s, what used to be known as East Pakistan split into another country now called Bangladesh (which is primarily home to the distinct ethnic culture of the Bengals), while what used to be known as West Pakistan became the country that is currently Pakistan. (Note that West Pakistan and East Pakistan were not geographically connected.)

India, Pakistan, Bangladesh, and Myanmar exist as separate nations to this day.

Current India

Most Indians today live in villages of about 1000 people that are segregated by caste, and usually have farming as the most popular occupation. About one fourth of modern Indians live in urban areas, which have less of an emphasis on the caste system. India currently has a democratic government with a president, who handles state matters, and a prime minister, who is in charge of the government.

Themes of India include as music, dance, religious festivals, literature, philosophy, ancient teachings, elaborate architecture (such as the Taj Mahal, as well as numerous lavish temples), sculptures, poverty, poor sanitary conditions, religious conflict, political unrest, poetry, curry, rice, mangoes, sugarcane, the sanctity of cows due to Hindu beliefs, vegetarianism (due to religious beliefs, many Indians are either vegetarians or they avoid beef and pork), and drama. Motion pictures are also highly popular among Indians today, and virtually every popular Indian film is filled with numerous song and dance sequences.

Current Pakistan

Pakistan is home to over 145 million people. It is located just west of India. Like Indians, Pakistani people have a very diverse ethnic mix. Pakistan is mainly a Muslim land, although other religions such as Hinduism and Christianity also exist in the country.

Pakistan has many cultural similarities to India other than India's caste system. Pakistani themes include political instability, family ties, wide temperature variations, poetry, art, rice, wheat, and movies.

Current Bangladesh

Bangladesh is located in a part of what used to be Eastern India, and currently borders India on both its east and west sides. Although small in land area, it has a population of over 130 million people. The country's southern section borders the Bay of Bengal in the Indian Ocean. Most of the country's inhabitants belong to the Bengal ethnicity and speak Bengali—in fact, the country used to be known as Bengal.

Bangladesh won its independence from Pakistan (which was formerly known as West Pakistan) in the early 1970s after a vicious war.

Bangladeshi themes include strong family ties, Islam, Hinduism, rice, milk, civil & political instability, soccer, a variation of the game "capture the flag," kite flying, music, dancing, architecture, monsoons, flooding, and tea.

Sri Lanka

Sri Lanka is an island located southeast of India. The majority of Sri Lankan people have their ethnic roots from Indian migrants that immigrated to the island at various time periods.

Sri Lankans are commonly split into distinct Sinhalese (a.k.a. Sinhala) and Tamil ethnic groups, which at times had their own kingdoms on the island. In the second millennium AD, Sri Lanka has been invaded or ruled by the Chinese, Malayans, Portuguese, Dutch and British. The country became independent in the mid 1900s.

Sri Lankan themes include gemstones, Hinduism, Islam, Christianity, Buddhism, social welfare systems, architecture, folk dancing, soccer, bike racing, coconuts, tea, and rubber.

Indian, Bangladeshi, Pakistani, and Sri Lankan Proverbs

Note: India has been a partially united land for much of history, and it is difficult to differentiate between proverbs of the current country divisions, especially in differentiating those from India and those from Pakistan. Most of the proverbs below have been categorized into a culture/region, including:

Hindustan: a region in India. Note that the term Hindustan can also be used categorized as the entire country of India, or to refer to the culture of Hinduism the religion.

Bengal: the culture and language of Bengali people, most of whom live in Bangladesh

Kashmir: a region in Northern India and parts of other countries such as Pakistan

Tamil: An ethnicity and language found primarily Southern India and in Sri Lanka

Sinhala / Sinhalese: The ethnicity and language that make up the majority in Sri Lanka.

Sanskrit: an ancient Indian language

A buffalo does not feel the weight of its own horns. (India)

Fate and free-will both play an equal role in destinies. (India)

There are as many characters as there are individuals. (India)

When a crow is killed by a storm, the fortuneteller says, "He died by my curse." (India)

Even if fed milk, a snake will still emit poison. (India)

The baby has not been born yet, and yet you assert that his nose is like his grandfather's! (India)

Most adults are attentive to what someone is doing, but children see beyond that. (India)

Pearls are worthless in the desert. (India)

A viper without fangs is like a piece of rope. (India)

The answerer is inferior to the asker. (India)

Regularity is the best medicine. (Hindustan)

Love your neighbor, but don't take down the separating-wall. (Hindustan)

No one can be a totally fair judge in his own case. (Hindustan)

In a treeless country, the castor plant is a big tree. (Hindustan)

Diet cures more than the surgical knife does. (Hindustan)

Sitting while you eat makes you large; standing while you eat makes you strong. (Hindustan)

Dig your well before you are thirsty. (Hindustan)

The person who is too humble becomes a scoundrel. (Hindustan)

The supreme excellence is not in being better than others, but in being better than your former self. (Hindustan)

The living things of the Earth depend on each other just like the limbs and organs of the body do. (Hindustan)

People don't trip on mountains, but they sometimes stumble on stones. (Hindustan)

An elephant, no matter how skinny, is valuable. (Hindustan)

Dependence on someone else can cause reoccurring disappointment. (Hindustan)

The speech, actions, manner of movement, and turban of each man differs from all others. (Hindustan)

Dogs fight with each other, but unite when they hear the voice of a jackal. (Kashmir)

If its not gossip, then why are you whispering it? (Kashmir)

Clean your heart and mind of negative thoughts. (Kashmir)

Bachelors want to get married, while married men regret that they did. (Kashmir)

(To most people), distant pepper is perceived as being sweet, and close sweets are perceived as being bitter. (Kashmir)

When pumpkins are watered, brinjals (*a small vegetable*) also get watered. (Kashmir)

(It's useless to attempt to) carry water in baskets. (Kashmir)

(Don't try to) cook six liters of food in a pot that only holds three liters. (Kashmir)

A simple meal at home is better than an elaborate one while away. (Kashmir)

Saving the mustard seeds that are in your hand might cause you to miss out on getting a watermelon. (Kashmir)

For every hundred lashes needed by the foolish, only one word is needed by the wise. (Kashmir)

If a man's beard is on fire, there are bound to be plenty of people who will want to warm their hands on the fire. (Kashmir)

(When well united and synergized), one plus one equals eleven. (Kashmir)

With the right trap, even an elephant can be caught. (Kashmir)

The innocent often pay for the acts of the guilty. (Kashmir)

The healthy person experiences a healthy world. (Kashmir)

Rice tastes good when it is cooked properly, and talking is good when it is said at the right time. (Kashmir)

Thunder is not the source of the rain. (Kashmir)

The message spoken to the daughter is often aimed at the daughter-in-law. (Kashmir)

The poor search for food, and the rich search for hunger. (Bengal)

You can have your nose broken easily if you put it in other people's business. (Bengal)

Non-violence is the best religion. (Bengal)

You can easily find a thousand teachers, but it is difficult to find a true disciple. (Bengal)

Even when many people attempt to travel the same road, there are some who walk and some who stumble. (Bengal)

Be careful of the teacher you choose and the water you drink. (Bengal)

Even if the caged bird has food to eat, he always dreams of the liberty of the forest. (Bengal)

What one has in the heart shows in the eyes. (Bengal)

If you want to be a true man, become good like the earth. (Bengal)

It requires lots of time to build a good name, but only a little time to ruin it. (Bengal)

An enemy's punishment is his envy. (Tamil)

Faith in medicine makes it effective. (Tamil)

A good husband might have a bad wife, and a bad wife might have a good husband. (Tamil)

Extreme hunger will cause a person to break through a stone wall and steal. (Tamil)

He who has studied himself is his own master. (Tamil)

The owl is small, but its voice is loud. (Tamil)

Kind words can conquer. (Tamil)

When you are shopping for a cow, make sure that the price of the tail is included. (Tamil)

When the wild pig's running (inadvertently) crushes the seed shells, the wild birds celebrate. (Sinhala)

When the dogs bark at the moon, the moon is not brought down because of it. (Sinhala)

During the daylight, a person will not fall into a pit that he fell into during the nighttime. (Sinhala)

The fool carries the burden. (Sinhala)

Don't believe everything you hear, and don't tell everything you believe. (Sinhala)

People searching for other people's faults often do not know their own. (Sanskrit)

The greatest hero is the person who controls his desires. (Sanskrit)

Wind sweeps the street clean. (Sanskrit)

Something done at the wrong time should be considered not done. (Sanskrit)

You can't cook one half of a chicken and expect the other half to lay eggs. (Sanskrit)

Middle Eastern Proverbs

Contents: Afghanistan, Arabia, Armenia, Azerbaijan, Hebrew, Iran, Kurdish, Turkey

AFGHANISTAN

Afghanistan has a mix of mountainous regions, deserts, and agricultural areas. There are a variety of ethnic groups in the area due to numerous changes and influences throughout the years. At various times in its history, Afghanistan has also been part of the same Empires as India and Iran.

Afghanistan's languages are Pashto and Dari (which are similar to Persian / Farsi). Most Afghans are farmers or nomadic farmers, while about 20% of the population lives in cities.

Some themes of Afghanistan include Islam, community bonds, extreme temperature variances, music, dancing, literature, art, a varied animal population (including many hound dogs), kite flying, shooting, wrestling, and *buzkashi* (a sport involving horsemen).

Afghan / Afghani Proverbs

In bad things be slow; in good things, be quick.

There is a path to the top of the highest mountain.

You stored your milk in a straining metal … and now you are complaining about bad luck?

There are twenty-five uncaught birds for a penny.

Everyone thinks his own thoughts are best.

You can use salt to prevent meat from rotting, but what will you use to prevent salt from rotting?

No rose is without thorns.

Community is not made by force.

The person who is cornered will fight.

In an ant colony, the dew is a flood.

What you see in yourself is what you see in the world.

The person who doesn't appreciate the apple will not appreciate the orchard.

ARABIA

Arabia is a term that generally refers to a group of countries throughout the Middle East region that have similar culture and language. Some African countries that speak Arabic are also sometimes referred to as part of Arabia. Throughout much of history, most Arabs were tribal people that were either desert nomads or farmers that formed small villages near Oasis.

The Arabia region and nearby territories is where many of the world's early cities and Empires began, including Sumer (c3000 BC-c2000 BC), Akkad (c2300s BC-c2100 BC), Mesopotamia (name of the region where many of these civilizations existed), Babylonia (on-and-off c2000 BC-c539 BC), Assyria (c2500 BC-600s BC), Canaanite Cities (c2000 BC-900s BC), Judah (on-and-off 900s BC-300s BC), and Judea (100s BC-100s AD). (Note: Judah and Judean Proverbs are covered in the Hebrew Proverbs section of this chapter.)

From around the 600s BC to 500 AD, some Arab regions also became under control of the Persian Empire, the Alexander of Macedon and successors Empire, the Seleucid Kingdom, the Roman Empire, and the Byzantine Empire.

In the 600s AD, most of Arabia was unified under religious leader Muhammad, who founded the religion of Islam (see the Islam chapter of this book for more info). Arab Muslim groups ruled much of Arabia and other territories until Mongols invaded and ruled in the 1200s to 1300s. The Crusaders also ruled some of Arabia for parts of the 1300s.

From the 1500s to the early 1900s, the Ottoman Empire became a major force in Arabia. The Portuguese also controlled several Arabic territories in the 1500s and 1600s.

By the early 1900s, British and other European groups established a presence in many Arabic regions, which soon comprised of over a dozen separated countries. By the mid 1900s, most Arab countries gained full independence from European influence.

Today, about half of all Arabs live in cities and towns, while the other half live in small villages. Most people have Arab ethnicities, but other cultural groups also exist in the region.

Current Middle Eastern Arab countries and regions include Bahrain, Iraq, Jordan, Kuwait, Lebanon, Oman, Palestine, Qatar, Saudi Arabia, Syria,

United Arab Emirates, and Yemen (also see the African Proverbs section for African Arab countries.)

Common themes of the Arab world include Islam (which is based on an Arabic holy book called the *Quran*), hospitality, strong family ties, hot summers, petroleum, camels, mustaches, dancing (including belly dancing), music, films, soccer, weapons, art, poetry, museums, architecture, the Al Jazeera television network, rice, bread, yogurt, cheese, dates, tea, stew, chickpeas, and lentils.

Note: Most Arab proverbs apply to the entire Arab region; however, I have accompanied some of them with a single country source.

Arabic / Arab / Arabian Proverbs

If you don't know where you are going, then look back to where you have come from.

Habit is the sixth sense that dominates the other five.

He who wants to sell his honor will always find a buyer.

The garlic complained to the onion, "You stink!"

If you count your friend's mistakes, he will desert you.

Many wars have been caused by a single word.

Wisdom consists of ten parts: nine parts silence, and one part a few words.

Examine what is said, not who is speaking.

A sense of humor is the pole that adds balance to our steps as we walk the tightrope of life.

You won't gain knowledge by drinking ink.

There has to be a first time for everything—even the most natural habits.

Don't celebrate someone's departing unless you know who will succeed him.

Call someone your lord…and he'll sell you in the slave market.

The person who predicts the future is lying, even when he is right.

Trust Allah (*God*), but tie up your camel.

How can the person who is eating dates prohibit the eating of dates?

It's better to be a free dog than a caged lion.

It's better to have a thousand enemies outside of the tent than one inside the tent.

There is no greater misfortune than your own.

Throw a resourceful person into a river, and he will probably come out with a fish in his hand.

Don't pour away your water due to a mirage.

If you stop every time a dog barks, then your road will never end.

If man's mouth was silent, then another part would speak.

A promise is a cloud; fulfillment is rain.

Example is better than law.

You will discover your true friends in moments of crisis. (Iraq)

If you conduct yourself properly, then fear no one. (Iraq)

All authors should prepare to encounter criticism. (Iraq)

Sometimes you need to sacrifice your beard in order to save your head. (Iraq)

Have faith in a stone and you will be healed by it. (Lebanon)

Love overlooks defects; hatred magnifies them. (Lebanon)

If a rich man eats a snake, people call it wisdom; if a poor man does the same thing, people call it derangement. (Lebanon)

The person who knew you when you were young will seldom respect you as an adult. (Lebanon)

Some men build a wine cellar after only finding one grape. (Lebanon)

When you return from a trip, bring back something for your family—even if it is only a stone. (Lebanon)

If anyone is not willing to accept your point of view, try to see his point of view. (Lebanon)

Lower your voice and strengthen your argument. (Lebanon)

Live near water, and ask not about sustenance. (Oman)

Birds align with grain, but not with the stick. (Oman)

If your motive is good, a farting donkey won't harm you. (Oman)

Build with silver and cover with gold. (Oman)

Every village has certain drawbacks to it. (Oman)

Nobody is perfect. (Palestine)

Hit the iron while it's still hot. (Palestine)

Do not drink poison to quench a thirst. (Palestine)

A small house is enough room for a thousand friends. (Syria)

In every village, there is a path that leads to the mill. (Syria)

Keep away from trouble and sing to it. (Syria)

A little spark can kindle a great fire. (Syria)

Choose the neighbor before the house. (Syria)

The person who deals in camels should make the doors high. (Syria)

Setting the conditions before you make an agreement is better than having an argument in the middle of the work. (Yemen)

ARMENIA

Armenian roots come from an ancient kingdom of Van that ruled from the 1200s to 800s BC. It was later assimilated into Median, Macedonian, and Roman Empires. Armenia was one of the first regions in the world to adopt Christianity as its religion, which it did in the early 300s AD.

In the 1500s, Armenia was part of the Ottoman Empire, and in the late 1800s, it aligned with Russia (later the USSR). Armenia became independent in 1990. The country's official language is Armenian

Some themes of Armenia include Christianity, literature (including legendary novelist Raffi), wine grape production, folk songs, opera, ballet, textiles, and mineral mining.

Armenian Proverbs

To be willing is only half the job.

If you chase two rabbits (at the same time), you won't catch either of them.

Even if the nightingale is in a gold cage, she still dreams of returning to the forest.

When someone's wealth improves, all of a sudden their house's columns appear to be crooked.

If you speak too much, you will learn too little.

The wolf is upset about what he left behind, and the shepherd is upset about what he (*the wolf*) took away.

There is no reason for war that reasonable men can't settle.

Clouds and thunder don't always result in rain.

A small cloud can hide the sun and the moon.

Men have three ears: one on the left of the head, one on the right of the head, and one in the heart.

Priest on the outside, Satan on the inside.

When the cart breaks down, advice is plentiful.

On a rainy day, many people volunteer to water the chickens.

AZERBAIJAN

Many of the people in Azerbaijan have Turkish or Persian heritage. Much of the country is mountainous, while other parts are low and level. Azerbaijan has many cultural ties to the bordering countries of Iran and Armenia.

Azerbaijan is primarily a farming and herding community, but about half its population lives in cities. Azerbaijan was a Soviet Republic for much of the 1900s, but declared independence in 1991. The country's main language is Azerbaijani.

Themes of Azerbaijan include poetry, philosophy, science, dry weather, cactuses, animal herding, cotton and tobacco farming, and petroleum.

Azerbaijani Proverbs

It's impossible to hold two watermelons in one hand.

Courage is ten, and nine is the ability to escape.

One hand washes the other hand, which in turn wash the face.

I attempted to draw the eyebrow, but I ended up poking the eye.

The forest can't be without its jackals.

Laughter is the remedy for 1001 illnesses.

The person who relies on his neighbor will remain without dinner.

HEBREW CULTURE / JEWISH CULTURE / ISRAEL

Hebrew was the language and culture of the Ancient Hebrews, who are the ancestors of the Jews (people of the religion of Judaism) (Judaism is covered in a separate chapter of this book).

The Jews were the main inhabitants of the Judah Empire (c1000s BC-586 BC) (Note: in 922 BC, the Empire split into separate Judah and Israel Empires, and Israel was conquered in 701 BC), the semi-independent Judah region (538 BC-300s BC), and the Kingdom of Judea (on-and-off from 100s BC-100 AD).

Beginning in the 500s BC, the Jews began using Aramaic more than Hebrew for ordinary everyday life, while Hebrew became the language used primarily in their religion.

After the Kingdom of Judea ended, Jewish people spread throughout the Middle East and to other regions. For many centuries after that, Hebrew was used among Jews mainly for religious, scholarly, and literary purposes.

In the 1800s, many Jews settled in Ancient Judean lands bordering the Mediterranean Sea, and they revived the Hebrew language. Many more Jews fled there during Nazi persecution in the 1930s and 1940s, and in 1948, the Jewish country of Israel was created with the support of the United Nations. Since then, there have been numerous wars and conflicts between Arabs and Israelis over the land.

About 80% of Israel's current population is Jewish, and most of the other 20% are Arabs.

Some Israeli themes include Judaism, music, dancing, technology, software, cell phones, weapons, an emphasis on the military, basketball, soccer, the Maccabiah Games (a Jewish athletic event held every four years), falafels (a food made from chickpeas), agricultural settlements such as the kibbutz, and the appreciation of ancient culture and architecture.

Note: For more Jewish-culture proverbs, see the Yiddish Proverbs section in the Central, Eastern, and Southern European Proverbs chapter.

Hebrew / Jewish / Israeli Proverbs

Don't be too sweet, or else you will be eaten up; but don't be too bitter, or else you will be spitted out.

The person who only accepts friends without faults will never have any real friends.

Don't trust someone who tells you all of his troubles and keeps you from all of his joys.

When con men meet a legitimately honest man, they are so bewildered that they consider him a greater con man than themselves.

Your friend has a friend, and your friend's friend has another friend—so know when to keep quiet.

A person worries about the past, distresses about the present, and fears the future.

Teach your tongue to say "I don't know" instead of to make up something.

Beware of the person who gives you advice according to his own interests.

There is no book that contains absolutely nothing bad, and there is no book that contains absolutely nothing good.

First learn, and then form opinions.

(Don't) sell the sun to buy a candle.

If someone is coming to kill you, get up early and kill him first.

Even the most expensive clock still shows sixty minutes in every hour.

A defendant's confession is worth a hundred witnesses.

Do not limit you children to your own learning, for they were born in a different time.

A good son-in-law is like the acquisition of a new son; a bad one is like the loss of your daughter.

Don't make a fence more expensive or more important than what it is fencing.

First improve yourself, and then judge others.

IRAN

Iran's history dates back to 3000 BC with the Elamite civilization. Much of Iranian culture comes from the Ancient Persian Empire that was unified in the 500s BC, and at one point made up one of the world's largest Empires. Over half of modern Iranians trace their roots back to Persian ancestry, while the rest of the population come from a variety of ethnicities and mixes. The country's main language is Persian (a.k.a. Farsi).

Iran has changed its borders frequently, and has had many native and foreign rulers, including (in loose chronological order) the Seleucid Dynasty, the Pathians, the Arsacid Dynasty, the Sasanian Dynasty, Arab Muslims, Turks, Mongols, the Safavid Dynasty (which at one point expanded into a large Empire in the 1500s and 1600s), Afghanis, Kurds, the Qajar Dynasty, the Pahlavi Dynasty, and the current Islamic Republic. Over time, the region has built a vivid history and culture.

Modern Iran contains cities and rural communities. Most cities have a mix of both traditional and modern characteristics. Rural communities are more resembling of earlier civilizations, and often based around farming. Throughout Iranian rural areas, there are also many nomads (frequent travelers).

Some common themes of Iran include strong bonds between friends and family, hospitality, Shi'i Islam, *Nowruz* (the Persian New Year celebration), science, architecture, literature, art, rugs, textiles, music, dancing, filmmaking, cats, joke telling, mustaches, petroleum, wrestling, weightlifting, soccer, melons, yogurt, rice, lamb, vegetables, stew, bread, kabob, and the appreciation of Iranian history and culture.

Iranian / Persian Proverbs

The night hides a world, but reveals a universe.

Solved riddles look easy.

Necessity can change a lion into a fox.

The way a house is decorated will tell much about its owner.

Don't just take love—experience it.

Every man is the king of his own beard.

You can close the city gates, but you can't close the people's mouths.

It's better to flee and stay alive than to die and become a hero.

A timely tear is better than a misplaced smile.

A sword in the hands of a drunken slave is less dangerous than science in the hands of the immoral.

Only a heart can find the way to another heart.

A wise man can laugh at his jokes.

A stone thrown at the right time is better than gold given at the wrong time

The elephant dreams of one thing, and the elephant driver dreams of another.

The fox uses his tale as a witness.

An egg thief becomes a camel thief.

The person who wants a rose must respect the thorn.

You can't pick up two watermelons with one hand.

A camel that wants fodder stretches out its neck.

Injustice all around is justice!

Do little things now; and big things will come to you.

Go and wake up your luck.

I used to complain because I had no shoes until I met a man who had no feet.

Another variation:

I used to complain because I had no shoes until I met a man who was dead.

While yearning for excess, we lose the necessities.

You can't please everyone.

A fool's excuse is bigger than his mistake.

You can't push on a rope.

A quality statement often gets no answer.

A greedy man is always poor.

Excessive praise is like an insult.

A single rose does not mean that it is spring.

A drowning man is not bothered by rain.

Curiosity is the key to knowledge.

Marriage is an uncut watermelon.

Thinking is the essence of wisdom.

The joy of finding something is often worth more than what is found.

KURDISH CULTURE

Kurds are a distinct ethnic group living in parts of Iran, Iraq, Turkey, Armenia, and Syria. They speak a variation of Persian called Kurdish. In the pre 1900s, most Kurds lived in nomadic animal herding tribes. Today, they often have agricultural or other conventional lines of work.

Kurdish themes include Islam, mysticism, great fighting ability, and a legendary sultan named Saladin.

Kurdish Proverbs

Don't throw away what will return against you.

A small key can open big doors.

Have meals with your friends, but don't trade (*do business*) with them.

Be swift if you are a hammer; be patient if you are an anvil.

Give a man some cloth…and he'll ask for some lining.

A good companion shortens the longest road.

You are as wise as your mind, not your years.

Dealing with yourself is harder than dealing with the rest of the world.

TURKEY

Turkey is a country in Europe and Asia. Throughout its history, Turkey has had a wide variety of people living in it, and the country's Turkish people (who make up about 90% of the population) have mostly a mixture of

Seljuk Turk, Persian, Arab, and Hittite heritages.   The country's main language is Turkish.

About two thirds of Turkish people live in cities or towns, many of which live in the capital of Istanbul (formerly called Constantinople), which was the capital of the Byzantine and Ottoman empires. A large percentage of Turkey's land is nearly barren and hard to farm on.

Common themes in Turkey include strong community ties, cooperation, music, literature, bazaars, baggy pants, Islam, cotton and tobacco farming, and animal herding.

Turkish Proverbs

Don't look at the shape—look at the character.

Every person admires his own character

One eats while another watches—that is how revolutions are begun.

Death is a black camel that lies down at every door. Sooner or later you must ride the camel.

No matter how much snow falls, it won't remain there all the way till summer.

There is not a single season without fruit.

A single bad experience is worth a thousand threats.

The place of your birth is less important than how you live.

Don't fall into a fire in order to avoid the smoke.

If you search for a faultless woman, you will remain a bachelor.

Western European Proverbs

Contents: Basque, Belgium, England, France, Ireland, Luxembourg, The Netherlands, Portugal, Scotland, Spain, Switzerland

BASQUE CULTURE

The Basque are a group of people living mainly in France and Spain on land near the Bay of Biscay and Pyrenees Mountains. There are about one million Basque people in that region, while about 150,000 others live outside of Europe. Many Basque speak their own language, which is very different to other nearby European languages, and is possibly the oldest European language currently in existence.

Themes of the Basque include apples, fishing, cow and sheep herding, Catholicism, iron mining, and shipbuilding.

Basque Proverbs

Things used to be that way, now they're this way, and who knows what they will be like later.

The sun shines the same on the good and the bad.

Before you get married, make sure you know what you are doing

A strong attack is half the battle won.

The person who wants everything to be just right often gets closer to the opposite.

Other people carry their faults up front—we carry ours behind our backs.
Meaning: People commonly notice and criticize other people's faults, but it is less common for someone to point out his own faults.

A small fountain quenches your thirst as well as a big one.

If you always tell the truth, you may lose your friends.

More people are threatened than beaten up.

A good listener needs few words.

Doing nothing and doing useless work are both the same thing

BELGIUM

Belgium is a small country with about 10 million people who speak Dutch, French, and German. Throughout its history, it has been influenced, ruled, or had settlers from the Celts, Romans, Franks, Hapsburgs, and Dutch.

Some Belgian themes include beer, parks, carnivals, paintings, and museums.

Belgian Proverbs

Note: For more proverbs commonly used among Belgian people, see the Netherlands section of this chapter.

Don't use another person's mouth unless it has been lent to you.

Honor is better than honors.

There is no use waiting for your ship to come in if you haven't sent one out.

ENGLAND

England is located on the island of Great Britain, and has a population of about 50 million people. The country has been a major force in world politics, economy, and culture for many centuries.

Celtic-speaking people lived in Great Britain in early times, and it later became part of the Roman Empire by the 50s BC. As the Roman Empire weakened in the 400s AD, England was invaded by Germanic and Nordic tribes such as the Angles, Saxons, and Jutes, who settled in and established kingdoms. Vikings also came to England in the 800s

In the mid 1000s, a French nobleman named William (Duke of Normandy) led a French-speaking group called the Normans, and conquered England. Over the years, the people and cultures of the Anglo-Saxons and Normans blended together, which resulted in the development of the modern English language.

In 1707, England united with other parts of the British island to form what later became known as the United Kingdom. At the same time, the British Industrial Revolution propelled Britain into the world's richest country, and the country also began gaining control of many other territories throughout the world.

Britain later became part of the winning sides in World Wars I & II (ending in 1918 and 1945, respectively), but suffered severe post-war economic depressions. Their colonial empire also weakened immensely, and by the 1950s, Britain had lost most of its vast number of worldwide colonies.

In the 1960s, the British economy began to improve. In the 1970s, Margaret Thatcher became the first ever woman prime minister of Britain. England's current prime minister is Tony Blair. Almost all English people today live in urban areas.

English themes include gardening, literature (noted for such writers as Geoffrey Chaucer, Charles Dickens, and William Shakespeare), visiting the neighborhood pub (public house), tabloids, newspapers, the British Broadcasting Corporation (BBC), soccer, cricket, rugby, music (including folk songs, as well as rock groups such as the Beatles and the Rolling Stones), concerts, ballet, dancing, movies, plays, sculptures, paintings, potatoes, barley, beer, Christianity, longstanding universities, textiles, aerospace manufacturing, and chemical production.

English Proverbs

A danger foreseen is half avoided.

Strike while the iron is hot.

He that is master of himself will soon be master of others.

Knowledge is a treasure, but practice is the key to it.

With all your knowledge, know thyself.

One does harm, and another bears the blame.

When everyone takes care of himself, care is taken of all

A place for everything, and everything in its place.

Better to be safe than sorry.

Praise the sea but keep on land.

My mind to me is a kingdom.

Nature is the true law.

One eyewitness is better than ten earwitnesses.

A good example is the best sermon.

Some are very busy and yet do nothing.

First come, first served.

Some have been thought brave because they were afraid to run away.

Half the world does not know how the other half lives.

He that is warm thinks all are so.

There is no time like the present.

There is a time to speak and a time to be silent.

Success makes a fool seem wise.

Everything has its time.

Skill and confidence form an unconquered army.

Self-preservation is the first law of nature.

Do not be in a hurry to tie what you cannot untie.

You may find your best friend or your worst enemy in yourself.

Two wrongs do not make a right.

A change is as good as a rest.

If he deceives me once, shame on him; if he deceives me twice, shame on me.

An artist lives everywhere.

Better to say nothing, than to say something not to the purpose.

What "they say" is half lies.

In a calm sea, every man is a pilot.

Don't dig your grave with your own knife and fork.

An ounce of prevention is worth a pound of cure

Creditors have better memories than debtors.

A full cup must be carried steadily.

He helps little that helps not himself.

Do not triumph before the victory.

Advice is least heeded when most needed.

Discretion in speech is more important than eloquence.

Poverty is no vice, but an inconvenience.

Actions speak louder than words.

Haste makes waste.

You never miss the water till the well runs dry.

A stitch in time saves nine.

Buy in the cheapest market and sell in the dearest.

A chain is no stronger than its weakest link.

Cursing the weather is never good farming.

A fool and his money are soon parted.

FRANCE

France has had a significant influence on the world for much of history, and the French language has been and continues to be one of the world's most widely used languages. France has been continuously inhabited for thousands and thousands of years, and has a very rich culture and history.

One of the most well known aspects of French history is the French Revolution (1787-1799), which led to the rise of Napoleon Bonaparte as France's emperor. Napoleon, who reigned from 1804 to 1814, expanded the Empire to large boundaries throughout and beyond Europe. However, he and his Empire quickly came crashing down after its brief period of dominance. The Current French Republic was established in 1959.

Some themes of France include wine, dining, wheat, dairy foods, philosophy, literature, poetry, art, music, ballet, architecture (including the Eiffel Tower), tourism, science, Christianity, Jerry Lewis appreciation, iron, steel, car manufacturing, technology, and skiing.

French Proverbs

Always talk big and you will never be forgotten.

Everyone thinks his own burden is heavy.

One day is as good as two for the person who does everything in its place.

Friends are lost by calling too often and by not calling often enough.

If the doctor cures, the sun sees it; but if he kills, the earth hides it.

A bad compromise is better than a good lawsuit.

A fault that is denied once is committed twice.

A man's value is that which he sets upon himself.

A small fire that warms you is better than a large one that burns you.

If you want to totally avoid being deceived, get married on February 30th.

To be willing is to be able.

Women will believe any lie that is wrapped in praise.

One dog's piss will not pollute the ocean.

It is a double pleasure to deceive the deceiver.

I have so much to do…that I am going to bed.

You cannot be very smart if you have never done anything foolish.

A rich man has more relatives than he knows about.

A throne is only a bench covered with velvet.

Why kill time when one can employ it?

A good meal should begin with hunger.

When you can't find peace within yourself, there is no use looking for it somewhere else.

A great fortune in the hands of a fool is a great misfortune.

Vive la difference.

The person who does not ask will never get a bargain.

There are more foolish buyers than there are foolish sellers.

Set your sail according to the wind.

All of the Earth's treasures can't bring back a lost moment.

War is much too serious a matter to be entrusted to the military.

Comparison is not (necessarily) proof.

Tough times don't last, but tough people do.

Late is worth more than never

Paris wasn't made in a day.

Impossible isn't (a word in) French.

Nothing is given as easily as advice.

To want to forget something is to remember it.

I love my friends—but I love myself more.

You need to break the shell in order to have the almond.

Better to prevent than to cure.

It would be a huge book that contained all the maybes said in a day.

When you rely too much on reason, you end up not relying enough on feeling.

There is no such thing as an insignificant enemy.

A person's reputation is like his shadow—sometimes it follows and sometimes it precedes him; and sometimes it is smaller and sometimes it is bigger than him.

The meaning is best known to the speaker.

The common property donkey is the worst saddled.

The only real way someone can stop criticism is to die.

Remember that everyone you ever meet is sure to fear something, to love something, and to have lost something.

Don't talk about a rope in the house of someone whose father was hung.

Example is the greatest of all seducers.

Sailors get to know each other better when there is a storm   (Corsica)

IRELAND

Ireland is an island west of Britain. The northeastern section, known as Northern Ireland, is part of the United Kingdom of Great Britain. The rest of the island is called the Republic of Ireland. In its history, Ireland has been subject to influences, migrations, and invasions by groups such as the Celts, Normans, Norses, English, and Scots.

The country's official languages are Irish and English. Ireland is particularly noted for its strong emphasis on Christianity, which is said to have been brought to the island in the 400s by a British / Roman man now known as St. Patrick.

Themes of Ireland include shamrocks, leprechauns, music (including harps and bagpipes), dancing (including the kind featured in *Riverdance*), soccer, hurling (a type of sport), storytelling, joke telling, art, theatre, literature, cows, potatoes, milk, wheat, and barley.

Irish Proverbs

Marriages are all happy—it's having breakfast together that causes all the trouble.

A glutton lives to eat; a wise man eats to live.

A good laugh and a long sleep are the two best cures in the doctor's book.

Good sense is as important as food.

No time for your health today, (will yield) no health for your time tomorrow.

Never burn a penny candle looking for a halfpenny.

Bricks and mortar make a house, but the laughter of children make a home.

There is no luck except where there is discipline.

Every eye forms its own fancy.

Say but little, and say it well.

A questioning man is halfway to being wise.

He is bad that will not take advice, but he is a thousand times worse that takes every advice.

LUXEMBOURG

Luxembourg is a small country that has German and French influences, but has remained a politically separate region since the 900s. The country's main language is Luxembourgish.

Themes of Luxembourg include wealth, art, and high iron and steel production.

Luxembourg Proverbs

Your wife and your wheelbarrow are two things that you should never lend to anyone.

A woman is as old as she wants to tell you she is.

THE NETHERLANDS (HOLLAND)

The Netherlands is a small and heavily populated country. Its 16 million inhabitants speak Dutch (a language related to German and English).

The Netherlands was inhabited in early times by Celtic and Germanic people, and then by a variety of other groups including the Saxons, Franks, and Frisians. The Netherlands has also been part of a number of European Kingdoms throughout its history.

In the 1500s and 1600s, the Dutch had a great influence on European art with artists such as Rembrandt.   Some other Dutch themes include bicycles, soccer, field hockey, ice-skating, architecture, proverbs, cheese, butter, pigs, steel, and shoes.

Dutch Proverbs

You can't shoe a horse while it is running.

The truth is lost when there is too much debating.

The person who is outside his door already has a major part of his journey behind him.

If you hear a lot of things, you will hear a lot of lies.

Deep swimmers and high climbers usually don't die in their beds.

Wise people can't answer the most foolish questions.

The strength of a tree lies in its roots—not in its branches.

He who undertakes too many things at once seldom does any of them well.

You can't hatch chickens from fried eggs.

Trees that are frequently transplanted rarely thrive.

A handful of patience is worth a bushel of brains.

Slowly but surely, the bird builds its nest.

It's vain to learn wisdom yet live foolishly.

If the rope is weak, pull gently.

Silence is the answer to many things.

Milk the cow, but don't pull off the udder.

There's more to dancing than a pair of dancing shoes.

Skill and assurance form an invincible combination.

A wise husband and a patient wife equal a peaceful home and a happy life.

A praying pirate is definitely a sign of danger.

PORTUGAL

Portugal neighbors Spain on its east and the Atlantic Ocean on its west. Most Portuguese people live towards the coastline, especially since Eastern Portugal has very bumpy land.

Over its early history, Portugal was inhabited or conquered by the Iberians, Celts, Romans, Germanic tribes, and Muslims. By the 1400s, the Portuguese began making many sea explorations. By the 1500s, they amassed a large overseas Empire that encompassed colonies in many parts of the globe, most of which they lost control of by the 1800s. From 1580 to 1640, Portugal was also united with Spain.

The current Portuguese government was formed in 1976. The nation's official languages are Portuguese and Mirandese.

Common themes of Portugal include Catholicism, cafes, soccer, the bullring (like bullfighting, but the bull is not killed), architecture, art, music, dancing, singing, fruit, fish, olives, wheat, wine (especially red "port" wine), and economic problems.

Portuguese Proverbs

The person who is well prepared has already won half of the battle.

Never cut what can be untied.

Not much can be done when everyone is giving orders.

Think of many things, but do just one at a time.

An hour of play discovers more than a year of conversation (does).

The dog wags his tail, not for you, but for your bread.

Visits always give a pleasure—if not the arriving, then the departing.

Hell is paved with good intentions, and roofed with lost opportunities.

SCOTLAND

Scotland is a country in the northern part of the United Kingdom. Scottish ancestry has many similarities to English ancestry, including Celtic, Roman, Anglo, and Norman influences.

In the 1600s, the Scottish Kingdom united with the English Kingdom, and in the 1700s they both became part of the United Kingdom of Great Britain. The Scottish people have three languages: English, Scots, and Gaelic.

Themes of Scotland include kilts, bagpipes, music, opera, ballet, dancing, storytelling, art, architecture, poetry, movies, actor Sean Connery, soccer, rugby, golf, whisky, oatmeal, cheese, wheat, barley, potatoes, hunting, and meat eating.

Scottish Proverbs

You will never know a man until you do business with him.

Don't be penny wise and pound (*dollar*) foolish.

Be a friend to yourself, and others will.

Better to bend than to break.

Better to be ill spoken of by one before all than by all before one.

Be happy while you're living, for you're a long time dead.

Every man's tale is good till another's be told.

Confessed faults are half mended.

Many a good tale is spoiled in the telling.

Be slow in choosing a friend, but slower in changing him.

A good diet cures more than doctors.

Self-assurance is two thirds of success.

SPAIN

Spain is one of the most influential countries in world history. The country's world exploration and conquests have resulted in various regions around the world becoming known as Latin America.

Like many other European nations, much of Spain's early history is marked by arrivals of Celts (around the 900s BC) and Romans (who ruled much of Spain from the 100s BC to the 400s AD). Spain was later conquered by Muslims and then by various Christian Kingdoms before uniting under King Ferdinand and Queen Isabella in 1479.

After the discovery of the Western Hemisphere in the late 1400s, Spain soon began colonializing the region. This caused the language of Spanish and the religion of Christianity to spread and eventually predominate throughout much of the Americas. By 1900, however, Spain had lost all of its overseas possessions.

Major themes of Spain include painting (including artists such as Pablo Picasso and Salvador Dali), gambling, bullfighting, Catholicism, coffee, olive oil, literature (including the works of Miguel Cervantes, who is covered in a separate chapter of this book), music, dancing, architecture, and mining.

Spanish Proverbs

Make sure you have many books and many friends—as long as they are good ones.

If you are choosing between bad company and loneliness, choose the second option.

Every season brings its joy.

Never advise someone to go to war or to get married.

If you want to be respected, you must respect yourself.

The person who plants the lettuce does not always eat the salad.

Ask for too much so that you can get enough.

It is beautiful to do nothing and then rest afterwards.

Look for the good, and let the bad come on its own.

The person seeking India's riches must have them within himself.

Three Spaniards, four opinions.

Give the grateful man more than he asks for.

The wind changes every day; a woman changes every second.

A person who talks a lot is bound to be right sometimes.

Don't talk too much—your ignorance exceeds your knowledge.

Even the best writer has to erase sometimes.

I dance to the tune that is played.

If you don't pay a servant his wages, then he will pay himself.

If someone cannot even keep his own secrets, don't count on him to keep someone else's.

Tomorrow is often the busiest time of the year.

Don't speak unless you can improve on the silence.

Changing one's mind is more often a sign of prudence than of ignorance.

The obscure we see eventually; the completely apparent takes longer.

The secret of patience is to do something else in the meantime.

Take hold of a good minute.

It is better if they say, "He ran away here" than "He died here."

Sell publicly and buy privately.

Buy from people who are desperate, and sell to newlyweds.

He that has a good harvest must be able to endure a few thistles.

The person that makes one basket can make a hundred.

Every person is a fool in some person's opinion.

Don't bite off more than you can chew.

Don't let anyone know about your silent (*secret*) money.

A meowing cat is never a good mouse catcher.

Say nothing when you are giving—only say something when you are receiving.

If you must battle your enemy, hit him where it hurts him most.

When the cat's away, the mice will play

Under a good cloak may be a bad man.

Don't sign a paper without reading it, or drink water without seeing it.

Talking about bulls is not the same thing as being in the bullring.

If you want to be respected, you must respect yourself.

When there is a famine, no bread is stale. (Catalonia)

At her wedding, the bride eats the least. (Catalonia)

A gentle breeze blowing in the right direction is better than a pair of strong oars. (Canary Islands)

SWITZERLAND

Switzerland is well known for its rivers, seas, lakes, and mountains (especially the Alps mountain system). Early Switzerland was part of the Roman Empire (0-400 AD), and also received an influx of Germanic tribal immigrants from the 200s AD to 500s AD.

The people of Switzerland speak a variety languages, including German, French, and Italian. The region's ancient Romansh language is also sparsely used in the country.

Some Swiss themes include education, a generous social welfare system, international trading and banking, watches, tourism, skiing, yodeling, granola, yogurt, cheese, chocolate, literature, philosophy, art, architecture, and science.

Swiss Proverbs

Sometimes you have to be silent in order to be heard

It's easier to criticize than to do better.

The poor lack much, but the greedy lack more.

Ask ten brewers and you will get eleven opinions.

When in doubt who will win, be neutral.

Love your neighbor, but don't pull down the hedge.

Northern European Proverbs

Contents: Denmark, Finland, Iceland, Norway, Sweden

DENMARK

Denmark is a peninsula and group of islands located north of Germany. It also includes the independently governed territories Greenland (the world's largest island) and the Faroe islands.

Danes migrated into Denmark beginning in the 500s AD. They later expanded the territory during the Viking area, which by the 1200s included many regions throughout Europe, including parts of Germany, Sweden, England, and later Norway.

By the 1900s, they had lost control of most of these lands, and in 1953, the current Denmark government was founded. Denmark is currently one of the richest countries (per capita) in the world. The country's main language is Danish; while English, Faroese, Greenlandic, German also have a significant presence there.

Danish themes include science, literature, music, ballet, theatre, freedom, the social welfare system, relationships without marriage, swimming, rowing, gymnastics, cycling, soccer, beaches, parks, education, furniture, shoes, dairy foods, eggs, and pork.

Danish Proverbs

When the feed box is empty, the horses bite each other

Things never go so well that someone should have no fear, nor so bad that someone should have no hope.

Food tastes best when you eat it with your own spoon.

Don't sail out farther than you can row back.

A person's character reaches town before the person does.

A timely ore (*penny*) is as good as a kroner (*dollar*).

It is a bad idea to take a thorn out of someone else's foot and put it into your own.

Many people love to praise right and do wrong.

The doghouse is not the place to store a sausage.

The endless saver always lives in poverty.

More than enough is too much.

Communicate more with yourself than you do with others.

No answer is also an answer.

It is better to ask twice than to lose your way once.

What you cannot say briefly you do not know.

No one is so tall that he never needs to stretch, and no one is so short that he never needs to stoop.

If you build according to every man's advice, you will have a crooked house.

So many heads, so many minds.

Truth must be seasoned to make it palatable.

You can't take a cow from a man who has no cows.

FINLAND

Finland contains numerous forests, hills, marshes, lakes, and rivers. The country has been a rather isolated for most of its existence, although it did become part of Sweden from the 1100s to 1800s, and then part of Russia until the early 1900s. Finnish is the country's main language, and Swedish also has a significant presence there.

Themes of Finland include wealth, nationalism, music, literature (including a well known epic called *Kalevala*), architecture, ceramics, skiing, track & field, fishing, ice hockey, saunas, grains, cows, dairy products, paper, lumber, equal rights, and education.

Finnish Proverbs

On the gallows, the first night is the worst.

A bark leaves no marks if you don't let the dog bite.

Don't judge a dog by its hair.

Being in love is like feeling the sun from both sides.

He who praises the past blames the present.

Great things often come from small beginnings.

The wise person is only cheated once.

ICELAND

Iceland is an island characterized by lots of snow, glaciers, and volcanoes (many of which are still active). Most Icelandic people trace their roots from Norwegian and British settlers that came to Iceland in the late first millennium AD. Along with Icelandic, its inhabitants also speak languages such as German, English, and various Nordic languages.

Themes of Iceland include ice, a generous social services system, a high cost of living, weaving, woodcarving, festivals, Christianity, chess, rock climbing, handball seafood, coffee, potatoes, sheep, literature, and printing.

Icelandic Proverbs

There's more to dancing than a pair of nice shoes.

You do not really know your friends from your enemies until the ice breaks.

When your neighbor's wall breaks, your own is in danger.

A story is only half told if only one side has been presented.

The twigs are rarely better than the trunk.

A man's will can be his paradise, but it can also be his hell.

All sails do not suit every ship.

Character is always corrupted by prosperity.

Pissing in your shoes won't keep your feet warm for very long

A sitting crow starves.

NORWAY

Norway is a mountainous country. Most people there have an ethnic background deriving from early Germanic tribal people. Throughout most of the second millennium, Norway has had ties with Denmark, and later with Sweden, until becoming independent in 1905. Norwegian is the primary language spoken in Norway.

Themes of Norway include plays, storytelling, festivals (many of which involve costumes), literature, libraries, art, seafood, cheese, furniture, petroleum, skiing, ice-skating, the internet, track & field, metals, jewelry, and music.

Norwegian Proverbs

It's too late to close the stable door after the horse has escaped.

Ask for advice, and then use your brain.

Heroism consists of hanging on one minute longer.

In every woman there is a Queen. Speak to the Queen, and the Queen will answer.

Afterthought is good, but forethought is better

Bad is called good when worse happens.

A sip at a time empties the cask.

You may go where you want, but you cannot escape yourself.

SWEDEN

Sweden is filled with many lakes and mountains. The country has a population of about 9 million people, almost all of who speak Swedish.

In the 800s AD and 900s AD, Sweden expanded its territory during the Viking era, but soon disbanded. Then in the 1100s, Sweden began conquering and uniting with most of its nearby Northern European countries, but by the 1500s it became independent again. In the 1800s it united with Norway, but in 1905 the countries split apart.

Swedish themes include economic prosperity, the social welfare system, mining, tourism, grains, festivals, music, opera, ballet, theatre, legendary film director Ingmar Bergman, arts & crafts, skiing & other winter sports, vacations, mountain hiking, soccer, and gymnastics.

Swedish Proverbs

Fear less, hope more; eat less, chew more; whine less, breathe more; talk less, say more; hate less, love more; and all good things will be yours.

Sweep before your own door first before you sweep before the doorsteps of your neighbors.

Don't throw away an old bucket until you know the new one holds water.

If you buy things you don't need, you are stealing from yourself.

Those who want to sing will always find a song.

Shared joy is double joy.

Don't cross the stream to find water.

Central, Eastern, and Southern European Proverbs

Contents: Albania, Austria, Bosnia & Herzegovina, Bulgaria, Croatia, Czech Republic & Slovakia, Estonia, Georgia, Germany, Greece, Hungary, Italy, Latvia, Lithuania, Macedonia, Malta, Poland, Roma, Romania, Serbia & Montenegro, Slovenia, Ukraine, Yiddish

ALBANIA

Albania is located east of Italy across the Adriatic Sea, and west of Greece. Albanians descend from the ancient Illyans. After a period of Roman rule and later ties with Constantinople, Albania was ruled by the Turks beginning in the 1300s.

Albania became an independent country in 1912. From the 1940s, it was an isolated country run by a socialist government, until a non-socialist government was implemented in 1992. Albania was recently influxed by many ethic Albanians fleeing Yugoslavia in 1999 due to the Kosovo conflict. The Tosk dialect of the Albanian language is the country's official language.

Themes of Albania include libraries, writer Ismail Kadare, Islam, Christianity, petroleum, mining, theatres, fruit, wheat, and cotton.

Albanian Proverbs

Patience is the key to paradise.

A day without work, (can yield) a night without sleep.

Those who know how to praise also know how to lie.

In nature, there is no such thing as a lawn.

You cannot hunt with a tied dog.

It is easy to cut the tail of a dead wolf.

AUSTRIA

Austria is located east of Germany and west of Hungary. It includes many mountains, forests, and rivers. In the 400s BC, the Celts came to Austria and established the kingdom of Noricum, and the Romans arrived later and made it a very prosperous area from the 200s BC to the fall of

Rome in the 400s AD. After many foreign invasions, the land became ethnically Germanic.

Austria was part of the Hapsburg Dynasty from the 1200s to the early 1900s, and in 1867, the dual monarchy of Austria-Hungary was established. World War I caused Austria-Hungary to dissolve, and Austria later united with Nazi Germany and joined the Axis powers of World War II. By 1945 they had lost the war, and after a decade of allied occupation, the Austrian government was formed in 1955. Austria's language is German.

Themes of Austria include skiing, tourism, science, art, architecture, literature, Christianity, music, theatre, museums, and steel.

Austrian Proverbs

For more proverbs commonly used by Austrians, also see the German Proverbs section in this chapter.

A light is still a light, even though the blind man cannot see it.

What I do not know will not keep me warm.

BOSNIA & HERZEGOVINA

Bosnia & Herzegovina is a very mountainous region that includes a variety of ethnic groups. It was settled by Slavs in its early history, and then was under rule of various groups including the Serbs, Croats, Hungarians, Ottoman Turks, and Austrians. In the 1900s, it united with Serbia, which later joined Yugoslavia. In 1992, the region became the independent country of Bosnia & Herzegovina. The country's main languages are Croatian, Serbian, and Bosnian.

Themes of Bosnia & Herzegovina include strong friendship and family ties, cafes, coffee, stuffed vegetables, folk songs, hiking, skiing, basketball, and soccer.

Bosnian & Herzegovinan Proverbs

Two things rule the world: reward and punishment.

Clean your own yard first before asking others to clean theirs.

A tree does not grow from the sky.

Someone who lies for you will also lie against you.

BULGARIA

Bulgaria is located north of Greece and Turkey, and borders the Black Sea to its east. Bulgaria was home to ancient Thracian civilizations, and was later conquered by the Romans and then by the Bulgars.

Bulgaria was conquered by the Turks in the 1100s, and it became independent country in 1908. From 1946 to 1989, it used a communist form of government, and in 1991 it implemented its current constitution. The country's main language is Bulgarian.

Themes of Bulgaria include wrestling, scenery, mountains, tourism, wheat, trade unions, cartoons, libraries, festivals, painting, and theatres.

Bulgarian Proverbs

A tree falls the way it leans.

If you want to drown, then don't torture yourself with shallow water.

A gentle word opens an iron gate.

If you can't be good, then be careful.

If you let everyone walk over you, then you become a carpet.

Nature, time, and patience are the three best doctors.

CROATIA

Croatia is a "C" shaped country, much of which runs along the Adriatic Sea. Croats are a type of Slavic people who arrived in the region around the 600s AD, and became part of the Hungarian Empire in the 1100s, although they maintained semi-independence.

After several territorial changes and foreign conquerors, Croatia became part of Yugoslavia in the early 1900s, and became an independent country in 1991. Croatian is the country's primary language.

Croatian themes include fruit, wine, olives, animated films, literature, textiles, and chemicals.

Croatian Proverbs

It is easy for someone to talk about fasting when he has a full belly.

A good friend is worth more than a bad brother.

If you deliberate for too long, you will end up with leftovers.

Don't measure a wolf's tail until he is dead.

If you ask for too much at once, you will come home with an empty bag.

CZECH REPUBLIC & SLOVAKIA

The Czech Republic and Slovakia have their roots in the Bohemia kingdom, which was settled in around the 400s AD primarily by the Czech people. By the 900s, it expanded to include other regions such as Slovakia.

After many other changes, in 1918 a republic union between Bohemia and other regions formed and became known as Czechoslovakia. From 1948, Czechoslovakia was dominated by the Soviets and communists, until the Soviet Empire collapsed in the early 1990s. In 1993, Czechoslovakia was split into the Czech Republic and Slovakia. Czech is spoken in the Czech republic. Slovakia's official language is Slovak, and Hungarian is also a popular language there.

Czech & Slovakian themes include music, filmmaking (especially animated films), caricatures, literature, toys, plays, and grains.

Czech / Slovakian / Czechoslovakian Proverbs

Every dog barks differently.

There is no wise response to a foolish remark.

What is soon ripe is soon rotten.

Consider each day of your life as the best.

Don't jump high in a room with a low ceiling.

Water is cheaper than medicine.

The way to be safe is to never feel secure.

Only in water can you learn to swim.

The person who God shows a treasure to must dig it out himself.

Custom and law are sisters.

ESTONIA

Estonia is a mainland plus about 1500 islands located near the Baltic Sea, west of Russia. The country has many lakes, forests, and rivers.

Despite its vulnerable position, Estonia was able to withstand many invaders until Danes took over in the 1200s. Other groups such as the Swedish and the Polish ruled some of the territory, and then the Russians (later the Soviets) took over in 1721. Estonia gained independence in 1991.

Estonian themes include literature, birds, theatre, newspapers, potatoes, and oil shale.

Estonian Proverbs

Sometimes silence is the proper answer.

The mistakes of other people are good teachers.

The town is new every day.

Earth is more precious than gold.

The work will teach you how to do it.

GEORGIA

Georgia is located in Eastern Europe / Southwestern Asia, within the Caucasus Mountains. Georgia was the site of ancient kingdoms of Iberia and Colchis.

Although Georgia is contained in mountains, the region has been subject to various invasions, rulers, or alliances. During its history, it has been ruled or invaded by Romans, Persians, Byzantines, Muslim rulers, Mogols, Turks, Armenians, and Ottomans. It later aligned with Russia (later the Soviet Union), and then gained independence in the 1990s. Georgian is the country's primary language, but other languages with a significant presence there include Russian, Armenian, and Azeri.

Themes of Georgia include pride in its ancient culture, hospitality, joke telling, great warriors, petroleum, coal, clothing, liquor, tea, poetry, literature, metalwork, and architecture.

Georgian Proverbs

Whoever I love is the most beautiful.

The person in a hurry usually arrives late.

The world can be conquered with words, but not with drawn swords.

GERMANY

Germany borders nine different countries, as well as the Baltic and North Seas. Germanic tribes first arrived in Germany around the 100s BC and drove out the Celts. Germany was able to remain one of few nearby European regions that was not conquered by the Romans. The region later became one of the centers of the Holy Roman Empire (not to be confused with the Ancient Roman Empire) around the 900s.

After many wars and conflicts that decreased its unity, Germany reunited in the 1800s into the German Empire, which dissolved after Word War I. In 1933, Adolph Hitler (an Austrian native who moved to Germany in 1913) became chancellor of Germany and established the Nazi dominated Third Reich. After several invasions of foreign lands, Hitler planned to take over the world. In 1939, he led Nazi Germany in an invasion of Poland, which led to Word War II.

Germany was defeated in 1945, and was soon split into four temporary Ally occupied zones. Shortly later, a dispute between the Soviet Union and other countries led to the spilt of Germany into a democratic West Germany and a Soviet controlled East Germany. The former capital city Berlin was also split, and marked by the infamous Berlin Wall. In 1989, the East German government was overthrown, and the Berlin Wall was for the most part destroyed. Germany fully reunited in 1990.

Themes of Germany include automobile manufacturing, engineering, steel, economic prosperity, book publishing, periodicals, literature, libraries, art, architecture, theatre, music, dance, technology, museums, vacations, festivals, Christmas, soccer, ice hockey, tennis, and volleyball.

German Proverbs

Work is good, as long as you don't forget to live.

Everyone's companion is no one's friend.

Truth that is poorly timed is as bad as a lie.

It is too much too believe everything, and it is too little to believe nothing.

The bridge between joy and sorrow is not long.

Confidence begets confidence.

To change and to change for the better are two different things.

Painted flowers have no scent.

Never give advice unless asked for it.

The belly does not have a conscience.

There are plenty of preachers who don't hear themselves.

The person who has no enemies also has no friends.

Blaming is easy; doing better is more difficult.

An old lie is often more popular than a new truth.

An enemy that is surprised is already half-defeated.

What good is it to run when you are on the wrong road?

It's hard to scare a person who thinks he will benefit from dying.

Don't throw away your old shoes before you have new shoes.

It's better to have no spoon than to have no soup.

Enough is better than too much.

A good lie finds more believers than a bad truth.

"It hasn't" doesn't (necessarily) mean "it won't."

If you want to be strong, conquer yourself.

When you sweep stairs, start at the top.

You can't direct the wind, but you can adjust your sails.

The fault of another is a good teacher.

Suit yourself to the times.

No person can like all, or be liked by all.

Your friend's enemy might be your best friend.

Many people can pack the cards; fewer can play the game.

Guard your mouth as well as you guard your chest.

When the thief is seen (stealing), he says he is joking; but when the thief is not seen, he steals.

Many people preach righteousness and perform sins.

Don't make a mouse of yourself, or else you will be eaten by cats.

Great speakers are usually liars.

Loving and singing are two things that should not be forced.

If you want to perform a good jump, sometimes you need to start by taking a step back.

GREECE

Greece is a peninsula and group of islands in Southern Europe. It has many mountainous areas, including Mount Olympus. Greece is particularly noted for its vivid history and its cultural influence on much of the world

Ancient Minoan and Mycenaean civilizations were located in Greece in early times. By the 700s BC, a group of Greek city-states formed. By the 300s BC, the city-states were conquered by Phillip II of Macedon, whose son Alexander the Great spread the Greek culture throughout his vast empire.

The Romans later conquered Greece in the 100s BC, and also assimilated much of the Greek culture. After the fall of Rome in the late 400s AD, the Byzantine Empire took over Greece shortly later, and ruled the region until the Ottoman Empire took over it in the 1400s. Greece became an independent country in 1832, and its current government formed in the late 1900s.

Greek themes include ancient architecture, ancient philosophy, theatre, literature, hot summers, olives, vegetables, bread, dairy foods, history, an emphasis on family, small businesses, low crime rates, soccer, hunting, Christianity, tourism, shipping, cotton, tobacco, and cement.

Greek Proverbs

You can tell who the good seamen are during a storm.

Don't trouble a quiet snake.

Eat and drink with your relatives, but do business with strangers.

A drop of wisdom is better than a sea of gold.

You can't hide behind your finger.

Listen to valuable statements even if they come from your enemy's mouth.

Every story can be told in different ways.

Many pupils have gained more wealth than their masters.

Many people know how to flatter; few know how to praise.

One minute of patience can result in ten years of peace.

A different man, a different taste.

Don't keep any secrets of yourself from yourself.

Alexander the Great wasn't tall.

Either remain quiet, or say things that improve the silence.

Even from an enemy a man can learn wisdom.

A woman prefers a man without money to money without a man.

Wonder is the beginning of wisdom.

Know yourself.

Nothing in excess.

HUNGARY

Hungarian people derive from a mixed ancestry of Magyars, Slavs, Turks, and Germanic people. In 1867, Hungary became part of a kingdom known as Austria-Hungary, which dissolved after Word War I. Hungary later became a Soviet-bloc nation, and in 1989 it gained independence. Hungary's main language is Hungarian.

Hungarian themes include Nobel Prizes, Catholicism, tourism, cafes, theatre, opera, literature, folk songs, folk dances, paprika, goulash (bean and meat soup), liquor, automobile manufacturing, libraries, and museums.

Hungarian Proverbs

A habit is first a wanderer, then a guest, and finally the boss.

Even the best tree sometimes has bad fruit.

Better to fear than to be frightened.

A man with good judgment does not make the goat his gardener.

Blushing is the paint of good habits.

In much talk there is much irrelevancies.

The owl tells the sparrow that her head is big.

The person who trusts is happy; the person who doubts is wise.

Just because a loan is old, that does not make it a gift.

Although pepper is tiny, its taste is intense.

It's hard to dance in chains.

It's natural to have some disagreement between husband and wife.

The amount of people—(equals) the amount of opinions.

A bashful beggar will have an empty wallet.

Do more things by wisdom than by force.

ITALY

Italy is a peninsula in Southern Europe noted for its natural beauty and rich history. The county has a population of about 60 million people, and has been a major influence on world culture during various periods of history.

Around the 1000s BC, Etruscan and Roman societies began spurning in Italy. In the 500s BC, the Roman Republic formed, which encompassed all of Italy by the 200s BC and continued to expand. This caused Roman culture to spread, as well as other cultures to become blended into it. A Roman Empire was officially established in 27 BC, which at one point grew to a vast size before beginning to decline in the 200s AD and coming to an end in 476.

In the 1000s, some Italian cities began growing into larger city-states, and later spurned a highly cultural period known as the Renaissance, lasting from the 1300s to the 1600s. After many various foreign rulers, Italy later became an independent and fully unified nation by the late 1800s. In 1946, the current Italian Republic was formed.

Italian themes include art (including artists such as Leonard da Vinci and Michelangelo), architecture, literature, soccer, basketball, cycling, shopping, lunch, Catholicism, churches, music (including classical music legend Vivaldi and opera star Luciano Pavarotti), filmmaking, museums, art galleries, wine, pasta, olives, fishing, designer clothing, sports cars, steel production, crafts, festivals, and the appreciation of history.

Italian Proverbs

All the brains are not in one head.

Not every truth is good to be told.

Don't judge a horse by its harness.

If a fox is preaching, then beware of your geese.

Good is good, but better beats it.

The person who enjoys good health is rich, even if he doesn't know it.

He that wants should not be bashful.

Beware of the person with nothing to lose.

A cage made of gold does not feed the bird inside of it.

There is no robber worse than a bad book.

As soon as a new law is made, a way around it is devised.

It is better to ride a donkey that carries you than a horse that throws you.

We learn from our mistakes.

The person who doubts nothing, knows nothing.

Experience runs a valuable school, but fools learn in no other.

If you dig a pit for others, you might fall into it yourself!

The poorhouse is full of honest people.

Every man is nearest himself.

The remedy is often worse than the disease.

To the person with little shame, the whole world is his.

Crooked logs make straight fires.

Necessity is a great teacher.

Moderation in all things.

Patience is a plant that does not grow in everyone's garden.

Yes and *no* rule the world.

To the person who watches, everything reveals itself.

The sun passes over filth and is not dirtied.

A thorn has a small point, but the person who feels it does not forget its sting.

Not every question deserves an answer.

I might have lost my ring, but I still have my fingers!

After the storm ends, the sun will shine.

Better untaught than ill taught.

Old thanks cannot be used for new gifts.

He who begins many things, finishes but few

The more the fox is cursed, the more prey he catches.

Yielding is sometimes the best way of succeeding.

Sometimes it is better to give your apple away than to eat it yourself.

It's no time to play chess when the house is on fire.

Rome was not built in a day.

A bow that is bent too far will break.

Preventing someone from falling is better than helping him get up.

If you stumble more than once over the same stump, you have no one to blame but yourself.

The person who offends writes as if it was written on sand, and the person who is offended reads it as if it were written on marble.

A wise person sometimes changes his mind, but a fool never does.

The best doctors are Dr. Quiet, Dr. Diet, and Dr. Merryman.

LATVIA

Latvia is a small country bordering the Baltic Sea and the Gulf of Rega on its west. In early times, it was occupied by Balts, and was later ruled by Vikings, Germans, Poland, Sweden, and Russia. It became an independent country in 1991. The majority of the population is Latvian, and about one fourth of it is Russian.

Latvian themes include manufacturing, textiles, music, dancing, theatre, art, and Christianity.

Latvian Proverbs

No matter how much you eat, save some seeds for sowing.

Every man forges his own destiny.

As long as you live, you learn.

LITHUANIA

Lithuanians derive from early native tribal people who united around the 1200s and expanded into an empire in the 1300s to 1500s. Lithuania was aligned with Poland from the 1300s to 1700s.

Lithuania has been dominated or had ties with Russia for much of the 1800s and 1900s. The country became independent in 1991. Its main language is Lithuanian, and Polish and Russian also have a presence there.

Themes of Lithuania include folktales, folk art, Christianity, music, museums, theatres, gypsum, flax, and potatoes.

Lithuanian Proverbs

All that glitters is not gold, and all that is sticky is not tar.

You can't blow against the wind.

Don't be too bold, or you will burn your eyes; but don't be too slow, or you will lose your share.

One day teaches the other.

MACEDONIA

Macedonia is located north of Greece, and borders three other countries. The majority of its inhabitants are Macedonian, and about 20% are Albanian.

Macedonia was part of the Roman Empire in early times. By the 600s AD, Slav immigrants entered the region, and from 1371 to 1912, the country was part of the Ottoman Empire. Part of Macedonia then became part of The Kingdom of Serbs, Croats, and Slovenes (which was the predecessor to Yugoslavia). In 1991, Macedonia became independent. Macedonian and Albanian are the country's two main languages.

Macedonia is not the same place as the nearby historical region in Greece and the current region in Greece that are also referred to as Macedonia.

Themes of Macedonia include poetry, theatre, economic problems, ethnic conflicts, Christianity, and Islam.

Macedonian Proverbs

A bear that dances in your neighbor's house might soon dance in yours.

If my neighbor is happy, my own work will go easier, too.

MALTA

Malta is a country of islands (one of which is also called Malta) located south of Sicily (Italy). Maltese people have a variety of heritages, due to its many foreign rulers throughout its history, such as the Romans, Arabs, Normans, French, and British. The current Malta republic was formed in 1974. Maltese and English are the country's official languages.

Themes of Malta include festivals, dancing, music, Catholicism, soccer, and architecture.

Maltese Proverbs

The person who thinks about his own grief forgets about the grief of others.

The law is not made for the rich.

The one who has had no experience of evil cannot know the worth of what is good.

The world teaches you more than your taskmaster.

Marriage without lovemaking means sad consequences and sorrow.

He is a fool who does not consider his own interests.

Asking is the sister of knowing.

One man's fault is another man's lesson.

He who does not fart lets out silent ones.

Enjoy yourself, for there is nothing in the world we can call our own.

POLAND

Poland borders seven different countries as well as the Baltic Sea. It became a kingdom in the 900s. In the 1300s, it united with Lithuania, and soon expanded its territory and became a dominant European power.

Poland later gradually lost much of its territory. By the 1700s, it was split up among Russia, Prussia, and Austria; but the country was later united as a Russian territory in 1815.

Poland gained independence from Russia after WWI, but was then dominated by the Russians (Soviets) beginning the 1940s before once again gaining independence in 1989. Polish is the country's official language.

Themes of Poland include Catholicism, potatoes, rye, literature, music, architecture, theatre, soccer, swimming, and boxer Andrew Golota.

Polish Proverbs

If each person would sweep before his own house, the city would soon be clean.

Pray once if you are going to fight, pray twice if you are going to sail, and pray thrice if you are going to get married.

Better no doctor at all than three.

God promised me a fur coat, and I am already sweating.

The news of a good deed travels far, but the news of a bad one travels even farther.

Under capitalism man exploits man; under socialism the reverse happens.

Do not push the river—it will flow by itself.

I'm human, and nothing that is human is strange to me.

A good run is better than a bad fight.

Truth can take you everywhere…including jail!

ROM / ROMA / GYPSY CULTURE

The Roma are a frequently traveling ethnic group that originated in India and later spread throughout Persia in the 1000s, to Europe around the 1400s, and to the rest of the world in recent years. There are about 3 million Roma today, many of which live in Eastern Europe.

The Roma have worked many jobs throughout their history, but are particularly well known for their male showmen and female fortunetellers.

Roma / Rom / Gypsy Proverbs

The journey is just as important as the destination.

The dog that trots about finds a bone.

It is better to be the head of a mouse than the tail of a lion.

We are all wanders of this earth; our hearts are full of wonder and our souls are full of dreams.

ROMANIA

Romania is bordered by the Black Sea on its east, and by five countries on its other sides. Romania includes the Carpathian Mountain chain. Romanians trace their ancestry to the native Dacians, as well as the invading Romans who came there around 100 AD.

The country officially became known as Romania in 1859 when Moldavia and Walachia united to form a country. Romania was a semi-independent Soviet satellite for part of the 1900s, and became wholly independent by the latter part of the century. Besides the Romanian language, Hungarian and German are also spoken in Romania.

Romanian themes include theatre, puppets, folk music, operas, dancing, folk art, peas, wine, woodcarving, costumes, periodicals, metalwork, and tourism.

Romanian Proverbs

The person taking legal action often gives up an ox to win a cat.

Without other people's companionship, even paradise would be an unlikable place.

Chooses a wife to please yourself, not others.

The eyes have one language everywhere.

Better late than never.

The blessing of having many children has never broken a man's roof.

SERBIA & MONTENEGRO

Serbia & Montenegro is forest-filled and mountainous, with some fertile plains. Serbs have been in the region since the 500s AD. It has been ruled partially or wholly by the Byzantines, Ottomans / Turks, and Russians. Over time, a distinct Montenegrin ethnicity also emerged due to various separations.

Serbia & Montenegro was part of a larger federation called Yugoslavia from 1929 until the various regions ceded in 1991, and then Serbia and Montenegro formed a new Yugoslavic Federation in 1992. The country was renamed Serbia & Montenegro in 2003. Today, Serbs form the majority of the country's ethnicity, and Montenegrins, Albanians, and Hungarians also have a major presence there. The main languages are Serbian, Croatian, Montenegrin, and Albanian.

Themes of Serbia include political turmoil, extended family groups, Christianity, seasoned ground meat, wine, cafes, folk stories, folk songs, festivals, handicrafts, poetry, filmmaking, gymnastics, and soccer.

Themes of Montenegro include extended family groups, architecture, church murals, art, literature, music, museums, hunting, and fishing.

Serbian & Montenegrin Proverbs

We won the war, but we lost peace.

Believing is easier than investigating.

Your ancestor's glory should not prevent you from winning your own.

It's better to blush once than to pale a hundred times.

Complain to someone who can help you.

You are not being honest if you burn your tongue and don't tell everyone else that the soup is hot.

If you humble yourself too much, you will get trampled on.

I am scratching myself where I am itching.

Grain by grain, a loaf; stone by stone, a castle.

SLOVENIA

Slovenia borders Italy on its west. The country has many mountains, valleys, rivers, and trees.

Slovenes came into the area around the 500s AD. It became part of the Charlemagne Empire in the 800, and later the Holy Roman Empire. The Austrians later had control of the territory until 1918 when the Kingdom of the Serbs, Croats, and Slovenes formed. Slovenia was later part of Yugoslavia in 1946, and became independent in 1991. Slovene is the country's main ethnicity and language.

Themes of Slovenia include manufacturing, a strong economy, Catholicism, literature, music, art, and theatre.

Slovene / Slovenian Proverbs

Speak the truth, but leave immediately after.

Never whisper to the deaf, or wink at the blind.

Life without holidays is like a long road without a gostilna (*place of food, drink, and socializing*)

Hunger is the best spice.

UKRAINE

Ukraine is located west of Russia. Most of the land contains plains, mountains, and rivers. Although commonly associated with Russia, Ukraine has had influences from the wide variety of groups that invaded it throughout history. By 1000 AD, it had been invaded by the Cimmerians, Scythians, Sarmatians, Goths, Huns, Bulgars, Avars, Khazars, Magyars, and Slavs. It was then conquered by the Mogols in the 1200s, and then fell to the Lithuanians in the 1300s, the Polish in the 1500s, and the Russians in the 1700s.

Ukraine is often noted for two recent peacetime tragedies: a severe famine in the 1930s, and the Chernobyl nuclear accident in 1986. Ukraine became an independent country in 1991. The country's main languages are Ukrainian and Russian, which are both similar.

Ukrainian themes include folk songs, dancing, literature, woodcarving, mosaics, Christianity, spas, heavyweight boxers and brothers Wladimir & Vitali Klitschko, skating (including Oksana Baiul), soccer, track & field, filmmaking, inflation, iron, and potatoes.

Ukrainian Proverbs

Fire starts with sparks.

No matter how hard you try, a bull will never give milk.

If you chase two hares (at the same time), you will catch neither of them.

Hey girl—if you eat cabbage, you will have a pretty face.

When you enter a great enterprise, free your soul from weakness.

A friendly word is better than a heavy cake.

You can get farther with a friendly word than with a club.

YIDDISH CULTURE

Yiddish is a language used by many European Jews and their descendants in everyday conversation as well as in literature.

The language's use began around the 800s, and it contains aspects of Hebrew, Aramaic, German, and later of Slavic. It has undergone several transitions, and remains popular among many Jewish people today.

Yiddish Proverbs

If you lose your self-respect, you also lose the respect of others.

Health comes before making a livelihood.

With a child in the house, all corners all full.

An imaginary sickness is worse than a real one.

Seek advice, but use your own common sense.

A person should stay alive, if only out of curiosity.

Every answer can result in a new question.

Being too nice can cost a lot.

If one soldier understood the thoughts of another, there would be no wars.

A person's worst enemy can't wish on him what he can think up himself.

Cold strengthens you more than hunger does.

A fool gives; a wise man takes.

A penny saved is a penny earned, but sometimes a penny is better spent than saved.

God created people because he loves stories.

"For example" is not the same as proof.

When brains are needed, brawn won't help.

If you keep on talking, you will end up saying what you didn't intend to say.

To learn the whole *Talmud* (a Jewish scholarly book) is a great accomplishment; to learn one good virtue is even greater.

Russian and Central Asian Proverbs

Contents: Kazakhstan, Kyrgyzstan, Russia, Tajikistan, Turkmenistan, Uzbekistan

KAZAKHSTAN

Most of Kazakhstan borders China and Russia. Most people in the country are either Kazakh or Russian, and these are also the country's main languages. Kazakhstan has a varied landscape that includes mountains and deserts.

In the 1200s and 1300s, the country was under Mongol rule, and from the 1400s to 1500s, the country established a Kazakh nomadic empire. In the 1800s it became under Russian (later Soviet) rule, and became independent in 1991.

Themes of Kazakhstan include Islam, iron, steel, sheep & goat herding, economic problems, storytelling, poetry, rugs, puppet shows, ballet, music, and dancing.

Kazakh Proverbs

Nothing is farther away than yesterday; nothing is closer than tomorrow

Every man in his life should plant a tree, build a house, and raise a son.

The world becomes new every 50 years.

You cannot choose your neighbors, but you can choose how to live with them.

People's lips are holy.

KYRGYZSTAN

Most of Kyrgyzstan borders China and Kazakhstan. The country is highly mountainous.

About half of the country's population is Kyrgyz (also spelled Kirghiz), and most of the rest are Russian and Uzbek. Kyrgyz and Russian are both official languages of Kyrgyzstan.

The Kyrgyz are a Turkic people who have been nomads for most of history. They were under Mongol rule in the 1200s. Kyrgyzstan was also part of the Qing (Manchu) Chinese dynasty in the 1700s, and became under control of the Russians (later the Soviets) in the 1800s, which caused much conflict. The country gained its independence in 1991.

Themes of Kyrgyzstan include Islam, animal herding, grains, potatoes, poetry, music, dancing, folk songs, and novelist Chingiz Aytmatov.

Kyrgyz / Kirghiz Proverbs

A hungry child does not play like a satiated child; and a satiated child does not play like a hungry child

The satiated do not understand the concern of the hungry.

Everything that a person has never seen before seems to look interesting.

There is no person without mistakes; there is no lake without frogs.

To the person who takes, six is not enough; to the person who gives, five is too much.

One who is extremely intelligence might turn crazy.

The wise can evade a thousand problems; the unwise can barely even evade one.

RUSSIA

Russia is located in Eastern Europe and in Asia. It is the world's largest country in land area, and the seventh largest in population (145 million).

Russia's environmental characteristics vary greatly throughout the country, but much of it is filled with mountains and rivers. Although there are about 70 different ethnicities in Russia, the vast majority of its population has Russian ethnicity.

Russia has had many influences and groups living and sometime ruling it, including various nomadic groups (700s BC-500s AD), and the Mongols (1200s-1300s).

By the 1500s, Russia began expanding under leaders such as Ivan IV (the first Czar/Emperor of Russia), Peter I, and Catherine II. After battling off Napoleon in the early 1800s and taking some of his territory, Russia later added many other territories such as Armenia and Georgia.

Russia continued to advance their domain, and after World War I, a new Soviet government emerged, which formed the Union of Soviet Socialist Republics (a.k.a. the Soviet Union or the USSR) several years later. By

1991, the USSR was split apart, and many of its republics were granted independence.

About three-fourths of current Russians live in urban areas, primarily in the Western section of Russia that is located in Europe.

Some themes of Russia include theatre, ballet, museums, literature, poetry, architecture, movies, machine building, textiles, lumber, iron, coal, cold winters, black market goods, ice hockey, volleyball, wrestling, boxing, weightlifting, and chess.

Russian Proverbs

A hammer breaks glass, but also forms steel.

Everything cannot be hung on one nail.

Trust, but verify.

Everyone has his own Czar (*Emperor*) in his head.

Every road has two directions.

If you are going to do something carelessly, it is better to give it up entirely.

There is no shame in not knowing—the shame lies in not finding out

Each day learns from the one before it, but no day teaches the one after it.

One day before you is better than ten years behind you.

If the child does not cry, the mother won't know what it wants.

Have a good time if you want—but don't overdo it.

It is easier to bear a child once a year than to shave everyday.

Asking is no sin, and being refused is no tragedy.

Custom is stronger than law.

A person never gets tired working for himself.

Do not spit into the well that you might need to drink out of.

Running away is not glorious, but often very healthy.

You can get used to anything—even hell.

Lie, but don't overdo it.

Friendship is one thing, and tobacco (*business*) is another.

Many people who have gold in the house are looking for copper outside.

Some people are masters of money, and some people are slaves of it.

TAJIKISTAN

Tajikistan is a highly mountainous country that borders China, Afghanistan, Kyrgyzstan, and Uzbekistan. Tajiks make up the majority of the population, while Uzbeks are also a major ethic group there. The country's official language is Tajik, which is very similar to Persian.

In early times, Tajikistan was part of the Persian Empire and then the Empire began by Alexander of Macedon. Arabs Muslims conquered the region in the 600s and 700s AD, and the Uzbeks ruled from the 1400s to 1700s. The Russians (later the Soviets) took over in the 1800s, and Tajikistan became independent in 1991.

Themes of Tajikistan include Islam, coal, cotton, costumes, festivals, horses, wrestling, The New Year celebration, and literature (particularly poetry).

Tajik Proverbs

Bread is bread; crumbs are also bread.

A big family is a rich family.

TURKMENISTAN

Turkmenistan is primarily a desirous region that borders the Middle East on its south and west. About 80% of he country's inhabitants are Turkmen, while several other ethnicities comprise the remaining 20%. The country's official language is Turkmen.

Nomadic tribes of Turkmen occupied the region in around the 1000s AD. They Russians (later the Soviets) conquered them in the late 1800s, and the country became fully independent in 1991.

Themes of Turkmenistan include Islam, horses, cotton, carpets, silk, literature (particularly poetry), and plays.

Turkmen Proverbs

If water is a Turkmen's life, then the carpet is his soul, and the horse is his wings.

If you have one day left in your life, take a horse; if you have two days, take a woman.

You reap what you sow.

UZBEKISTAN

Uzbekistan has a population of about 25 million people, about 70% of which are of the Uzbek ethnicity. The main language is Uzbek, and secondary languages are Russian and Tajik.

The Uzbeks ethnicity derives from a mixture of Turkic and Mongol people. Most of them came into the current area of Uzbekistan around the 1500s, and by the late 1800s, the region became controlled by Russia. Uzbekistan became an independent country in 1991.

Themes of Uzbekistan include a strong economy, cotton, sheep machinery, Islam, literature (particularly poetry), music, and architecture.

Uzbek Proverbs

Have breakfast yourself; share lunch with your friend; and give dinner to your enemy.

Don't choose a house—choose neighbors. Don't choose a path—choose traveling companions.

Where there is water, there is life.

A word said is a shot fired.

He who possesses knowledge possesses the world.

Oceanian / South Pacific Proverbs

Contents: Australia, Fiji, New Zealand, The Samoan Islands, Tonga

AUSTRALIA

Australia is a large island / small continent located "down under," south of Indonesia and Papa New Guinea. Australia was inhabited by native Aboriginals for approximately 50,000 years, who numbered about 700,000 when European settlers arrived on the continent in the late 1700s (although they knew about the continent since the early 1600s).

The British soon set up a settlement of criminals and seamen in Australia, which caused many deaths of native Aborigines due to diseases and modern weaponry. In 1900, Britain declared Australia a commonwealth territory, and it remains so today.

Australian themes include coal, diamonds, the greeting "G'day mate," actress Nicole Kidman, actor Mel Gibson, Steve & Terri Irwin from the show *The Crocodile Hunter*, kangaroos, gambling, beer, eating a wide variety of animals, festivals, music, dancing, literature, and Aboriginal culture.

Australian Proverbs

A bad worker blames his tools.

Those who lose dreaming are lost.

In the planting season visitors come singly, and in harvest time they come in crowds.

Half a loaf is better than none.

The clash of ideas brings forth the spark of truth.

We are all visitors to this time, this place. We are just passing through. Our purpose here is to observe, to learn, to grow, to love; and then we return home.

FIJI

Fiji is a large group of islands, and contains a wide variety of ethnic groups, such as Polynesians, Melanesians, Indians, Europeans, Chinese, and people who emigrated from surrounding South Pacific islands. Fiji was a colony of Britain for about a century until declaring independence in 1970.

Themes of Fiji include ceremonies, kava root drinks, music, dancing, and crafts.

Fijian Proverbs

Life is like this: sometimes sun, sometimes rain.

Each bay, its own wind.

NEW ZEALAND

New Zealand is a group of two large islands and several smaller ones. New Zealand is located in the middle of nowhere, far from virtually any other land whatsoever.

New Zealand was occupied in earlier times by Polynesian Maori people who arrived there around 800 AD. European exploration in the 1600s caused the British to attempt to coloniolize New Zealand in the mid 1800s. Fighting persisted for decades between the native Maori and the British, and after a period of British dominion, New Zealand gradually became self-governed in the 1900s.

Most New Zealanders have European ancestry, while the Maori constitute about 10 percent of the population. Several minority groups also exist.

New Zealand themes include wood crafting, music, dancing, rugby, meat (especially sheep), seafood, vegetables, dairy foods, restaurants, legendary writer Katherine Mansfield, legendary climber Sir Edmund Hillary, yachting, and a recent movement to preserve Maori culture.

New Zealander Proverbs

A house full of people is filled with different points of view.

Don't spend time with people who don't respect you.

A little axe, when well used, brings lots of food.

Can I pull down the sun with a forked stick, or prevent it from running its course?

Walk in the valley of our ancestors, learn of the history, and marvel at the beauty.

There is more than one way to achieve a goal.

Take time to enjoy life's roses.

Persist as tenaciously as you persist in eating.

Survival is the treasured goal.

THE SAMOAN ISLANDS

The Samoan islands contain primarily Polynesian people similar to groups such as the Tongans, Hawaiians, Tahitians, and New Zealand Maori. The islands are politically split into American Samoa and (Western) Samoa. The main languages spoken are Samoan and English.

Samoan themes include fishing, tourism, coconuts, bananas, education, and social organization.

Samoan Proverbs

In every generation there are some outstanding chiefs.

A careless person will be taken by surprise by his observant enemy.

The person with burnt fingers asks for tongs.

It is useless to shake the branch that bears no fruit.

Let each person do his share of the work.

TONGA

Tonga is a group of islands in the South Pacific. Most of its inhabitants have a Polynesian ethnic background. The country's main languages are Tongan and English.

Tongan themes include social organization, coconuts, bananas, pineapples, fishing, and handicrafts.

Tongan Proverbs

A cowardly hyena lives longer.

To enjoy is to learn

Native American Proverbs, Quotes, and Chants

The Native Americans (also known as the Indians or the American Indians) are the original inhabitants of the Americas (North, South and Central America including the Caribbean / West Indies Islands; all of which is also called the New World or the Western Hemisphere). Before we get into their various proverbs, quotes and chants, here is a brief background and history of them.

Origins

Some scientists and archeologists believe that the Native Americans were people who originally came to the Americas from Asia around 13,000 BC, but possibly as early as 33,000 BC. This was a time when there was much more dry land on the earth than there is today, including a land route from Asia to North America. As centuries passed, much of the earth's land submerged under water due to severe climate changes.

Other groups contend that Native Americans do not derive from Asian immigrants.

Early Native American Life

Very early groups of Native Americans were probably hunter-gatherers who formed small groups of about 30 people, and frequently moved. They developed several hunting weapons and strategies. As the environment changed, many Native American lifestyles changed, and farming also developed in several regions

Spreading Throughout the Americas

Various groups of Native Americans spread from North America to other parts of the Americas. By 10,000 BC, they had reached most parts of the Americas, and by 6000 BC, various groups extended from the northernmost to the southernmost regions of the Americas. (Note that other groups of Asian people known as the Inuit Eskimos and the Aleuts came to the Western Hemisphere in another period of migration—however, these groups are usually not grouped under the category "Native Americans")

As Native Americans spread across the Americas, various groups formed many different languages and ways of life, ranging from the huge cities of the Aztecs and Mayans in Central America, to the various villages of

Native American people that hunted and farmed in eastern North America, to the frequently traveling peoples in southern South America.

Keep in mind, however, that there were hundreds of different tribes of Native Americans with many different lifestyles and languages.

General Life

For most groups of Native Americans, life was centered on getting food (through hunting, fishing, farming and/or gathering) and other necessities, as well as adapting to seasonal variances of the environment.

Some other common life themes among Native Americans included interacting and cooperating with one's family and community, splitting up tasks among various people, getting married, the trading of goods and services, and the variety of religions and rituals practiced throughout the Native American world.

Children and Adolescents

A strong emphasis in Native American communities was placed on children, who were considered sacred, and were taught through experiences, lessons, and games. A common practice among various communities was to put boys (and sometimes girls) who were in their early teens through a special initiation ceremony, where they had to overcome harsh conditions under their own reliance to become officially considered adults.

Families and Groups

Family played a major role in most Native American communities, many of which lived and cooperated within large family groups. Other communities formed special groups that were not based on relation, but were organized by age groups.

Tribes and Larger Groups

Native Americans who lived in one region and had similarities were considered a tribe. Some tribes also had subdivisions. Additionally, in some instances, tribes joined together to form federations, most notably the Iroquois League a.k.a. the Five Nations (originally formed in the 1100s and comprised of the Mohawk, Onondaga, Oneida, Seneca, and Cayuga tribes. The Tuscarora joined them in the early 1700s and made them the Six Nations).

Also, primarily in South of what is currently the United States, several large empires formed, including the Aztec empire (in Mexico), the Inca empire (in South America along the Andes Mountains), and the Maya Empire (near Central America).   The Natchez Indians also had an empire type state in the southeastern region of what is now the United States

Sports and Games

Sports were often an important part of Native American life for both children and adults, and various groups participated in events such as running races, aiming contests, and many kinds of sports played with balls, hoops, sticks and/or spears. The Aztec and Mayan groups often took these game a little too seriously, and sometimes sacrificed the captain of the losing team to the gods.

Many Native Americans also played various guessing games.

Wars Between Native Americans

Wars sometimes erupted between various tribes due to disputes that got out of hand, although some tribes and smaller groups usually tried to avoid wars. Native American Empires in South and Central America often had formal armies.

European Contact

European contact with the Americas began after Columbus landed on one of the Islands of the Bahamas (probably San Salvador) in 1492. (The Bahamas are located near Florida and Cuba). Estimates of the Native American population at that time run from about 30 to 120 million, most of whom lived in what is now South American, Central America, and Mexico.

Europeans such as the Spanish, Portuguese, English and French later began arriving, exploring, and settling in many parts of the Americas, and soon had a very horrible impact on Native American life.

European Impact

The Europeans often tried to destroy Native American culture, and disputes also developed over land. Many wars developed between Native Americans and Europeans, which were for the most part won by the Europeans, who had tremendous advantages in numbers, technology, and large-scale organization. The European countries also fought with each other over control of the New World.

The further influx of settlers in the Americas caused tremendous damage to Native American societies. They often lost their land and were forced to move. Additionally, their food supply often decreased because of the settlers influence, and many Native Americans starved. Illnesses also killed a large number of Native Americans. And the introduction of liquor by the Europeans also resulted in many Native Americans becoming alcoholics.

As the United States developed into an individual nation in the late 1700s, treaties were often signed that gave Indians territories called reservations, although Americans frequently reneged on such treaties.

Throughout the Americas, Native American mistreatment continued for many decades, but by the mid to late 1900s, Native Americans began receiving equal rights.

Native Americans Today

About 40 to 50 million Native Americans live in Latin America, while millions of other people in Latin America have partial Native American ancestry. In the United States, there are about two to three million Native Americans citizens, who form over 500 different tribes. Some live on Native American reservations and other designated areas, while many others live in urban areas and have assimilated with the general American lifestyle. Canada also has a significant Native American population.

Native American culture is still strong today, but many Native American groups fear that it is slowly dissolving, especially since many of the hundreds of its languages are disappearing.

Native American Proverbs and Quotes, Organized by Tribe

Note: This section is more focused on Native Americans in what is currently the United States and Canada. Most Native Americans in Mexico, South America, and Central America make up a large part of the populations and ancestry of the people. See the chapters on Proverbs of those regions for more info on those areas and their proverbs.

Contents: Arapaho, Arikara, Blackfoot, Cherokee, Cheyenne, Crow, Hopi, Huron, Mohawk, Navajo, Nez Perce, Omaha, Onondaga, Pawnee, Pueblo, Sauk, Seneca, Shawnee, Shoshone, Sioux, Suquamish, Yampiraka, Yokuts, Other

ARAPAHO

The Arapaho used to hunt on the Great Plains of North America. They lived in teepees and followed buffalo herds, which were their major source of food. They were constantly at war with other Indian tribes.

The Arapaho believed in a powerful spirit world. Many actions and objects had symbolic meaning for them, and they performed various rituals and religious ceremonies, most notably the sun dance.

When white settlers tried to take their land, the Arapaho attempted to fight them off, but in the 1860s they made peace agreements and moved to reservations. There are about 5,000 modern day Arapaho, most of which live in Wyoming and Oklahoma.

Arapaho Proverbs

All plants are our siblings. If we listen, we can hear them speaking.

If you wonder often, the gift of understanding will come.

May our thoughts reach the sky where there is holiness

ARIKARA

The Arikara lived near the in the Missouri River in the Dakotas. They were expert farmers, and very proficient in growing corn and other crops. They also hunted a variety of game. The Arikara led very religious and ceremonial lives.

The area they occupied caused many conflicts with white traders, and led to many battles with Americans in the 1800s. These battles along with smallpox epidemics caused many Arikara deaths. In the mid 1800s, the Arikara set up at a reservation, and many of the approximately 2000 current Arikara live in a reservation in North Dakota.

Arikara Quote

Chief White Shield
(1798-1878) Arikara leader

Skin color makes no difference… My skin is red, but my grandfather was a white man. But why should that matter? It is not the color of the skin that makes me good or bad.

BLACKFOOT

The Blackfoot were a nomadic buffalo-hunting society that lived in Alberta and Montana. They were known as a strong military power that dominated both neighboring tribes and white settlers for many years.

When buffalo herds were scarce in the late 1800s, many Blackfoot died of starvation, and the community turned to farming. Today, there are about 15,000 Blackfoot, most of who still live in Montana and Alberta.

Blackfoot Proverbs

Life is not independent from death—it only appears that way.

There are plenty of different paths to a deep understanding of the universe.

Blackfoot Quote

Crowfoot
(1836-1890) Great warrior who became head chief of the Blackfoot, and promoted peace with other tribes and with whites

What is life? It is the flash of a firefly in the night. It is the breath of a buffalo in the wintertime. It is the little shadow that runs across the grass and loses itself in the sunset.

CHEROKEE

The early Cherokee farmed and hunted in the southern Appalachian region. By the 1500s, they had devised many kinds of tools, and lived in log cabins. They also celebrated various ceremonies, many of which were agriculturally related.

In the 1800s, they began adopting several aspects of white culture, such as a republican government, as well as techniques in farming, weaving, and home building. In 1821, they devised a system of writing their language, and it quickly became popular among them. Within a few years, almost the Cherokee nation became versed in it, and by 1828, a newspaper was started called the *Cherokee Phoenix*.

Later, the Cherokee were driven off and horribly mistreated by white settlers and the US government. In their forced move, thousands of them died. Now most Cherokee live in Oklahoma and North Carolina. There are currently about 300,000 Cherokee in North America today, making them the most populous Native American tribe in the United States.

Cherokee Proverbs

Don't allow yesterday to expend too much of today.

There is a right time and place for everything.

Listen—or your tongue will keep you deaf.

Cherokee Quote

High Eagle

I see the universe; I see myself.

CHEYENNE

The early Cheyenne farmed, fished, gathered and hunted in the Minnesota/ Lake Superior region. By the mid to late 1700s, they moved to the Great Plains, where they lived in tepees and hunted buffalo. In the early 1830s, they divided into Northern and Southern groups.

Their spiritual beliefs included the existence of a separate above ground and below ground god, as well as four spirits at the four points of the compass. They elaborately preformed the sun dance ritual, and they also used sacred good luck bundles. The Cheyenne were grouped into various society groups such as social, dance, medicine, spiritual, and military.

The 5,000 current day Cheyenne live mostly in Montana and Oklahoma.

Cheyenne Proverbs

Don't judge with the eyes—use the heart instead.

Watch out for the man who says nothing and the dog who does not bark.

Our first teacher is in our own heart.

Do not judge a person until you have walked two moons in his moccasins.

CROW

The Crow used to be farmers that were part of the Hidatsa tribe living in North Dakota. In the early 1700s, they moved west and became travelers who lived in teepees and followed herds of buffalo. They also became successful traders of horses, bows, shirts, and feather items.

The Crow believed in supernatural visions that were triggered by fasting in isolation, and agonizing one's body with skewers. They also performed many elaborate tobacco-related ceremonies.

The Crow were frequently at war with neighboring tribes, but were friendly with white settlers and soldiers. In 1825, they signed a friendship treaty with the US government, and beginning in 1851, the US government established the Crow reservation through another series of treaties.

About 5,000 current day Crow tribe members live on the Crow Indian Reservation in Montana. Modern day Crow often operate through a tribal council, and participate in many traditional ceremonies.

Crow Proverbs

People's eyes say words that the tongue cannot pronounce.

Stand in the light when you want to assert yourself.

The laws of man change, but the laws of the spirit stay the same.

You already have everything needed to become great.

Crow Quote

Shes His

The earth you see is not just earth—it contains the blood, flesh, and bones of our ancestors... It is consecrated.

HOPI

The Hopi (a subdivision of the Pueblo tribe, who are covered in this chapter) were a secretive and isolated society that participated very heavily in various ceremonies and rituals. One very notable and bizarre ceremony of theirs is the Snake Dance, where performers dance with live snakes in their mouths.

There are currently about 10,000 Hopi, the majority of which live on the Hopi reservation in Arizona. One Hopi village called Oraibi was founded about 800 years ago, and is considered one of the longest continuously occupied villages in the US.

Hopi Proverbs

Let no one say negative things about those who are not present.

A community that lacks faith in itself cannot survive.

Everything has form, power, and inner meaning.

Never get involved in someone's decisions about his belongings.

If two different bowls both get the job done, then what difference does it make if one bowl is dark and the other is pale.

Don't be afraid to weep—it will free your mind from sad thoughts.

Take your children where you go—and don't be ashamed.

There is never a valid reason for arguing.

No answer is also an answer.

You must live your life from start to finish; no one can do it for you.

HURON

The Huron lived in villages near the St. Lawrence Rivers, and mainly practiced agriculture, with a secondary emphasis on hunting and fishing. The Huron had a very organized society, split into various levels of chiefs and groups that extended from local levels all the way to a council that headed the entire Huron nation. Most current day Huron live in Oklahoma.

Huron Proverbs

Let your nature be known and expressed.

Listen to nature's voice—it contains treasures for you.

Huron Quote

Deganawidah
(Lived in 1500s and 1600s) Leader who helped found the Iroquois confederacy

A council fire shall be kindled for all the nations. It shall be lit for the Cherokee and the Wyandot. We will also kindle it for the seven nations living toward the sunrise, and for the nations that live toward the sunset. All shall receive the Great Law and labor together for the welfare of man.

MOHAWK

The Mohawk used to live in New York near the Mohawk River. The Mohawk lived in bark-covered structures known as long houses. The men hunted, and the women farmed crops and gathered other wild crops. The Mohawk were particularly well known for their fierce and highly skilled warriors.

The Mohawk were among the five original nations in the Iroquois League. After the Revolutionary War, many Mohawk moved to Canada. Today, most of the tribe's approximately 7,000 members live in Canada, and some live in New York.

Mohawk Proverbs

Life is both giving and receiving.

Listen to her—our Earth, our Mother; listen to what she is saying.

Mohawk Quotes

Peter Blue Cloud
(1935-) Mohawk writer

From a grain of sand to a great mountain, all is sacred.

Hiawatha
(Lived in the 1500s) Onondaga and Mohawk leader

What is past is past—it is the present and the future that concern us.

NAVAJO

The Navajo lived in scattered collections of homes across vast areas. They had religious lives with a wide variety of rituals, many of which are still performed by modern day Navajo. The Navajo call themselves *Dine*, meaning "the people."

They are currently about 200,000 Navajo, making them second largest Native American tribe in the US. Most of them occupy the Navajo reservation, which is the nation's largest reservation and encompasses over 16 million acres of land in parts of Arizona, New Mexico, and Utah.

Navajo Proverbs

A spear is a big responsibility.

I am one with the Earth.

All around me my land is beauty.

Navajo Chants

I have been to the end of the Earth.
I have been to the end of the waters.
I have been to the end of the sky.
I have been to the end of the mountains.
I have found none that are not my friends.

The Earth is beautiful
Its feet, they are beautiful
Its legs, they are beautiful
Its body, it is beautiful
Its chest, it is beautiful
Its breath, it is beautiful
Its head-feather, it is beautiful
The Earth is beautiful.

In harmony may I walk.
With harmony ahead me, may I walk.
With harmony behind me, may I walk.
With harmony above me, may I walk.
With harmony underneath my feet, may I walk.
With harmony all around me, may I walk.
It is done in harmony.

I see the Earth.
I am looking at her and smile because she makes me joyful.
And the Earth is also looking back at me and smiling.
May I walk joyfully and lightly upon Her.

May there be joy.
May there be success.
May there be good health.
May there be well being.

The mountains—I become part of it.
The flowers, the evergreen tree—I become part of it.

The morning moisture, the clouds, the bodies of water—I become part of it

The wilderness, the water drops, the pollen—I become part of it.

NEZ PERCE

The Nez Perce originally lived in the region where the borders of Idaho, Oregon, and Washington meet. They formed small villages near salmon-filled streams, and lived in large lodges that housed many families together. In the 1700s, many of them acquired horses and became bison hunters, and also developed a war related culture.

In the mid 1800s, gold was discovered on their lands, and caused their community to be disrupted by white miners and settlers. This led to the Nez Perce War of 1877, where the Nez Perce troops were outnumbered twenty to one by the US troops, and surrendered after several months of bloodshed. About 4,000 Nez Perce currently live in America, many of which reside in an Idaho reservation.

Nez Perce Quotes

Chief Joseph aka Thunder-Coming-Up-Over-the-Land-From-the-Water (1840-1904) Leader known for his integrity and honor

It does not require many words to speak the truth.

No man can think for me.

The earth and myself are of one mind.

I believe much trouble and blood would be saved if we opened our hearts more.

Too many misinterpretations have been made ... too many misunderstandings.

I am tired of talk that comes to nothing.

The Earth is the mothers of everyone, and everyone should have equal rights upon it.

You might as well expect the rivers to run backward than to believe that any man who was born free should be contented to be penned up and denied liberty to go where he pleases.

OMAHA

The Omaha used to live in the Ohio River Valley along with ancestors from other Native American tribes. The Omaha later separated from other groups, and around 1700 they moved to Nebraska. In their seasonal lives, they planted crops in the spring, moved west and hunted buffalo in the summer, returned to their village with dried buffalo meat and also harvested their crops in the fall, and then hunted deer in the winter. They also lived with an elaborate social organization.

The Omaha currently live primarily in Nebraska and Iowa. The city of Omaha is named after them.

Omaha Proverbs

Ask questions from your heart, and you will receive answers from your heart.

Dreams are wiser than men.

It is easy to show braveness from a safe distance.

The clear sky and the green fruitful Earth are good; but peace among men is better.

Misfortune happens even to the wisest and best men.

ONONDAGA

The Onondaga used to live in New York, and were predominantly farmers and hunters. They formed a social structure where the adult males of each community formed a council that was headed by village chiefs. They were also part of the Iroquois League.

About 1000 Onondaga currently live in a New York reservation.

Onondaga Proverbs

There are no secrets or mysteries—there is only common sense.

We give back thanks to our mother, the earth that sustains us.

We give thanks back to the Sun that has looked upon the Earth with beneficial eyes.

PAWNEE

The Pawnee used to live in what is now Nebraska and primarily farmed in their villages, but also went to the plains a couple times a year to live there and hunt buffalo. Pawnee men sported a very interesting look: they shaved their heads but left a small scalp lock that they stiffened with various materials, and pointed upwards.

The Pawnee were very religious, and much of their religious activity revolved around corn, which they viewed as a sacred gift. They also believed that some stars were gods. Additionally, like most other tribes, they had shamans that were regarded as having mystical and special powers.

In the late 1800s, attacks from other tribes and an influx of white settlers caused the Pawnee to move to what is now Oklahoma. Today, there are around 3,000 Pawnee, most of whom live in Pawnee, Oklahoma.

Pawnee Proverbs

What happened in the past and cannot be stopped should not be lamented over.

Let us see—is this real this life that I am living?

PUEBLO

The Pueblo have lived in the same location longer than any other people in the US or Canada. They are descendants of a group called the Anasazi, who are known to have built multistory buildings as early as the 700s. By the 1300s, the Pueblo lived in the Rio Grande valleys.

The Pueblo were very religious and ceremonial, and they emphasized the ideal of building harmony with the universe. Many current Pueblo have retained much of the attributes of ancient Pueblo lifestyle. Subdivisions of the Pueblo include the Zuni and the Hopi (see the section on Hopi in this chapter for more info).

Pueblo Proverbs

Never sleep while your meat is cooking on the fire.

People seeking a myth will usually find one.

We are grateful to the Mother Earth.

I add my breath to your breath that we shall be as one people.

SAUK

The Sauk were once part of a large group of several Indian tribes, and lived close to another related tribe called the Fox. They initially lived in Canada and Michigan, but were driven out by the Iroquois and moved to Wisconsin, Illinois, and Iowa.

In 1804, they gave up much of their land to the US, and most of them moved again. But many of them were later led by a renowned warrior named Black Hawk in trying to regain one of their villages, which led to the Black Hawk War of 1832 where they were defeated. Most of the 1000 current Sauk live in Iowa and Oklahoma.

Sauk Proverbs

Look at your own moccasin tracks before pronouncing someone else's faults.

You can't purchase friendship—you have to do your part to make it.

SENECA

The Seneca used to live in western New York and eastern Ohio. They were the largest of the five tribes that joined in 1100 to form the Iroquois League. The Seneca used to live on hills near a river, and surrounded themselves with fences to prevent attacks. In the villages, several related families often lived together in long houses.

Today, there are about 9,000 Seneca, and most live on reservations in New York.

Seneca Proverbs

Before leaving your host, give him a little present—it will serve as a little courtesy, and will not offend.

The more often you ask how much farther you have to go, the longer your quest will feel.

Every fire is the same size when it begins.

SHAWNEE

The Shawnee used to live in the Eastern and Midwestern United States. They performed many agriculture and warrior-related ceremonies, many of which involved dancing. Today, most Shawnee live in Oklahoma, and number about 5,000 people.

Shawnee Proverb

Respect everyone, but lower yourself to no one.

Shawnee Quotes

Tecumseh
(1768-1813) Shawnee Indian chief who led an intertribal alliance that resisted white rule.

Never trouble anyone regarding his religion—respect him in his beliefs, and demand that he respect yours

Tenskwatawa a.k.a. He-Who-Opens-The-Door
(1768-1834) Leader and religious man also known as "The Prophet." He was Tecumseh's brother.

Tenskwatawa has never spoken a lie or an impurity, and never will

I have been shown how to open the door that has shut us out from joy.

I have been a slave to liquor since first I tasted it—but never again will I drink any.

SHOSHONE

The Shoshone (a.k.a. Snake) used to live in the barren desert regions in what are currently the outskirts of Nevada, Idaho, Wyoming, California, and Utah. They formed small, isolated family groups that traveled and searched for food such as wild seeds, roots, fish, insects, birds, and small land animals. They also spent a lot of time singing, dancing, and telling stories.

Later, they acquired horses from the Spaniards, and became buffalo hunters. In the 1800s, the Shoshone moved to Native American reservations.

Today, there are about 10,000 Shoshone, most of which live in Wyoming, Nevada, Idaho, and Utah.

Shoshone Proverbs

Some people are smart but not wise.

SIOUX

The Sioux (pronounced Soo) used to live in the Northern Plains of North America. The Sioux were renowned for their extremely effective fighting ability. In 1876, they refused US government orders to enter a reservation, which caused a group of US troops to attack them. Although the Sioux didn't have the technological power that US troops had, the Sioux emphatically defeated and devastated the US troops in what was later known as "(US Lieutenant Colonel George A.) Custer's Last Stand."

US Army troops later came in and forced the Sioux to enter the reservation. But shortly later, some Sioux refused, which resulted in more fighting between the Sioux and Americans in what was later known as the Sioux wars.

Today, many of the 40,000 current day Sioux live on reservations in the northern plains, while others live in various US urban areas, and a few thousand live in Canada.

The Sioux (also known as the Dakota) are usually categorized into three groups: Santee (Dakota), Yankton (Nakota), and Teton (Lakota). The Lakota are covered in detail in a separate chapter of this book

Sioux Proverbs

Frogs don't drink up all the water in the ponds they live in.

Inner peace and love are God's greatest gifts.

Be self-loving—go outside yourself and take action. Be peaceful, and be focused on the solution.

Sioux Quotes

Chief Sitting Bull
(1831-1890) Leader and medicine man

The earth has received the sun's hug, and we shall see the results of that love.

I was eager to learn and to do things, and thus I learned quickly.

If a man loses anything and goes back and carefully looks for it, he will find it.

Crazy Horse
(1842-1877) Determined and fierce warrior and leader

All we wanted was peace and to be let alone

Wovoka (a.k.a. the Cutter)
(1858-1932) Religious figure of Sioux and other tribes

Always do right. It will give you satisfaction in life.

Ohiyesa a.k.a. Charles Alexander Eastman
(1858-1939) Physician and writer

The man who preserves his selfhood is ever calm and unshaken by the storms of existence.

Silence is the cornerstone of character.

Friendship is held to be the severest test of character.

It has been said that the position of woman is the test of civilization, and that of our women was secure. In them was vested our standard of morals and the purity of our blood. [For the Native American,] The wife did not take the name of her husband nor enter his clan, and the children belonged to the clan of the mother. All of the family property was held by her, descent was traced in the maternal line, and the honor of the house was in her hands...

Thus she ruled undisputed within her own domain, and was to us a tower of moral and spiritual strength... [Before the arrival of the "white man,"] you could not find anywhere a happier home than that created by the Indian woman. There was nothing of the artificial about her person, and very little disingenuousness in her character.

SUQUAMISH

The Suquamish and their ancestors lived in the Puget region (in Washington state) for thousands of years. They lived in small villages, and had great skill in making such things as canoes and baskets. They were also great at fishing.

Most Suquamish currently live on a Port Madison Indian Reservation in Washington.

Suquamish Quotes

Chief Seattle (Seathl)
(1790-1866) Leader who promoted peace between whites and Native Americans; the city of Seattle, Washington is named after him

> All things share the same breath—the animal, the tree, the man, and the air shares its spirit with all the life it supports.

> The earth and myself are of one mind

> All things are connected. Whatever befalls the earth befalls the children of the earth.

> We are part of the earth, and it is part of us.

> Every part of the soil is sacred to my people.

YAMPARIKA

The Yamparika lived mostly in Colorado and Kansas. They were primarily buffalo hunters, and were also renowned warriors. Like the Shoshone, they were once part of a group called the Comanche.

Yamparika Quotes

Chief Ten Bears
(1792-1872) Leader and peacemaker

> My heart is filled with joy when I see you here, like when the brooks fill with water when snow melts in the spring; and I feel as glad as ponies do when the fresh grass starts growing at the beginning of the year.
> I heard of your coming when I was many sleeps away, and I made but a few camps before I met you. I knew that you had come to do good to me and my people. I looked for the benefits that would last forever, and so my face shines with joy as I look upon you.

I want no blood upon my land to stain the grass. I want it all clean and pure. And I wish it so that all who go through among my people may find peace when they come in, and leave with it when they go out.

YOKUTS

The Yokuts (also known as the Mariposan) occupied parts of California. They were divided into about 50 tribes, each with its own dialect and territory. Chiefs, who were sometimes women, headed their tribes.

The Yokuts were a hunter-gatherer community. They wore very little clothing, and performed many ceremonies and rituals. They also had unique village jobs such as a local jester, and undertaker.

There are about 1500 Yokuts today, most of which live in California.

Yokuts Chant

My words are tied in one with the great mountains, with the great rocks, with the great trees, in one with my body and my heart. All of you see me, one with this world.

OTHER NATIVE AMERICAN PROVERBS & QUOTES

Proverbs

I seek strength, not to be better than my brother, but to battle my most significant enemy: myself.

Even a small mouse has anger.

Quote

Unknown Native American Chief

My heart laughs with joy because I am in your presence... Oh, how much more beautiful the sun is today then when you were angry with us!

American (United States) Proverbs

The United States of America (a.k.a. the USA or the US) is among the largest (with a land area of 3.6 million square miles) and most populous (287 million people) nations in the world. The country consists of 50 states that resemble semi-independent countries, as well as the District of Columbia capital, and several island territories that are partially self-governed.

The United States is noted for its wide diversity of people from various backgrounds. This has created both a unified culture, as well as many distinct cultural differences throughout the country. This unique environment has spurned many great proverbs. Before we explore those proverbs, here is a brief background of the country.

Native Americans in America

Native Americans (a.k.a. American Indians) were the only inhabitants of the Western Hemisphere (the Americas—North, Central, and South America, and the Caribbean Islands) for thousands of years. Some scientists and archeologists believe they are people who came from Asia to North America somewhere between 33,000 BC and 13,000 BC.

There is no telling how many Native Americans inhabited the Western Hemisphere before Europeans arrived there in 1492 AD, but estimates run from about 30 to 120 million throughout the Western Hemisphere, and anywhere from 1 to 15 million in what is now the United States.

European Discovery

The European world was unaware of the entire Western Hemisphere for most of history. In 1000 AD, Vikings from Greenland briefly explored part of the North American. In 1492, a group led by Italian navigator Christopher Columbus landed on an island in the Bahamas of the Caribbean (probably San Salvador).

Forming the 13 American Colonies

The Spanish, Portuguese, English and French soon explored and conquered many parts of the Western Hemisphere, and in the 1500s and 1600s, many English settlers arrived in the easternmost region of what is now the United States, and formed the original 13 American Colonies. People from other parts of the world also settled in America.

Slavery and African Americans

In the early 1600s, Africans who had been captured and sold to European traders were transported and sold in America. Initially, they had the same legal status that was granted to white indentured servants, but by the mid 1600s, their bosses began enslaving them permanently.

American Revolution

In 1763, Britain gained control of most North American territories, and the population in Colonial America (which was still limited to primarily the easternmost part of what is currently the United States) was at over one million. British leaders taxed Americans and restricted their freedom, resulting in the Revolutionary War that started in 1775.

On July 4, 1776, the colonists declared their independence, and by 1783, they defeated the British. In 1787, a group of Americans wrote the US Constitution.

Extending Westward

Through various wars and purchases, US territory and settlement extended westward, and by the mid 1800s, the nation extended all the way from the Pacific Ocean to the Atlantic Ocean.

Economic Growth

In the late 1700s to mid 1800s, the US experienced economic growth due to such factors such as the invention of the cotton gin and the reaper, the gold rush in the West, and the introduction of large-scale manufacturing.

The Civil War

Over issues such as slavery, an American Civil War between the North (Union) and South (Confederacy) began in 1861. The Union was victorious after four years of fighting that claimed the lives of about 360,000 Union and 260,000 Confederate troops. Slavery was abolished throughout the US following the war.

Big Business to WWII

After the Civil War, the US underwent tremendous industrial growth due to investment banking, new inventions, communication advancements, progress in transportation, and development in industries such as coal, petroleum, steel, machinery, automobiles, and clothing. Many people moved from farms to work in cities.

In 1917 the US entered World War I, and played an important role in the Allied victory in 1918. The economy then grew at a frantic pace in the 1920s, but in 1929 a stock market crash triggered a severe and lengthy economic depression.

The Depression didn't fully end until Word War II, which the US fought in from 1941 to 1945 and played a key role in defeating Germany and Japan.

Post World War II

The post World War II period marked another period of economic growth in the US, as well as a time of tremendous social progress. In the 1960s, a civil rights movement soon brought greater equality and freedom to all people in America. Other major themes in post WWII America included a conservation movement, a war in Vietnam, and a growth in advanced technology.

US Languages

The main language of the United States is (American) English, although many variations exist, such as Ebonics, Southern, Texan, New Englander (including Bostonian), Midwestern, and New Yorkese.

Because of its multiculturalism, many other languages are spoken in the US, particularly Spanish.

American Themes

Some American themes include multiculturalism, economic prosperity, business, corporate America, democracy, politics, civil rights, patriotism, television, music, dancing, nightclubs, movies, pop culture, magazines, books, literature, dining out, collecting things, beaches, parks, playgrounds, vacations, baseball, football, basketball, golf, comedy, lawsuits, art, obesity, abundance, the social security system, psychiatrists, diet fads, beer, and fast food.

American Proverbs

A fault confessed is half redressed.

Success has many fathers, but failure is an orphan.

Hunger finds no fault with moldy corn.

Every man is occasionally what he ought to be perpetually

If we blame others for our failures, then we should also give others credit for our successes.

After all is said and done, more is said than done.

The opportunity of a lifetime is seldom so labeled.

The tiger crouches before he leaps upon his prey.

An ounce of proof is worth a ton of assertions.

Human nature is the same all the world over.

One who cannot respect himself cannot respect another.

Self-help is the best help.

An ounce of discretion is worth a pound of wit.

Boys will be boys.

Don't cry over spilt milk.

The unknown is always great.

The simplest things are the most startling.

The road to the head lies through the heart.

Better to risk a little than to lose the whole.

If you can't stand the heat, get out of the kitchen.

You can lead a horse to water, but you can't make it drink.

It takes two to make a bargain.

Loose lips sink ships.

Man is greater than the tools he invents.

Variety is the spice of life.

Don't put robbers to work in a bank.

You made your bed, now lie in it.

Don't make a mountain out of a molehill.

Scratch my back and I'll scratch yours.

There are two sides to every story—and then there's the truth.

We'll cross that bridge when we get to it.

If you make yourself into a doormat, people will wipe their feet on you.

Don't count your chickens before they've hatched.

A penny saved is a penny earned.

Don't bite the hand that feeds you.

We may give advice, but we cannot give conduct.

Why buy the cow when you can get the milk for free?

A smile is worth a thousand words.

At the center of climb is "I"

Doctor's faults are covered with earth, and rich men's with money.

If you are always dwelling in trouble, change your address.

A crooked cornstalk can have a straight ear.

There's no use asking the cow to pour you a glass of milk.

Don't mistake chicken dung for an egg.

When the bait's worth more than the fish, it's time to stop fishing.

What goes around comes around.

If slavery isn't wrong, nothing's wrong.

Observe with the eyes; listen with the ears; shut the mouth. (Hawaiian)

Do not disturb the water that is tranquil. (Hawaiian)

Strive for the summit. (Hawaiian)

The quickest way to double yur money is to fold it over and put back it in yur pocket. (Cowboy)

Never miss a good chance to shut up. (Cowboy)

It don't take no genius to spot a goat in a flock of sheep. (Cowboy)

If yuh ever find yurself in a hole, the first thin' to do is stop diggin'. (Cowboy)

There's two theories to arguin' with a woman—and neither one works. (Cowboy)

Good judgment comes from experience, and a lotta uh that comes from bad judgment. (Cowboy)

If yur ridin' ahead of the herd, take a look back every now and then to make sure it's still there. (Cowboy)

Lettin the cat outta the bag is a whole lot easier'n puttin' it back. (Cowboy)

Timin' has a lot to do with the outcome of a rain dance. (Cowboy)

If it don't seem like it's worth the effort, it probably ain't. (Cowboy)

The biggest rascal you'll probably ever need to deal with watches you shavin' his face in the mirror every mornin'. (Cowboy)

Never ask a barber if he thinks yuh need a haircut. (Cowboy)

After weeks of beans and taters, even a change to taters and beans is good. (Cowboy)

Never take to sawin' on the branch that's supportin' you—unless you're bein' hung from it. (Cowboy)

When you're trying' somethin' new, the fewer people that know about it, the better. (Cowboy)

Yuh don't need decorated words to make yer meanin' clear. Say it plain, and save some breath for breathin'. (Cowboy)

Never lie unless yuh have to, and if yuh don't have a dang good lie, stick to the truth. (Cowboy)

It's best to keep yer troubles pretty much to yerself, 'cause half the people yu'd tell 'em to won't give a dang, and the other half will be glad to hear yu've got 'em. (Cowboy)

The length of a conversation don't tell nothin' 'bout the size of the intellect. (Cowboy)

There be treasure in them thar hills. (Pirate)

Once out yonder tis only the rules that can save you—the rules of us pirates, that is. (Pirate)

Where's the loot? (Pirate)

The truth, the whole truth, and nothing but the truth. (Legal)

When the law is against you, argue the facts. When the facts are against you, argue the law. When both are against you, change the subject. (Legal)

Buy on the rumor; sell on the news. (Wall Street)

Buy low, sell high. (Wall Street)

An analyst is only as good as his last idea. (Wall Street)

North American Proverbs

(Also see the chapter on American (United States) Proverbs.)

Contents: Canada, Mexico

CANADA

Canada is the world's second largest country in land area (after Russia), although it has a medium sized population of 32 million people. The country has a wide variety of geographical features, including mountains, rivers, lakes, islands, plains, lowlands, and continental shields. Canadians have a wide variety of ethnic backgrounds, although more than half of its people have British or French ancestry.

Native Americans and Intuit Eskimos first inhabited Canada until a wave of European explorers arrived there in the 1500s. France initially took over much of Canada, but France was soon involved in a longstanding rivalry with Britain over the region.

By the mid 1700s, Canada was under British rule, although people of both British and French ethnicities inhabited the area. In 1931, Canada became an equal partner of Britain, and in 1982, Canada became fully independent. Its official languages are English and French.

Canadian themes include cold weather, ice hockey, lacrosse, football, skiing, fishing, national parks, the Canadian Broadcasting Corporation, pro wrestling, literature, painting, music, ballet, Christianity, beer, actress Pamela Anderson, actor Jim Carrey, actor Mike Meyers, actor Michael J. Fox, media personality Tom Green, lumber, paper, and steel.

Canadian Proverbs

You can't catch skunks with mice.

The devil places a pillow for a drunken man to fall upon.

Walk a mile in my moccasins to learn where they pinch.

When you talk about the sun, you will see her beams.

Do not yell "dinner" until your knife is in the loaf.

Canada is a country with two official languages and no official culture.

Through other people's faults, wise men correct their own.

MEXICO

Mexico was the site of many Native American civilizations in the first millennium AD, including the Maya and Aztec, who were both conquered by Spanish explorers in the early 1500s. In the early 1800s, Mexican rebels were able to negotiate independence from Spain.

In the mid 1800s, America initiated a war with Mexico called the Mexican War, which resulted in Mexico's loss of areas that currently make up Western and Southwestern United States.

Mexico later endured many civil wars and political rebellions until the early 1900s. The recent election of Vicente Fox to the Mexican presidency in 2000 ended a longstanding political domination of the Institutional Revolutionary Party.

Most Mexicans have either European and/or Native American ancestry. Of Mexico's 100 million inhabitants, about 18 million live in the Mexico City metro area.

Mexican themes include Catholicism, silver, economic problems, literature, murals, music, movies, television, soccer, bullfighting, baseball, boxing (including legendary fighter Julio Cesar Chavez), sombreros, corn, beans, rice, salsa, coffee, and squash.

Mexican Proverbs

The rat who only knows about one hole will soon be caught by the cat.

Since excuses were invented, no one is ever in the wrong.

He who speaks too much is tiresome; he who speaks to little is boring.

He who assists everybody assists nobody.

Speak plain—call *bread* bread, and *wine* wine.

He who lingers around will hear bad things spoken about him.

One timely shout is better than constant talk.

He who follows his own advice must take the consequences.

If you want to live in peace, you must not tell everything that you know, nor judge everything that you see.

It's a bad start of the week for the man who is hanged on a Monday. *Note: In Mexico, Monday (Lunes) is the first day of the week.*

Trust your best friend as you would your worst enemy.

A golden cage is still a cage.

The person who asks for little deserves nothing.

He who knows nothing neither doubts nor fears anything.

If you don't honor your wife, you are dishonoring yourself.

Central American Proverbs

Contents: Belize, Costa Rica, El Salvador, Guatemala, Honduras, Nicaragua, Panama

BELIZE

Belize is a small country with about 250,000 people, and contains a variety of ethnicities, as well as languages such as Creole, Spanish, English, and various Native American languages. Belize has lots of jungles, as well as mountains, swamps, and barrier reefs.

The country was originally inhabited primarily by the Native American Maya civilization. Upon European arrival, it became subject to battles over it by the British and Spanish in the 1600s and 1700s, and became known as British Honduras. Britain ruled Belize until it gained independence in the late 1900s

Themes of Belize include multiculturalism, music, corn, beans, stew, alcohol, and timber.

Belizean Proverbs

Don't hang your hat higher than you can reach.

Blood cannot be washed out with blood.

If a man gives you a basket to carry water, it means that he hates you.

Never drop the bone to catch the shadow.

There is no use in wiping your butt before you defecate.

COSTA RICA

Costa Rica was originally occupied by various Native American tribes. It was slowly settled in by groups of Spaniards beginning in the 1500s, although mainland Spain remained relatively uninterested in the region. Costa Rica became independent in the 1800s, and became a fully democratic nation by the late 1800s. Most Costa Ricans have primarily Spanish ancestry.

Costa Rican themes include publishing, Catholicism, coffee, bananas, cocoa, a variety of plants and animals, movies, music, art, parks, and holidays.

Costa Rican Proverbs

Once does not mean frequently, and twice does not mean constantly.

A mind can make a heaven out of hell, or a hell out of heaven.

The last to breathe is the first to drown.

All people have their friend and their enemy within themselves.

Every word has three definitions and three interpretations.

EL SALVADOR

Though small in size, El Salvador has over six million residents. The countries historical roots lie mainly in the Native American Cuzcatlan Kingdom. After various divisions, El Salvador was unified in the early 1800s. Most El Salvadorians have European and/or Native American ancestry.

Themes of El Salvador include coffee, Catholicism, cotton, folktales, paintings, political turmoil, and poverty.

Salvadorian / Salvadoran Proverbs

Better to prevent than regret.

Where there is life, there is also hope.

GUATEMALA

Most Guatemalans have mixed Latin / Native American ancestry. The country has many mountains and tropical rainforests.

Guatemala was home to parts of the Native American Maya and Yucatan civilizations, and was then ruled by the Spanish beginning in the 1500s until receiving independence in the early 1800s. Following about a century of rule by dictators, Guatemala has had numerous and widespread political conflicts and turmoil.

Themes of Guatemala include coffee, festivals, Easter, Independence Day, a wide variety of diverse lifestyles throughout the country, isolation, foreign import products, soccer, parks, high birth rates, and emigration.

Guatemalan Proverbs

Better to eat beans in peace than to eat meat in distress.

A good name hides thievery.

Don't despise someone for telling the truth.

Your true enemy lives in your own house.

HONDURAS

Much of Honduras is covered with mountains, plants, and trees. Honduras was at one time part of the Native American Maya civilization before Spanish explorers and settlers caused widespread oppression and disease among many of the region's Native American population. Honduras became independent in the 1800s. Most Hondurans have mixed European / Native American ancestry.

Themes of Honduras include tamales, bananas, corn, coffee, political turmoil, droughts, hurricanes, strong family bonds, poverty, soccer, tourism, and Catholicism.

Honduran Proverbs

Perseverance will kill the prey and win the prize.

Even the supreme cloth is bound to have one faulty thread.

NICARAGUA

Nicaragua was one of the regions where the Native American Maya civilization thrived. It was later ruled by Spain until becoming independent in the 1800s, although it remained aligned with other neighboring countries until 1938.

The US opposed Sandinista political party ruled Nicaragua for about three decades until Violeta Chamorro's presidency, which lasted from 1990 to 1996.

Themes of Nicaragua include holidays, baseball, literature, art, political turmoil, and music.

Nicaraguan Proverbs

It takes two to start an altercation, but only one to end it.

Fleeing and running are not the same thing.

There is taste in variety, and variety in taste.

Many things are too bad to be blessed, and too good to be cursed.

PANAMA

Panama is well known for its location between Central and South America. The country contains a frequently used man-made ship passage called the Panama Canal. Panama has many various ethnic groups and mixes, but the majority of Panamanians have mixed European / Native American ancestry.

After seeding from Spain in the 1800s, Panama used to be part of Columbia (a country Panama borders to the southeast) until it became independent in 1903. Many people have heard of Panama's former covert ruler Manuel Noriega, who was overthrown in 1989 by US troops.

Themes of Panama include storytelling, beans, rice, corn, beer, multiculturalism, baseball (including legendary player Rod Carew), boxing (including legendary fighter Roberto Duran), basketball, beaches, festivals, and music.

Panamanian Proverbs

The leafiest tree doesn't always have the juiciest fruit.

Half of an orange tastes just as sweet as a whole one.

Caribbean / West Indies Proverbs

Contents: Bahamas, Cayman Islands, Cuba, Dominican Republic, Haiti, Jamaica, Puerto Rico

BAHAMAS

The Bahamas is a group of 700 islands. In the late 1400s and early 1500s, all of the Native Americans who lived there were forced by Spaniards to be shipped off to work in Haiti. Today, most Bahamian people have African and/or European ancestry, and speak English.

Themes of the Bahamas include gambling, celebrations, dancing, tourism, and financial services.

Bahamian Proverbs

Cunning is superior to strength.

Half a loaf is better than none.

CAYMAN ISLANDS

The Cayman Islands are well known as a tourist center as well as a place for financial services.

The Spanish discovered the Cayman Islands in the 1500s, but never attempted to move in. The British later made the Cayman Islands a dependant of Jamaica, and then coloniolized it when Jamaica gained its own independence. Most Cayman people are British, African, or mixed ancestry

Cayman Proverbs

If it's not broken, don't fix it.

Measure twice, cut once.

CUBA

Cuba is one large island plus a group of about 1500 surrounding smaller islands. It makes up a large percentage of the land area in the Caribbean Sea region.

Arawak and Ciboney Native Americans primarily occupied the islands until Spanish explorers arrived in the 1500s. The Native American population gradually declined, and the Spanish brought in African slaves from the 1700s until slavery was abolished in the late 1800s. After struggles for independence in the late 1800s, Cuba became independent in 1902 primarily due to the Spanish-American War.

Communist leader Fidel Castro made Cuba a socialist state in the late 1950s, causing poor US-Cuba relationships, as well as the infamous events of the Bay of Pigs Invasion in 1961, the Cuban missile crisis in 1962, and the Elian Gonzalez incident in 1999. Most Cubans have Spanish and/or African ancestry.

Cuban themes include *Scarface* character Antonio "Tony" Montana, cigars, baseball, boxing, communism, carnivals, voodoo, libraries, museums, painting, dancing, music, legendary writer Jose Marti, and actress Daisy Fuentes.

Cuban Proverbs

Seven sons of one mother, and each one of a different mind.

A lie runs until truth catches up to it.

Brief encounters can result in long relationships.

When money talks, everyone else is silent.

How can you trust anyone who doesn't know how to blush?

Every head is a world.

Life is short; but it barely takes a second to smile.

Listen to what they say about others, and you will know what they say about you.

Do not be excessively timid or excessively confident.

DOMINICAN REPUBLIC

The Dominican Republic is the eastern region of an island (Hispaniola) that also contains the nation of Haiti. Most Dominicans have mixed African / European ancestry and speak Spanish. The land is very mountainous and has a wide variety of plants.

The Dominican Republic has been under rule of Spanish, French, and Haitians at various times, and in 1843, it split off from Haiti. It is currently an independent country with ties to the United States.

Dominican themes include hurricanes, Catholicism, sugar exporting, tourism, poverty, music, dancing, the Carnival festival, rum, rice, beans, bananas, sweet potatoes, baseball (including legend Sammy Sosa), and cockfighting.

Dominican Proverbs

A rainbow would be considered even more beautiful if it wasn't free.

Other people's burdens are what kill the donkey.

The current nature of this planet is to celebrate the dead saints and persecute the living ones.

It is not the load that kills—it is the excessive load.

HAITI

Haiti is located on the Western section of the same island that contains the Dominican Republic. Haiti is very mountainous, and overpopulated in the flatlands. Almost all Haitians have African or mixed African / European ancestry. Haitians speak Haitian Creole (an English dialect), as well as French.

Native American originally lived on the island that now contains Haiti and the Dominican Republic, but almost none of them survived due to incoming Spaniards who caused widespread disease, and also enslaved the Native Americans and subject them to brutal working conditions.

The French later took over the Western part of the island. African slaves were brought to the island, but rebelled and gained freedom and Haitian independence by 1804. At that time, the entire island was known as Haiti.

In 1843, the island was split into the separate nations of Haiti and the Dominican Republic, and the entire island became known as Hispaniola. Many political problems continued to ensue in Haiti to this day.

Themes of Haiti include voodoo, beans, rice, sweet potatoes, poverty, coffee, oppressive child labor, carnivals, music, gambling, cockfighting, and soccer.

Haitian Proverbs

Salt does not brag that it is salted.

Stumbling is not the same as falling.

Little by little, the bird builds its nest.

The goat that has many owners will be left to die in the sun.

Being careful is not being a coward.

Beyond the mountain is another mountain.

Spread piss doesn't foam.

To speak French does not mean that you are smart.
Note: French is sparsely spoken language in Haiti that is usually used to try to impress others or show them up.

JAMAICA

Jamaica is an island nation noted for its natural beauty and year round warm climate, which have made it a highly frequented tourist spot. Most Jamaicans speak a local dialect of English known as Jamaican Creole, which is similar to Creole languages used in places such as Belize, Grenada, and St. Vincent. Jamaican Creole has aspects of West African languages, Spanish, and French.

Jamaica was originally inhabited by the Arawak Indians, who named the island *Xaymaca*, meaning land of wood and water. Spaniards claimed the land in the late 1400s and enslaved the Arawak, most of whom later died due to disease and horrid working conditions. The Spaniards also brought enslaved Africans to Jamaica.

In the late 1600s, the British took over Jamaica, but met continued opposition by a group of Africans called Maroons who had escaped slavery. The Maroons and the British signed a peace treaty in the early 1730s, and the British Parliament abolished slavery in Jamaica in the early 1830s. By 1944, Jamaican calls for increased freedom caused Britain to concede Jamaica some rights of self-government, and in 1962, Jamaica became a fully independent nation.

Today, over 90 percent of Jamaica's population has either African or mixed African / European ancestry. Other ethnicities on the island include Chinese, Indian, and Syrian.

Jamaican themes include tourism, music (especially folk music and reggae), reggae legend Bob Marley, reggae star Shaggy, dancing, storytelling, poetry, bobsledding, cricket, soccer, sprinting, Christianity, churches, Rastafarianism (a religion and political movement), mining, buses, herbs & spices (especially allspice), rum, bananas, sugar, and coconuts.

Jamaican Proverbs

Note: I have included the Jamaican Creole version of these proverbs, with translations and explanations given where needed.

- One one coco fill up a basket.
Fill your basket one item at a time.

- I noh come to yah bout how horse dead an' cow fat.
I didn't come to hear about how the horse is dead and the cow is fat.
Meaning: Enough with the irrelevant details.

- Poun ah fret cyaan pay ounce ah det
A pound a fret can't pay an ounce a debt.

- Pit inna di sky, it fall inna yuh eye.
Spit in the sky, it falls in your eye

- Mi come yah fi drink milk, mi noh come yah fi count cow!
I came here to drink milk—I didn't come here to count cows!
Meaning: Quit deceiving me, and deliver what you spoke of!

- De chil mus creep befo him walk.
The child must crawl before he walks.

- Man dat carry strah noh fe fool wid fiyah.
A man carrying straw should not fool around with fire.

- All yuh hear no good fo speak.
Not everything you hear is good for saying.

- What good a educayshun if him got noh sens.
What good is an education if he doesn't have any (common) sense.

- Howdy an tenk yu noh broke noh skware.
(Saying) howdy and thank you don't break any squares.
Meaning: Saying howdy (hi) and thank you are not bad things, and there is often much to be gained by using such greetings.

- Yu mek yu sail too big fi yu boat, yu sail wi capsize yu.
If you make your sail to big for your boat, it will capsize (upset or overturn) you.

- All kine ah fish eat man, but only shark get de blame.
All kinds of fish eat man, but only sharks get the blame.

- Tek whey yuh get tell yu get whey yu waant
Take what you can get until you can get what you want

- Yu shek man han, yu noh shek im heart.
You shake a man's hand—you don't shake his heart.
Meaning: What you see on the outside doesn't necessarily show you the truth behind things.

- Too much callaloo mek peppa pot stew bitta.
Too much callaloo (greens, okra, seasoning, or crabmeat) can make the stew bitter or unpleasant tasting.

- Di hiya di monki clim, di more him expose.
The higher the monkey climbs, the more he exposes.

- If yu wan haf a bred, beg smaddy buy i', but if yu wan a wun, buy i' yuself.
If you want half of a bread, then beg somebody to buy it for you; but if you want a whole one, buy it yourself.
Meaning: If you want something done right, do it yourself. If you ask others to do something for you, they will probably do it lackadaisically.

- Waant aal, lose aal
Want all, lose all.
Meaning: Excessive greed or perfectionism usually doesn't pay off.

- De bes a filed mus hab weed.
Even the best field must have (some) weeds.

PUERTO RICO

Puerto Rico is a mountainous island with political ties to the United States. Puerto Rico contains a variety of ethnic groups, the majority of which have Spanish and/or African ancestry.

Arawak Native American groups originally lived on the island, and Spanish settlers arrived there in the 1500s, and soon brought in African slaves. Puerto Rico began an independence movement in the 1800s, and the country was eventually ceded to the US by Spain in 1898 after the Spanish-American War. By 1952, the island became a semi-independent self-governed Commonwealth of Puerto Rico associated with the US.

Themes of Puerto Rico include multiculturalism, music, dancing, literature, art, rice, beans, stews, rum, consumerism, actress Rita Moreno, actor Jose Ferrer, baseball (including legends Roberto Clemente and Ivan Rodriguez), and boxing (including legend Felix "Tito" Trinidad).

Puerto Rican Proverbs

The night forms a cover for sinners.

God's greatest act was to make one day follow another.

Do not fear a stain that disappears with water.

What might not happen in a year might happen in an instant.

The day after is the student of the day before.

Hurriedness is not necessarily the daughter of foolishness, and delay is not necessarily the daughter of cowardice.

There is a remedy for everything except death.

A good beginning is half the work done.

I will do anything except bear the responsibility of guarding a house that has two doors.

Never say no due to pride, or yes due to weakness.

South American Proverbs

Contents: Argentina, Bolivia, Brazil, Chile, Columbia, Ecuador, Guyana, Paraguay, Peru, Suriname, Uruguay, Venezuela

ARGENTINA

Argentina is located in southern South America. The country borders the Atlantic Ocean, and along with its western neighbor Chile, it extends down to the southernmost region of South America. Argentina contains a wide variety of geographic features.

Historians are uncertain of Argentina's early history, but by the 1500s, Spanish settlement began there, and by the late 1700s, the Argentinean city of Buenos Aires was the capital of Spain's Western Hemisphere colonies. By the early 1800s, Argentina became independent of Spain (although it did not have set boundaries until much later).

The Argentinean government has been subject to many changes in the last fifty years, including on-and-off leadership by the well known Peron family and its supporters. Most Argentineans have Spanish and other European ancestry.

Themes of Argentina include beef, *gaucho* (cowboy) culture, music, dancing, soccer (including legend Diego Maradona), polo, soap operas, wine, coffee, tea, and literature.

Argentine Proverbs

The tongue that belongs to a fake friend is sharper than a knife.

What is greatly desired is not believed when it comes.

A dog that always barks gets little attention.

A man who develops himself is twice born.

One door is shut, but a thousand are open.

The person that learns well also defends himself well.

BOLIVIA

Bolivia used to contain such Native American groups such as the Tiwanaku, Aymara, and later the Inca, who were invaded by the Spaniards in the 1500s. Bolivia became an independent country in the 1800s, but it later lost territories to Chile and to Paraguay. Most Bolivians have Spanish and/or Native American ancestry.

Bolivian themes include hats, Catholicism, churches, soccer, the Carnival festival, poverty, cocaine, dancing, music, sculptures, and paintings.

Bolivian Proverbs

An altercation is like buttermilk—the more you stir it, the sourer it gets.

Diligence is the mother of good fortune.

If you marry wise judgment, peace will become your brother-in-law.

One grain will not make up an entire granary, but it does its part along with the others.

BRAZIL

Brazil contains half of the land area of South America, and has a population of 175 million people. Brazil borders every other South American nation except for Chile and Ecuador. The country contains an immense variety of geographical features. Portuguese is the official Brazilian language.

The history of Brazil's early inhabitants is uncertain. By the 1500s, the Portuguese began settling in, and were also joined later by some French and Dutch settlers.

In the early 1800s, the Portuguese King John VI fled to Brazil to avoid Napoleon's invasion of Portugal. When he moved back to Portugal a few years later, Brazil claimed its independence. Brazil became a democracy in the late 1900s.

Most Brazilians have European, African, and/or Native American ethnicity, and some Brazilians have full or partial Asian ancestry.

Brazilian themes include music, dancing (including the samba), the Carnival festival, soccer (including legendary players Pele, Ronaldo, and Rivaldo), literature, meat, beans, shrimp, art, architecture, theatre, strong family ties, car appreciation, volleyball, beaches, tennis star Gustavo Kuertan, soap operas, the internet, nakedness, mining, coffee, and oranges.

Brazilian Proverbs

Between the beginning and end, there is always a middle.

One man's happiness is another man's sadness.

Do not put the cart before the horse.

A timely no beats a hasty yes.

CHILE

Located in southern South America bordering the Pacific Ocean, Chile is easy to spot on a map because of its unique long and narrow shape. It also consists of many small islands near the mainland.

Native American groups such as the Mapuche and Aymara lived in Chile until Spanish arrival in the 1500s. After winning independence form Spain in the early 1800s, Chile later won coastal territory from Bolivia in a war in the late 1800s. Chile currently has a democratic government.

Chilean themes include poetry (including Nobel Prize Winners Gabriela Mistral and Pablo Neruda), economic prosperity, tolerance, soccer, skiing, mining, music, the Ricky Ricardo song "Santiago Chile," and fishing.

Chilean Proverbs

Anguish is our worst advisor.

Never defecate more than what you eat.

God cures, and the doctor gets paid.

COLUMBIA

Colombia borders the Pacific Ocean, the Caribbean Sea, Panama, and five other countries. The country is named after Christopher Columbus.

A wide variety of Native American groups occupied Colombia prior to European discovery. In the 1500s, Spaniards came to Colombia and put it under the rule of Peru. Colombia gained independence from Spain in the early 1800s, but struggled with a civil war in 1840. After the war, Colombia has had alternating periods of major political problems and political stability, which continue to this day.

Most current Columbians have European and/or Native American ancestry, and some have partial or full African ancestry.

Columbian themes include Catholicism, festivals, coffee, cocaine & heroine (including legendary drug trader Pablo Escobar), emeralds, art, literature, folk music, dancing, folktales, corn, beans, coconuts, rum, beer, libraries, regional variations of lifestyles, soccer, baseball, auto racing, bullfighting, gambling, and strong family ties.

Colombian Proverbs

The person who recognizes his major mistakes is on the road to wisdom.

The person who gives away his belongings will slowly become a beggar.

It's better to be the pot than the lid.

Suit the behavior to the occasion.

ECUADOR

Ecuador borders the Pacific Ocean, and is named after the Equator line due to the country's location. Ecuador contains parts of the Amazon River and Andes Mountains. It is also home to Cotopaxi, the world's highest active volcano.

Ecuador was conquered by the Incas in the 1400s and the Spaniards in the 1500s, who put it under the control of Peru. It gained independence from Spain in the 1800s. Most Ecuadorians have Native American (the majority of which are Quechua) and/or Spanish ancestry, although many distinct ethnic groups exist there.

Ecuadorian themes include Christianity, religious festivals (particularly baptism), *quinceaneras* ("sweet 15" celebrations for girls), the Carnival festival, ponchos, sandals, *fanesca* (a popular soup), chili sauce, arts & crafts, soccer, cockfighting, music, dancing, beauty contests, and a strong emphasis on family.

Ecuadorian Proverbs

The pot that belongs to many is stirred poorly and boiled even worse.

Hands that give also receive.

Every secret is eventually revealed.

GUYANA

Guyana is a small country that borders the Atlantic Ocean. The country has a diverse population, most of whom speak a Guyanese Creole variation of English.

Originally inhabited by Native Americans, Guyana was colonized by the Dutch in the 1600s, who soon brought in African slaves to the region. Britain purchased the region in the 1800s and abolished slavery shortly later. Many Indian and Asian immigrants later came to the Guyana. In the late 1900s, Guyana became self-governed.

Guyanese themes include music, literature, art, festivals, Islam, Hinduism, Christianity, and cricket.

Guyanese Proverbs

Never shop for black cloth at nighttime.

Don't try to force your foot into every stocking.

Not all who go to church go there to pray.

Not all of a scholar's knowledge comes from what he learned from his teacher.

PARAGUAY

Native American Guarani tribes lived in Paraguay when Spaniards began settling there in the 1500s. Paraguay gained independence in the early 1800s, but by the late 1800s, the country suffered extreme losses of lives and land in a war with surrounding territories. After having a longtime military based government beginning in the mid 1900s, Paraguay elected a civilian president in 1993.

Most modern Paraguayans have Spanish and Native American Guarani ancestry, although other ethnicities and mixes also exist in the country.

Themes of Paraguay include rivers, strong family ties, tea, music, dancing, soccer, basketball, Catholicism, corn, rice, coffee, marijuana, and cassava.

Paraguayan Proverbs

It is a rarity to find someone who can weigh other people's faults without putting his own thumbs on the scale.

Gratitude ranks as the least of virtues, and the lack of gratitude is the worst of vices.

The miserable only keep track of your misses and never count your hits.

PERU

Peru is located in Western South America and borders the Pacific Ocean. The country contains many mountains and rainforests. About half of Peruvians are Quechua Native Americans, while most others have Spanish and/or Native American ancestry.

Peru used to form the foundation of the Inca Empire. The Spaniards came in and ruled Peru from the 1500s until the country gained independence in the 1800s. In the late 1800s, Peru lost a war with Chile, and suffered economically for many years. Peru has had many governmental changes in the last few decades.

Peruvian themes include mythology, ancient architecture, handicrafts, music, dancing, art, theatre, literature, festivals, soccer, bullfighting, and cockfighting.

Peruvian Proverbs

Money isn't advice.

The tree of silence yields the fruit of inner peace.

Little by little, a person can get very far.

A continuous drip polishes a stone drip-by-drip.

SURINAME

Suriname is a small country that borders the Atlantic Ocean. It is known for its tremendous diversity, and includes such ethnicities as Indian, Javanese, African, Chinese, Native American, and Dutch. Languages spoken in the country include Dutch, English, Sranan (a Creole dialect), and Hindi.

Originally inhabited by Native Americans, Suriname was settled in by a various European explorers beginning in the 1500s. By the 1600s the Dutch had a huge influence there, and brought African slaves until slavery was abolished in the 1800s. Various settlers also came to the country, and it remained a Dutch colony until gaining independence in the mid to late 1900s.

Surinamese themes include multiculturalism, Christianity, Hinduism, Islam, Judaism, Confucianism, African religions, Native American religions, high birth rates, art, rice, and bananas.

Surinamese / Surinamer Proverbs

If a person shaves you with a razor, do not shave him with broken glass.

Knowledge is priceless.

URUGUAY

Uruguay borders the Atlantic Ocean.   It used to be inhabited by the Charrua Native Americans. Beginning in the 1500s, both the Spanish and the Portuguese lay claim to various parts of Uruguay at various times. By the 1700s, the Spanish had gained control of the region, but Uruguay became independent by 1811.

By 1821, it was conquered by Portugal and incorporated into Brazil, but a revolt led to another Uruguayan independence by 1828.   The current civilian Uruguayan government was instituted in 1985.

Most Uruguayans have Spanish and/or Italian ancestry, and some have partial or full African or Native American ancestry.

Uruguayan themes include animal herding, grains, *gaucho* (cowboy) culture, the Carnival festival, alcohol, barbequing beef, music, dancing, literature (including the well known book *Ariel*), soccer, and horse racing.

Uruguayan Proverbs

Better to lose a minute in your life than your life in a minute.

Cunning is superior to force.

What is done at night appears in the day.

VENEZUELA

Venezuela borders the Caribbean Sea. It contains a heavily populated coastal area, as well as many mountains and plains throughout the rest of the country. Venezuela also contains Angel Falls, the world's largest waterfall.

The country was settled in and ruled by the Spaniards beginning in the 1500s. In the early 1800s, Venezuelans defeated the Spanish under a leader named Boliviar, a Venezuelan native and freedom fighter who also helped gain liberation for the territories that currently make up Panama, Columbia, Ecuador, Peru, and Bolivia. Although once united, these regions soon split part.

Venezuela became a democracy in the 1960s after a succession of military dictators, but the country continues to have political turmoil. Most Venezuelans have European and/or Native American ancestry, or partial/mixed African ancestry.

Venezuela's economy currently relies heavily on petroleum, and it is the only current OPEC member located in the Western Hemisphere.

Venezuelan themes include salons, beauty contests, dancing, music, the Carnival festival, soap operas, cornmeal bread, literature, soccer, baseball, and a local variation of bullfighting.

Venezuelan Proverbs

Blood is inherited; character is earned.

Forgiving an enemy is a requirement; trusting him is not.

Preface to Folktales Section

Folktales are stories that are commonly told throughout a particular region or culture. They can generally focus on a wide variety of subjects, although the one's chosen for this book have an underlining lesson in their theme.

Folktales are generally passed down orally before being written down, and although the main theme of a particular folktale remains the same, the details, minor themes, and the style of telling it differs from source to source.

Aesop's Fables

Aesop's Fables have been told for over two and a half millenniums. They have been handed down verbally for much of that time, and are originally attributed to a Greek man named Aesop who lived in the 500s BC.

Aesop was a slave who frequently told witty, sharp and lesson-producing stories. The people enjoyed them so much that Aesop was eventually granted his freedom.

As his tales have been passed down through time, changes have been made, and new stories have been added that were never actually told by Aesop. Nevertheless, all those stories have been grouped together and become collectively known as Aesop's Fables, and are interwoven with the folklore of Greece and much of the rest of the world.

AESOP'S FABLES

The Traveler's Complaint

A man who was about to go traveling saw his dog standing near the door yawning. The man complained to the dog, "Why are you just standing there like that yawning, when we are running late for our trip! Stop messing around, and come here this instant so we can leave."

The dog replied, "Actually, I was just standing here waiting for you!"

The Boy in the River

One day, a boy swimming in a river got caught in a current and was in danger. He spotted a man nearby and shouted out for help.

The man said, "You should have never went in that water, and this is not the proper behavior for children, and just wait till I tell your parents, and…"

The boy interrupted him and said, "Sir, please help me now, and you can scold me afterwards for as long as you want!"

The Mouse's Adventure

A young mouse was about to take his first trip outside of the mouse hole. Before he left, his mother warned him to watch out for danger.

The excited mouse eagerly went out, but just minutes later he came frantically running back with a terrified look on his face.

"What happened?" his concerned mother asked.

"Well," replied the young mouse, "first I saw this friendly animal with beautiful soft fur, a long tail, and gleaming green eyes. It made an inviting 'purring' sound, and I was about to go introduce myself to the gentle creature.

"But then I saw a ferocious monster with red hair and vicious claws, and it made a terrifying noise like 'Cock-a-doodle-do!' I was so scared that I immediately ran away and came back here."

"My son," replied the mother, "that so-called 'friendly' animal you saw is a cat, and it eats mice like you and me. And that 'ferocious monster' you saw is a rooster, and it does not eat mice. Remember this lesson, my son: Appearances can be deceiving."

The Fox and the Grapes

A hungry fox spotted some delicious looking grapes on a vine that was caught on a tree branch. The fox eagerly began jumping and trying to get the grapes. After many unsuccessful tries, she turned around and walked away, saying to herself, "Well, they probably weren't ripe anyway."

The Shepherd's Warning

A shepherd heard his enemies approaching. He ran over to his donkey and exclaimed, "Quick, donkey, we must go now or else we are sure to be captured!"

The donkey replied, "Do you think that if your enemies conquer me, they will put double the load that you put on my back everyday?"

"No," the shepherd answered.

"Well then," the donkey continued, "as long as I will be carrying the same load, what difference does it make to me whose loads I am carrying?"

The Mother Crab's Complaint

A mother crab told her son, "Just look at how you walk that way, crooked and one sided. You should walk straight and forward."

The son replied, "OK—show me how and I will do it."

So the mother began trying to do it, but soon discovered that her walking was as crooked as the son's due to the structure of a crab's body.

The Boy's Dilemma

A boy put his hand into a container of almonds. He grasped as many almonds as he could hold, but when he tried to pull his hand out, it did not fit out of the container's neck. The boy was unwilling to let any of the almonds go, and soon began crying at his dilemma.

Finally, he let half of them out and was able to get his hand out, and realized how such a petty and trivial matter had caused him a problem.

Dispute in the Desert

A traveler wanted to cross a section of the desert, and agreed to pay a donkey owner to use his donkey while the owner would walk alongside and act as a guide. Several miles into their voyage, it had become scorching hot, and the traveler stopped to rest.

Since they were deep into the desert and there was no other alternative, the traveler laid down in the donkey's shadow for shade. But the guide protested, and said, "Hey, that's my donkey, and that's my shade. I should be the one resting there."

"Wait a minute!" the traveler replied. "I paid you so I can use this donkey. I have every right to rest under its shade."

"No," the guide retorted. "You paid to ride my donkey, but I still retain the rights to its shade!"

"The rights to its shade?" the traveler incredulously responded. "Oh come on now, that is the comment of a fool."

The guide angrily replied, "You think you can insult me? How dare you say that to me!"

They continued to argue, and soon began fighting. As they shouted and fought, the donkey grew terrified and galloped away and out of site.

The Swan's Singing

A man bought a swan and a goose from the market. He planned to kill the goose for food, and keep the swan to listen to its singing. The next night, he went to get the goose to kill for his meal, but since it was dark, he could not tell them apart and grabbed the swan by accident.

As the man prepared to cut off the bird's head, the swan began singing so that the man could distinguish its identity, and thus the swan's life was saved.

The Fishermen's Early Celebration

Several fishermen felt something heavy caught on their net, and began celebrating because they assumed that they had a very large catch.

When they finally decided to pull up the net after fifteen minutes of celebrating, they were dismayed to find that it was full of sand and stones, and contained only three small fish.

The Donkey Tricks the Wolf

A donkey noticed a wolf was about to pounce on him. The donkey began limping, and calmly announced, "Wolf, I wouldn't do that if I were you. I have just stepped on a sharp thorn, and if you eat me, the thorn will cut up your throat. Let me lift up my hoof first, and then you can pull out the thorn before you eat me."

The wolf was very surprised at the donkey's behavior. He thought, "This donkey is really stupid. He should be running for his life right now, but instead, he is letting me eat him. And he is even making sure that I don't get cut by the thorn in his foot. What an idiot!"

The donkey lifted his hoof in the air, and the wolf stood behind him and searched for the thorn. Then all of a sudden, the donkey gave a powerful kick to the wolf's head, sending him sprawling several feet in the air and falling on his back.

As the donkey ran away, the hurt wolf thought to himself, "That donkey is definitely not as stupid as I thought!"

The Cat's Meal

A cat caught a rooster, and began thinking of a morally justifiable excuse to kill and eat him. The cat told the rooster, "You bother people by crowing at night and not letting them sleep, and that is why you deserve to be eaten."

The rooster replied, "Actually, my noises help people get up in time so they won't be late for their duties."

"Ok, fine," the cat replied, "but I am hungry, so I am going to eat you anyway!"

The Mice and the Cat

The mice met together one day to discuss how they could deal with the always-dangerous cat that lurked around the house. After many mice presented plans that the others rejected, one mouse suggested, "Let's hang a bell around the cat's neck—that way, we will always know where it is, and can plan accordingly."

The mice praised his suggestion with enthusiasm, and were all elated to know that their cat problem was solved. But then one of them remarked, "You are all overlooking one thing—who is going to put the bell on the cat!"

The Difference Between Salt and Cloth

A merchant tied some baskets full of salt to his donkey and head for the bazaar. There was lots of salt, and the donkey struggled to carry the heavy load. As they crossed a shallow river, the donkey accidentally slipped and fell, and about half of the salt was washed away in the water.

The merchant was upset over the loss, but the donkey was glad that the heavy load had been lightened. When they reached the bazaar, the merchant traded his salt for cloth, and loaded it in baskets and tied it to the donkey.

As they headed home and reached the same river, the donkey remembered what happened with the salt. He pretended to slip and fall into the water so that his load could once again be lightened. But the donkey's plan backfired—the cloth did not wash away. Instead, the bags of cloth soaked up water and became twice as heavy, and the donkey had to carry the heavier load the rest of the way home.

The Donkey Hears Grasshoppers Chirp

A donkey was enamored with the sound of grasshoppers chirping. He went over to the grasshoppers and said, "I really love your singing. I must know what you eat that gives you such lovely voices."

The grasshoppers replied, "We eat dew."

After hearing this, the donkey decided that he would eat only dew like the grasshoppers. He did, and three weeks later, the donkey died of starvation.

The Goose and the Golden Eggs

One day, a poor man spotted a new goose among the various birds he kept in his yard. When he and his wife came to feed it the next day, the goose began making some noises, and out of it came a solid gold egg.

Each day after that, the goose laid another gold egg, which the man and his wife eagerly collected. They soon became very rich, and bought lavish items and hired servants. In time, their lifestyle had become so expensive that they could not be supported by the goose's output.

"One egg a day isn't nearly enough," the man lamented to his wife. "We can barely afford our high dollar lifestyle anymore."

"I agree," she responded. "We should cut the goose open now so we can get all the eggs at once."

"Great idea, honey!" the man replied as he reached for a knife. He cut the goose open, but there were no gold eggs inside the now-dead goose.

The Lion and Dolphin Alliance

A lion walked by a beach and saw a dolphin in the water. He went to the dolphin and said, "We should form an alliance."

The dolphin replied, "OK."

A few days later, the lion was in battle with a bull, and called for the dolphin to assist him. The dolphin heard this and wanted to help, but he had no way to reach the land.

The next day, the lion angrily came to the dolphin and exclaimed, "You traitor—you did not help me against the bull I was fighting yesterday."

The dolphin retorted, "Don't blame me—blame Nature instead, which gave me power in the sea, but not in the land."

Mulla Nasrudin Folktales

Mulla (a.k.a. Hodja or Hoca) Nasrudin is the starring character in a vast number of amusing tales told in regions all over the world, particularly in countries in or near the Middle East. Each tale depicts Nasrudin in a different situation, and through his viewpoint they humorously reveal commentary and lessons on various life themes. The great allure of the Mulla Nasrudin tales is that they are funny as well as lesson filled, philosophical, and thought provoking.

The Mulla Nasrudin Character

Mulla, Hodja, and Hoca are titles from various areas of the world that in early times were used to signify a learned man.

The character Mulla (/ Hodja / Hoca) Nasrudin is sometimes wise, sometimes foolish, and sometimes both. He is a unique spin on a wise sage or philosopher character.

Much of Nasrudin's actions and can be described as illogical yet logical, rational yet irrational, bizarre yet normal, and simple yet profound. What adds even further to his uniqueness is the way he gets across his messages in unconventional yet very effective methods.

Origins and History

Mulla Nasrudin tales have been passed down for many centuries. It is thought that the Mulla Nasrudin character is based on a real man who lived in the 1300s. However, many countries claim to be the origin of the actual Mulla Nasrudin character and his tales, and it remains uncertain where the man lived and the stories started.

But whatever the origins of Mulla Nasrudin are, pinpointing them has become a trivial point. As generations went by, new stories were added, others were modified, and the character and his tales spread to broader regions. The types of themes and wisdom in his tales have become legendary products of a variety of people's observations and imaginations. And although most of them depict Nasrudin in an early small village setting, the tales deal with concepts that have relevance to today's universe and people.

Today, Mulla Nasrudin stories are told in a wide variety of regions, and have been translated into many languages. (It can only be assumed that some regions independently developed a character similar to Mulla Nasrudin, and the stories have become assimilated together.)

In many regions, Mulla Nasrudin is a major part of the culture, and is quoted or alluded to frequently in daily life. Since there are thousands of different Nasrudin stories, one can be found to fit almost any occasion.

Sufis (who are covered in the Sufism chapter of this book) also use Nasrudin stories frequently as learning and meditation tools, similar to the way Zen Buddhism practitioners use koans (see the Zen Buddhism chapter for more info on koans).

Also Known As

In different regions, the character goes by such aliases as:

Mulla Nasrudin

Hodja / Hoca Nasreddin

Nasreddin Hodja / Hoca

Effendi

Variations of Mulla:	Molla, Mullah, Mollah, Maualana
Variations of Nasrudin:	Nasreddin, Nasruddin, Nasiruddin, Nastradin, Nasreddine, Nasredin, Nastradhin, Nasrettin, Nastratin, Nasr Eddin, Nasr Ud Din, Nasr Id Deen, Nasirud Din, Nasr Ed Dine, Stradin
Variations of Hodja / Hoca:	Hocca, Hodscha, Khoja, Hoja, Hogia, Hodza, Hogea, Hodza, Khodja, Chotza, Chotzas, Joha, Juha
Variations of Effendi:	Ependi, Afandi, Efendi

MULLA NASRUDIN FOLKTALES

The Moving Friend

"Nasrudin," a friend said one day, "I am moving to another village. Can I have your ring, so that I will remember you every time I look at it?"

Nasrudin replied, "Well, you might lose the ring and then forget about me. How about I don't give you a ring in the first place—that way, every time that you look at your finger and don't see a ring, you will definitely remember me."

Clothes Shopping

Nasrudin was shopping for clothes. He tried on a coat, and then took it off, and said to the storeowner, "Well, I don't really want this. Take it and give me a pair of pants instead."

The storeowner did, and then Nasrudin put the pants on and began walking out of the store. The storeowner stopped him and said, "Sir, you forgot to pay me for those pants."

Nasrudin replied, "I exchanged the coat for these pants."

The storeowner said, "But you did not pay for that coat, either."

Nasrudin responded, "Of course I didn't—why would I pay for something I chose not to take!"

The Loan Request

A friend asked Nasrudin, "Can I borrow 1000 toman from you for three months."

"Well," Nasrudin replied, "I can fulfill half of your loan request."

"OK; that's fine," the friend said, "I'm sure I can get the other 500 toman somewhere else."

"You misunderstood me," Nasrudin replied. "The half of your loan request I agreed to was the time: the three months. As for the 1000 toman, I cannot give it to you."

Can I Borrow Your Donkey?

A man knocked on Nasrudin's door. When Nasrudin opened it, the friend asked, "Can I borrow your donkey?"

"I would love to help you," Nasrudin replied, "but I have already lent it to someone else."

Just then, a loud donkey noise came from Nasrudin's yard.

"Hey," the man said, "I just heard the donkey make a noise from your yard!"

Nasrudin quickly retorted, "Do you mean to tell me that you are going to take the word of a donkey over mine?"

Sack of Vegetables

Nasrudin snuck into someone's garden and began putting vegetables in his sack. The owner saw him and shouted, "What are you doing in my garden?"

Nasrudin confidently responded, "The wind blew me here."

"That sounds like BS to me," the man replied, "but let's assume that the wind did blow you here. Now then, how can you explain how those vegetables were pulled out from my garden?"

"Oh, that's simple," Nasrudin responded. "I had to grab them to stop myself from being thrown any further by the wind."

"Well," the man continued, "then tell me this—how did the vegetables get in your sack?"

"You know what," Nasrudin said, "I was just standing here and wondering that same thing myself!"

What in the World Were You Smuggling?

Nasrudin the smuggler was leading a donkey that had bundles of straw on its back. An experienced border inspector spotted Nasrudin coming to his border.

"Halt," the inspector said. "What is your business here?"

"I am an honest smuggler!" replied Nasrudin.

"Oh, really?" said the inspector. "Well, let me search those straw bundles. If I find something in them, then you are required to pay a border fee!"

"Do as you wish, "Nasrudin replied, "but you will not find anything in those bundles."

The inspector intensively searched and took apart the bundles, but could not find a single thing in them. He turned to Nasrudin and said, "You have managed to get one by me today. You may pass the border."

Nasrudin crossed the border with his donkey while the annoyed inspector looked on. And then the very next day, Nasrudin once again came to the border with a straw-carrying donkey. The inspector saw Nasrudin coming and thought, "I'll get him for sure this time."

He checked the bundles of straw again, and then searched through Nasrudin's clothing, and even went through the donkey's harness. But once again he came up empty handed and had to let Nasrudin pass.

This same pattern continued every day for several years, and every day Nasrudin wore more and more extravagant clothing and jewelry that indicated he was getting wealthier. Eventually, the inspector retired from his longtime job, but even in retirement he still wondered about the man with the straw-carrying donkey.

"I should have checked that donkey's mouth more extensively," he thought to himself. "Or maybe he hid something in the donkey's rectum."

Then one day he spotted Nasrudin's face in a crowd. "Hey," the inspector said, "I know you! You are that man who came to my border everyday for all those years with a straw-carrying donkey. Please, sir, I must talk to you."

Nasrudin came towards him and the inspector continued talking. "My friend, I always wondered what you were smuggling past my border everyday. Just between you and me, you must tell me. I must know. What in the world were you smuggling for all those years? I must know!"

Nasrudin simply replied, "donkeys."

The Donkey Seller

Nasrudin brought his donkey to sell at the bazaar, but every time a customer wanted to inspect it, the donkey began biting and being uncooperative. One man asked Nasrudin, "Do you really expect to sell a donkey that behaves like that?"

Nasrudin replied, "Not really; I just brought him here so other people would experience what I have to put up with every day!"

Nasrudin Gets Engaged

Nasrudin got engaged to a woman. The fiancée's mother invited Nasrudin to her house to ask him some questions.

"Tell me," she said, "are you sure this is the first time you are getting married?"

"Yes," Nasrudin replied, "I swear on my two kids that I have never been married before."

The Baby is Crying

Late one night, Nasrudin's baby started crying. Nasrudin's wife turned to him and said, "Husband, go take care of the baby. After all, he is not only mine—he is also half yours."

Nasrudin sleepily remarked, "You can go stop your half from crying if you want, but I choose to let my half continue to cry."

Complaints About Nasrudin's Wife

One day, the local people complained to Nasrudin, "Your wife is always walking here and there, going to all sorts of different places. It is improper for a woman to do that. Tell her that she should stop moving around so much."

"OK," Nasrudin said. "If she ever comes to our house, I will be sure to tell her."

Nasrudin Wants a Divorce

Nasrudin went to the village judge and asked to divorce his wife. When the judge asked what her name was, Nasrudin replied, "Man…I don't know."

The judge curiously asked, "Well, how long have you been married to her?'

"Five years," Nasrudin replied.

The judge incredulously responded, "Do you mean to tell me that after five year of marriage, you do not know your wife's name?"

"That is correct," said Nasrudin.

"Why not?" asked the judge.

"Because," Nasrudin explained, "I did not have social relations with her."

Man Searches for Joy

One day, Nasrudin began talking to a man from another town. The man lamented to Nasrudin, "I am rich, but I am also sad and miserable. I have taken my money and gone traveling in search of joy—but alas, I have yet to find it."

As the man continued speaking, Nasrudin grabbed the man's bag and ran off with it. The man chased Nasrudin, and Nasrudin soon ran out of his sight. He hid behind a tree, and put the bag in the open road for the man to see.

When the man caught up, he located the bag, and his facial expression immediately turned from distress to joy. As he danced in celebration of finding his bag, Nasrudin thought to himself, "That is one way to bring joy to a sad man."

Nasrudin Eats Dates

A man noticed Nasrudin eating dates with their seeds, and asked, "Why are you eating the seeds of those dates?"

Nasrudin remarked, "Because the merchant who sold them to me included the weight of the seeds in his price."

Grammar

Nasrudin was ferrying a traveler across a lake. As they spoke on various subjects, Nasrudin made a minor grammatical error. The traveler remarked, "You who wears a turban and calls himself a Mulla—have you ever studied grammar extensively?"

"No," Nasrudin admitted, "I have not covered that subject in depth."

"Well then," the traveler replied," you have wasted half of your life!"

Several minutes later, Nasrudin turned to the traveler and asked, "Have you ever learned how to swim?"

"No," the traveler responded.

"Well then," Nasrudin replied, "you have wasted all your life—for there is a hole in the boat, and we are sinking!"

Across the River

Nasrudin was standing near a river. A man on the other side of the river shouted to him, "Hey! How can I get across the river?"

"You are across!" Nasrudin shouted back.

When Will the End of the World Be?

Philosopher: "I have been traveling, researching, and contemplating for years, trying to determine when the end of the world will be—yet I still have not found out the answer. Mulla, do you know when the end of the world will be?"

Nasrudin: "Yes—I have known that information for a long time."

Philosopher: "Well, will you share this knowledge with me?"

Nasrudin: "Of course. When I die, that will be the end of the world."

Philosopher: "Are you certain that will be the end of the world?"

Nasrudin: "It will be for me."

The Pot

Nasrudin borrowed a pot from his friend. The next day, he gave the pot back to the friend, and also gave him another smaller pot. The friend looked at the small pot, and said, "What is that?"

"Your pot gave birth while I had it," Nasrudin replied, "so I am giving you its child."

The friend was glad to receive the bonus, and didn't ask any more questions.

A week later, Nasrudin borrowed the original pot from the friend. After a week passed, the friend asked Nasrudin to return it.

"I cannot," Nasrudin said.

"Why not?" the friend replied.

"Well," Nasrudin answered, "I hate to be the bearer of bad news…but your pot has died."

"What?" the friend asked with skepticism. "A pot cannot die!"

"You believed it gave birth," Nasrudin said, "so is why is it that you cannot believe it has died."

The Town Gossip

The Town Gossip: "Nasrudin, I just saw a huge tub of *choresht* (stew) that some men were transporting."
Nasrudin: "What's it to me?"
The Town Gossip: "They were delivering it to your house."
Nasrudin: "What's it to you?"

The Stranger's Request

One day, Nasrudin was repairing his roof, and was interrupted by a stranger knocking on his door.

"What do you want?" Nasrudin shouted down to him from the roof.

"Come down so I can tell you," the stranger replied.

Nasrudin angrily climbed down the ladder. "Well!" Nasrudin snapped at the stranger, "What is so important?"

"Can you spare some money for this poor old man?" asked the stranger in a near whisper.

Nasrudin started to climb up the ladder and said, "Follow me up to the roof."

When they both reached the roof, Nasrudin turned to the stranger and said, "No, you can't have any money. Now get off my roof!"

Avoiding Criticism

Nasrudin and his son were traveling with their donkey. Nasrudin preferred to walk while his son rode the donkey. But then they passed a group of bystanders, and one scoffed, "Look—that selfish boy is riding on a donkey while his poor old father is forced to walk alongside. That is so disrespectful. What a horrible and spoiled child!"

Nasrudin and his son felt embarrassed, so they switched spots—this time Nasrudin rode the donkey while his son walked.

Soon they passed another group of people. "Oh, that's detestable!" one of them exclaimed. "That poor young boy has to walk while his abusive father rides the donkey! That horrible man should be ashamed of himself for the way he is treating his son. What a heartless parent!"

Nasrudin was upset to hear this. He wanted to avoid anybody else's scorn, so he decided to have both himself and his son ride the donkey at the same time.

As they both rode, they passed another group of people. "That man and his son are so cruel," one bystander said. "Just look at how they are forcing that poor donkey to bear the weight if two people. They should be put in jail for their despicable act. What scoundrels!"

Nasrudin heard this and told his son, "I guess the only way we can avoid the criticism of others is to both walk."

"I suppose you are right," the son replied.

So they got off the donkey and continued on foot. But as they passed another group of people, they heard them laughing. "Ha, ha, ha," the group jeered. "Look at those two fools. They are so stupid that both of them are walking under this scorching hot sun and neither of them is riding the donkey! What morons!"

Note: The next two stories portray Nasrudin as the village judge.

Judge Nasrudin's Ruling on the Cow-on-Cow Homicide

A neighbor ran into Judge Nasrudin's room and asked him, "If one man's cow kills another's, is the owner of the first cow responsible?"

"It depends," Nasrudin cautiously answered.

"Well," said the man, "*your* cow has killed *mine*!"

"Oh," answered Nasrudin. "Well, everyone knows that a cow can't think like a human. So obviously, a cow isn't responsible. And therefore, its owner isn't responsible either."

"Excuse me, Judge," the man interrupted, "I made a mistake. What I meant to say is that *my* cow has killed *yours*!"

Judge Nasrudin sat in contemplation for a few moments. "Now that I think about it more carefully," he announced, "this case is much more complex then I initially though."

Judge Nasrudin turned to his assistant and said, "Please bring me that big blue book on the shelf behind you…"

You are Right

Judge Nasrudin was listening to a case. After hearing the plaintiff present his side, Nasrudin remarked, "You are right."

Then the defendant presented his side, and Nasrudin remarked, "Yes, you are right."

Nasrudin's wife had been listening to the case, and incredulously remarked, "Nasrudin, that doesn't make any sense—how could you say that the plaintiff is right, and then also say that the defendant is right?"

Nasrudin responded, "You know what—you are right, too!"

Nasrudin Has Left the Building

Nasrudin was a part time teacher, but got bored of the repetitive routine. One day at the beginning of class, he asked his new pupils, "Do you know what I am about to teach you?"

"No," they responded.

"Well then," Nasrudin said, "Since you don't have enough background information, there is no point in me trying to teach it to you." And with that statement, Nasrudin left the building.

The next day, he came to the class and asked them, "OK—do you know, or don't you know?"

Thinking that they were on to his trick, the students responded, "Yes, we know."

"Well then," Nasrudin replied, "if you already know, there is no point in me telling you!" And with that, Nasrudin left the building.

The next day, he came to the class and once again asked them, "Do you know, or don't you know?"

The students, once again thinking that they were on to his trick, replied, "Half of us do, and half of us don't."

"OK, fantastic," Nasrudin replied. "Now the half of you that do know can tell the other half that you that don't!" And with that statement, Nasrudin left the building.

The Turban is Mine

Nasrudin's old friend Eynolla came to visit him one day from a far away village.

"I want to introduce you to a few people," Nasrudin told Eynolla.

"OK," replied Eynolla, "but please lend me a turban, for I am not properly dressed."

So Nasrudin lent him the turban, and they went and visited one of Nasrudin's friends. "This is my friend Eynolla," Nasrudin said, "but the turban he is wearing is mine."

Eynolla was deeply annoyed by the remark. He waited until they left the friend's house, and then said to Nasrudin, "Why did you make such a comment, saying that the turban I am wearing is yours? Do not make such a comment on our next visit!"

So they made their next visit, and this time Nasrudin said, "This is my friend Eynolla—and the turban he is wearing is his; not mine."

As they left, Eynolla once again expressed his annoyance, exclaiming, "Why did you go to such lengths to say that the turban was mine and not yours. Don't do it on our next visit."

So as they made the next visit, Nasrudin said, "This is my friend Eynolla…and I have nothing to say about whether or not the turban he is wearing is his or mine."

Selling a Turban

Nasrudin went to the mayor's palace one day, and wore an elaborate turban on his head in hopes of selling it to the mayor.

"Wow!" said the mayor, "what a magnificent turban! I have never seen anything like it. How much will you sell it for?"

"Fifty thousand toman," Nasrudin calmly replied.

A merchant happened to be in the court and heard this. The merchant was familiar with Nasrudin's slickness, and was also familiar with the value of goods. He turned to the mayor and remarked, "That price surely does not correspond to the market value of such an item."

The mayor heard this, and asked Nasrudin, "Your price sounds very expensive."

"Well," Nasrudin replied, "the price is based on how much I bought it for, and I paid a lot for it because I knew that there is only one mayor in the entire universe who has taste exquisite enough to buy such a turban."

Upon hearing this compliment, the mayor immediately demanded to his servants that Nasrudin be paid full price for the turban. Nasrudin walked over to the merchant and said, "You might know the market values of turbans, but I know the market value of complimenting the mayor."

The Neighbor's Garden

Nasrudin spotted some ripe oranges in his neighbor's garden, and wanted to take one. He took his ladder up to the dividing wall, climbed to the top of the wall, and pulled the ladder over.

As he began climbing down to his neighbor's side, he suddenly heard the voice of his neighbor exclaiming, "What are you doing here!"

Nasrudin confidently replied, "I am selling ladders."

The neighbor countered, "Does this look like the place for selling ladders?"

"Well now," Nasrudin replied, "do you think that there is only one place to sell ladders?"

The Punishment

Nasrudin told his son to go get some water from the well. Before the son left, Nasrudin slapped him and shouted, "And make sure you don't break the jug!"

The boy began crying, and a bystander noticed this and said, "Why did you hit him? He hasn't done anything wrong."

Nasrudin replied, "Well, better to hit him now than to hit him afterwards if he does end up breaking it. That would be too late."

The Right Language

A man was caught in a river current, and hanging on to some rocks to avoid being carried away. Another man saw this, and said, "Give me your hand so I can help you out." The man in the river heard this, but did not cooperate.

Nasrudin saw this happening. He walked over to the man in the river, and asked, "What do you do for a living?"

"I collect taxes," the man replied.

"Then *take* my hand," Nasrudin said, and the man finally cooperated.

Nasrudin turned to the other man who was watching, and remarked, "Tax collectors speak the language of *take*, not the language of *give*."

Nasrudin Defends Himself in Court

Nasrudin was in court for stealing a watermelon. The Judge exclaimed, "Nasrudin, I must give you a fine for what you have done."

"There is no need to do that," Nasrudin said. "You can just use this against all the credits I have accumulated for the times I didn't steal anything."

African Folktales

Africa is one of the world's most abundant sources of folktales. Here are some of them:

Note: For info about the African continent, see the African Proverbs chapter.

Up to the Giraffe's Knees

One day, a giraffe was standing in a pond while a monkey was sitting in a nearby tree. The monkey, who was not a good swimmer, saw the giraffe and asked him, "How deep is that pond?"

The giraffe replied, "The water is only up to my knees."

The monkey heard this and went in the water. Shortly later he was near-drowning and shouting for help. The giraffe quickly rescued him and took him out of the pond.

The monkey angrily looked at giraffe and yelled, "Why did you trick me!"

"I didn't tell you that the pond was shallow," the giraffe retorted. "I said that the water level was up to my knees—that doesn't mean the water isn't deep. After all, I am much taller than you, and just because the water isn't deep for me, it doesn't mean that it will be the same for you!"

Fortune Teller

One day, a young man named Essien went to the forest and decided to cut some wood. He had never cut wood before, and throughout his life he had neglected learn the skill and observe other people cutting wood.

Essien climbed up a tree and sat onto a branch, and began cutting the very branch he was seated on! A local man observed him and remarked, "Why are you cutting a branch that you are sitting on? Aren't you going to fall down with it?"

Essien snapped back, "Listen, I have cut off branches this way many times, and I have never fallen down!"

He continued cutting, and moments later, the branch gave way and Essien fell to the ground. The fall caused him painful injuries that took weeks to recover from.

When he finally recovered, Essien sought out the wise man and remarked, "Wow! I have seen first hand that you have great powers, and can predict the future. Please, Mr. Wise Man and Fortune Teller—tell me when I will die."

"What?" the wise man replied, "I cannot do that! Your question is foolish—how can I know when you will die? I am not a fortuneteller. And I am not even an experienced woodcutter, either. The only reason I knew you were going to fall off of the tree branch is because I used common sense!"

Rival Storytellers

Two rival storytellers attended a dinner party. When dinner was finished, one of them began telling a story. "I once visited another land," he said, "where everything was humongous. In fact, I saw a bird that was so big, it took an hour just for it to fly by me!"

The other storyteller heard this and remarked, "Yes, I have been there too and can confirm that. And when I was there, I saw a tree so big that it took me two hours just to walk by it."

The first storyteller shouted out, "No, you are mistaken—that is impossible. There is not a tree that big in this entire world!"

The second storyteller responded, "The tree I described must have existed—after all, if it didn't, then where would the bird you described have been able to sit down!"

Frogs Fall in Milk

Two frogs fell into a bowl of milk and couldn't get out. As they both treaded milk, one said to the other, "I am tired, and I will not tread anymore. I will accept death."

Upon speaking those words, he allowed himself to sink, and soon drowned to death.

The other frog was also tired, but he continued to tread. After more time had passed, his treading caused the milk fat to turn into butter. He used the butter to jump out of the bowl and to safety.

The Traveler

An elaborately dressed man was traveling to a party. On his way, a farmer approached him, handed him some peanuts, and said, "Here is some food for your journey."

The man replied, "I am about to eat rare gourmet food—I have no use for peanuts!" He threw the peanuts in the mud, and left.

As the man traveled further, he encountered a river that was more torrid than usual, and concluded that he could not make it across. He had to turn back and head for home. On his way back, it grew late in the evening, and the man's belly yearned for food.

He remembered the peanuts he causally tossed away earlier. He returned to that spot, and had no choice but to laboriously pick the peanuts out of the mud one by one for his dinner.

The Red and Blue Coat

Yerodin and Lumumba were very close friends and neighbors whose homes were separated by a narrow path between their yards.

One day, a local trickster decided that he would test their longtime friendship. The trickster put on an elaborate two-color coat that was split down the middle: red on the right, and blue on the left. He walked on the path between the two houses while Yerodin and Lumumba were farming. The trickster made a loud whistle while he was in the middle of the path, and both friends momentarily looked up and noticed him.

Then a few minutes after he had passed by, Yerodin said to Lumumba, "Did you like the flamboyant red coat that man was wearing?"

"Red coat?" Lumumba replied. "No, you are mistaken. I saw him too when he walked between us, and his coat was blue."

"Listen," retorted Yerodin, "I saw the coat clearly and I am sure that it was red."

"No, no, no; you are wrong," replied Lumumba. "I am absolutely sure that it was blue."

Yerodin began getting annoyed, and replied, "Hey, I know what I saw, and that coat was not blue. It was definitely red. I am sure about this!"

"You are not very observant," Lumumba quickly replied, "and stubborn as well. Only a fool would not recognize that the coat was blue."

"Oh, so you think that I am stupid, huh?" shouted Yerodin. "Well, you are actually the stupid one, because the coat was red!"

They began to shout and argue more intensely, and their shouts turned into fighting. As they battled, they suddenly heard a man laughing. They looked up, and saw the trickster wearing the two-color coat with both colors facing them.

They stopped fighting and yelled out the trickster, "You despicable man! We have been the best of friends for years, and now look what you have started between us!"

"Don't blame me," the trickster replied, "I am not the one who made you two fight each other."

"What are you taking about?" Yerodin and Lumumba skeptically asked.

The trickster continued, "Both of you were speaking the apparent truth in your argument. But the reason you ended up fighting is because you only considered my coat from your own point of view!"

Birbal Tales and Other Indian Folktales

Folktales are very popular in India, and the country has an abundant number of them. Many of these folktales involve a character named Birbal.

Note: For more info on India, see the Indian Proverbs chapter.

Birbal

Birbal stories have been told and retold throughout India (particularly in Northern India) for many generations, and are popular among both children and adults. They are based on an actual man named Birbal who served for many years on the court of Emperor Akbar the Great.

Emperor Akbar and the Nav Ratna

Akbar (whose full name was Jalaludden Mohammed Akbar Padshah Ghazi) was the Mughal (Ruling Dynasty) Emperor of India, and one of the most successful world leaders in history. He reigned from age 18 in 1560 all the way to his death in 1605.

During his reign, Emperor Akbar relied on many people for different areas of expertise and knowledge, especially since he was illiterate (although he kept that a secret from almost everyone).

Birbal was part of a prestigious group of those court attendants known as the Nav Ratna (nine jewels of the Mughal Crown) of Emperor Akbar's court. One of the Nav Ratna was a financial genius, another was a great historian, and another was an expert in chivalry.

Birbal

Birbal was Emperor Akbar's favorite Nav Ratna, and noted for his great wit, intelligence, wisdom, and problem solving ability. He had several administrative and military duties, and also served as Emperor Akbar's main and trusted advisor. In fact, Emperor Akbar enjoyed Birbal's wit and humor so much that they were also close friends, which made many of the other court attendants envious.

BIRBAL TALES

The Scholar's Challenge

A scholar heard about Birbal's witty reputation, and went to Akbar's Court to challenge him. Birbal accepted the scholar's challenge. Then the scholar asked Birbal, "OK—do you want to answer fifty easy questions, or one difficult question."

"One difficult question," Birbal answered.

"OK." The scholar replied. "What came first? The chicken or the egg?"

Without any hesitation, Birbal confidently responded, "The chicken."

"How do you know?" asked the scholar.

"We agreed on only one question," Birbal replied, "so no second question please!"

And Akbar and Birbal left the Palace Court without saying another word to the scholar.

The Theft Investigation

A wealthy man came to Akbar's Court one day and said to Birbal, "I have been robbed of my valuable gold necklace."

"Do you have any idea who stole it?" Birbal asked.

"I am fairly certain it was one of six servants," the man replied, "but I have no idea which one is the thief."

"OK," said Birbal, "I will come to your house tomorrow in the afternoon to investigate. Make sure all your servants are there."

So the next day, Birbal came to the man's mansion, and was accompanied by a magician. Birbal announced to the wealthy man and the servants, "I am investigating a theft, and this magician will help me determine who the thief is."

The magician said some mystic chants that caught everyone's attention, and then took six sticks out of a bag and handed them to Birbal. Birbal gave each of the servants a stick, and remarked, "These sticks are all the same length, but by the spell of this powerful magician, any thief who touches one will cause it to grow three centimeters. Tomorrow, we will inspect the sticks and be able to determine who the thief is."

So the next day, Birbal came back and asked the servants to hand the wealthy man the sticks. As he examined them, the wealthy man exclaimed, "This is strange. None of these sticks grew, but the butler's actually shrunk tree centimeters!

"Then he is the thief," Birbal remarked. "After all, only a man's guiltiness would cause him to fear the stick would grow, and thus would impel him to cut the stick so that he wouldn't be caught."

Water and Well Dispute

A tricky man sold his well to a farmer. The next day, the farmer went to draw water from the well, but the tricky man stopped him and said, "I sold you the well, not the water. You cannot draw my water from the well. I still own the water."

The farmer was upset, so he went to the Emperor's court and described the situation to Birbal. Birbal called over the tricky man to the Palace and asked him, "Why don't you let this farmer use the well's water? After all, you sold him the well."

The tricky man quickly replied, "I only sold the well to the farmer, not the water. He has no right to draw my water from the well!"

Birbal thought for a moment, and then said, "OK, fine. But listen— since you sold the well to this farmer and you claim that the water is still yours, then you have no right to keep your water in his well. You must either pay rent to the farmer to keep your water in his well, or pay him to use his well so you can remove your water from it!"

The Test

Several men went to the Royal Palace and requested to become Emperor Akbar's Royal Advisor. Akbar told them, "Only the person who passes my special test will get the job."

He then took off his coat and put in on the floor. "Cover me from head to toe with this coat," Akbar commanded.

All the men tried, but one by one they failed. When they covered his lower body, his upper body remained uncovered, and when they covered his lower body, his upper body remained uncovered.

Then Birbal entered the court, and Akbar asked him if he could complete the task. Birbal paused for a moment, and then politely asked Akbar, "Could you pull up your knees for a second?" Akbar did, and Birbal easily covered him from head to toe with the coat.

The Emperor's Mustache

Emperor Akbar enjoyed asking his court attendants many bizarre hypothetical questions. One day he asked them, "How should we punish someone who pulls on my mustache?"

One man replied, "He should be beheaded."

Another said, "He should surely be hanged."

And another said, "He should be fed to the tigers."

The Emperor heard these responses and then turned to Birbal and asked, "What do you think?"

Birbal though for a moment and replied, "He should be given fruit."

"What?" the Emperor incredulously replied. "Have you gone insane? Do you have any idea what you are saying?"

Birbal calmly replied, "I have not gone insane, Sir. I know what I am saying."

The Emperor angrily retorted, "Then how can say something like that?"

Birbal politely responded, "Because the only person who would dare do such a thing is your grandson!"

The Monkey and the Pea

Akbar and Birbal were out hunting. They were both riding on horses, and they stopped to feed their horses some peas. Just then, a monkey ran down from a tree and snatched a huge handful of the peas.

As the monkey ran back up the tree, one of the peas fell from his hands. The monkey tried to grab it, but in his attempt to catch that one pea, he dropped all of the other peas he was carrying. They all fell to the ground, and the horses ate them.

After Akbar and Birbal watched this happen, Birbal remarked, "Dear Emperor, if you are ever in an excessively greedy mood, just remember what happened to that monkey!"

OTHER INDIAN FOLKTALES

King of the Jungle

One day, Tiger attacked Fox, and Fox yelled, "How dare you attack me—I am the King of the Jungle!"

Tiger was extremely surprised to hear this. He snapped back, "That's preposterous. You are not the King."

"Yes I am," replied Fox. "All the animals are terrified of me. They run from me whenever I approach them. If you want proof, just come with me and I will show you."

So Fox went into the forest and Tiger followed him. They came to a herd of zebras. When the zebras saw Tiger standing behind Fox, they quickly darted away in fear of Tiger.

Then Tiger and Fox traveled further, and came to a group of deer. The deer spotted Tiger behind Fox, and they, too, quickly fled in fear of Tiger.

Fox turned to Tiger and said, "You saw it for yourself, didn't you. That should be enough proof for you. The animals flee at the very sight of me. I am the King of the Jungle!"

Tiger responded, "Yes—at first I thought you were lying, but indeed I have seen it with my own eyes. Please forgive me for attacking you, Great King." And Tiger quickly dashed away.

The Sly Fox Dupes the Crow

A lady was making *bhajiyas* (an Indian snack food). A hungry crow noticed the bhajiyas, and quickly swooped down and grabbed one in its beak. She flew up to a tree and was about to begin eating, but was interrupted by a sly fox that said, "Oh Crow, I was just thinking about your lovely voice—please sing for me and give me the honor of partaking in such a beautiful sound."

The Crow enjoyed hearing the compliments, and eagerly began singing. But once she opened her mouth, her bhajiya fell to the ground. The sly fox picked it up and ran away with it.

An Elephant is...

There once was a gated garden that contained a large elephant. As it made a loud trumpeting "praaaaah," three blind men that were walking nearby heard the noise.

"What in the world was that?" the first man asked.

"Oh—that is an elephant," the second man replied.

"What is an elephant?" the third man inquired.

"To be honest, I am not exactly sure what it is," said the second man.

"Well, let us find out," said the first man.

So the first man stretched out his arm and hand and walked forward until his hand touched the elephant's ear. He ran his hand along the ear and proudly concluded, "An elephant is flat and wide like a big fan!"

The second man then embarked on his own investigation. He stretched out his arm and hand, and soon made contact with the elephant's tail. He traced his hand along it and said, "No, you are mistaken. An elephant is nothing like a fan. In fact, it is thin and narrow like a rope."

The third man set out to resolve the dispute. He stretched out his arm and hand as he walked forward, and he reached the elephant's middle body. As he examined it with his hand, he retorted, "You both have it all wrong. An elephant is not like a rope, nor is it like a rug. It is actually solid and thick, like a wall."

Each man held to his own viewpoint, and the three men began arguing and shouting. Each of them left the argument convinced that he was right.

Always Fearing Everything

A forest-dwelling elephant had been living a peaceful life, but one day a king spotted her and said to his servants, "Take that elephant to the palace garden and have the instructors train her."

They did as he said, but the palace trainers were cruel and they constantly beat the elephant. She was terrified of them, and escaped the palace and ran all the way to the Himalayas.

After many years passed, the king had forgotten about the elephant, but the elephant still hadn't moved on from her experience at the royal garden. She was still frightened and worried, and grew excessively thin because she barely ate.

One day, a tree-sprite told her, "Don't be afraid all of the time—you are not in the palace garden anymore. Stop the excessive worrying, for you are free now."

Pumpkins and Nuts

A man was resting under a nut tree. He looked a few yards to his side and noticed a big pumpkin growing on a thin vine near the ground.

"The ways of nature are foolish indeed," the man thought. "Why should a big strong tree like the one above me hold nuts, while a thin weak vine holds a large pumpkin. It should be the other way around."

But at that moment, a small nut from high up in the tree fell and hit him on the head. The man looked up into the branches and thought, "I guess my presumption was mistaken. After all, if it was a big pumpkin that fell out of the tree and onto my head, it might have killed me!"

The Guru's Next Life

Note: This story deals with reincarnation, a belief common among Hindus (and many other people around the world) that a person's soul is reborn in another body when a person dies, unless the person has achieved liberation.

A guru was peacefully sitting outside when he had a flash vision and foresaw what he would be in his next life. The guru called over his main disciple and told him, "I have taught you for a very long time, and now I need you to do something for me."

The disciple replied, "Oh, I will do anything you ask me, guru."

The guru continued, "OK, let me describe the situation. I have just found out that I am going to die soon, and be reborn as a piglet in the litter of that sow in our yard. It will be easy to tell me apart, due to a large mark on my forehead. When I am reborn as that pig, I want you to kill it so that I will be released from a pig's life. Will you do this for me, my disciple?"

The discipline was sad to hear this news, but loyally replied, "Yes, guru."

Several days later, the guru died, and the sow had a litter of pigs, one of which had a mark on its forehead just like the guru predicted. When the disciple saw this, he pulled out a knife and was about to slit the pig's throat. But he was interrupted by the pig, who yelled out, "Stop—don't do it! When I asked you to kill me, I did not know what a pig's life would be like—but now that I have experienced it, I like it, and want to live on. Please let me go."

Other Folktales

Here are some other folktales from various parts of the world:

Sweden: The Boys Hunts a Fox

A boy spotted a sleeping fox in the forest. The boy slowly picked up a big stone and crept up near the fox.

He silently thought, "I am going to kill this fox, and then sell its skin. With the money I make, I am going to buy some wheat and plant it in my family's fields. And I'll bet that when people are passing by the field, they are going to notice my wonderful wheat. If they come near it, I will shout to them and tell them to stay away. And if they don't listen to my first warning, then I will shout even louder…"

As the boy was thinking this, he really shouted out loudly and woke the sleeping fox. The startled fox ran away, and the boy was left holding the stone in his hand.

Germany: The Barber Plays a Trick

A merchant, a barber, and a bald man were traveling together. They stopped to sleep, and they decided to take turns watching for trouble—the barber would watch first, the merchant second, and the bald man third.

While the barber was performing the first watch, he decided to play a trick on the merchant, and he took out his razor and shaved the merchant's head completely bald. Then when the merchant's turn came to keep watch, the barber woke him up.

The merchant, still half asleep, felt a breeze on his head. When he touched it with his hands and noticed there was no hair on it, he thought, "That stupid barber made a mistake and woke up the bald man instead of me!"

Macedonia: The Greeting

Itar Pejo walks past a rich man.
Rich Man: "Hey, why didn't you greet me and bow?"
Itar Pejo: "Why should I?"
Rich Man: "Why? Because I have six hundred gold coins, that's why!"
Itar Pejo: "So what if you do. Why should it mean anything to me? They are yours, not mine."
Rich Man: "Yes, they are mine, but I can give you three hundred."

Itar Pejo: "Well, if you give me three hundred, then we will both have the same amount of money, and using your rationale, there will be no reason for me to bow to you."

Rich Man: "Well, what if I decide that I don't want to be rich anymore, and give you all six hundred gold coins? Then what?"

Itar Pejo: "If you give me all of them, then I will have six hundred coins, and you will have zero. And then using your rationale, you will be the one bowing to me!

Rich Man: "OK, Fine. I must be getting along now."

Itar Pejo: "A greeting and respect are not bought with money!"

Indonesia: New Shirt

Si Kabayan was sitting outside and crying. A friend saw him and asked, "Why are you crying?"

"Because I just got a new shirt," he replied.

"But that is good news. Why does it make you cry?" the friend asked.

Si Kabayan responded, "Because it will get old."

Indonesia: The Blue Cat

An ancient Indonesian king had a deep love for his vast collection of cats, especially one particular white-furred cat he treasured the most.

Early one morning, the king awoke from a dream and rushed to his fortune-teller and exclaimed, "I dreamt I had a blue cat that brought me and my kingdom great luck and prosperity. But then the blue cat ran from the palace, and all of the good fortune immediately vanished. Fortune-teller, you must interpret this dream for me."

The fortune-teller responded, "We must find a blue cat, for it is sure to bring you all the great things from your dream. Without it, you and your kingdom will be doomed to bad fortune."

The king immediately ordered his entire kingdom to find the blue cat. But despite their best efforts, not one had been located after several weeks. The king nervously feared that his kingdom would be doomed soon, and offered a reward of great riches as well as his daughter's hand in marriage to any man who found the elusive cat.

Upon hearing this, one young man became determined to get a blue cat, especially since he adored the princess. Lo and behold, he presented the king with a blue cat the very next day.

The king was relieved. He sat the cat on the throne with him, and his kingdom seemed to prosper just like the fortune-teller had forecasted it would. The king was pleased, and gave the young man the riches and the princess' hand in marriage.

But rumors persisted throughout the palace that the young man had simply painted a cat blue and tricked the king. In fact, everyone except the king noticed that the "blue" cat was the same size and had the same colored eyes as the now-absent white cat that used to be the king's favorite. Nevertheless, nobody told the king about the prevailing suspicions.

Then one day the blue cat was missing. The king panicked, and ordered everyone in his palace to search for it. Hours passed before someone finally spotted it in the palace garden. But it had fallen into water and most of its blue dye was washed off.

The king saw this and was immediately enraged. "I must kill my daughter's husband for what he has done!" the king declared.

The princess, who had grown to love her husband and did not want to see him harmed, exclaimed, "Father, my husband made you the blue cat you wanted, and your kingdom has been happy ever since."

The king retorted, "He has endangered my kingdom by giving me a counterfeit. That blue cat he gave me is actually the white cat I already had! My luck depends on a blue cat."

The princess responded, "The 'good luck' of the blue cat is dependent on what you believe, and my husband's actions have showed you this. Everything was OK when you thought that the white cat was a blue cat. Your white cat is just like the 'lucky' blue cat if you think it is."

Iran: What Are You Doing?

A busy businessman was walking towards the bazaar one day, and noticed a man wearing simple clothing lying in the grass, leisurely enjoying himself in the sunlight in the midst of all of the business going on around him. After watching him lay there for a few minutes, the businessman curiously asked, "What are you doing?"

The man replied, "I am just enjoying this moment."

"Listen," the businessman retorted, "you should be working. It is a weekday."

"Well," the man said, "I usually just work a few days a week until the late morning running my business. It is pretty fun, but I don't want to do it all day, and although I am not wealthy, I am financially secure. So I just spend the rest of the day as I wish, and right now I am enjoying the sunlight and watching the people go by, and later on I will go to the teahouse and chat with a few friends."

"This is nonsense!" the businessman replied. "I have a much better way for you to live your life. Look at me. I am rapidly expanding my business as we speak, and am building factories making textiles. You should get up right now, abandon what you have been doing, and do something more useful."

"What?"

"Get up, go work on your business right now until night and make more money."

"And then what."

"And then get up tomorrow and work from sunup till sundown."

"And then what?"

And then you can work hard for 60 or 70 hours a week like me, and use your money and build a big business, and build a future."

"And then what?"

"And then you can buy a big house."

"And then what?"

"And then maybe after years of devoting yourself and making money, then you can just relax, go outside and sit in the sun, and enjoy life—just like I will be doing in ten years from now."

"Tell me this," the man replied. "What am I doing right now?'

Nepal: Tiger Hunting

A needle, a seed, a rock, and a hammer were in the jungle one day. They found an empty tiger's cave, and devised a plan to hunt the tiger. They all took their positions, and waited for the tiger to return.

When the tiger finally arrived, he went to sit down, and he landed on the needle. As the tiger shouted in pain, the seed jumped into the tiger's eye, and the rock tripped him so that he fell right under where the hammer was waiting. When the timing was right, the hammer dropped onto the tiger's head, hitting him extremely hard and killing him.

Thus, through their good planning, organization, and unity; a needle, a seed, a small rock, and a hammer accomplished the impossible-looking task of killing a tiger.

Preface to Religion Section

The next few chapters cover various religions, and their writings, sayings, quotes, etc.

It is not my goal to promote or dispromote any types of religion or belief in this chapter and in this book. The following religion-related chapters are primarily focused on drawing out wisdom and spiritual subjects from various texts and quotes.

Throughout the chapters, I have only chosen references to God that are in the most general sense, or are used to establish certain philosophical and spiritual points.

I have also included "non-religious" thought such as atheism and agnosticism in a separate chapter, as well as schools of thought such as deism, pantheism, and humanism in another chapter.

Judaism

Judaism began as the religion of the ancient Hebrews. According to Jewish scriptures, the religion's early foundations began with the prophet Abraham (a nomad and leader from the Middle East) around the 1900s BC; and then after many Hebrews were enslaved in Egypt as several centuries passed, the Jewish God YHWH (a.k.a. Elohim) and the prophet Moses freed the enslaved Hebrews around the 1300s BC. According to the scriptures, God led them out of Egypt in a move known as the Exodus, and established a covenant with them.

The Hebrews / Jews later moved into an area known as Canaan in the 1200s BC, and had an Empire or major presence there on-and-off from around the 1200s BC to the 100s AD (see the Jewish Proverbs section of the Middle Eastern Proverbs chapter for more info on this Empire.)

Religious historians point to Judaism as among the world's earliest monotheistic (having one God) religions. Aspects of Judaism have also integrated into many of the world's other religions, including Christianity and Islam. There are about 14 million Jews in the world today.

Central to the Jewish faith is the scripture known as the *Tanakh* (alternate spelling *Tanach*, a.k.a. the *Jewish Bible*). The *Tanakh* is one of the earliest texts in world history that is still widely read today, and is also a central text among Christians, who refer to it as the *Old Testament Bible*.

The *Tanakh* is a series of various works combined, and is considered by many scholars to have been written, edited, and organized into its current form over a period lasting from around 1300 BC to 90 AD. It is organized into three parts: *Torah*, *Nevi'im* (Prophets), and *Ketuvim* (Writings). Many well-known Biblical proverbs come from a section / book in the *Ketuvim* that is aptly named *Proverbs*.

Many Jews also study a series of "Rabbinic" Judaism texts known as the *Mishnah*, the *Talmud* (which also contains the *Mishnah*), and the *Midrash*, which are based on teachings, traditions, and various commentaries that were passed down orally, and then written from the 200s AD to 600s AD.

Some other themes of Judaism include the various laws contained in the *Tanakh*, *synagogues* (temples), *rabbis* (religious leaders), holidays such as *Rosh Hashanah* (New Year), *Yom Kippur* (Day of Atonement), and *Pessach*/Passover (which commemorates the Exodus), *kashrut*/kosher dietary laws, *Shabbat*/Sabbath (the day of rest in each week), circumcision, *mitzvah* (a commandment, duty, or good deed), and *bar* & *bat mitzvah* ceremonies signifying the passage into early adulthood.

Tanakh / Old Testament Bible Passages

Note: The Tanakh is usually organized into Books, then Chapters, and then Verses. Each passage below is followed by those identifications in parentheses. These passages are based on the widely used King James Version (KJV) Bible translation, with some minor changes made for improved clarity.

And God said unto Moses, "I am that [/ *who*] I am"… (Exodus 3:14)

…Let my people go… (Exodus 8:1)

You shall not bear false witness against your neighbor. (Exodus 20:16)

The Lord lifts up his countenance upon you, and gives you peace. (Numbers 6:26)

… The Lord is one. (Deuteronomy 6:4)

… Behold, I will do a new thing; now it shall spring forth; shall you not know it? I will even make a way in the wilderness, and rivers in the desert. (Isaiah 43:18-19)

For now I will break his yoke off of you, and will burst your ropes of bondage. (Nahum 1:13)

Create in me a pure heart… and renew a right spirit within me. (Psalms 51:10)

I am a stranger in [/ *on*] the earth... (Psalms 119:19)

Discretion shall preserve you; understanding shall keep you. (Proverbs 2:11)

Happy is the man that finds wisdom, and the man that gets understanding. (Proverbs 3:13)

My son, keep sound wisdom and discretion; and do not let them depart from your eyes. (Proverbs 3:21)

Keep your heart with all diligence; for out of it are the issues of life. (Proverbs 4:23)

…Wisdom is better than rubies; and all the things that may be desired are not to be compared with it. (Proverbs 8:11)

A fool finds it sporting to do mischief, but a man of understanding delights in wisdom. (Proverbs 10:23)

A gossip reveals secrets, but he that is of a faithful spirit conceals the matter.
(Proverbs 11:13)

He that diligently seeks good procures favor; but he that seeks mischief, it shall come unto him. (Proverbs 11:27)

Every prudent man deals with knowledge, but a fool lays open his folly. (Proverbs 13:16)

The wisdom of the prudent is to understand his way, but the folly of fools is [self] deceit. (Proverbs 14:8)

All the days of the afflicted are evil; but he that is of a merry heart has a continual feast. (Proverbs 15:15)

Better is a dinner of herbs where there is love than a stalled ox [*kept in a stall for fattening*] with hatred. (Proverbs 15:17)

A man has joy by the answer of his mouth; and a word spoken in due season, how good is it! (Proverbs 15:23)

How much better is it to get wisdom than gold!... (Proverbs 16:16)

...He that rules his spirit [is better] than he that takes a city. (Proverbs 16:32)

He that has knowledge spares his words, and a man of understanding is of an excellent spirit. (Proverbs 17:27)

He that answers a matter before he listens to it, it is a folly and shame unto him.
(Proverbs 18:13)

…There is a [type of] friend that sticks closer than a brother. (Proverbs 18:24)

He that gets wisdom loves his own soul; he that keeps understanding shall find good. (Proverbs 19:8)

Cease, my son, to hear the instruction that causes you to err from the words of knowledge. (Proverbs 19:27)

Even a child is known by his doings… (Proverbs 20:11)

He that goes about as a gossip reveals secrets—therefore, meddle not with him that continuously runs his mouth. (Proverbs 20:19)

A prudent man foresees the evil and protects himself from it…(Proverbs 22:3)

Do you see a man diligent in his business? He shall stand before kings… (Proverbs 22:29)

Do not labor excessively to be rich—use your wisdom and cease doing so. (Proverbs 23:4)

For as he thinks in his heart, so is he…(Proverbs 23:7)

For a just man falls seven times, and rises up again… (Proverbs 24:16)

A word fitly spoken is like apples of gold in settings of silver. (Proverbs 25:11)

He that has no rule over his own spirit is like a city that is broken down and without walls. (Proverbs 25:28)

Boast not of tomorrow—for you know not what a day may bring forth. (Proverbs 27:1)

As water reflects face to a face, so does a heart reflect man to a man. (Proverbs 27:19)

Great men are not always wise, and neither do the aged [always] understand judgment. (Job 32:9)

For, see, the winter is past, the rain is over and gone. The flowers appear on the earth; the time of the singing of birds has come, and the voice of the turtle is heard in our land. (Song of Solomon 2:11-12)

To every thing there is a season, and a time to every purpose under the heaven:

A time to be born, and a time to die;
A time to plant, and a time to pluck up that which is planted;
A time to kill, and a time to heal;
A time to break down, and a time to build up;
A time to weep, and a time to laugh;
A time to mourn, and a time to dance;
A time to cast away stones, and a time to gather stones together;
A time to embrace, and a time to refrain from embracing;
A time to get, and a time to lose;
A time to keep, and a time to cast away;
A time to tear, and a time to sew;
A time to keep silence, and a time to speak;
A time to love, and a time to hate;
A time of war, and a time of peace. (Ecclesiastes 3:1-8)

So I perceive that there is nothing better than that a man should rejoice in his own works, for that is his portion… (Ecclesiastes 3:22)

The fool folds his hands together, and eats his own flesh. (Ecclesiastes 4:5)

Better is a handful with quietness than both the hands full with travail and vexation of spirit. (Ecclesiastes 4:6)

Behold that which I have seen: it is good and comely for one to eat and to drink, and to enjoy the good of all his labor that he takes under the sun all the days of his life which God has given him, for it is his portion. (Ecclesiastes 5:18)

It is better to hear the rebuke of the wise, than for a man to hear the song of fools.
For as the crackling of thorns under a pot, so is the laughter of the fool—this also is vanity. (Ecclesiastes 7:5-6)

For to him that is joined to all the living there is hope: for a living dog is better than a dead lion. (Ecclesiastes 9:4)

I returned, and saw under the sun, that the race is not [always] to the swift, nor the battle to the strong, neither yet bread to the wise, nor yet riches to men of understanding, nor yet favor to men of skill; but time and chance happens to them all. (Ecclesiastes 9:11)

Both riches and honor come of you, and you reign over all; and in your hand is power and might; and in your hand it is to make great and to give strength unto all. (I Chronicles 29:12)

Mishnah, Talmud, and *Midrash* Passages

If I am not for myself, who will be for me? And if I am only for myself, what am I?   And if not now, when?

The sun will set without your assistance.

Who is honored? He who honors mankind.

Slander no one, whether brother or not your brother, whether a Jew or not a Jew.

Live well. It is the greatest revenge.

Examine the contents, not the bottle.

Do not conclude that someone is good before you have observed how he acts at home.

Never expose yourself unnecessarily to danger.

Christianity

Christianity is based on the teachings of Jesus Christ, who lived in the 00s BC and 00s AD. In fact, the year 0 on most calendars around the world is based on the birth of Jesus, although the current consensus is that he was actually born closer to the year 4 BC.

Jesus was born and raised Jewish, and then preached a distinct new religious teaching somewhat related to Judaism. He lived in the Roman province of Palestine (current Israel, Palestine, and Jordan), and spent much of his life in the cities of Nazareth and Jerusalem. He spoke mainly Aramaic.

After gaining a following of people and transmitting his ideas to twelve disciples known as Apostles, Jesus was later crucified (executed by being nailed to a cross) by his opponents, probably in 30 AD or 33 AD. Christians believe that Jesus died for people's sins, and he was resurrected after his death, spent 40 more days on Earth and spoke to several people, and then ascended to Heaven. Christians use the cross as a symbol of Jesus and their religion.

The various sects of Christianity differ on their view of the divinity of Jesus, but most believe that he was the son of God, or God in human form. Most Christians also believe in a divine Trinity, or three forms of God: God the Father, God the Son (Jesus), and God the Holy Spirit.

Christianity became the state religion of the Roman Empire in the 300s AD, and has spread worldwide over time. There are about 2 billion Christians in the world today, making it the world's most followed religion.

Central to the Christian faith is the book titled the *Bible*, which is considered the most influential, widely translated, and best selling book ever. The *Bible* contains a section known as the *New Testament* in addition to the Jewish *Tanakh* scriptures, which Christians refer to as the *Old Testament*. (See the chapter on Judaism for info on and passages from the *Old Testament / Tanakh*)

The *New Testament*, which is a collaboration of several different works, was written around 30 AD to 120 AD, and compiled into its current organization in the 300s. Of the 27 books in the *New Testament*, the first four (Matthew, Mark, Luke, and John) are referred to as the Gospels. They make up about half of the New Testament, and are considered accounts of the life and messages of Jesus.

There are three main branches of Christianity: Roman Catholicism, Eastern Orthodoxy, and Protestantism. Protestantism contains many various sects / denominations, including Adventist, Amish, Anglican, Baptist, Christian Science, Episcopal, Lutheran, Mennonite, Methodist, Pentecostal, Presbyterian, and Society of Friends (Quaker). Another notable branch of Christianity is the Church of Latter-day Saints (Mormon).

Some Christian themes include holidays such as Christmas (celebration of the birth of Jesus) and Easter (feast / celebration of the resurrection of Jesus), baptism (a holy ceremony involving water), churches, priests, mass (the main Catholic religions service), the Catholic organizational hierarchy headed by the pope, the Sabbath (the day of rest in each week), and penance of sins (used mainly by Catholics and Orthodox).

New Testament Bible Passages

Note: The Bible is generally organized into Books, then Chapters, and then Verses. Each passage below is followed by those identifications in parentheses. These passages are based on the widely used King James Version (KJV) Bible translation, with some minor changes made for improved clarity.

Blessed are the pure in heart... (Matthew 5:8)

Blessed are the peacemakers... (Matthew 5:9)

Let your light so shine before men, that they may see your good works... (Matthew 5:16)

And why do you behold the speck that is in your brother's eye, but don't consider the beam that is in your own eye? Or how can you say to your brother, "Let me pull out the speck out of your eye," and at that time a beam is in your own eye? ...First cast out the beam out of your own eye; and then shall you see clearly to cast out the speck out of your brother's eye. (Matthew 7:3-5)

Ask, and it shall be given you; seek, and you shall find; knock, and it shall be opened unto you—for everyone that asks receives; and he that seeks finds; and to him that knocks it shall be opened. (Matthew 7:7-8)

Therefore in all things, whatsoever you would have others to do to you, you should also do so to them... (Matthew 7:12)

For what is a man profited, if he shall gain the whole world, and lose his own soul? Or what shall a man give in exchange for his soul? (Matthew 16:26)

...Unless you are converted and become like little children, you shall not enter into the kingdom of heaven. (Matthew 18:3)

... Love your neighbor as yourself. (Matthew 19:19, and also in Matthew 22:39)

...Many are called, but few are chosen. (Mathew 22:14)

And if a house is divided against itself, that house cannot stand. (Mark 3:25)

And as you would have others do to you, you should do to them likewise. (Luke 6:31)

A good man brings that which is good from the good treasure of his heart... (Luke 6:45)

For what is a man advantaged if he gains the whole world, and loses himself or be cast away? (Luke 9:25)

...Take heed, and beware of covetousness; for a man's life does not consist of the abundance of the things that he possesses. (Luke 12:15)

...The kingdom of God is within you. (Luke 17:21)

Don't be surprised that I said unto you, "You must be 'born again.'" (John 3:7)

You shall know the truth, and the truth shall make you free. (John 8:32)

... Love one another. (John 13:34)

...If you have any word of encouragement for the people, say it. (Acts 13:15)

That they should seek the Lord, if haply they might feel after him, and find him, though he be not far from every one of us; for in him we live, and move, and have our being... (Acts 17:27-28)

Therefore, you who teach another, do you not teach yourself? You who preach that a man should not steal, do you steal? (Romans 2:21)

...If the roots are holy, so are the branches. (Romans 11:16)

And don't be conformed to this world; but be transformed by the renewing of your mind... (Romans 12:12)

Be in harmony with each other… (Romans 12:16)

If it is possible, as much as it depends on you, live peaceably with everyone. (Romans 12:18)

Let us therefore follow after the things which make for peace, and things wherewith people may elevate one another. (Romans 14:19)

Don't you know that you are the temple of God, and that the Spirit of God dwells in you? (I Corinthians 3:16)

Let no man deceive himself. If any man among you seems to be wise in this world [just because of a faulty public opinion], let him become a "fool" so that he may be wise. (I Corinthians 3:18)

… I will not be enslaved by anything. (I Corinthians 6:12)

There are no temptations that come to you that are not [also] common to others… (I Corinthians 10:13)

…[Unless you] speak with words that are easily understood, how will it be known [by anyone] what is spoken [by you]? [It will be like] you are speaking into the air. (I Corinthians 14:9)

Be not deceived: evil communications corrupt good character. (I Corinthians 15:33)

Now the Lord is that Spirit, and where the Spirit of the Lord is, there is liberty. (II Corinthians 3:17)

We are troubled on every side, yet not distressed; we are perplexed, but not in despair; persecuted, but not forsaken; cast down, but not destroyed; (II Corinthians 4:8-9)

While we look not at the things that are seen, but at the things which are not seen; for the things that are seen are temporal; but the things that are not seen are eternal. (II Corinthians 4:18)

… Let us cleanse ourselves from all impurities of the body and spirit… (II Corinthians 7:1)

…Whatsoever a man sows, that shall he also reap. (Galatians 6:7)

Therefore, as we have the opportunity, let us do good unto all people...(Galatians 6:10)

And be renewed in the spirit of your mind; (Ephesians 4:23)

And be kind to one to another, tenderhearted, forgiving one another, (Ephesians 4:32)

Make the best of the [/ *each*] moment [/ *time*]... (Ephesians 5:16)

Finally, brethren, whatsoever things are true, whatsoever things are honest, whatsoever things are just, whatsoever things are pure, whatsoever things are lovely, whatsoever things are of good report; if there be any virtue, and if there be any praise, think on these things. (Philippians 4:8)

And that you study to be quiet, and do your own business, and work with your own hands, as we commanded you, that you may walk honestly toward them that are without, and that you may have lack of nothing. (I Thessalonians 4:11-12)

... Elevate and encourage one another... (I Thessalonians 5:11)

Test all things; and stick to what is good; (I Thessalonians 5:21)

... Do not become weary of doing good. (II Thessalonians 3:13)

That they do good, that they be rich in good works, ready to distribute, willing to communicate; storing up for themselves a good foundation against the time to come, that they may lay hold on genuine life. (I Timothy 6:18-19)

...[God gave us a spirit of] power, love, and sound mind; (II Timothy 1:7)

Don't get involved in foolish and ignorant issues, knowing that they begin quarrels. (II Timothy 2:23)

Unto the pure all things are pure... (Titus 1.15)

...Avoid foolish questions, and genealogies, and contentions, and strivings about the law—for they are unprofitable and vain. Warn a conflicting person once, and then once again [if necessary], but no more than that. (Titus 3:9-10)

My brethren, consider it all joy when you fall into diverse challenges. Know this, that the trying of your faith develops perseverance. And let perseverance have her supreme work, that you may be supreme... (James 1:2-4)

Blessed is the man that endures during challenges... (James 1:12)

But those of you who only hear the word are deceiving your own selves. For anybody [who] hears [the] word but does not apply it is like a man who looks at his face in a mirror, sees himself and then goes his way, and without delay forgets what manner of man he was. (James 1:22-24)

... Resist the devil, and he will flee from you. Draw near to God, and he will draw near to you... (James 4:7-8)

... What is your life? ... (James 4:14)

But, beloved, be not ignorant of this one thing: that one day is with the Lord as a thousand years, and a thousand years as one day. (II Peter 3:8)

He that does not love does not know God; for God is love. (I John 4:8)

Islam

Islam began was founded by Muhammad in the 600s AD in Arabia. Islam shares some of the core beliefs of Judaism and Christianity, and also recognizes many prominent figures of those religions, including Jesus, Moses, and especially Abraham. Muslims (people who follow the Islam faith) consider Muhammad to be God's last messenger.

Muhammad was born in the Arabic city of Mecca around 570 AD. In the early 600s, he began preaching a new religious doctrine with some similarities to the Christian and Jewish religions, and he became a religious leader who attracted a group of followers.

However, Muhammad met opposition with Meccans who followed Mecca's traditional religious practices, and he decided to regroup in the city of Medina (a.k.a. Yathrib). After sending many of his followers to Medina, Muhammad made a pilgrimage from Mecca to Medina in 622, and established a Muslim community there. That pilgrimage, referred to as *hijra*, is the starting date on the Muslim calendar.

In 630, Muhammad and the Muslims conquered Mecca, and by the time of Muhammad's death in 632, they controlled most of Arabia. Muslim leaders such as Abu Bakr and his successors extended that territory throughout Arabia and beyond, and a united Muslim Empire lasted until the 1200s.

There are currently about 1.3 billion Muslims worldwide. The regions with the highest Muslim populations are mainly in Asia and Northern Africa, particularly in Indonesia, Pakistan, Bangladesh, and Middle Eastern countries.

Islam is an Arabic word that means submission / surrender to God. Muslims refer to God as *Allah*, an Arabic term that is not exclusive to Islam, and is used by many Middle Easterns who belong to other religions.

Islam is based on a holy scripture known as the *Quran* (alternate spelling *Koran*), which is a major influence on the conduct and lifestyle of Muslims. The book was written and put into its current form in the 600s AD. Like other religious scriptures of the world, the *Quran* has been translated into many languages; however, Muslims emphasize that the only authentic *Quran* is the original Arabic version.

Muslims also study *Hadith*, which are written recordings of the sayings and acts of Muhammad. There are numerous collections of *Hadith*, and Muslims often differ on which ones they consider authentic.

Some themes of Islam include *mosques* (houses of worship), *tahara* (ritual purification), *salat* (prayer, performed five times daily), *shahadah* (a proclamation of faith / bearing witness to God), *sawm* (a.k.a. *saum* or *siyam*; fasting from sunup to sundown during the Muslim month of *Ramadan*), *zakat* (almsgiving), and repentance for sins. Another main aspect of Islam is *hajj*, a pilgrimage to Mecca that Muslims are expected to perform at least once in their lifetime if health and finances permit.

Most Muslims belong to two main sects of Islam: Sunni and Shi'i (a.k.a. Shi'a or Shiite). Sunnis constitute about 85% of Muslims; Shi'is comprise about 10%, and are found primarily in Iran, as well as in Iraq and several other countries.

Quran Passages

Guide us on the right path... (1:6)

...[Why] Would you exchange what is better for what is worse?... (2:61)

...Wherever you turn, there is Allah's presence [/ *appearance* / *face*]...(2:115)

Remember Me, and I will remember you... (2:152)

... [The righteous are] steadfast in trial and adversity... (2:177)

Fight in Allah's cause against those who attack you, but begin not transgressions; for Allah loves not transgressors. (2:190)

...Do good, for Allah loves those who do good. (2:195)

Kind speech and forgiveness is better than charity followed by injury... (2:263)

... The grace of Allah is infinite... (3:74)

Let there be among you a community that invites goodness, enjoins what is right, and forbids what is wrong. Those are the people that will succeed. (3:104)

... [Those who guard (against wrong)] do not knowingly persist in what [wrong] they have done. (3:135)

...If you patiently persevere and guard against evil, it will be a determining factor of affairs. (3:186)

...When you judge between people... judge with justice...(4:58)

… [Allah] knows what you hide and what you reveal… (6:3)

Vision does not comprehend Him [*Allah*], and He comprehends [all] vision. He is the [knower of the] subtle, the aware. (6:103)

…Every soul gets what it deserves on none other than itself… (6:164)

… Eat and drink, but do not be excessive… (7:31)

…Be patient and persevering; for Allah is with those who patiently [/ *firmly*] persevere. (8:46)

…Maintain the straight path, and do not follow the path of the ignorant. (10:89)

…Whoever follows the right way does so for [the good of] his own soul, and whoever goes astray does so to his own detriment… (10:108)

…Allah does not change the condition of a people until they change it within themselves [*within their hearts / souls*]…(13:11)

… A good word is like a good tree. Its root is firm and its branches are in heaven, and it yields fruit in every season… But an evil word is like an evil tree uprooted from the earth. It has no stability. (14:24-26)

…Nothing on earth or in heaven is hidden from Allah. (14:38)

Allah imposes being just, doing good, and giving to family [/ *community*]; and He forbids all shamefulness, injustice, and rebellion…(16:90)

Whoever goes rightly, does so for his own soul; and whoever goes astray, does so to his own detriment. And the bearer of a burden cannot bear the burden of another…(17:15)

You shall not follow what you do not know—you must use your hearing, sight, and heart [/ *brain*]. (17:36)

Do not turn your face in contempt from others, nor walk insultingly [/ *arrogantly*] through earth. (31:18)

... He [*Allah*] is aware of what is in [people's] hearts [/ *brains* / *thoughts*]. (35:38)

... Avoid excessive suspicion... (49:12)

... Allah is aware of all you do. (57:10)

It is the most hateful sight to Allah when you say what you do not practice. (61:3)

And so I call witness by the sunset's glow,
And by the night and all that it drives on,
And by the moon when it becomes full,
That you shall surely travel from one stage to another. (84:16-19)

The preoccupation of abundance [in material wealth] diverts you [from higher things], (102:1)

Distress goes to all slanderers and libelers. (104:1)

He [*Allah*] neither begets, nor was he begotten. (112:3)

Muslim Proverbs, Teachings, Etc

Note: Most of these are based on or derived from Hadith entries.

The most ignorant one is he who does not learn from the world's changes. The richest one is he who is not trapped by greed.

Be generous but not wasteful; be economical but not stingy.

Feed the hungry, visit the sick, and free the captive who is unfairly confined.

Giving something to a needy man yields one reward, and giving the same amount to a needy relative brings two: one for the charity, and another for honoring the family.

Avoid greed, for greed in and of itself is poverty.

Be persistent in good actions.

The best man is he whose life is long and actions are good. The worst man is he whose life is long and actions are bad.

The quest for knowledge is every Muslim's obligation.

Seek knowledge from the cradle to the grave.

The person who gives life to learning does not die.

There is no greater wealth than wisdom, no greater poverty than ignorance, and no greater heritage than culture.

The truly learned are those who apply [/ *practice*] what they know.

Knowledge that remains on the tongue is very superficial; the main value and excellence of knowledge is to apply it.

Learn to know yourself.

Whoever knows his own self knows God.

Do what you should do when you should do it; don't to do what you shouldn't do; and when it is unclear, wait until you are more sure.

It is best to leave alone the things that do not concern you.

No one is truly true except he who is true in word, action, and thought.

Speak rightly or be silent.

Protect and honor the earth, for the earth is like your mother.

A bad [but] learned man is the worst of men; a good learned man is the best.

Time spent learning [/ *contemplating*] is better than time spent praying.

A variation of this:

An hour of contemplation is better than a year of prayer

All actions are judged by the motives that cause them.

Being alone is better than being in bad company, and being in good company is better than being alone; being silent is better than speaking of evil, and speaking of good is better than being silent.

Give the laborer his pay before his sweat is dry.

Riches do not originate from an abundance of material wealth, but from a contented mind.

Do not get involved in long religious discussions—they only result in making religion a complicated and confusing subject. God made religion easy and simple.

A true Muslim does not slander or abuse others.

Aim for compassion, and avoid oppression and impurity. Compassion is grace, and a lack of it is disgrace.

Make peace between one another.

The most honorable among you are those who carry themselves with the most outstanding conduct.

Sufism

Many people consider Sufism a mystical branch of Islam. Others define it as a mystical and spiritual teaching that is distinct from Islam, but is linked to Islam because most Sufis (people who practice Sufism) also follow Islam and intermix it with Sufism. Some historians trace the origins of Sufism to times that predate the founding of Islam.

Many Sufi teachings have some similarities to eastern philosophies such as Taoism, Zen Buddhism, and Confucianism (all of which are covered in separate chapters in this book).

Sufis have produced an enormous amount of literature over time, which accounts for a large percentage of the general philosophical works of the Middle East, as well as from nearby regions in India and Africa. Some Sufi philosophers that are well known in the western world include Jalal Al-Din Rumi and Hazrat Inayat Khan, who are both covered in this chapter.

Sufi Proverbs

Grasp the moment; you can't power a mill with water that has already passed by.

Those that have time and search for a better time will lose time.

Abundance can be had simply by knowingly receiving what has already been given.

Knowledge without its application is like water without wetness.

Never be enslaved to principles.

We are in this world, but not of it.

Behind every adversity lies a hidden possibility.

Bringing joy to one heart with love is better than one thousand repetitive prayer recitings.

Watching someone else eating will not satisfy you hunger; the spiritual experiences of others will not satisfy your yearning.

The treasure of joy is closer to you than you are yourself—so why should you go searching from door to door?

If you pick up a bee due to kindness, you will learn the limitations of kindness.

There would be no such a thing as counterfeit gold if there weren't real gold somewhere.

When a pickpocket sees a saint, all he sees are his pockets.

Wise company can also make you wise.

Asking good questions is half of learning

There is a difference between spending a night with a lover and a night with a toothache.

I searched for God, and found only myself. I searched for myself, and found only God.

A person who seeks God through logical proof is like someone who searches for the sun with a lamp.

Sufi Quotes / Passages

Amr ibn Uthman al-Makki

The Sufi acts corresponding to whatever is most fitting for the moment.

(Shaykh) Abu'l-Hasan Ash-Shadhili
(Lived in 1100s and 1200s) North African Sufi spiritual figure

The Sufi views his own experience as tiny bits of dust made visible by a ray of sunlight: neither real nor unreal.

(Farid Ud-Din/Al-Din) Attar
(Lived in 1000s and 1200s) Iranian Sufi Poet and writer of many books

[The Valley of] Understanding can be arrived at in various ways.

Your own heart is the living place of the Universe's essence.

Salih always told his students, "If you constantly knock at someone's door, one day it will be opened to you."

Rabia heard him say this and remarked, "Salih, how much longer do you intend to preach this in the future tense, saying 'will be opened?' Was the door ever closed?"

Salih bowed in acknowledgement.

Rabi'a
(Lived in 700s and 800s) Sufi poet

…Do not allow anyone to oppress your soul.

Where part of you goes, the rest of you will eventually follow.

Hafiz

You yourself are your own obstacle—rise above yourself.

I caught the joy virus last night when I was out singing beneath the stars.

Abu Hamid Al-Ghazali
(1058-1128) Influential Iranian-Middle Eastern Sufi philosopher and writer

…The distinctive aspect of mysticism is something that cannot be understood by study, but only by dhawq [*tasting / immediate experience*]… There is a big difference between knowing the meaning and the causes of health and satiety, and being healthy and satisfied.

Khawwas

All wisdom can be expressed in two phrases: What is done for you—allow it to be done. What you must do yourself—make sure you do it.

Abu Sa'id Ibn Abi'l Khayr
(967-1049) Persian Sufi poet

Take a step away from yourself—and behold—the Path!

… Know that you know nothing and are no one.

Kashani

The lower self is preoccupied with showing itself in ways that will gain other people's good opinions.

The lower self quickly gets bored of things. If it in someway is successful in getting what it wants, it will still not be satisfied. The lower self is unstable.

Qushayri

...[The lower self] constantly demands a person to act vainly in order to be complemented by others. Verily, there are plenty of spiritual seekers and holy people who are therefore controlled by their lower self.

Sufayan (or Sufyan) al-Thawri
(?-777) Sufi leader and teacher

If someone tells you, "You are a wonderful person!" and this pleases you more than if he said, "You are a bad person!" know that you are still a bad person.

Al-(or Ah-) Hujwiri
(?-1075) Sufi scholar and writer

[Once, Ibrahim bin Adham read an inscription a stone that said:] "You are not practicing what you know, so why do you seek what you do not know?"

There are two kinds of speech and two kinds of silence. Speech is either truth or falsehood, and silence is either realization or unattentiveness. The words of one who speaks the truth is better than silence, but for the person who makes up lies, his silence is better than his speech.

Bayazid (or Abu Yazid al) Bistami
(800-874) Sufi of Northwestern Iran

Early on, I was mistaken in four aspects. I endeavored to remember God, know Him, love Him, and seek Him. When I had reached the later stage [*or I had got there*], I realized that He remembered me before I remembered Him, He knew of me before I knew of Him, He loved me before I loved Him, and He sought me before I sought Him.

For thirty years I sought God. But when I reassessed the situation, I realized that it was He who sought me.

The thing we tell of can never be found be seeking, yet only seekers find it.

Al-Antaki

Act as if there were no one on earth but you, and no one in Heaven but God.

Ahmad Ibn Ata'Allah
(Lived in 1200s) Sufi master and writer

Whatever you think concerning God—know that he is different from that!

Al-Hallaj
(888-922) Sufi from Baghdad

I saw my Lord with the eye of the heart. I said, "Who are you." He said, "You."

(Muhammad) Ibn' Arabi
(1165-1240) Arabic Sufi teacher and writer of hundreds of books

Those who cherish God in the sun witness the sun, and those who cherish Him in living things observe a living thing, and those who cherish Him in lifeless things view a lifeless thing, and those who cherish Him as a unique and unequalled being see Him as such.

Beware of committing yourself exclusively to a specific belief so that you disbelieve everything else, or else you will miss out on much good—in fact, you will miss out on recognizing the authentic truth. God, the all-present and all-powerful, is not limited to any single belief. Wherever you turn, there is the face of Allah.

The entire world is truly imagination. Only He [God] is real reality. Anyone who understands this knows the secrets of the spiritual path.

(Maulana) Jalal Al-Din (or Jalaluddin) Rumi
(1207-1273) Iranian Sufi poet; among his writings include the very well known *Mathnawi*

A person cannot live in "if."

Be concerned with what you truly value; let the thief steal something else.

Conventional opinion hampers our souls.

You already possess the powerful mixture that will make you well—use it.

Appear as you are; be as you appear.

Each person has been made for some specific work, and the longing for that work has been put into every heart.

Ah! Joyous is the soul that saw its own faults.

The satiated man and the hungry man do not see the same thing when they look at a loaf of bread.

…People don't observe themselves, and thus they blame one another.

Your mission isn't to look for love, but simply to search and locate the barriers within you that have formed against it.

We waste our energy designing and carrying out plans to become what we already are.

The act of trying to find the way home is what convinces us we are lost. We're not lost; we're not alone; and we've never even left home.

Oh tongue; you are an infinite fortune. Oh tongue; you are also an infinite ailment.

Treasures and armies do not make a king. A true king is a king within himself.

Become your own fortune… Seek the bounty within yourself.

All darkness is followed by sunshine.

Outside of the concepts of misdeed and good deed, there is a field. I will meet you there.

If you—wandering Sufi—are looking for the supreme treasure, do not look outside. Look within, and seek that.

Although we appear to be asleep, there exists a wakefulness in us that guides the dream, and that will also eventually frighten us back to the truth of who we are.

Everything you observe has its roots in the unseen world. The forms may change, but the essence stays the same. Every awesome sight will disappear, and every sweet word will fade away; but do not be dejected—for their source is eternal, growing, branching out, and giving new life and new joy. Why do you weep? The source is in you, and this whole world is springing up from it.

Hazrat Inayat Khan
(1882-1927) Indian musician and Sufi teacher who is accredited with bringing Sufism to the West

No one should allow his mind to be a vehicle for others to use; he who does not direct his own mind lacks mastery.

The secret of life is balance, and the absence of balance is life's destruction.

A responsible person is worth more than a thousand men who labor.

All things become wrong when they are not in their right time or when they are not in their proper place.

You need not do something today [just] because you did it yesterday.

Worrying about the faults of others is an unnecessary addition to the worry we have over our own faults.

While man judges another from his own moral standpoint, the wise man looks also at the point of view of another.

Overlook the greatest fault of another, but do not partake of it in the smallest degree.

Do not take the example of another as an excuse for your own wrongdoing.

When speech is controlled, the eyes speak; the glance says what words can never say.

It is seldom that too little is said and too much is done, but often the contrary.

Many feel, a few think, and fewer still there are who can express their thoughts.

Wisdom is not in words; it is in understanding.

Speaking wisdom is much easier than living it.

One word of the truly inspired answers a hundred questions and avoids a thousand unnecessary words of explanation.

The mind is its question, and it is itself its answer.

Every soul has a definite task, and the fulfillment of each individual purpose can alone lead man aright; illumination comes to him through the medium of his own talent.

The present is the reflection of the past, and the future is the re-echo of the present.

The mystic retains something of childhood all through his life.

Wisdom existed before the wise; life existed before the living; love existed before the lover.

We start our lives trying to be teachers; it is very hard to learn to be a pupil.

Words that enlighten are more precious than jewels.

One single moment of a sincere life is worth more than a thousand years of a life of falsehood.

Reason is the illusion of reality.

Reality itself is its own evidence.

Many evils are born of riches, but still more are bred in poverty.

The whole world's treasure is too small a price to pay for a word that kindles the soul.

To be really sorry for one's errors is like opening the door of heaven.

Life is an opportunity, and it is a great pity if man realizes this when it is too late.

Insight into Life is the real religion, which alone can help man to understand Life.

To learn the lesson of how to live is more important than any psychic or occult knowledge.

The more a man explores himself, the more power he finds within.

He is an unbeliever who cannot believe in himself.

Man looks for wonders; if he only saw how very wonderful is the heart of man!

It is more important to know the truth about one's self than to try to find out the truth of heaven and hell

The source of the realization of truth is within man; he himself is the object of his realization.

There is no greater scripture than nature, for nature is life itself.

A study of life is the greatest of all religions, and there is no greater or more interesting study.

The lover of nature is the true worshipper of God.

As a child learning to walk falls a thousand times before he can stand, and after that falls again and again until at last he can walk; so are we little children before God.

God is the answer to every question.

What limits God? His name.

Vilayat Inayat Khan
(1916-) Worldwide spiritual teacher; son of Hazrat Inayat Khan

Have the courage to face the light of your own being.

Do you think that you aren't free? You *are* free, but you do not know
that you are free—and it is your not knowing that you are free that is
your limitation and your imprisonment. Realize your freedom, and you
are free.

Al-Suhrawardi
(Lived in 100s and 1200s) Sufi writer and theologian who lived in Baghdad
and Bengal / India

For people who hear about the Sufi teaching and put it into practice, it
becomes wisdom in their hearts, and others who listen to them will
benefit. But for those who hear but do not put it into practice, Sufism is
just talk that will be forgotten after several days.

Hinduism

Hinduism derives from various ancient religious beliefs. Its origins are uncertain, but it is believed to be influenced by the religion of the Ancient Indus Valley culture in India whose roots predate 2000 BC, combined with the ancient religion of various Aryan people who came to the region at various times, particularly around 1500 BC. As those ancient teachings flourished in the region, they developed into the distinctive religion of Hinduism.

Over time, Hinduism has become a diverse religion that varies widely among its practitioners, and also has developed many various scriptures. These scriptures are commonly put in such groups as the *Vedas*, the *Upanishads*, the *Mahabharata* (which contains the central Hindu text titled the *Bhagavad Gita*), the *Ramayana*, the *Puranas*, and many others. Most of these date from before 1500 BC to as late as 1000 AD.

It is difficult to determine whether Hinduism is monotheistic or polytheistic, and some conclude it is both and neither, and that it also differs between different sects of Hinduism. In Hinduism there are various gods such as *Brahma* (the Creator), *Vishnu* (the Maintainer), *Shiva* (the Destroyer), and many others. However, there is also a concept known as *Brahman* (not to be confused with the aforementioned Brahma, which is often considered like an agent of Brahman), which is often described as "the essence," the absolute, the supreme spirit, the ultimate reality, or God.

Hinduism also has a concept called *Atman*, which can be defined as breath / soul / universal soul / inner self / inner God / vital principle. Some people feel that a message of Hinduism is to realize that Brahman is Atman.

A main theme of Hindu belief is the idea that people's souls transfer (reincarnate) into a new body after death, and that this process happens over and over in a continuous cycle called *samsara*. Throughout these lives, a soul accumulates *karma* based on good or bad deeds, which always eventually come back to the soul. Hindus see most things that happen to someone as the result of karma accumulated in his/her current and former lives. Hindus also believe that the cycle of samsara can be escaped when a soul reaches a stage known as *moksh*a (liberation).

Most Hindus practice meditation and yoga. Another main theme of Hinduism is a social system where people are placed into a specific caste (social level based on a certain hierarchy) due to their heredity.

Hinduism is considered the source of many principles prevalent in Buddhism and Jainism. Today, India is still the primary land of Hinduism, but the religion is also followed in many other regions, including Malaysia, East Africa, regions nearby India, and many island countries. There are approximately 1 billion Hindus today.

Bhagavad Gita Passages

Note: These passages are clarified adaptations of the translation by Kashinath Trimbak Telano.

The undisciplined person eats too much, or doesn't eat enough. The undisciplined person sleeps too much, or doesn't sleep enough... The spiritual discipline that destroys suffering goes to the person who eats the proper amount of food, does the proper amount of exercise, performs the proper amount of work [/ *play*], and gets the proper amount of sleep.

The intelligence that is clear understands action and inaction, what should be done and what shouldn't be done, danger and the absence of danger, and freedom and bondage.

Although all people seem to be on different paths, they are all traveling to one goal: the goal of Self-Realization.

Through meditation, the Higher Self is seen.

...[The mind is] difficult to control, but it can be conquered... through regular practice.

There is no need for this weakness [of yours]—it is not worthy of you. Get rid of this base weakness of spirit; arise and conqueror your foes!

He who is not self-restrained will have no steadiness of mind or perseverance in the pursuit of self-knowledge. There is no tranquility for the person who doesn't persevere in the pursuit of self-knowledge—and without tranquility, how can there be happiness?

There is no existence for what is unreal, and there is no non-existence for what is real—to know the correct conclusion for both of these things is to know the truth. What pervades all of this is inexhaustible and indestructible—nothing can bring about its destruction.

It is better for a person to do his own duty, even if imperfectly, than to do another's duty well performed.

The devoted and discipline person who control's his mind will attain tranquility and oneness.

Know that nature and spirit both are without beginning, and that all developments and qualities to be produced from nature.

When one sees eternity in temporal things, and infinity in finite things; then one has pure knowledge.

The person with devotion... attains the highest tranquility; but the person who is without devotion... is tied down by his desires.

Devoted people cast off attachment and perform action to attain purity of self, with the body, the mind, the understanding, or even the senses— all free from individualistic notions.

A person whose self is not attached to external objects obtains the happiness that is in one's self, and by concentrating of the mind... obtains indestructible happiness

...[The devoted person who understands the truth] thinks he does nothing at all when he sees, hears, touches, smells, eats, moves, sleeps, breathes, talks, excretes, takes, opens his eyes, or closes his eyes... He knows that the senses deal with the objects of the senses.

A man should elevate his self by his Atman [*breath / soul / universal soul / inner self / inner God / vital principle*]. The Atman can be a person's friend, but it can also turn into his enemy. A person's self-control will make his Atman his friend, but without self-control, it will behave like his enemy.

When a man sees all the variety of things as existing in one, and all as emanating from that, then he achieves harmony with Brahman [*"the essence," the absolute, the ultimate reality, or God*]. This inexhaustible supreme entity, being without beginning and without qualities, does not act, and is not tainted... though stationed in the body.

Other Hindu Scripture Passages

You should keep your mind pure, for what a person thinks, he becomes—this is the eternal mystery... When the mind is silent... you can transcend the mind. (*Maitri Upanishad*)

Words cannot express the joy of a soul purified by spiritual meditation that has achieved harmonious oneness... (*Maitri Upanishad*)

The mind can be the source of bondage, or can be the source of liberation. (*Maitri Upanishad*)

Brahman [*"the essence,"* the absolute, the ultimate reality, or God] shines forth, vast, self-luminous, inconceivable, subtler than the subtle. He is far beyond what is far, and yet here very near at hand. He is seen here, dwelling in the cave of the heart of every conscious being. (*Mundaka Upanishad*)

He who knows Brahman [*"the essence,"* the absolute, the ultimate reality, or God] becomes Brahman. (*Mundaka Upanishad*)

Ask to know the infinite (*Chandogya Upanishad*)

The spiritual migration of life takes place in one's mind. (*Upanishads*)

The miserable tend to constantly notice other people's faults, even if they are as small as a mustard seed; and continuously shut their eyes against their own faults, even if they are as large as a vilva fruit. (*Garuda Purana*)

... The wise and intelligent practice attaining self-knowledge. (*Viveka Chudamani*)

Children and other family and acquaintances can free a father's debts, but no one can free another person's bondage. Other people can remove someone else's pain that is caused by something like a weight on the head, but only one's own self can end the pain caused by something like hunger. A sick person can get better through treatment such as an improved diet, but cannot be improved through treatment undergone by others.

Reality can be experienced only with one's own experience, but not through someone else's. (*Viveka Chudamani*)

…Wise men should seek to understand the truth of their own nature. (*Viveka Chudamani*)

[*The beginning of the world:*] There was neither non-existence nor existence; there was no air, nor the sky beyond it. What covered it? And where? And what contained it? Was water there, an unfathomed depth of water? There was neither death, nor was there immortality. There was no divider of night and day.

That One Thing, breathless, and breathed by its own nature—apart from it there was nothing else whatsoever. Darkness was concealed by darkness; all was indiscriminate chaos. Everything that existed then was void and formless, and by the great power of heat, that One Thing was born. Then desire arose—the primal seed born of the mind [/ *spirit*].

Sages who searched with their heart's thought know the existent's kinship in the non-existent. Their separation extended; what was above it, and what was below? There were begetters, powerful forces, free action here and energy up there.

Who really knows and who can declare from what origin this creation comes from? And the entity of this creation after it came about—who knows how it came into being?

He, the first origin of this creation, whether he formed it all or did not form it, he who observes this world in highest heaven... he knows it—or perhaps even he does not know. (*Rg / Rig Veda*)

Jainism

Jainism began in India in the 500s BC by a man known as Mahavira, who Jains regard as a hero and victor who found his Way to salvation. He is said by some to have lived near Siddhartha Gautama (the founder of Buddhism), and that they were both familiar with each other's teachings.

Jainism has some similarities to various aspects of Hinduism, but also has many distinct differences. The main themes of Jainism include asceticism (self-deprivation), self-discipline, *ahimsa* (non-injury to all living things), a love for all living things, non-attachment, *ratnatraya* (three jewels on the path to liberation: right belief, right knowledge, and right conduct), and purifying the *jiva* (soul). Jains follow this path in order to achieve *moksha* (liberation from karma).

Like Hinduism, Jainism is also based on karma, which accumulates in one's soul based on the soul's actions. Many Jain principles for achieving liberation are done to stop new karma and cleanse already acquired karma.

There are about 5 million Jains today, virtually all of whom live in India.

Jain Scripture Passages and Teachings

One who knows the inner [/ *spiritual*] [self] knows the external [universe] as well. One who knows the external [universe] knows the inner [/ *spiritual*] [self] as well. (*Akaranga Sutra*)

He who denies the world, denies the self; and he who denies the self, denies the world. (*Akaranga Sutra*)

See! There are men who control themselves; others pretend only to be houseless… (*Akaranga Sutra*)

You are your own friend… (*Akaranga Sutra*)

Understand one philosophical view through the understanding study of another. (*Akaranga Sutra*)

…Some, though instructed, have no good conduct. Let that not be your case! (*Akaranga Sutra*)

In the case of obtaining anything in excess, one should not hoard it. (*Akaranga Sutra*)

I have heard and realized that bondage and salvation are both within yourself. (*Akaranga Sutra*)

Even if a man overcomes thousands of powerful foes, it is even better if he conquers only himself. (*Uttaradhyayana Sutra*)

Fight the fight within—why fight external foes? He who overcomes himself through himself obtains joy. (*Uttaradhyayana Sutra*)

It is difficult to conquer oneself—but when that is conquered, everything is conquered. (*Uttaradhyayana Sutra*)

Like a wise man, trust nobody, and always be on the alert... (*Uttaradhyayana Sutra*)

Those who praise their own doctrines yet disparage other peoples' doctrines are not solving any problem. (*Sutra Kritanga*)

Discipline is the way to achieve liberation. (*Shilapahuda*)

Have benevolence towards all living things. (*Tattvartha Sutra*)

Rendering help to another is the function of all human beings. (*Tattvartha Sutra*)

Consider the family of humankind one. (*Jinasena, Adipurana*)

All living beings long to live.

Non-violence is the highest religion.

A soul's greatest mistake is not recognizing its real self, and can only be corrected by recognizing itself.

Know yourself, recognize yourself, and be immersed by yourself—and you will attain God-hood.

Every soul is independent.

Sikhism

Sikhism was founded in the 1400s in India by Guru Nanak. Sikhism is a distinct religion, but also has some similarities to a wide variety of other religions and eastern philosophies, including Hinduism, Sufism, Islam, Taoism, Buddhism, and Christianity.

For Sikhs, the concept of God is less of a personality-based being, and more accurately described as the Ultimate Reality / One / Truth, which is timeless, formless, unborn, self-existent, and above and within everything. Sikhs (people who follow the religion) consider themselves on a spiritual path to attain oneness with the Truth, to know it, and to live it.

Guru Nanak is the most venerated figure in Sikhism, and was also followed by nine other gurus. Central to Sikhism is the scripture known as the *Sri Guru Granth Sahib*, which was written primarily in 1604 and added to in 1704, and records various hymns from a variety of people, including those of Guru Nanak. The *Sri Guru Granth Sahib* is considered the "Final Guru" in the Sikh lineage of Gurus.

Sikh men wear turbans and have beards, and all have the surname *Singh*, which means lion. All Sikh women have the surname *Kaur*, which means princess. Both Sikh men and women wear a bracelet on their right wrist. Since Sikhs have been persecuted for much of history, many Sikhs often carry swords as a symbol of their willingness to defend their beliefs.

Some other themes in Sikhism include cooperation, commitment, righteousness, the importance of work, the equality of people, and an emphasis on the Sikh community.

There are currently about 22 million Sikhs in the world today, most of whom live in Punjab, India.

Sri Guru Granth Sahib Passages

[There is] one universal reality [/ *being*], and Truth is its Name.
Note: Known as "Ikk oan kaar sat naam" in its original Punjab language, this statement is the opening of the Sri Guru Granth Sahib, and is the main theme of Sikhism.

Realization of Truth is higher than all else; higher still is truthful living.

By purity of heart alone, the holy eternal is attained.

By conquering my mind, I have conquered the whole world.

Treat others as you would be treated yourself.

We know the Truth when our Soul knows the Way; and cultivating our bodies, we sow the seed of God.

Where speech will not succeed, it is better to be silent.

Yoga does not consist of going to distant places… or wandering around the world, or in ritual bathing.   To live pure amidst the world's impurities—this is practicing true yoga.

The world is a garden and the Lord is its gardener, cherishing all and neglecting none.

Why do you go to the forest to search for God? He lives in everything and is yet ever distinct—he lives with you, too.   Like a flower's fragrance and a mirror's reflection, God dwells inside everything. Seek him… in your heart.

He [*God*] is always near—don't think he is far... Recognize him within yourself.

… The wise practice spiritual wisdom.

Gather spiritual wisdom within your mind.

The jewel of spiritual wisdom was placed within the universe.

Let spiritual wisdom be your food, and compassion your attendant.

Let understanding be the anvil, and spiritual wisdom the tools.

Practicing truth, self-discipline and good deeds, the Gurmukh [*God-oriented person*] is enlightened.

Zoroastrianism

Zoroastrianism was founded by Zarathushtra (a.k.a. Zoroaster) around 1200 BC, although estimates on this date vary greatly. In early times, Zoroastrianism was the religion of Ancient Persia, and is considered by many to have a major influence on Judaism, Christianity, and Islam. By the 600s AD, Islam had replaced Zoroastrianism in most regions. Today, most of the current 200,000 Zoroastrians live in India, and the rest live in Iran and other parts of the world.

Zoroastrianism's main theme is choosing good over evil, and having good thoughts, good words, and good deeds. Zoroastrianism emphasizes that people have the free will to make the choice of good over evil.

A related ideal of Zoroastrianism is the concept of *Asha*, a term that refers to such things as truth, wisdom, righteousness, progression, and justice. Asha is the principle that Zarathushtis (people who follow Zoroastrianism) pattern their lives on.

The main deity of Zoroastrianism is *Ahura Mazda*, which translates to "Wise Lord" or "Lord Wisdom." Zarathushtis often use fire as a symbol of Ahura Mazda, and many Zoroastrian rituals and ceremonies are accompanied by fire.

The Zoroastrianism's main text is the *Avesta*, which has many parts and was put in final form around the 600s AD, although it is based on various texts and teachings complied and passed down for many centuries, many of which were destroyed during the times of Alexander of Macedon.

Zoroastrian Scripture Passages and Sayings

Note: Most of these are passages from the Avesta

Make your own self pure... [Every man] can win purity for himself by cleansing his heart with good thoughts, good words, and good deeds.

Doing good to others is not a duty—it is a joy, for it increases your own health and happiness.

If someone does not perform a duty owed to another, he becomes a thief of the duty.

In the family, may discipline overcome indiscipline, peace [overcome] hostility, charity [overcome] stinginess, devotion [overcome] arrogance, and truth speaking [overcome] false speaking.

He has gained nothing who has not gained the soul. He shall gain nothing who shall not gain the soul.

Think good and be righteous.

Be good, be kind, be humane, and be charitable; love others, console the afflicted, and pardon those who have done you wrong.

In this world... may peace triumph over discord.

That nature alone is good which refrains from doing unto another whatsoever is not good unto its own itself. (From the *Dadistan-i-Dinik*)

Shinto

Shinto is a religion native to Japan. It began in its earlier form around 300 BC, and was more resemblant of its current form around 400 AD.

Shinto is based on the belief of various *kami*, which are supernatural spirit beings / essences / forces that animate everything in the world. Shinto emphasizes themes such as family, community, tradition, nature, purity, cleanliness, harmony, *makoto* (sincerity), *jinja* (shrines), the sacredness of Mount Fuji, and rituals such as the annual *matsuri* (festival).

Shinto does not have a formal religious doctrine. There are several groups of Shinto scriptures, such as the *Kojiki* and the *Nihongi* (a.k.a. *Nihonshoki*), which were written in the 700s AD, and mainly contain creation accounts, tales of deities and/or people, and recordings of Japanese history. Shinto adherents also study various other early Japanese texts.

Shinto has had and continues to have a great deal of influence on Japanese culture and society, and is the origin of many Japanese customs such as removing shoes before entering a house, and taking a daily bath. It was also the official state religion of Japan from 1871 to 1945.

Although Shinto has a major influence on virtually all Japanese people, only about 4 million people consider themselves Shinto.

Shinto Sayings / Teachings

Makoto [*sincerity*] is the single virtue that binds the divine and man in one.

The best and surest way to be one with the divine is makoto [*sincerity*].

With makoto [*sincerity*], there is virtue.

Makoto [*sincerity*] is the mother of knowledge.

In governing, let us govern with true makoto [*sincerity*].

Makoto [*sincerity*] is the mind of the kami [*gods*]… if one has a mind of makoto, the kami will surely respond. (Ekken Kaibara, *Divine Injunctions*)

Time spent laughing is time spent with the kami [*gods*].

Admitting a fault is the beginning of righteousness.

The world is one great family.

Respect your ancestors.

Even in one single leaf on a tree, or in one blade of grass, the awesome Deity presents itself.

Our eyes might see unleanliness, but let not our *minds* see unleanliness. Our ears might hear some unlceanliness, but let not our *minds* hear uncleanliness.

Baha'i

The Baha'i faith is considered the newest of the world's widely practiced religions. Baha'i grew from the teachings of Persian (Iranian) man named Siyyid Ali Muhammad, who became known as the Bab. Beginning in 1844, the Bab attracted a large group of followers to his new theological movement, which has some relation to Shi'i Islam traditions. The Bab also predicted the coming of a new prophet.

The followers of Bab were persecuted and many of them were killed, and in 1850, opponents of the Bab executed him. His religious movement continued, and in 1863, a Babi (follower of the Bab movement) named Mirza Husayn Ali Nuri was recognized as the prophet that the Bab predicted, and became known as the prophet Baha'u'llah, which means Glory of God.

Baha'u'llah attracted many followers throughout his life, although he was persecuted numerous times by his opponents and was exiled and imprisoned on several occasions. He died in 1892, and the Baha'i religion continued to grow and spread dramatically, and currently has 7 million adherents.

The Baha'i faith emphasizes such themes as world unity, equality, and service to humanity. It also recognizes figures central to Judaism, Christianity, Islam, Hinduism, Zoroastrianism, and Buddhism.

Baha'i practices include daily prayer sessions, daily study of various sacred writings by Baha'u'llah and other Baha'i figures, and an annual nineteen-day period of fasting from sunrise to sunset.

Baha'u'llah Writings

It is not for him to pride himself who loves his own country, but rather for him who loves the whole world. The Earth is but one country, and mankind is its citizens.

The true seeker must, before anything else, cleanse his heart.

Strive to be shining examples for all of mankind.

Let your vision be world embracing, rather than confined to your own self.

The most beloved of all things in my sight is justice.

The well being of mankind, its peace and security, are unattainable unless and until its unity is firmly established.

How could you forget you own sins and busy yourself with the faults of others… Breathe not the sins of others so long as you yourself are a sinner.

Blessed and happy is he that arises to promote the best interests of the peoples and kindred of the Earth.

Be fair in your judgment, and guarded in your speech.

…[Be] a joy to the sorrowful.

My first counsel is this: possess a pure, kindly and radiant heart…

Native American Religions

The Native American culture has a wide and diverse variety of religions among their various tribes. A large percentage of Native Americans today practice their traditional religion. Several New Age religious practices (of both Native Americans and other people) also encompass various aspects of Native American religions.

In many ways, the religions of Native Americans overlap with the general Native American culture, proverbs, teachings, sayings, etc., which are covered in this book in the chapter on Native American Proverbs, Quotes, and Chants; and the chapter on The Lakota Native Americans.

Although it is difficult to refer to the various Native Americans under a single generalization, many of them have some prevalent themes in common, including:

the existence of spirit power in everything, which referred to by some Native Americans as *wakan*

the unity between the human world, nature, and the spirit world

the view of nature as the place where humans and spirits interact

an emphasis on living in balance and harmony with nature and with the spirit world

an interdependence of life forms

an emphasis on society, communal harmony, kinship, and cooperation

the sacredness and spiritual significance of nature and the earth; particularly objects in nature such as mountains, rivers, rocks, stars, and plants; as well as many animals, such as eagles, hawks, crow, owls, and deer.

the view of everything in its physical sense, its subtle sense, and its spiritual sense

symbols such as the circle and the number four (see the Lakota Native Americans chapter for more info on those symbols.)

the existence of a Great Power or Great Mystery, and various other gods an emphasis on health

an emphasis on self-discipline, and performing various tests of physical ordeals

purification practices, fasting, and vision-seeking

an emphasis on warrior culture

rituals, stories, dancing, art, chants, and music (mainly singing & drumming),

shamans

Native American Religion Quotes

Red Jacket a.k.a. Segoyewatha
(Lived in 1700s and 1800s) Seneca leader and orator

> We also have a religion that was given to our forefathers, and has been handed down to us, their children. It teaches us to be thankful, to be united, and to love one another. We never quarrel about religion.

Black Elk
(1863-1950) Lakota (Teton Sioux) holly man and writer

> ...[Peace] comes within the souls of men when they realize their relationship, their oneness with the universe and all its powers, and when they realize that at the center of the Universe dwells the Great Spirit, and that this center is really everywhere. It is within each of us. (From his book *The Sacred Pipe*)

A Lakota seer

> We are earth people on a spiritual journey to the stars. Our quest, our earth walk, is to look within, to know who we are, to see that we are connected to all things, and that there is no separation, only in the mind.

Shooter
Lakota (Teton Sioux) man

> All birds, even those of the same species, are not alike, and it is the same with animals and humans. The reason Wakan Tanka [*the Great*

Mystery, the supreme spiritual power in Sioux belief] does not make two birds, or animals, or human beings exactly the same is because each is placed here by Wakan Tanka to be an independent individual and to rely upon itself.

Zitkala Sa a.k.a. Red Bird a.k.a. Gertrude Simmons Bonnin
(1876-1938) Sioux Leader, writer, and musician

…The voice of the Great Spirit is heard in the twittering of birds, the rippling of mighty waters, and the sweet breathing of flowers. If this is Paganism, then at present, at least, I am a Pagan.

From the Creation Account of the Omaha

In the beginning, everything was in the mind of Wakonda [*God*].

Ohiyesa a.k.a. Charles Alexander Eastman
(1858-1939) Physician and writer

(Excerpts from his book *The Soul of the Indian*)

The original attitude of the American Indian toward the Eternal, the "Great Mystery" that surrounds and embraces us, was as simple as it was exalted. To him it was the supreme conception, bringing with it the fullest measure of joy and satisfaction possible in this life.

That solitary communion with the Unseen which was the highest expression of our religious life is partly described in the word bambeday, literally "mysterious feeling"…

The Indian loved to come into sympathy and spiritual communion with his brothers of the animal kingdom, whose inarticulate souls had for him something of the sinless purity that we attribute to the innocent and irresponsible child. He had faith in their instincts, as in a mysterious wisdom given from above; and while he humbly accepted the supposedly voluntary sacrifice of their bodies to preserve his own, he paid homage to their spirits in prescribed prayers and offerings.

…[The Indian] saw miracles on every hand—the miracle of life in seed and egg, the miracle of death in lightning flash and in the swelling deep! Nothing of the marvelous could astonish him; as that a beast should speak, or the sun stand still. The virgin birth would appear scarcely more miraculous than is the birth of every child that comes into the world, or the miracle of the loaves and fishes excite more wonder than the harvest that springs from a single ear of corn.

Let us not forget that, after all, science has not explained everything. We have still to face the ultimate miracle;—the origin and principle of life! Here is the supreme mystery that is the essence of worship, without which there can be no religion, and in the presence of this mystery our attitude cannot be very unlike that of the natural philosopher, who beholds with awe the Divine in all creation.

Every act of his [*the Indian's*] life is, in a very real sense, a religious act. He recognizes the spirit in all creation, and believes that he draws from it spiritual power. His respect for the immortal part of the animal, his brother, often leads him so far as to lay out the body of his game in state and decorate the head with symbolic paint or feathers.

African Religions

It is estimated that about 100 million Africans currently practice one of the 60+ different traditional African religions.   African religions are intertwined with African culture, proverbs, folktales, teachings, sayings, etc., which are covered in this book in the chapters on African Proverbs and African Folktales.

Although there is a diverse variety of African religions, many of them have several themes in common, such as:

the sacredness of the universe

the relation that things in the universe have between one another

the existence of a Supreme Creator God and various other gods

an emphasis on society, communal harmony, kinship, humanity, and cooperation

the existence of the spirit world, and the human interaction with it

various rituals, prayers, ceremonies, temples, and shrines

the divineness of nature

the religious significance of the sky, star, sun, and moon

the existence of an above world (the sky and its contents), an immediate world (the surface of the earth), and a sprit world below.

African Religion Proverbs, Quotes, Chants, Prayers, Etc.

Note: Most of these are identified by tribe and by country in parentheses, or by country only.

Nuer (Sudan) Prayer

Le us be at peace, let people's souls be relaxed… Remove all evil from our path.

Bushmen (South Africa) Prayer

When the moon dies every month, let the sin in me die with it. When the moon is reborn each month, let the good in me be reborn with it.

Galla (Ethiopia) Prayer

Dear God, at dawn I thank you for the good night you gave me, and ask you to give me a good day. Dear God, at dusk I thank you for the good day you gave me, and ask you to give me a good night.

Yoruba (Nigeria) Chant

The sun shines and directs its hot ray to us; the moon rises in its glory. The rain will come again and the sun will shine again, and God's vision moves over it. Nothing is hidden from him.

Pygmy (Zaire) Chant

In the beginning was God; today is God; tomorrow will be God. Who can make God's image? He has no body. He is like a word that comes from your mouth—that word; it is no more. It is past, and still lives—so is God.

Gikuyu (Kenya)Teaching

God has no father or mother, and no wife or children—He is all alone. He is not a child, nor is He an old man—He is the same today as He was yesterday. He does not eat food, and he does not have messengers.

Zulu (South Africa) Proverb

God is he who is of Himself.

Banum (Cameroon) Proverb

[*God is*:] He-who-is-everywhere

Bacongo (Congo) Proverb

[*God is*:] The marvel of all marvels

Yoruba (Nigeria) Proverb

Character is religion.

Igbo (Nigeria) Proverb

If you say yes, your [personal] God will also say yes.

Burundian Proverb

God knows the things of tomorrow.

Ovambo (Angola) Proverb

God has nothing hidden from him.

Hutu (Rwanda/Burundi) Proverb

If you pray to God for blessings at the same time you are sitting on a fireplace, he will give you ashes.

Ethiopian Proverb

We do not see God, we only see His works.

More African Proverbs

God conceals himself from the mind of man, but reveals himself to his heart.

God will outlive eternity

Humanism

Humanism is a term that can refer to many things, but in its general sense in modern times, it is the emphasis on human value, human needs, human life, human interest, humanity, society, and living a good, joyous, and useful life.   The general Humanist movement and philosophy is not necessarily part or not part of any other beliefs.

Since it is difficult to pinpoint what humanism is, it is also difficult to trace a history of it. Of course, throughout history, there have been many people that have emphasized a concern for one another and for human values, although not necessarily as far as taking it beyond religious beliefs. Many religions also preach a humanistic message.

Humanist quotes

Old Testament (Scripture of Judaism and Christianity) *Bible*

… Love your neighbor as yourself… (Leviticus 19:18)

Mishnah (Text of Judaism)

Who is honored? He who honors mankind.

New Testament (Scripture of Christianity) *Bible*

Therefore in all things, whatsoever you would have others to do to you, you should also do so to them… (Matthew 7:12)

… Love your neighbor as yourself. (Matthew 19:19, and also in Matthew 22:39)

… Love one another. (John 13:34)

Therefore, as we have the opportunity, let us do good unto all people…(Galatians 6:10)

And as you would have others do to you, you should do to them likewise. (Luke 6:31)

And be kind to one to another, tenderhearted, forgiving one another, (Ephesians 4:32)

… Elevate and encourage one another… (I Thessalonians 5:11)

Let us therefore follow after the things which make for peace, and things wherewith people may elevate one another. (Romans 14:19)

Muslim Teachings based on Hadith (Recorded Acts & Sayings of Muhammad)

Make Peace between one another.

Aim for compassion, and avoid oppression and impurity. Compassion is grace, and a lack of it is disgrace.

A true Muslim does not slander or abuse others.

Sri Guru Granth Sahib (Scripture of Sikhism)

Treat others as you would be treated yourself.

Shinto Saying

The world is one great family.

Buddhist Teachings based on sayings of the Buddha Siddhartha Gautama

Practice love, and give joy.

Be loving and kind.

In doing good, consider not just yourself, but also all of the universe's beings.

Cultivate loving-kindness.

Jainism Teachings / Scripture Passages

Have benevolence towards all living things. (*Tattvartha Sutra*)

Consider the family of humankind one.

Zoroastrianism Teachings / Scripture Passages

Doing good to others is not a duty—it is a joy, for it increases your own health and happiness.

Be good, be kind, be humane, and be charitable; love others, console the afflicted, and pardon those who have done you wrong.

That nature alone is good which refrains from doing unto another whatsoever is not good unto its own itself.

Writings of the Baha'i prophet Baha'u'llah

The Earth is but one country, and mankind is its citizens.

The well being of mankind, its peace and security, are unattainable unless and until its unity is firmly established.

Blessed and happy is he that arises to promote the best interests of the peoples and kindred of the Earth.

Jonathan Swift
(1667-1745) Irish writer of *Gulliver's Travels* and other books

We have just enough religion to make us hate, but not enough to make us love one another.

Voltaire a.k.a. Francois Marie Arouet
(1694-1778) French writer and philosopher

I know of no great men except those who have rendered great service to the human race.

William Pitt
(1708-1778) English statesman

We need a religion of humanity. The only true divinity is humanity.

Thomas Paine
(1737-1809) Influential English-American writer

The world is my country, all mankind are my brethren, and to do good is my religion.

Red Jacket a.k.a. Segoyewatha
(Lived in 1700s and 1800s) Native American Seneca leader and orator

> We also have a religion that was given to our forefathers, and has been handed down to us their children. It teaches us to be thankful, to be united, and to love one another. We never quarrel about religion.

Friedrich Wilhelm Nietzsche
(1844-1900) Influential German scholar and philosopher

> Since humanity came into existence, man has enjoyed himself too little. That alone is our original sin.

(Swami) Vivekananda
(1863-1902) Indian humanist and spiritual leader who tried to combine Indian spirituality with Western culture

> The only God to worship is the human soul in the human body.

(Swami) Sivananda
(1887-1963) Indian yoga master

> Doing good to others is the highest religion.

Adlai Stevenson
(1900-1965) American politician and Presidential candidate who also confounded the United Nations

> The human race is a family. Men are brothers. All wars are civil wars.

Katherine Hepburn
(1907-2003) American actress

> I believe there's nothing we can know except that we should be kind to each other and do what we can for other people. (*Ladies Home Journal* October 1991)

Sun Myung Moon
(1920-) Korean religious leader who founded the Unification Church

> I look at all the major world religions of the world as one big family.

Various Religious Theistic Quotes

Here are some various theistic (pertaining to God and the belief in God) quotes:

Origen
(Lived in 100s and 200s) Egyptian Greek Christian theologian, philosopher, and Biblical scholar

> God must not be thought of as a physical being, or as having any kind of body. He is pure mind. He moves and acts without needing any tangible space, size, form, color, or any other property of matter.

Saint Augustine (of Hippo)
(354-430) Christian bishop and philosopher

> God is an infinite circle whose center is everywhere and whose circumference is nowhere.

Meister Eckhart
(Lived in 1200s and 1300s) German mystical theologian

> God's seed is in us. With a wise and diligent farmer, it will thrive and grow up to God, whose seed it is; and correspondingly it will bear fruits of God-nature. Pear seeds grow into pear trees, nut seeds into nut trees, and God-seed into God.

Saint Catherine of Siena
(1347-1380) Christian Italian preacher and religious scholar

> All the way to heaven is heaven.

Joseph Albo
(Lived in 1300s and 1400s) Jewish scholar and theologian

> God is that which has no definition.

Francis Howgill
(1618-1669) Quaker (A Christian group) Preacher

> Men substitute tradition for the living experience of the love of God.

Blaise Pascal
(1623-1662) French mathematician, physicist, philosopher, and theologian

It is the heart that perceives God, and not the reason.

Isaac Newton
(1642-1727) One of the greatest scientists ever

The existence of a Being endowed with intelligence and wisdom is a necessary inference from a study of celestial mechanics.

Immanuel Kant
(1724-1804) Influential German philosopher

The human heart refuses to believe in a universe without a purpose.

William Cowper
(1731-1800) English Poet

Nature is but a name for an effect whose cause is God.

Joseph Joubert
(1754-1824) French philosopher

It is easy to understand God as long as you don't try to explain him.

Friedrich Von Schiller
(1759-1805) German dramatist and poet

The universe is one of God's thoughts.

Henry David Thoreau
(1817-1862) American writer, philosopher, and naturalist

The unconsciousness of man is the consciousness of God.

Edgar Cayce
(1877-1945) American meditation expert and author

He who understands nature walks with God.

(Sir) James Jeans
(1877-1946) English physicist and mathematician

If the universe is a universe of thought, then its creation must have been an act of thought.

From the intrinsic evidence of his creation, the Great Architect of the Universe now begins to appear as a pure mathematician.

Albert Einstein
(1879-1955) German-American physicist who is recognized as one of the greatest scientists of all time

I want to know His [*God's*] thoughts…

Swami (Papa) Ramdas
(1884-1963) Indian spiritual leader

Man is indeed God playing the fool.

Niels Bohr
(1885-1962) Danish physicist who won the Nobel Prize for Physics in 1922

It makes no sense to say the universe has no sense.

J.B.S. Haldane
(1892-1964) British geneticist

In ultimate analysis, the universe can be nothing less than the progressive manifestation of God.

(Sri) Nisargadatta Maharaj
(1897-1981) Indian spiritual leader

God is perfection itself, not an effort at perfection.

Theodore Munger
(Lived in 1800s and 1900s?) Christian minister

…No man can know himself as he is, and all the fullness of his nature, without also knowing God.

Isaac Bashevis Singer
(1904-1991) Jewish Polish American writer who won the Nobel Prize for Literature in 1978

God is the sum of all possibilities.

Sun Myung Moon
(1920-) Korean religious leader who founded the Unification Church

God is formless. If you think He is big, He is infinite; and if you think he is small, his is infinitesimal.

God is the subject of the heart. He has feelings of boundless sorrow and joy.

Sathya Sai Baba
(1926-) Indian spiritual leader

Steady perseverance alone will tame your mind, and it is only through a tamed mind that you can experience God.

Allan Sandage
(1926-) American astronomer who co-discovered the Quasar

God to me is a mystery, but is the explanation for the miracle of existence—why there is something instead of nothing. (From *NY Times*, March 12, 1991)

Gerhard Staguhn
(1952-) American physicist

If there was a big bang, the universe must have consisted of an infinite amount of energy concentrated in a single point. God knows where that came from.

Carl W. Miller

Belief in God is acceptance of the basic principle that the universe makes sense; that there is behind it an ultimate purpose.

Omraam M. Aivanhow

Wherever there are no limits, where Infinity and Eternity and Immortality exist, that is where God is.

Jewish Rabbinic Quote

God is like a mirror. The mirror never changes, but everyone who looks at it sees a different face.

Bengali Proverb

Unless a man is simple, he cannot recognize God, the Simple One.

Kurdish Proverb

Search yourself, and you will find Allah [*God*].

Ukrainian Proverb

God is looking for those who come to Him.

Religious scientist saying

God, the creator of the universe, can never be against learning the laws of what he has created.

Deism and Pantheism

DEISM

Deism is difficult to specifically define, but in general, Deists believe that there is a God, but that we can only rely on reason to perceive any religious matters. Most Deists also believe that God only revealed himself through the creation of the universe, and has not revealed himself in any other way since.

Deism was particularly popular in the US in the 1700s and 1800s as a distinct school of religious thought that was a response to both atheism and traditional theistic religions. Some of the founding fathers were considered deists, and many scholars believe that at least several of the early US presidents were either Deists, or on the borderline of being Deists.

Deist Quotes

Note: The people quoted here are not necessarily deists.

Thomas Paine
(1737-1809) Influential English-American writer

> Do we want to contemplate his power? We see it in the immensity of the creation. Do we want to contemplate his wisdom? We see it in the unchangeable order by which the incomprehensible whole is governed. Do we want to contemplate his munificence? We see it in the abundance with which he fills the earth… In fine, do we want to know what God is? Search not the book called the Scripture, which any human hand might make, but the Scripture called the Creation. (From *Age of Reason*)

Thomas Jefferson
(1743-1826) 3rd American president, scientist, writer, and lawyer

> Question with boldness even the existence of God; because if there be one, he must more approve of the homage of reason than that of blindfolded fear.

Henry David Thoreau
(1817-1862) American writer, philosopher, and naturalist

> There may be Gods, but they care not what men do.

Matthew Arnold
(1822-1888) English writer

All things seem to have what we call a law of their beings; whether we call this God or not is a matter of choice.

PANTHEISM

Pantheism is similar to Deism, and is also difficult to pinpoint what exactly it defines, but in general, Pantheism identifies the Universe and nature as all or part of the ultimate reality. It is not quite theism, and not quite atheism (the idea that there is no God), although pantheist thought generally is on the borderline of both. Some scholars feel that pantheism is belief in God, but that God to pantheists is not like the God with personality and certain qualities that is part of traditional theistic thought.

The term *pantheism* was first used in the 1700s, although pantheistic thought has definitely been around throughout history. Some people attribute various philosophies throughout the West and East as having pantheistic qualities.

Pantheist Quotes

Note: The people quoted here are not necessarily pantheists

Pantheist Saying

God is everything, and everything is God.

Baruch Spinoza a.k.a. Benedict de Spinoza
(1632-1677) Jewish/Pantheist Dutch philosopher and theologian

The more we understand individual things, the more we understand God.

All things which are, are in God. Besides God there can be no substance, that is, nothing in itself external to God.

The more you understand yourself and your emotions, the more you necessarily love God.

Matthew Arnold
(1822-1888) English writer

All things seem to have what we call a law of their beings; whether we call this God or not is a matter of choice.

John Burroughs
(1837-1921) American writer and naturalist

Can we describe form to infinite space? No more than we ascribe personality to God.

Joy in the universe, and keen curiosity about it all—that has been my religion.

Frank Lloyd Wright
(1869-1959) American architect and writer

I believe in God, only I spell it Nature.

Pablo Casals
(1876-1973) Legendary Spanish cellist and conductor

God, Nature. I call God Nature, or Nature God. And then comes this other thought: I am a miracle that God or Nature has made.

Hazrat Inayat Khan
(1882-1927) Indian Sufi teacher who is accredited with bringing Sufism to the West

The lover of nature is the true worshipper of God.

There is no greater scripture than nature, for nature is life itself.

Carl Sagan
(1934-1996) American astronomer and legendary science writer

But if by "God" one means the set of physical laws that govern the universe, then clearly there is such a God. This God is emotionally unsatisfying... It does not make much sense to pray to the law of gravity.

Atheism and Agnosticism

ATHEISM

In general, atheism is the idea or assertion that there is no God or divine beings. Some people label it as non-belief in God.

Although some sort of religion has predominated virtually the entire world over the last five thousand or so years, there has been some atheistic presence in most places in most of recorded history.

As for the time before recorded history (known as prehistory), history scholars are uncertain as to whether humans were theistic or atheistic. One archeological finding of an ancient human buried in Iraq was found to have decomposed flower petals in the dirt surrounding the body. Researchers believe that the flowers were put there by others in some sort of formal burial process. Some archeologists point to this find to suggest that early humans might have followed rituals or religious practices, although the issue of early religions is still relatively unknown.

Atheistic Quotes

Note: The following people quoted here are not necessarily atheists

Heraclitus
(Lived in 500s and 400s BC) Greek philosopher

> The universal process was not created by any God or any person. It infinitely was, is, and always will be, an everlasting fire.

Democritus
(Lived in 400s and 300s BC) Greek philosopher who enjoyed humor, and also came up with a theory of atoms

> Nothing exists except atoms and empty space; everything else is opinion.

Lucretius
(Lived in 00s BC) Roman / Latin philosopher and poet

> Nature is observed doing everything spontaneously of herself, without the influence of the Gods.

Charles De Montesquieu

(1689-1755) French philosopher

If triangles made a God, they would give him three sides.

Denis Diderot
(1713-1784) French philosopher and writer

If you want me to believe in God, you must make me touch him.

Thomas Paine
(1737-1809) English-American writer

My own mind is my own church.

Chevalier de Lamarck
(1744-1829) French naturalist

Life is purely physical phenomenon.

Napoleon Bonaparte
(1769-1821) French emperor who believed he was totally invincible

Everything is more or less organized matter.

If I had to choose a religion, then the sun as the world's life giver would be my God.

Auguste Comte
(1798-1857) French philosopher

The universe shows no proof of an all-directing mind.

John Stuart Mill
(1806-1873) British philosopher and economist

My father taught me the question, "Who made me?" cannot be answered, since it immediately suggests the further question, "Who made God?"

Walt Whitman
(1819-1892) American writer

There is no God more divine than yourself.

Charles Bradlaugh
(1833-1891) English philosopher and reformer

The atheist does not say, "There is no God," but he says, "I known not what you mean by God; the word God is to me a sound conveying no clear or distinct affirmation." (From his essay "A Plea for Atheism")

Mark Twain a.k.a. Samuel Langhorne Clemens
(1835-1910) Legendary American writer and lecturer

In religion and politics, people's beliefs and convictions are in almost every case gotten at second-hand, and without examination.

There is no God, no universe, no human race, no earthly life, no heaven, no hell. It is all a dream, a grotesque and foolish dream. Nothing exists but you. And you are but a thought—a vagrant thought, a useless thought, a homeless thought, wandering forlorn among the empty eternities! (From his short novel *The Mysterious Stranger*)

Thomas Hardy
(1840-1928) English poet and novelist

I have been looking for God for fifty years and I think if he had existed I should have discovered him.

Friedrich Nietzsche
(1844-1900) Influential German scholar and philosopher

There cannot be a God because if there were one, I could not believe that I was not He.

There is not enough love and goodness in this world to allow us to give some of it away to imaginary beings.

The concept of God was invented as the opposite of the concept of life.

Thomas Alva Edison
(1847-1931) Legendary American inventor

…Nature made us—nature did it all, not the Gods of the religions.

Remy de Gourmont
(1858-1915) French novelist, philosopher, poet, and playwright

God isn't all that exists. God is all that doesn't exist.

H.L. Mencken
(1880-1956) Influential American writer

When I die, I shall be content to vanish into nothingness... I do not believe in immortality, and have no desire for it.

Katherine Hepburn
(1907-2003) American actress

I'm an atheist, and that's it. I believe there's nothing we can know except that we should be kind to each other and do what we can for other people. (*Ladies Home Journal* October 1991)

Howard Kreisner
Talk show host

...I realized God was an extension of my imagination...

Starhawk
Writer

The cosmos is interesting rather than perfect, and everything is not part of some greater plan, nor is all necessarily under control.

Rick Reynolds

I believe to this day what I believed when I was eight—science.

Anonymous

Thank God I am an atheist.

AGNOSTICISM

Agnosticism does not take either side of religious beliefs or atheism. In general, agnostic thought states that it is indeterminate and impossible for humans to know (through experience) whether or not there is a God / Gods / divine beings.

Some people also feel that the term agnosticism also includes the related idea that it has yet to be determined but may or may not be able to determine whether or not there is a God / Gods / divine beings. So basically, the term agnostic generally refers to those who make no assertions of belief either for or against God / Gods / divine beings.

The term *agnosticism* originated in the late 1800s by T.H. Huxley, although there have clearly been people with agnostic beliefs throughout known history.

Agnostic Quotes

Note: The people quoted here are not necessarily agnostics

Protagoras
(Lived in 400s BC) Greek philosopher

> As to the Gods, I have no way of knowing if they exist or not, or what they are like.

Thomas Jefferson
(1743-1826) 3rd American president, scientist, writer, and lawyer

> Question with boldness even the existence of God; because if there be one, he must more approve of the homage of reason than that of blindfolded fear.

Ernest Renan
(1823-1892) French writer on a variety of topics

> Agnostic's Prayer: O God, if there is a god, save my soul, if I have a soul.

Clarence Darrow
(1857-1938) American lawyer, writer, and public speaker

> If there is any God in the universe, I don't know it. Some people say they know it instinctively. Well, the errors and foolish things that men have known instinctively are so many we can't talk about them. (From the book *Why I Am an Agnostic, and Other Essays*)

> I feel... that whether the universe had an origin, and if it had, what the origin is, will never be known by man. (*Why I Am an Agnostic, and Other Essays*)

Francis Thompson
(1859-1907) English Poet

Agnosticism is the everlasting perhaps.

Misc. Quotes on Religious Related Topics

Here are some more quotes about God, religion, and the Universal essence / origin that I couldn't fit into any of the other categories.

About God

Simonides
(Lived in 500s and 400s BC) Greek Poet

The longer I contemplate the subject of God, the more enigmatic [/ *obscure*] it becomes.

Voltaire a.k.a. Francois Marie Arouet
(1694-1778) French writer and philosopher

God is a comedian playing to an audience that is too afraid to laugh.

If God made us in His image, we have more than repaid the compliment.

If God didn't exist, it would be necessary to invent him.

William Blake
(1757-1827) English writer, mystic philosopher, and artist

Jesus Christ is the only God. And so am I. And so are you.

Friedrich Wilhelm Nietzsche
(1844-1900) Influential German scholar and philosopher

Which is it: is man one of God's blunders, or is God one of man's blunders?

The creator wanted to look away from himself—and consequently, he created the world.

I cannot believe in a God who wants to be praised all the time.

I would only believe in a God who knows how to dance.

If a God created the world, then he must have created man... as an eternal source of amusement in the midst of his rather dull eternity.

The "Kingdom of Heaven" is a condition of the heart; not something will come upon the earth or after death... The "Kingdom of God" is not something that one expects; it has no yesterday, and no day after tomorrow; it will not arrive in a thousand years; it is an experience of the heart; it is everywhere, it is nowhere.

Jules Renard
(1864-1910) French writer

I don't know if God exists, but it would be better for His reputation if He didn't.

Paul Valery
(1871-1945) French Poet and Essayist

God made everything out of nothing, but the nothingness shows through.

R. Buckminster Fuller
(1895-1983) American poet, philosopher, inventor, and architect

God is a verb, not a noun.

Arthur C. Clarke
(1917-) English scientist and writer

It may be that our role on this planet is not to worship God, but to create him.

Sun Myung Moon
(1920-) Korean religious leader who founded the Unification Church

You should speak with your mind—your inmost self. If it is sympathetic with others, you can become one with God and automatically know the truth of the Universe.

James W. Riley

When God sends rain…rain is my choice.

Bob Stokes

The world is proof that God is a committee.

About Religion

Thomas Paine
(1737-1809) English-American writer

Every religion is good that teaches man to be good.

George Sand
(1804-1876) (Female) French novelist

I appreciate and respect your faith, but cannot share it with you.

Henry David Thoreau
(1817-1862) American writer, philosopher, and naturalist

Your religion is where your love is.

Mabel Collins
(1851-1927) British writer and spiritual writer

Religion is always man-made. It cannot therefore be the whole truth.

George Bernard Shaw
(1856-1950) Irish writer on a variety of subjects who won the Nobel Prize for Literature in 1925

There is only one religion, though there are a hundred versions of it.

Henri Bergson
(1859-1941) French philosopher who won the Nobel Prize for Literature in 1927

The emotion felt by man in presence of nature certainly counts for something in the origin of religions.

Miguel de Unamuno
(1864-1936) Spanish philosopher and writer

The skeptic does not mean he who doubts, but he who investigates or researches, as opposed to he who asserts and thinks that he has discovered.

Mohandas Karamchand "Mahatma" Gandhi
(1869-1948) Indian leader against British rule who successfully used a movement based on nonviolence to build social and political progress

God has no religion.

Carl Jung
(1875-1961) Influential Swiss psychologist and psychiatrist

Religion is a defense against the experience of God.

Emil Brunner
(1889-1966) Swiss Protestant theologian

The God of the "other religions" is always an idol. (From his book *Revelation and Reason*)

Isaac Bashevis Singer
(1904-1991) Jewish Polish American writer who won the Nobel Prize for Literature in 1978

Doubt is part of all religion. All the religious thinkers were doubters.

Swami Muktananda
(1908-1982) Spiritual scholar

…God never made an agreement with any [religion]… All religions are of fairly recent origin, but God has existed since the beginning of time. He could not have signed a contract with any religion founder saying, "You are my exclusive salesman."

Sun Myung Moon
(1920-) Korean religious leader who founded the Unification Church

I look at all the major world religions of the world as one big family.

Julian P. Johnson
American spiritual seeker and author of *The Path of the Masters* (1939)

There is no such distinction as true and false religion, for every man's religion is for him true and genuine.

Stuart Holroyd
Writer of books such as *The Elements of Gnosticism* (1994)

> Religion is not so much man's attempt to know God as his attempt to know himself.

Rachel Naomi Remen
Author of *Kitchen Table Wisdom* (1996)

> Religion is a bridge to the spiritual—but the spiritual lies beyond religion. Unfortunately, in seeking the spiritual we may become attached to the bridge rather than crossing over it.

Homer Simpson
Character from the television show *The Simpsons*

> And what if we picked the wrong religion? Every week, we're just making God madder and madder!

Anonymous

> No religion has a monopoly on spirituality.

About the Universal Essence / Origin

Paul Henri Thiry Baron d'Holbach
(1723-1789) German French philosopher

> The universe shows us nothing save an immense and unbroken chain of cause and effect.

Charles Darwin
(1809-1882) Legendary English naturalist and scientist who wrote the groundbreaking book *On the Origin of Species by Means of Natural Selection*

> My theology is a simple muddle: I cannot look at the universe as the result of blind chance, yet I can see no evidence of beneficial design, or indeed of design of any kind.

Bertrand Russell
(1872-1970) English writer and logician who won the Nobel Prize for Literature in 1950

The universe may have a purpose, but nothing we know suggests that, if so, this purpose has any similarity to ours.

Christopher Morley
(1890-1957) American writer and journalist

My theology, briefly, is that the universe was dictated but not signed.

Steven Weinberg
(1933-) American nuclear physicist who co-won the Nobel Prize for physics in 1979

The more the universe seems comprehensible, the more it also seems pointless.

Heinz R. Pagels
(1939-1988) American physicist and writer of books such as *The Cosmic Code*

I think the universe is a message written in code, a cosmic code, and the scientist's job is to decipher that code.

What is the universe? Is it a great 3-D movie in which we are all unwilling actors? Is it a cosmic joke, a giant computer, a work of art by a Supreme Being, or simply an experiment? The problem in trying to understand the universe is that we have nothing to compare it with.

Stephen Hawking
(1942-) Legendary English physicist who has written many best selling books including *A Brief History of Time*

The whole history of science has been the gradual realization that events do not happen in an arbitrary manner, but that they reflect a certain underlying order, which may or may not be divinely inspired.

Even if there is only one possible unified theory, it is just a set of rules and equations. What is it that breathes fire into the equations and makes a universe for them to describe?

The usual approach of science of constructing a mathematical model cannot answer the questions of why there should be a universe for the model to describe. Why does the universe go to all the bother of existing?

Douglas Adams
(1952-2001) British writer most known for the science fiction novel *The Hitchhiker's Guide to the Galaxy* and the Hitchhiker series of books

There is a theory which states that if ever anybody discovers exactly what the Universe is for and why it is here, it will instantly disappear and be replaced by something even more bizarre and inexplicable. There is another theory which states that this has already happened. (From *The Hitchhiker's Guide to the Galaxy*)

Copyright and Translation Information

Note: This book is not endorsed, affiliated, or sponsored by any persons written about in this book; or by any other companies, products, trademarked terms, or copyrighted material affiliated with them, including, but not limited to Mary Kay Ash, Mary Kay Cosmetics, Hillary Clinton, Oprah Winfrey, *The Oprah Winfrey Show*, Phil Jackson, Vince Lombardi, Casey Stengel, Scotty Bowman, Michael Jordan, Mike Tyson, Olga Korbut, Wilma Rudolph, Babe Ruth, Napoleon Hill, The Ralston Society / Ralston University Press, the Napoleon Hill Foundation, any translations/translators consulted upon in this entire book, or any other companies, products, trademarked terms, or copyrighted material affiliated with those translators/translations.

Note: Many of the quotes used in this book, particularly but not limited to those published from the 1920s to today, are used in this book under fair use, and are protected by copyright by their various respective copyright owners.

Translation Notes

Most translations of foreign material are Rodney Ohebsion's adaptations of various translations.
-*The Analects*: Rodney Ohebsion's clarified adaptation based on several public domain translations
-*Tao Te Ching*: Rodney Ohebsion's clarified adaptation based primarily on the translations of James Legge and JH McDonald.
-*Chuang Tzu*: Rodney Ohebsion's clarified adaptation based primarily on the James Legge translation. Passage Titles added by Rodney Ohebsion.
-*Lieh Tzu*: Rodney Ohebsion's clarified adaptation of the Lionel Giles translation. Passage titles added by Rodney Ohebsion.
-Zen / Buddhist Proverbs, Teachings, Sayings, and Koans: Rodney Ohebsion's clarified adaptations based on a variety of sources. Koan titles added by Rodney Ohebsion.
-*The Art of War*: Rodney Ohebsion's clarified adaptation of the Lionel Giles translation
-*The Art of Worldly Wisdom*: Rodney Ohebsion's clarified adaptation of the Joseph Jacobs translation
-*Essays*: Rodney Ohebsion's clarified adaptation of the Charles Cotton translation
-*Philosophical Dictionary*: Rodney Ohebsion's clarified adaptation of the H.I. Woolf translation
-*Maxims* and Other Rochefoucauld Writings: Rodney Ohebsion's clarified adaptation of the J.W. Willis Bund & J. Hain Friswell translation

-Leonardo da Vinci's Notebooks: Rodney Ohebsion's clarified adaptation of the Jean Paul Richter translation

-Cyrus The Great's Human Rights Charter: Rodney Ohebsion's clarified adaptation of the United Nations translation

-The Prince: Rodney Ohebsion's clarified adaptation of the W.K. Marriott translation.

-The Bible (Tanakh / Old Testament & New Testament): Rodney Ohebsion's clarified adaptation of the King James Version (KJV) Translation

-The Quran: Rodney Ohebsion's clarified adaptation based on several translations.

-Bhagavad Gita: Rodney Ohebsion's clarified adaptation of the Kashinath Trimbak Telano translation.

-Other Hindu Scripture translations: Rodney Ohebsion's clarified adaptation of a variety of sources.

-Other Religious Scripture Passages: Rodney Ohebsion's clarified adaptation of a variety of sources.

Most foreign quote translations from sources not listed above are based on a variety of sources, most of which are public domain, and most are adapted for better clarity by Rodney Ohebsion.

Usage Permissions for Material from *A Collection of Wisdom*

I, Rodney Ohebsion, am very lenient in allowing other writers (of books, articles, or websites) to use my original material from *A Collection of Wisdom*. Please contact Immediex Publishing at www.immediex.com for permission.

For small portions, I will usually allow you to use material for free as long as you clearly indicate you got it from this book, and you mention www.immediex.com For larger portions, I may or may not require payment, depending on what you want to use it for, and how much material you want to use.

I have also written several articles based on material in this book that are available for free one-time reprint in any publication. Please go to www.immediex.com for these articles.

FOR CONTACT INFO, GO TO www.immediex.com

For retail or wholesale orders of *A Collection of Wisdom*, visit

www.immediex.com